The Adventures of a Super Hero's Insurance Adjuster.

By D. L. Carter.

This is a work of fiction. Names, characters, businesses, places, events, locales, and incidents are either the products of the author's imagination or used in a fictitious manner. Any resemblance to actual persons, living or dead, undead or elvish, or actual events is purely coincidental but if you happen to meet any of them please let the author know. The author has made a reasonable attempt to avoid using anyone else's title, logo and super name. No infringement on existing powers is intended.

No part of this book may be reproduced in any form or by any electronic or mechanical means, including information storage and retrieval systems, without written permission from the author, except for the use of brief quotations in a book review.

ISBN-13:978-0692338230
(D. L. Carter LLC)
ISBN-10: 0692338233

Cover Illustration Copyright © 2011 by D. L. Carter
Paperback and e-book copyright © D. L. Carter

With thanks to:

Carol, Sarah and Esther – for writing advice, encouragement and reading the

drafts,
Ed – for putting up with the constant typing and for doing the dishes;
and the inventor of The Latte – for instances of assistance and support too numerous to mention.

TABLE OF CONTENTS

Chapter One..	6
Chapter Two...	22
Chapter Three..	35
Chapter Four..	41
Chapter Five..	49
Chapter Six..	64
Chapter Seven...	83
Chapter Eight...	96
Chapter Nine..	108
Chapter Ten...	116
Chapter Eleven..	133
Chapter Twelve..	144
Chapter Thirteen..	153
Chapter Fourteen...	166
Chapter Fifteen..	178
Chapter Sixteen...	188
Chapter Seventeen..	196
Chapter Eighteen...	206
Chapter nineteen...	215
Chapter Twenty...	225
Chapter Twenty-one..	240
Epilogue..	263
By the same author	266

Neque cuiquam mortalium injuriae suae parvae vindentur.1.

1. Nobody underestimates his own troubles. Plutarch

Brevis ipsa vita est sed malis fit longior2.

2 Life is short, but trouble makes it longer. Ovid.

Quod si ita est, aeternum victurus sum 3.

3. If this is true, I'm going to live forever. UltraMan

Dramatic Personae (includes, but is not limited to)

The Heroes	Secret identity	Powers
Ultra Man	Craig Duane	Flight, Strength, Super Speed, Resilience
Purple Lightning	Oliver Franks	Super Speed, Resilience
The Mysterious West	Lacey Hendley	Flight, Magic
Tye Dye	Edward Bishop	Extreme light manifestation
Captain Fabulous	Captain Fabulous	Stretching, Resilience.
Urban Renewal	Robert Kirk	Strength. Resilience
Flash Heat	Jessie Lymph	Projected Temperature Blast
Captain Smash (retired)	Mr. Crunch	Invulnerability. Strength
The Thump	Mrs. Crunch (MIA)	Strength
The Power	Jason Crunch Jr. (MIA)	Strength

The Villains	Secret Identity	Powers
Nuclear Man	Douglas MacLean	Projectile vomiting of toxic and radioactive materials
The Mystress of the Night	Joan Hendley	Magic
The Shriek	Steven Holtzman	Projected Sound Blast
Mr. Ooze	Oscar Walters	Highly adhesive corrosive mucosal liquid
Major Calamity	Jacob Finkelstein	Flight (uses stolen weapons)
The Blast	Andrew Sutter	Projected AirWave Blast

Intentions as yet unidentified
The Ice Queen - - - - - - - - ?

Chapter One.

The New Jersey Morning Sun.
Attempts to capture Nuclear Man failed last evening when he projectile-vomited radioactive and toxic chemicals over the floor between himself and the arresting officers. While the Super Support SS.C. ™ Hazmat equipment was being airlifted to the site, Nuclear Man was able to retrieve his crutches and shuffle, unimpeded, to his getaway vehicle parked in a nearby handicapped zone.

"Heads up!" shouted The Mysterious West, as she swooped past Ultra Man on her specially designed side-saddle broom, her multiply-beaded braids attacking her own face with all the vigor of Medusa's snakes.

Ultra Man, leader of the Northeast U.S. Region Super Team, didn't bother dodging; he knew better. When West was flying it was safer to let her do all the fancy maneuvering.

Unnerving, but safer.

Instead, Ultra Man tracked her flight path with only a fraction of his attention while he braced himself against the rising wind. When this battle had started, just minutes ago, there had been a gentle breeze rattling down the urban concrete canyon, but with every spell she cast The Mysterious West stirred up energies, stirred up the Elements. Most especially, she stirred up the air.

Hopefully, they'd be able to finish this fight before... Ultra Man shuddered, remembering the lecture he'd received only last month... before *something* happened he'd have to explain to The Weather Channel and the Environmental Protection Agency. Or worse, to Ali Brent, the S.S.C.'s stubborn, annoying, irritating Northeast Region's Event Site Supervisor and senior insurance assessor. She'd said it last time; if he let them make another mess with the weather, she'd make him clean up the mess using his own old underwear. Shaking off all thoughts involving Ali Brent and underwear, Ultra Man returned his concentration to the ongoing fight.

His visor protected his eyes from the thin but fast-flying dust as he scanned the area for larger debris – as well as for the Villains they'd interrupted robbing a nearby hospital. He pulled off the plastic bag plastered against his thigh by the wind and concentrated on staying airborne and hovering roughly in one place. Since he wasn't entirely sure, even after all these years, and all that SS.C. sponsored research, how it was he was able to fly, his concentration was more well-intentioned than directed.

A glitter of green coming up fast from the ground caught his attention. Ultra Man grabbed a hunk of vinyl siding flying past and swung it up to protect his face. The handful of crystal green muck spattered against the improvised shield, missing Ultra Man's gloved fingers by mere inches. The next two missiles met a similar fate. When a few seconds passed without a further attack, Ultra Man took a quick glance around the dripping vinyl, scanning the battleground. Far below he spotted Mr. Ooze squelching his way across an apartment complex forecourt, scraping green residue from his face, arms and bare chest as he tried to build up enough muck for another missile.

Ultra Man's lips curled and he swallowed hard to keep his midnight snack where it belonged. (Note to self: - no veggie special - extra spicy - burritos when on call). Hovering midair a few hundred feet away, The Mysterious West stuffed ingredients pulled from the pockets of her vest into a spell pouch. The faint shimmer of the air surrounding her showed her personal Ooze-repelling spell was in place.

Down on the ground a purple blur zapped across the road and wrapped itself around Mr. Ooze. The purple color intensified and updrafts of air thrust more trash into the sky. After a few minutes Ooze staggered, clutched at his chest and fell to his knees. Ultra Man grinned and dropped his makeshift shield. The last member of the Super Team, Purple Lightning, having successfully knocked out Mr. Ooze, took a victory lap around the block, slowing toward normal speed. Ultra Man wiggled his jaw sideways to activate the communicator inside his mask.

"P.L., report!"

P.L.'s voice vibrated in his ear with the familiar high speed distortion. "Ccccirccccuit ccccompletedddd. Nnnnno signnnnn oooofffff Nnnnuclear Mannnn oooooorrrrrr Shrreeeiiiikkkkkk."

Ultra Man let out a breath he wasn't aware he'd been holding as his fists unclenched within his bronze gloves.

"What about the Mystress of the Night?" he demanded.

Mysterious West glanced over from where she was constructing yet another spell pouch, her braids lashing across her face.

"She's still out there somewhere," she shouted against the rising wind. "I can smell her."

"Interesting talent," mused Ultra Man as he tensed his shoulders and waited while his Power lifted him a few yards higher. "I don't remember hearing about it during the briefing."

The Mysterious West only snorted.

Rotating, he scanned the pavements, buildings, roads stretched out beneath him. The wind drove flurries of loose trash and dust along the empty midnight streets; dragging the last few autumn leaves from scraggly roadside trees. Beneath him, P.L. jogged down the streets at a speed merely five or six times that of a normal man.

"Don't see her," P.L. began.

A ball of light flew across the forecourt hitting a wall behind where P.L. had been shattering the bricks into hundreds of tiny, hot, and above all, sharp pieces. P.L. zigzagged and staggered as debris sprayed across his path. Recovering in milliseconds, he shot off for another pass around the block, building up speed as he skittered back and forth dodging balls of light The Mystress threw after him. Cursing, Ultra Man adjusted his flight path. So far The Mystress was ignoring him, concentrating on sending spells toward P.L. and The Mysterious West.

Not, thought Ultra Man, grinning as he increased his speed, *a good idea.*

A gust caught the Villainess's latest spell package, smearing it against the apartment building wall – which promptly started to dissolve. Ultra Man cursed under his breath. The Super Clean crew was not going to be pleased with this site. He could just *see* the interdepartmental memos.

"Aim's no better, girl," shouted Mysterious West, drawing back her arm and casting a bundle down and to her right. "You still throw like a baby."

West must have augmented her aim with a spell, Ultra Man realized when, despite the swirling wind, Mysterious West's pouch descended straight and true. Striking the ground behind The Mystress, its contents surged out, sending grey clouds fountaining up and out. The Mystress of the Night swore, gathered her flowing robes tight to her body and ran. The charms and bags tied to her belt slammed against her thighs as she fled a sticky grey fog that crawled along the pavement behind her. Dragging a small red package out of her belt, the Mystress cast it at the cloud. Ultra Man tensed his arms, changed direction, heading for the questionable shelter of the apartment building. Having previous experience of occasions when the Witches' powers met, he knew better than to be caught in the backwash. Behind him the grey fog flashed red and purple, then boiled up to merge with the thick Jersey City smog.

Emerging a few seconds later from his shelter behind a satellite dish, Ultra Man leapt into the air. Below him Mr. Ooze was back on his feet and staggering down a narrow alley, leaving crystal green footprints glowing on the ground. Purple Lightning, buffeted by winds, dodging sparks and colored lights generated by the battling sisters, slowed until his body was almost visible and bravely kept working his way close to the battling witches. That left Ultra Man with the responsibility of catching the sticky Villain.

"P.L. Help West. Distract the Mystress," ordered Ultra Man, "I'm going after Ooze."

A mutter from Mysterious West was his only answer to what, even he would admit, was an unnecessary order. A high, yowling buzz told him that P.L. was trying to say something but his microphone hadn't caught up with his words. Ultra Man dodged through a forest of satellite dishes, over the building and down – hopefully to come up behind the fleeing Villain. Unfortunately for his flight powers, the Mystress and West had continued casting spells in the few minutes his back was turned and the wind was now driving directly toward him, forcing him back into the sky. He practically had to claw his way down to the ground.

Sheesh, where was gravity when you needed it?

His final landing was graceless and clumsy, but at least he ended up on his feet.

Any landing you can walk away from yada yada.

Unfortunately, while he'd been battling the element of air, Ooze had vanished.

"Are Ooze and the Mystress still together?" demanded Ultra Man as he jogged along, following the green trail. He was reluctant to risk taking flight again in this turbulent air.

P.L. rounded a corner ahead of him, skidding to a stop, leaving smoking marks on the pavement. Drawing a steadying breath, P.L. faced his team leader, then he raised one hand and pointed straight up.

Ultra Man tilted his head and stared at the pre-dawn sky. A sky filled with writhing, boiling, multicolored clouds.

Dark, looming clouds.

Heavy, nasty, unfriendly, *portentous* clouds.

Lightning skittered across the sky, highlighting the tornado forming above them.

The vast, dark funnel, positioned directly above a building containing a couple of hundred innocent sleepers and a hospital with an unknown number of ill, vulnerable civilians.

Ultra Man groaned as the funnel descended toward them.

"Aw, shit," was all he said.

Less than an hour later:

"Has The Colonel developed anything to take this stuff out of suede?" asked Ali Brent, pulling her boots free of the crystal green ooze congealing on the sidewalk.

"You're joking, right?" snorted Norman Spike. "He's got more important stuff to worry about."

Norman leaned against his van to yank yet another layer of protective gear over his clothes. The Super Support SS.C. ™, Super Clean Team ™ logo (a gold bucket and mop with silver wings) on his baseball cap glittered under the crime scene lights as he waved his gloved hand at the chaos around them.

"Look at this! Mister Ooze really did a number on this street. Hell, on this whole block. It's gonna take days to clear this mess. The only thing we've found that works on Ooze's ooze is liquid nitrogen, and you know what that does to concrete." He scanned Ali top to toe and held out a hand to halt her progress into the scene. "What happened to your work boots?"

"They're all in decontamination. Damaged my last pair at that Nuclear Man site yesterday. I was there for hours, barely got home, then they called me out for this. I've only had three hours sleep," she said, yawning broadly as she looked around the event site.

The air was filled with settling concrete dust, pieces of torn fabric, paper, and other unidentifiable debris. Water, both clean and foul, poured from shattered pipes to flood down the street. Ali stared down at her shoes and the mess under their soles and sighed. Between the Ooze and the water, there were few places safe to put her feet.

Norman didn't say anything, but out of the corner of her eyes, Ali saw his shoulders stiffen under his layers of clothing. *Oops.* She'd forgotten he'd been with her on that site yesterday, and he'd stayed there working while she'd headed into the office. She didn't have to see his eyes to know they were blood-shot behind his protective glasses. His thick grey hair stuck out from under his Super Clean baseball cap in jagged spikes, and his hands trembled as he tugged at his suit – probably from caffeine poisoning.

"What am I saying? You're running on even less. Norm, are you going to be all right?"

Norman gave her a one-shoulder shrug and continued attaching gizmos and gadgets to the belts that crisscrossed his chest. "You know me, my strength is that of a thousand men, etc., etc.," he replied, opening the rear of his van wider. "Prelim scan shows no radiation or dangerous toxins. Paper suit should be enough. Just be careful where you put your feet."

"Too late."

He handed her a folded blue suit and paper shoe covers and continued assembling and checking his gear. Ali watched Norman's preparations for a moment, considering whether or not to send the exhausted man home. The problem was, she didn't have anyone else to call instead, if he was unable to work. And, until he complained or fell over, she needed him on-site. There wasn't a better Site Examiner in the SS.C., and he wouldn't thank her for removing him for as trivial an excuse as mere exhaustion. Hell, Norman was so loyal and driven he would probably be coming in to work three weeks after he was dead.

"Who do we hold responsible for this morning's mess?" Ali examined the decimated city block again and bit back another yawn. Her jaw creaked and complained but held.

"Let's see," Norman rubbed absently at his unshaven chin, "I've heard it was the full team, Ultra Man with The Mysterious West and Purple Lightning on our side. We were lucky today; the only one Mr. Ooze had with him was the Mystress of the Night."

"Uh huh, and where were Nuclear Man and the Shriek?"

"I heard that The Mystress of the Night – while she was hexing it out with The Mysterious West - said that he had a cold or something, so we don't need to break out the Hazmat suits or worry about the EPA today. And since The Shriek used his powers in Buffalo five days ago, he's not expected on scene for, maybe, another two days."

Ali closed her eyes for a moment in gratitude for small blessings. Just for a moment. Too long and she'd fall asleep standing up. Shivering, she drew in a breath of chill pre-dawn air. Poets and health nuts could rave all they wanted about the benefits of getting up early, but personally, Ali considered nothing could beat a decent night's sleep.

In her next life, she resolved, she'd be a professional mattress tester. Maybe then she could catch up on lost "Z's."

"Nuclear Man must be the wimpiest Super Villain of all time," said Ali as she shrugged the paper suit up over her shoulders and zipped it closed. "The other day, he held off a dozen cops by throwing up. Today he's out with the sniffles?"

"Given the extreme measures I have to use to clean up after him, I don't agree with you there, Ali. Anyway, I hear his cancer has metastasized to his liver. That would make anyone cranky. Besides, would you prefer that The Blast worked this area? Or Major Calamity? *They're* not wimps."

Ali remembered the pile of reports that had landed on her desk the last time The Blast got testy up in the Pacific Northwest region. Afterward, it'd been necessary to destroy Seattle's famous Space Needle for safety reasons. To further annoy the locals, The Blast had written to the Mayor of Seattle, offering to complete the destruction at a lower fee than the demolition contractors.

The arrogant putz.

Fortunately for Ali, The Blast seemed content with harassing the West Coast. Nuclear Man's team didn't come out to play too often. And with the visits from traveling Super Villains whose actions could never be predicted, and the League of Evil Geniuses, she was kept pretty busy. The rest of the local criminals were surprisingly un-Super and, therefore, were not her problem. Super Support Co ™ (and Super Clean ™) dealt only with the fall-out from Supers and Villains - and that was quite enough. Thank you and Goodnight.

She winced as she lifted her boots again, tugging against the adhesion from the drying ooze.

"No, I suppose it could be worse," Ali muttered, reaching into her car for her attaché case, "So, where are the survivors?"

Norman jerked his thumb toward a stunned collection of people in various stages of dress, huddling within a circle of Salvation Army vans and ambulances.

"Over there. No injuries reported beyond being shaken up, which, considering the destruction, was a hell of a lucky break for everyone. Especially us. Ultra Man managed to get everyone out before the apartment building collapsed. He saved them all."

Ali chewed on the inside of her cheek to keep from groaning at Norman's effusive praise and the beatific expression of admiration on his exhausted face. There were times when she just wanted to slap some cynicism into him. Sixteen years of cleaning up behind the local Super Team, and Norman was still a devoted fan who considered it an honor to be woken out of a sound sleep and sent out into the freezing cold at 2 am to clean up after someone else's Super carelessness.

She glared at the mess in front of her. Piles of cracked concrete, shattered steel and glass. Broken buildings and broken lives. Three years on the job and she wasn't a fan, but then, she never had been. She knew the Super Team members far too well to admire them, and her disgust grew with every site she picked her way through, every devastated family she interviewed, every multistory, multifamily apartment building reduced to pancake powder.

Norman settled his face mask in place, powered up a hand-held scanner and wandered off, poking his instruments under pieces of broken concrete. Overhead, police and news helicopters buzzed back and forth over the scene in some erotic dragonfly dance, illuminating the ground beneath with their searchlights.

The hiss and squelch of tires behind Ali had her turning and biting back a curse. A low, smooth stretch limo slid to a halt beside Norman's van, just short of a line of Ooze's ooze. Its darkened passenger window powered down, revealing the narrow-nosed, hatchet face of her immediate superior. Ali kept her face impassive with an effort.

Nigel Hackham, of Hackham, Breackham, Bendit and Crunch, legal advisers to the Super Teams of North America and a significant part of the Board of Directors of Super Support Corp, beckoned to Ali with one slender, black-gloved hand. She trudged over to his car concentrating on keeping a professional demeanor. There was something about Nigel's fake British style that got on her last nerve and tap-danced. He'd raised being cool and superior to the level of a martial art and frequently used it to bludgeon his junior staff.

"Ms. Brent! Such efficiency. All suited up and ready to work. Excellent." He made no move to open the door and join her in the chill air. Instead, he sipped his designer coffee and wound the window up a few inches to keep the warm air inside. "Since your shoes are already destroyed, Ms. Brent, I wonder if you would do me a favor and deliver the "hold harmless" forms to the survivors. You can bring them into the office with your preliminary site report."

Ali glanced down at her boots and groaned. The green goop had bonded the paper covers to her shoes. Not that there had been any hope of saving the boots from the first moment she'd stepped out onto the site. She could try to have them cleaned, but one quick spin through a liquid nitrogen wash and there'd be nothing left but dust. Consequently, the grunt she gave her boss could have been agreement or a smothered profanity, but she held out her hand and accepted the thick stack of paper. She waited briefly for thanks. Instead, the window powered up and the limo slid way.

She considered, and discarded, thumbing her nose at the disappearing limo. Not because it was childish, but because she was too tired. Turning to face the wreckage, Ali watched as a few enterprising reporters argued with the police at the blockade.

"*Must be newbies*, she thought, stumbling on the uneven ground.

The police had arrived early enough to prevent the media from perpetrating another assault on the survivors. Ali presented her S.S.C. ID to the cop with the most phones (seems like too many phones?) and other devices hanging from his uniform and was waved through the barriers without delay.

Each time she ducked under crime scene tape, her hands got sweaty and her heart hammered in her throat. She might not be a Super or a cop, but *this* was her contribution to the justice system. Her chance to stand for the victims. Filling in insurance evaluations wasn't as flashy as the things the Supers did, and she didn't get credit in the press or invited to celebrations at the White House. But, when it came down to it, clean-up was essential. Without her and her team, the cumulative effect of Super/Villain battles would leave quite a few cities resembling post-Beirut landscapes. She was proud of her team and their work. The silent, unheralded heroes in paper suits – *the Super Clean Team*™.

"Ta-da," she whispered. Chuckling a little, she schlepped and glopped her way through the muck toward the survivors.

Despite the personal danger, Ali did not wear a face mask, making her one of perhaps ten people in the whole Super Support Corp who went out barefaced to meet the world. The four SS.C. lawyers had to surrender their anonymity to do their jobs effectively. Their rationale was much the same as Ali's. It was hard enough to get people to trust lawyers without wearing masks. How much trust would people offer an insurance adjuster if they couldn't look her in the eye? Of course, her job was more than to be the S.S.C. liaison with insurance companies. Sometimes she felt like an overworked mix of spin-doctor, PR rep, trauma counselor, babysitter, and media consultant.

Immediately after she had passed under the barrier, the barking voices of the reporters sounded, chasing after her. They hadn't noticed her approach, and now she was out of their reach and ignoring them, but that didn't stop them from trying to get her to turn. To give them a soundbite. Get her face on video.

The questions were all familiar. *"Who was she?" "What was she doing?" "Who did she know?" "What did she know?" "Did she know any of the Superteam members?" "Was it true about Captain Fabulous?"*

Ali ignored the noise, just as she had on every other occasion, and kept her back to the cluster of cameras. She knew the risk she ran walking around a Super Event site barefaced. If she was recognized, there were stalkers and criminals, friends and families of those sent to jail by Supers, who could see her, remember her, and track her. See her as a way to get revenge. Not to mention the pathological fans trying to find a way to get close to their heroes. Each time she stepped onto a site she had to wonder. Maybe this time they would identify her, find some clue and track her down? Ali kept her eyes forward and chin up and pushed that concern away. She was fortunate to be blessed with ordinary, forgettable features. The mid-brown hair and eyes, medium height and a middling figure wouldn't, and didn't, get her many serious admirers. (As if she had the spare time to look for them.) On the other hand, these reporters had no idea they'd seen her many times before, and within a few hours wouldn't recognize her even if she came up and spit in their lattes.

Three years on the job and no one had identified her – an SS.C. record. It was faintly annoying. What woman wanted to be that ordinary? That forgettable? Even if it did save her job? Her life?

Then again, there might be a simpler reason as to why no one ever guessed who she was. Why would anyone pay any attention to her when there could be Super beefcake wandering around in his underclothes?

I mean, really. People had to have their priorities.

The survivors were pretty much as Ali expected. Several were sitting, stunned and silent, on the back steps of the ambulances. A few were being prevented from trying to get back into their shattered dwellings by police, sweating in their unnecessary Hazmat suits. Most were wandering vaguely about, mumbling to the neighbors whose existence they wouldn't even acknowledge on any other day of the week. Ali waited until someone noticed her and nudged those standing nearby to let them know she'd arrived.

Ali's hand clenched on the handle of her attaché case as the crowd formed around her. She studied it, looking for the heckler, the know it all, the troublemaker. They were bound to be there. There was one of each in every group. With a little luck, she'd be able to keep them under control tonight. Humans under stress could become dangerous creatures at very short notice. She took a few steps back when it seemed she was about to be surrounded, keeping a careful eye on the tiny, little women scattered through the crowd. Bitter experience told her they were the ones who could cause the most trouble. Heaven protect her from little old ladies with sharp walking sticks. She still bore the scars.

"Good Morning. I'm the Site Supervisor from Super Clean ™, a subdivision of the Super Support Corporation," said Ali, pitching her voice to carry to the edge of their group – and no further, "First of all, I'd like to say how sorry I am that your lives have been disrupted this way. The Super Teams try at all times to limit involving civilians in their crime-fighting efforts. Unfortunately, on this occasion they were not able to do so. We will be doing the best we can to get your lives back on track as soon as possible."

Her audience nodded without really understanding what she was saying. Good. At least, good for the Company. Gritting her teeth, she plowed on with her scripted speech.

"I am here to help you with practical insurance issues. To that end, I have some paperwork for you all to fill out. Don't worry, it won't take long. Afterward, we'll be transporting you to a hotel where rooms are standing by. Don't worry about cost. For those of you who have the recommended Super Hero Intervention Rider on your home insurance policies, we'll help you contact your SS.C. later today to get your settlement as quickly as possible. They will be responsible for the cost of your hotel stay. We will have S.S.C. representatives at the hotel to assist you with immediate needs. For anyone who doesn't have the rider, there are some special charity funds that provide assistance to those in your situation. We will assist you with applications to those, as well."

There was more life in their faces now. Shock was giving way as they began to understand the reality of what had happened. Before the panic, the self-preservation and self-serving mindset could set in, Ali started moving through the crowd handing out bundles of paperwork and souvenir Super Team ™ pens. To her complete absence of surprise, a few people insisted on going through her bag of pens until they found the one with their favorite Supers logo on it. The Ultra Man ones went fastest. (No surprise there. He'd actually been here this morning, and people wanted a memento.) When the crowd backed off a little, Ali continued in her calm, even, 'trust me' voice.

"To begin with, I need you to complete these basic identification forms. If you remember the name of your insurance SS.C. that would really help. I'll need to talk to each of you before we put you on the buses."

"Ultra Man grabbed me out of bed and flew me out the window," cried a youngster Ali guessed might be seven, jumping up and down in front of her, waving his arms through the air. "Brrrrrrrdddddddd. Just like that!"

"Well, the Super who makes a brrrrrdddddd sound is Purple Lightning," Ali told him in the singsong voice adults used with unfamiliar children. Leaning down to smile at him, she added, "It's the sound of his shoes on the ground."

"Nah," said the boy, running off between the silent adults, his hands held out in front of him. "It was Ultra Man! Brrrrrrrrrrrrrrrrrddddddddddddddd...."

Ali chuckled to herself and followed him.

Handing out the paperwork and pens took a little time; especially as she had to explain over and over what she needed the survivors to do. She pushed back her rising impatience, reminding herself that they were hardly expected to be at their best at this hour of the morning – and under these circumstances. Operating on three hours' sleep, she wasn't too good herself. Once the paper was handed out, she pulled a clipboard out of her attaché and turned her professional smile on the nearest adult.

"Can you tell me anything about the layout of your apartment building?"

"I can help you with that," said a small man who'd been sitting morosely on a pile of broken concrete. "I'm the building Super." He laughed self-consciously. "Well, not *that* kind of Super."

"Great," Ali laughed politely with him for about two seconds – like she hadn't heard every variation on 'Super' puns there was - and hauled out a sketchbook. "Just give me an outline. How many apartments on each floor, how they're arranged and numbered. Location of stairs and elevators. It will help with identifying any recovered property."

"Sure." The building Super retreated to his seat and started doodling. "We had a basement. All the families had little storage lockers down there. Nothing much. A place to keep exercise bikes and things. Might be they're still intact."

"Could be." Ali made a note and left him to his artwork. Passing slowly through the crowd, she collected names, apartment numbers, work numbers, and (probably incorrect) insurance information until her face ached with the effort of maintaining her damned professional smile. Somehow, she managed to keep smiling while enduring repeated descriptions of shaking walls, flying debris, and exaggerated tales of rescue. Acting as if she'd never heard such remarkable tales of rescue and bravery – with so little coffee in her system – was almost beyond her ability. Still, she smiled, nodded, took notes, and went on.

One elderly couple proudly held up an overweight striped cat and an empty, dusty birdcage.

"Captain Ultra Man came through the door as if it wasn't there. He grabbed me, grabbed my husband, and the next thing we knew we were out here. A second later my fuzzy baby here drops into my arms and my husband's holding the cage. Captain Ultra Man's Fabulous."

"No, he's *Ultra Man*. Captain Fabulous works out of our Southwest office." Ali bit the inside of her cheek and waited for the few beats until she regained her composure. Imagining the reactions of both Supers if they ever heard that combined title almost had her giggling - a sure sign she was short on sleep.

"Ah. Did you see a purple light when this was happening?"

The lady blinked and her eyes widened. "Well, yes. I think so. How did you know?" she turned to her husband, "Did you see it, honey?"

The old man nodded, clutching the empty birdcage that constituted all his remaining worldly goods. That and saggy, fireman red pajamas.

"Then it was the Purple Lightning who got you and your pet out," said Ali. "Ultra Man doesn't move as fast as P.L., so if he'd done the rescue, you would've seen him. All you see when P.L.'s about is a flash of purple light."

"Oh." Disappointment faded the bright light out of the woman's eyes and her chin began to tremble. "I was so looking forward to telling my granddaughter about it. She's in Ultra Man's fan club. We were going to try and get an autograph for her."

"None of the Super Team members are permitted to give out signatures," said Ali, in a flat, don't-push-me-on-this-one voice.

The elderly couple gave her matching glum looks and wandered off. Ali sighed and kept moving. She'd never understood people. They complained if the cable SS.C. interrupted their service for half an hour – no matter what the reason – but let the Super Team come into town, tear down their homes, and all they cared about was getting the most famous of the Supers to perform their personal rescues. Those who worked for the S.S.C. still talked about the old man who had drowned insisting he was going to wait for The Night Walker to rescue him, even though The Walker was seven years' dead at the time. People. She didn't understand them, and most days she didn't want to.

Ali jumped as the phone at her waist trembled. She pulled it free and turned her back on the crowd. "Site Supervisor."

"Site Examiner." Norman's electronically altered voice crackled out of the small speaker in his face mask. "Contamination review complete. We're clear for next stage."

"Finally," said Ali, glancing up at the brightening sky. She wanted to get the survivors off the site before they got a clearer look at what had happened to their homes. Before they recovered from their shock and started doing something stupid, like climbing through the wreckage trying to find precious tokens of their lives.

Or, more dangerous, calling a lawyer.

She thumbed the dial on the phone down to the secure broadcast setting and lifted it to her mouth again. "This is Site Supervisor. Site cleared. Everyone in!"

The distant growl of engines starting overwhelmed the buzz of the helicopters and hissing police scanners. Within minutes, a parade of vehicles rumbled toward the police roadblock, following the path Norman had already marked as clear of Ooze's ooze. The crowd of reporters swelled and swarmed as they approached. Two black buses, with privacy windows activated, followed by five huge, black semi-trailers inched past as the barricades were moved. The police had their hands full for a few minutes keeping the reporters away from the cavalcade. Ali watched the semis maneuver through the damage, seeking places to park, concerned that, once again, she might get blocked in. Apparently, her most recent carefully phrased email was having the desired effect. Both her car and Norman's van still had a clear path out.

"All right," said Ali to the watching survivors as the vehicles hissed to a halt, "The buses in front are for you. They'll take you to the hotel. I advise you not to talk to the reporters." Again, she was buried under the weight of their mass disappointment. Hunched shoulders and pouting lower lips were directed at her, and she could see that one or two were measuring the distance between the buses and the TV vans as if planning escapes. Ali waved her hand to regain their attention. "Remember, people, you're barely dressed. Is this how you want to be seen over breakfast on TVs around the world?" She nodded to one stocky, hairy gentleman who was spared embarrassment only by aged boxer shorts and a blanket. He pulled the blanket tighter around his shoulders when it would've given better service, in Ali's opinion, around his waist.

"I have been informed that there will be arrangements made for a press conference after you've had a chance to clean up and rest. There's no pressure on you to participate in that conference, which will be held later this morning." She clapped her hands to get them moving. "Okay, if you would start making your way to the buses, please. I'll take the forms back. Thank you."

Ali herded the last stragglers to the buses, where she handed a copy of her list of names to the publicity rep. The two women exchanged tired shrugs. Then the rep settled her mirrored glasses back on her nose, pulled down the bill of her Super Clean ™ baseball cap and tried to get the last of the victims onto the bus.

Of course, a few ignored the advice regarding the reporters. Someone always did. Currently, the boy was entertaining a TV crew with his imitation of 'Ultra Man's' rescue noise. The elderly couple – obviously thinking they couldn't take a chance at their age and wait for their fifteen sound bites of fame - was performing for another group.

'Whatever, thought Ali, turning back to the debris field. *It's their decision.*

She stretched, arching her back. Fatigue poisons were building up in her body and fogging her mind. She blinked swollen eyelids over gritty eyes. Dawn light was creeping across the site, sending dancing shadows over the remains of the buildings. Ali reached into a pocket of her attaché and pulled out a bottle of caffeine pills. She swallowed two and waited. When she could focus again, she headed for the black trucks.

Protective suit-clad workers were emerging from the semis and assembling a field office with practiced moves. The Super Clean logos on the prefab building and their suits glowed. Even from close up, it was hard to tell male from female in the bulky suits. With their security face-masks, it was impossible to tell one from another, unless you could read the coded designs printed on the backs.

"Well, good morning, Site Manager," Ali said to an individual who was watching the unloading.

He, or she, nodded.

"I have a rough map of the apartments," continued Ali, handing over the building Supervisor's rough drawing. "Please note the existence of basement storage units. See if you can access them early. I want you to have something precious and personal retrieved for each family and taken to the hotel by the end of the day. Hand it to the public relations rep for distribution."

"Got it," said the Site Manager, his voice rendered anonymous by the device in his mask.

Ali sighed in relief. Now she'd passed her responsibilities on to this S.S.C. worker drone, her body sagged. Her bag slipped from her shoulder and caught on her elbow. She dragged a hand across her face and let out a slow breath before straightening her spine and putting the strap back where it belonged. Her day was far from over.

"I'm heading into the office," she said. Even with the caffeine jolting through her system, her tongue felt thick and heavy, and she had to concentrate on forming each word, "Fax me an eval when you complete each section of the site. I need a timeline for reconstruction as soon as possible."

"Got it," said the site manager again, and turned away.

As Ali made her way to her car, the now stained shoe coverings caught on sharp edges, threatening to pull her off her feet. She was breathing hard and trembling by the time she reached the undamaged pavement.

The sudden popping of her ears and a blast of cold air warned her of a new arrival on the scene. She pressed her lips together hard to protect her fillings from the chill.

"Hey, Ali. Long time, no see."

Ali didn't turn. The familiar voice made her back stiffen and she raised her chin in sheer self-defense. She opened her car door, tossed her attaché case onto the passenger seat and sat down to start unzipping her ruined footwear.

"Ultra Man," she finally acknowledged her voice sharp. "On-site, you are supposed to use my title. Didn't you see Mr. Crunch's memo?"

"*Excuse me,* Ms. Site Supervisor."

He shuffled his brilliantly polished brown boots, even as he hovered two inches above the pavement. It was safer, considering the amount of ooze on the ground. Ali glanced down at her ruined shoes, then glared at him, her fingers clenching. She ran her gaze up and down him, keeping all expression from her face as she examined the familiar bronze and forest green armor that was designed to conceal the perfect, muscular body – and failed. The square, bronze-toned mask hid his green eyes. His helmet covered most of his face, but a few perfectly tousled, sandy curls peeped out to outline the freckled square jaw-line of the football jock from hell.

Now that the cold air announcing his arrival had dissipated - even from a distance of a few feet - she could feel the heat pouring off his body. All Supers put out a little extra heat when they were using their abilities, but Ultra Man was a furnace. Maybe because he had so many abilities, and he used them simultaneously. Ali wasn't a Super-Power theorist and didn't care that much about the *why* of their abilities. Mostly she tried not to think about them at all, except in relation to her job.

Along with the heat came the subtle scent of hard-working man, not unpleasant, and uniquely Ultra Man. From the almost pornographic messages posted on Ultra Man fan websites, it appeared that the scent of him was memorable. Certainly, those women who'd been rescued by him, or claim to have been rescued by him, all went on about it at length. It was altogether possible that someone down in The Colonel's lab was working on replicating those pheromones. Properly merchandised, as an aftershave perhaps, the scent would make the S.S.C. a fortune. If they weren't, well, maybe she should suggest it.

Everyone in the Company was supposed to keep an eye out for merchandising possibilities. After all, *something* had to pay for the cleanup crews. The insurance money was never enough.

And anything to do with Ultra Man was sure to sell.

It was hard for most people to believe he'd only been working for the Super Support Co. for five years. With his reputation for miraculous rescues and phenomenal Powers, people expected him to be much older and wiser than a mere mortal. Ali had no such expectations. She knew better. She got a headache whenever he was around. She also experienced frustration, irritation and a whole lot of other – *ation's*. So, she kept her head down and concentrated on unsticking the zipper on her left boot.

"How have you been, Ali? Site Supervisor."

"Keeping busy."

Her body shivered, despite her determined efforts not to react to the animal magnetism that was part of his Super Power package. His voice was dark, smooth, and went down easy, like a Guinness on a warm day. Ali groped under the front seat for her dwindling supply of empty plastic shopping bags.

(*Note to self: grocery shop on the way home or be prepared to eat the only thing still in your fridge - the baking soda deodorizer pack.*)

Finding a bag without holes in the bottom, she dropped the first boot in it and then bent to work on her second foot. The mundane task of pulling off her shoes took most of her remaining strength.

"Uh. Yeah." Ultra Man treated the still-standing buildings across the street to his much-photographed penetrating stare before smiling down at her again. "Busy morning."

"So I see. Did someone forget to tell you that you are supposed to stop Mysterious West from battling The Mystress directly?" Ali snapped, tilting her head to glare up at him. "Did you miss that email?"

"I read it," began Ultra Man, "but in battle situations, it's hard to direct which Super comes up against which Villain. We have to adapt, adjust, stay flexible, and respond to the flow of the battle."

"Save it for the press conference. I know better. Those two –!" Arrggh. You know when their spells start bouncing off each other, the damage they do is so much worse. Look at that mess!" Rising anger cleared her mind. Ali waved a hand at the city block, now almost stripped bare of buildings. "What did they call down? An F-five tornado?"

"F two," Ultra Man said, his lips pressing flat and tight over his perfect teeth. "Three, at most. And they kept it under control. Besides West had it taken down within seconds of it forming."

Ali's low growl communicated her disbelief. "Fortunately, no one was hurt," she said. "You should be very grateful that I'm not going to be at the debriefing for this. I'm going to be too busy organizing the clean-up."

"Oh, I dunno," said Ultra Man in the quiet, clear voice so beloved of TV microphones, "I kind of miss having you spend an hour lecturing me on preserving public safety."

Ali hunched back over her feet.

Damn the man. Usually she was the most even-tempered of women, but when he was around she went from zero to furious in two seconds out of sheer habit. She took several deep breaths and tried to think of flowing rivers and gently traveling clouds. When that didn't work, she focused her best withering glare on

Ultra Man.

"What's on your mind?" She asked after a few minutes passed and he was still floating there, watching her, completely un-withered.

"I was wondering if you were free Friday evening. Maybe you'd like to go with me to that charity bash?"

She didn't give him a chance to finish. "No."

The second boot thudded into the shopping bag and Ali swung her bare feet into her car. With a sharp tug, she slammed the door, gave him one last, furious look as she fastened her seatbelt and drove away.

Ultra Man rose higher to watch the progress of Ali's little car until she had safely navigated through the mess. She was usually a careful driver – unless she was trying to get away from him – but he knew she'd been awake and on duty for three days, and he was concerned. Even mad and exhausted, she navigated successfully around the masses of civilians, police, and trucks, and zoomed off in the direction of the freeway.

His shoulders sagging, he crossed his arms over his chest, drifting forlornly across the event site, absently following the artificial sound of the PR rep's voice. He realized the rep was trying to organize the reporters for the usual post-battle press conference, a task he'd heard Mr. Crunch refer to as 'herding cats' and changed direction. For some reason, the cameramen and photographers wanted the destroyed apartment complex as a backdrop for their sound bites. The PR rep was trying to turn them toward the mostly intact garage with the still-lit hospital logo on it. It was too soon to tell who was going to win.

He wasn't ready to face the press yet. Purple Lightning had the right idea. By volunteering to follow the Villains he was spared this particular aggravation. Ultra Man turned away from the cameras and settled to the ground beside the remaining member of his Superteam.

The Mysterious West flipped her braids back over her shoulders and tugged her tunic straight. Cameras and microphones by the dozen were being rounded up and trained in their direction. Ultra Man pretended to be blind to their existence and deaf to their shouted questions. Instead, he watched The Mysterious West. He'd noted a couple of times during the last few battles that she'd landed on some structure instead of keeping her broomstick hovering under her own power, that she'd seemed a little breathless during her spell casting. Even now, an hour after the fight had ended, she was moving slowly, panting a little. Ultra Man caught West's eye and maneuvered until his broad back was between her and the TV cameras. On the sidewalk nearby, he could see a number of civilians complete with digital cameras and hand-held video cams all aimed in their direction. Rubber-neckers, ghouls – he'd never figured out a good title for those who came to stare at the suffering of others. He shifted position again. Right now, he was too tired, too frustrated, to deal with them. No matter where the battle took place – the north slope of Mt Ararat at two A.M., near an undersea volcano at three in the afternoon, behind forty-seven feet of steel-reinforced concrete three days after the crack of doom (doom or dawn?)– somehow people with cameras glued to their faces would appear. And they'd expect him to sign autographs (against Company policy), smile for the damn camera (not his idea of fun, but required of him by his contract) and listen, patiently, to whatever inanity and twaddle they wanted to spout. There were times when he thought that it would be easier saving the human race on a daily basis if he just didn't have to deal with the actual humanity.

"Many thanks," said Mysterious West, ducking down behind his broad-chested form and whipping out a compact from one of her pockets. Flipping it open, she inspected herself critically. "I'm gettin' too old for this," she told him before surreptitiously touching up her dark red lip-gloss, refreshing her blush. "What do you think, boy? Am I ready for my close up, Mr. De Mille?" she joked, then looked up into Ultra Man's face. "Hey, what's the matter, baby? How'd things go?"

"Bad," he replied in a low grumble. "You know, I've battled sea monsters, bank robbers and creatures from other worlds. Why is it I can't get a date?"

"Dates, you can get. Do get. It's her. It's tougher when she's 'the one.'" West patted him on the arm, her bracelets chiming. "Better luck you'll be having next time," she consoled him, her voice dropping to a whisper as she snapped the compact shut. "If you need, I have some charms that can bring a woman's heart to heel. It's dangerous magic, so I recommend you to wait. Better do it the ordinary way. What takes hard work to make, lasts longer."

"Well, magic doesn't seem like playing fair," said Ultra Man, and blushed at West's wicked chuckle.

"Fair? In love, no one plays fair, boy. You think those muscles of yours are fair?"

Ultra Man's smile faded. "I can't take it again. She just shut me down. I didn't even get to *ask* her out. She knew what was coming and," he paused, staring at his special scuff resistant boots. "I don't know why I even try. Anyone else can talk to her. Why does she freeze me out? She doesn't even give me a chance. I should just give up."

"No, love, you know you're not going to give up."

"You don't understand. She looks at me and I get this chill, straight through to the heart. Stops me dead in my tracks. I'm wasting my time, and I know it. I should accept it. She doesn't want me. It wouldn't kill me to date someone else. A few years from now, I could be laughing at myself and all the time I wasted on her while sitting on the couch beside some other woman who loves me."

"Ha!"

Ultra Man shrugged. "What's wrong with me, West? Why can't I just move on? Would it kill me to acknowledge she's just not interested?"

Mysterious West just smiled, and after a moment the corners of Ultra Man's mouth turned up as well.

"You're right. I can't do it. I can't give up on her."

"Keep the faith, boy. Momma will fix," She glanced around to where the PR rep was beckoning. "Hey, looks like they're ready for us. Professional face, baby."

She flashed him a smile, brilliant white against her dark skin, straightened her shoulders, and sauntered toward the cameras.

Ultra Man took a deep breath, straightened his shoulders, and allowed his features to settle into the familiar mask, even though most of it couldn't be seen beneath his visor. He could tell Mysterious West had to work harder every day to put that spring in her step, that confident, spicy swagger that was her trademark. He bent to pick up a discarded fragment of spell-cloth and rubbed it between his fingers. Her retirement joke was becoming less funny. Soon, too soon for Ultra Man, Mysterious West would retire, and he would be without his mentor, partner, and friend.

Now, despite everything, he had to appear confident, assured, and strong. That was the image he was trained to project, no matter what happened. Of course, it wasn't hard when you were putting your fist into some bad guy's face. But when facing the press? No, that wasn't so easy. Tucking the fragment inside his glove, he fixed his 'dashing' smile in place, and floated over to his mark, readying himself to throw his scripted words into the News machine.

Chapter Two.

The truth about Captain Fabulous' love nest. Photo along top of page 2, 3, 4, 5, 6, and fold out page 12.
London: News of the Screws.

Editorial Staff meeting
Northern Star Daily
35 cents per issue. Weekly discount rate - including Sunday edition $2.25. E-book and Print.

"Can't take it again ... she," said the tiny image of Ultra Man on the TV screen as he turned away. The screen image jumped and skipped as the person holding the camera phone scrambled to get the gesticulating Ultra Man back in frame again. Ultra Man was standing in the moonscape-like wreckage of the apartment building, facing the vague colored fog that was all any camera would record of The Mysterious West. Her damned magic field confused both light and sound. So while they could occasionally pick up a word or two of Ultra Man's, West's replies were little more than the buzzing of bees. "Freeze me.... out ... chill ... straight through to the heart ... stops me ... dead ... kills me ... Can't do it."

"This is the greatest thing to ever happen to our paper." The editor stalked across the room and slammed his hand down near his computer screen. The monitor shuddered and swayed on the table, held upright only by the piles of paper that surrounded it. The editorial staff studied pens, tablets, blank note pages, and awaited enlightenment. "Fortunately for us, the guy who shot this film showed it to a cousin of his who works for us, instead of calling around the TV guys. God, what an idiot. Can you imagine what the networks would have paid for this?" The editor paused to grin and rub his hands together. "Never mind. His innocence is our gain. With this in our possession, we've got a full news cycle's jump on the existence of a new Villainess. We can set the pace. Set the tone. A chance like this doesn't fall into the hands of a newspaper more than once a decade, and we are going to milk it for every inch of advertising space we can sell." His staff exchanged puzzled glances. The editor – who had paused, waiting for applause and celebration - growled and started prowling again. "What? You can't see it. You can't read between the lines. You've just seen film of Ultra Man admitting he's terrified of a Super Villainess. "*She*," he said. "*Can't take it*," he said."

He waited for a chorus of questions in vain. A few minutes passed before the first member of his staff responded.

"Perhaps we should watch it again," said his political specialist. "I didn't hear '*Villainess.*'"

"Who said Supers use the word '*Villainess*'?" demanded the editor. "They've probably got their own in-house terminology for the criminals. Besides, so what if you don't hear the word, can't you hear what he's not saying? Read his body language." The editor rewound a few seconds of video, hit the pause button. "Look at him. That is the posture of a man who has just been beaten to within an inch of his life." He tapped a thick finger against the tiny TV screen. "Look at his shoulders – tensed, hunched. I saw men standing like that often enough when I was on the sports beat. That is the body of a man who has just seen himself at death's door. Hopeless. Helpless. Defeated. Isn't it wonderful?"

There were a few mumbles of comment now. Not very enthusiastic, but demonstrating some interest, some slow awakening to the possibilities.

"Are you sure that....?" began one less experienced individual.

"Of course I am. We're going to go to press saying there is a new Super Powered Villainess on the scene and – this is the perfect storm – she's so powerful *Ultra Man* is afraid of her! If we wait for the S.S.C. to confirm her existence, we'll get the same spoonful of preprocessed propaganda that everyone else gets. Dry, dull, unemotional list of Powers, drained of all sex appeal. But, if we act now, then we get to lead the pack. It will be our take. She'll be *our* Villainess."

The editor paused, his eyes unfocused as he contemplated the future. The future of his paper with its own signature, patron Villainess. The New York Times senior editor – *may he rot in hell, the snobby bastard* – couldn't claim a Villain or a Super of his very own. This particular scoop might just rupture his ulcer and wouldn't that be the icing on the cake.

"Problem is," observed the City Beat editor, rudely interrupting dreams of glory, "we haven't any information to go on. Just this little clip. What are we going to do with this?"

"Be creative! A new Villainess, fresh from her first battle. You know how she must be feeling. She's alone. By now, all the Super Teams will be ranged against her. Write that story. Her story."

"I thought we were a newspaper," muttered one reporter to his nearest neighbor, "not a soap opera...."

He glanced up, met the editor's gaze, and his mouth dried. No one actually moved or thought about moving. It was as if all the cells in all the other reporters' bodies spontaneously shifted three inches away, leaving him exposed to the editor's laser-beam stare.

"And, uh, we should write about how we're being forced to speculate because the S.S.C. haven't yet released any facts," he finished, fast.

"Good recovery," said the editor. "Give me an outline within the hour. Now, we need some color.... A picture.... That moron cousin of Albert's wasn't there early enough to get a shot of her, and there've been millions of photos taken of Ultra Man...." He kicked the art director's chair. "You, Floyd, earn your money. I want an artist's impression for the front page."

"We don't have a description, boss. Haven't been able to get close to the survivors," Floyd protested as he caught the sketchpad that came flying across the room. "We need somewhere to start."

"Let's see. Yeah, you're right. First, we need a name. Ultra Man said she chilled him, froze him, with a glance. Think, people. Who is she?"

"Um....Chill Out. Chill Girl. Snow Flake. Snow Maid," suggested one reporter.

The editor shook his head and resumed pacing.

"Miss Ice. Ms. Ice. Ice Maid," said another.

"Nah, that makes it sound like she should be selling snow cones on the Jersey Shore."

"Ice Queen," said the head of the Sunday Magazine, directing a glare toward the Metro beat's Goth assistant.

"That's it," cried the editor, stabbing one thick finger toward Floyd. "Until we know better, we'll call her Ice Queen. Yeah, that works." He ignored the faint protests from those seated safely in the back; instead, he loomed over the art director's chair. "Ice Queen sounds good to me."

"Maybe she won't like it, boss. She's probably got her own title for herself."

"Too bad if she does." The editor dismissed the threat potential of an unknown Villainess. Even bad guys knew they had to keep the press alive to keep giving them air time and ink. "If she wants to tell us who she really is, I'm willing to listen. I'm a reasonable guy. I'll give her front page today and, when she contacts us to clear it up, we'll give her the front page tomorrow. You know Joe Q Public; he'll eat it all up with a spoon. The first announcement. The controversy when we get more information. All of it. It'll all sell! For now, Floyd, try for something stunning in silver and blue. We know that one glance from her and Ultra Man is on his knees, so we know she's strong, powerful, has presence.... *Gravitas*...."

Floyd's pencil flew across the page. "So, you're looking for something in a D cup?"

It was mid-morning when Ali reached the not-at-all-secret headquarters of the Super Teams™. The Super Support SS.C. ™ tower glowed as it speared above the Jersey City skyline, a single finger of copper and silver raised at New York City across the harbor. A few decades before, New York had refused the first Super Teams permission to build their headquarters within any of its boroughs. The mayor at that time had claimed he didn't want to increase crime by having the S.S.C. and the Supers acting as trouble magnets. (A decision vigorously protested by the New York Times city editor.) Eventually, the S.S.C. had set up shop in Jersey City, waving their existence and prosperity defiantly at the city across the sound.

The huge S.S.C. logo in front of the building turned on its base, held aloft by statues of the 'originals' - the five members of the first Super Team. Ali wasn't old enough to remember the first man walking on the moon, or even the day the 'first' Supers stopped their random rescues, formed the SS.C. – and hired their first lawyer. To be honest, she hadn't paid much attention to Super history in school. When she was growing up, the Super Teams had been as much a part of the scenery as police, politicians and pimples, and she'd cared more about the pimples. After taking the job with the S.S.C., she'd been too busy just getting through the day to pay attention to the mythos of the Company.

By the time Ali was within three blocks of the S.S.C. building, she and her car had already undergone four unobtrusive security scans. Now, at the entrance to the employee's garage, three guards equipped with electronic scanners and sniffing dogs waved her to the side of the road. Ali's eyes drifted shut and she slumped in her seat as they searched her car. The whole car shook when the youngest slammed his scanner against the passenger side door. Ali graced the boy with a narrow-eyed glare that dissolved into a smile when she saw the terror on the youngster's face.

"Ooze," the boy hissed to his superior, backing away from the car. "I'm picking up Ooze's chemical signature."

The older man patiently tapped keys on the scanner and shot a sympathetic glance in Ali's direction.

"We'll have you on your way in a minute, Site Supervisor," he said, and then held up the readout for the youngster. "Now see here, George, this gauge here says there are less than three ounces of Ooze in the car. Nowhere near enough for there to be a full-grown Villain hiding in the trunk. Likely the Site Supervisor stepped in something at an event site. Happens all the time. Now, you go ask her nicely to show you her shoes "

Ali reached over to open her passenger side door, pointed at the floor and waited while the guards – using special handling equipment – opened the top of the bag and poked the ruined suede boots with tiny probes. The guards went into a huddle, whispered into communicators all the while Ali struggled to stay awake.

"Sorry, Site Supervisor," said the senior guard, "You're over the allowed contamination by 3.7 grams. You have to enter through Decom entrance. Your car will be impounded, examined, and if necessary, decontaminated. I'll flag it as urgent, so, if you're lucky, it'll be ready for you to pick up before the end of business today."

"Thanks," muttered Ali, well aware that her business day could last until after midnight. "Ask them to change the oil while they have it."

She drove a few more blocks to the 'secure' parking entrance, into the car elevator, and handed her keys over to another anonymous person in a Hazmat suit. Yet another security guard emerged from the side doors and used safety prongs to lift the plastic bag out of her car and into a wheeled, hazardous materials box. Ali followed him along the too-brightly lit for her tired eyes corridors. Fortunately, her escort wasn't feeling chatty and satisfied himself with maintaining a professional, alert watch over Ali and her dangerous plastic bag of shoes, all the way down to Decomtam Ali's feet squeaking on the chill floor was the only sound as they walked deeper into the building. When they reached the locked, bolted, and secure airlock that was the entrance to Decontam, Ali pressed the buzzer and waited, trying to ignore her guard and the TV screens embedded in the wall near the door.

It was almost impossible to escape TVs in the S.S.C. building. In the main building, TV sets were positioned beside each receptionist and secretary, and on and in every flat surface. It wasn't even possible to escape in the bathrooms. The SS.C. hadn't gone as far as to put them in the stalls, but the talking heads yammered endlessly from sets on the wall between the hand dryers. Usually, Ali was able to tune them out, but today she was so tired that the voices echoed behind her eyes. She leaned against the wall to rest while the nearest set rattled on about The Blast's blackmail threat to deface Mount Rushmore being thwarted by the local Super Team, sixteen police sharp shooters, and the fire departments of five counties.

Finally, the door to Decontamination clicked open with a rush of disinfectant-scented air and Ali entered alone. The only occupant of the small foyer was a small, scowling woman sitting at the intake desk. She stopped slapping the bejeezus out of a computer when Ali's Hazmat box rolled to a stop beside the counter.

"You again." The woman, grey-haired, pale-eyed and almost as wide across her shoulders as she was tall, regarded the sticky mess without enthusiasm. "What is it this time?"

"Hey, Deloris. Ooze's ooze," said Ali.

The woman used the end of a pencil to pull down the edge of the plastic, peered into the bag and tutted.

"Might as well toss these," she advised, "by the time we've finished with them, there'll be nothing left but dust."

"What a surprise," Ali groaned, rubbing her tired eyes. "What about my work boots? Are any of them back yet?"

Deloris tapped a few keys to pull up Ali's file and read slowly, tugging at her lower lip with highly polished, two-inch long, green and bronze striped nails. Ali sniffed but said nothing. She found it difficult to respect anyone who decorated their body with Super color schemes.

"Lessee. Currently, on my list, we have three sets work boots, size nine. First set condemned – chemical and/or radiation contamination beyond safe limits even after processing. What *were* you playing in? Ah, yes, Nuclear Projectile Vomiting Man site. The second set – destroyed during treatment." She glanced up at Ali. "How many does that make it this year? Nineteen pairs? A bit hard on your stuff, aren't you? The Colonel will not be pleased."

"I'm first or second On-Site, it gets messy."

"I expect it does," said Deloris absently, returning her attention to the screen. "Looks like your third set survived, but they're not ready for pick up. They need to be re-soled. The Colonel has them. Try Thursday."

Ali nodded and waved at the ruined suede.

"Do me a favor? Send these boots out for Decontam anyway. If they're destroyed, at least I'll have a record. Maybe this time, I'll get reimbursed."

"No problem." Deloris put on a pair of thick, insulated gloves and used a pair of tongs to place the Hazmat box into a larger, metal box. She sealed and labeled the package, dropped it onto a conveyor belt, then printed out a receipt. "I'll send a note down to The Colonel and put in an order for more replacements. Looks like you're going to need them."

A quick spin through the chemical showers and Ali was "decontaminated." Her guard vanished, leaving Ali, now smelling faintly of citrus, to make the trip to her office on the fifth floor alone. When the elevator doors opened, Ali staggered out into the Legal Department's wide foyer. Uniforms and insignia's of Supers past and present were displayed in protective reinforced glass cases along the walls, along with photographs of famous event sites. A few curious civilians wandered between the displays, suitably awed, while they waited for the honor of being admitted past the banks of secretaries. Ali ignored them, striding off down a side corridor. She stopped in at Nigel's office to hand the '*hold harmless*' forms to his secretary.

"You missed the morning meeting," said Lena, looking down her nose at the dust-covered papers, but making no move to take them.

"Being in two places at one time isn't my Superpower," drawled Ali and dropped the bundle on Lena's desk.

"Too bad," said Lena, as she reached for a handful of tissues, dusting the papers clean before putting them into a folder with the S.S.C. logo embossed in silver. "Would help though, wouldn't it?" she said.

"Hardly," muttered Ali, turning to leave. "That would just mean there'd be two of me to be exhausted."

Originally, the sign on Ali's desk had read simply, *Ali Brent, Assistant Insurance Assessor,* and she'd shared a tiny room in a sub-subbasement with six other overworked drones. Over the years, she'd been promoted and promoted again. Now her door read Site Supervisor *and* Northeast Regional Supervisor. Her office crept closer and closer to the center of power, until she was just down the corridor from the offices of the S.S.C. lawyers - Hackham, Breakham, Bendit and Crunch, and one floor down from the office of Control – the ultimate authority and C.E.O. of the S.S.C.

"More responsibility," she mused, running her hand over her nameplate before pushing the door open. "Less sleep. No life."

Inside, Ali's two personal assistants and her secretary were arranging papers on a long side table. They paused and favored her with suspicious looks as she entered. No doubt they already knew about the midnight call out. If they'd missed the morning news reports, then the faintly sour citrus smell of the Decontam spray would warn them that Ali had just come in from an event site. She stopped in the middle of a floor littered with still more piles of paper, tapped her fingers rapidly on her attaché, and grinned at them.

"Bad news, Eliza," she said, and a small blonde woman flinched, "I've got another four hundred and twenty-six files to add to your collection."

Eliza, Ali's secretary, nudged a trashcan forward with her foot. "Stack 'em in this secure round file. I'll get back to them sometime this century."

"Good plan," Ali agreed, ignoring the trashcan, she dropped the files into an empty cardboard box on the table. "Naomi, I'm assigning this new site to you."

A slender girl with caramel brown skin and black eyes groaned, clutched at her throat and sank to her knees. "No. Please. Mercy, I beg you," she cried. "I'm swamped."

The corner of Ali's lips quirked as she watched Naomi's performance. This particular one was a little over the top, so she'd have to give it only seven out of ten. Although the Canadian judge might have given her higher marks, just for the chin tremble. After all, she was demonstrating considerable Creativity and Technical Skill.

"Come on, Naomi, I know your workload. I've just signed off on one of your sites as completed. Another has all paperwork submitted and we're just waiting for payment. Besides, this one is easy. If everyone is telling the truth, only three of the households are completely uninsured, the rest claim to have the recommended riders."

"Well, that's okay, then,' said Naomi, brightening and coming to her feet.

Ali waited until she accepted the box before adding, "And we need to contact the DMV about the one hundred and seven squashed cars in the garage next door. Hopefully, they're insured, too."

Naomi's eyes narrowed. "Witch," she muttered.

"Why, thank you," said Ali, with a bow and a smile before turning to Eliza. "Did I miss anything interesting in this morning's meeting?"

"We spent an hour discussing the upcoming charity event. I managed to keep you off all of the committees - again. And I managed to keep you from being volunteered for any *duties* on the night. You may thank me later. I've put a list of suitable rewards on your desk, beginning with reassignment to our Hawaii office."

"Such efficiency," drawled Ali, in a reasonable imitation of Nigel Hackham. "Anything else?"

"They discussed *thinking* about hiring a Supervisor for the Midwest. Next week, maybe, they'll talk about thinking of starting actual recruitment."

"Wonderful," said Ali, frustration and fatigue making her voice sharp. "In the meantime, what are we supposed to do? We're drowning trying to keep up with the event sites of two regions."

"Maybe you should go to the occasional meeting and say that," suggested Eliza.

"Emails are easier," said Ali, with a shrug and started sorting through the reports that had accumulated since she'd left at midnight. "That way, you don't have to look Mr. Breakham in the eye when suggesting he spend money."

The girls laughed and Ali sat down at her desk. Powering up her computer, she opened the spreadsheet showing assignments completed, pending, and stalled. Her little group of three, and the central region group of five in Ohio were handling enough work to keep twice that number of people busy, and Ali had to keep up with all of them -as well as staying in contact with her colleagues in the other regions. The delay replacing the Midwest Supervisor was wearing her down. She needed someone to take back that half of her workload. She needed a vacation. She needed one night's sleep without a midnight call. From the look of things, none of those needs were likely to be met any time soon.

"For them to take this much time means that someone has a relative they want the S.S.C. to hire,' Ali mused, dropping a handful of junk mail into the trash and tucking the remainder under a collector's quality 'The Thump' paperweight, "and it's taking longer than they thought to bury all the bodies."

"Cynic," said Eliza.

"Realist," countered Ali, resting her forehead against the computer screen. "Did they say anything about my request for more on-site staff? I need another person to be approved to do emergency call-outs."

"I'm sorry, they put that down for later debate," Eliza replied. "Said something about the expense of the security of another naked face not being something they want to undertake right now. Not if they're planning on hiring someone for the Midwest slot."

Ali bared her teeth at the screen and shook her head.

"I didn't really expect them to do anything immediately, but I can't keep doing this. I'm asleep on my feet." Sagging, Ali propped her elbows on her desk and pressed her fingers against her temples. "What else?" she asked, closing her eyes.

"Nothing much. I gave the reports on the airport, 43$^{rd.}$ street, and the Elizabeth wharf site on your behalf. You've been thanked for your hard work, by the way. Don't you just feel the love? The bids have been approved and work started on the Rhode Island site. Mr. Breakham asked for a written update on today's event ASAP."

"Surprise, surprise." Turning her head, Ali opened her eyes just enough to stare at the fax machine that was already spitting out page after page of tightly printed text. "Oh goodie, a light day at the office. Maybe we'll take the afternoon off and go holiday shopping."

Eliza picked up another pile of paper and started sorting. "Sure. The amount of time we spend sipping coffee and filing our nails, I don't know how we justify taking our exorbitant salaries."

Ali's only response was a snort.

While her assistants resumed their work, Ali pulled her notes out of her bag and tried to get her thoughts in order. She reached into a side drawer, pulled out another package of caffeine tablets and dry swallowed two. Pulling a face at the bitter taste, she rested her forehead on her hand while she waited for the chemicals to perk up her system, and thought about this morning's confrontation with Ultra Man.

Maybe fatigue was the reason she'd let him annoy her again. She managed to avoid him most of the time, an easier task than expected despite them working for the same S.S.C., in the same region. Usually, by the time she got to a crime scene, he and his team were long gone. Weeks could pass and she didn't have to acknowledge his existence. But when she did run into him, he seemed to be driven by some perverse twist in his personality to keep hitting on her. She'd tried ignoring him, saying 'no' in fourteen different languages, had even taken out a sworn statement that she wouldn't go anywhere with him *even* if he were the-last-man-on-earth. Yet, time would pass, she'd run into him again and earn herself another unwanted proposition.

She knew his powers were flight, endurance, and strength. It was frustrating to learn that they also included incredible denseness of the head.

It was almost midnight when Ali got home. Pausing just inside her apartment to kick off the new shoes she'd picked up instead of eating lunch, she curled her aching toes into the thick carpet. The living room light was on - not a good sign - and there were empty junk food packages scattered across the couch that hadn't been there this morning. She took a few cautious steps into the apartment and braced for the next disaster.

"Hey, girlfriend, you're out of ice cream."

As far as Ali could tell, the voice could have come from the kitchen, her bedroom, living room, or the aching cavern between her ears. She dropped a box of paper and her computer onto her living room table before staggering to the kitchen to dump the grocery bags.

A purple blur surrounded, then preceded her through the swinging door. By the time Ali reached the kitchen table, the blur had resolved itself into a tall, purple-clad, black man, his neatly shaven head glowing by the light of the open refrigerator.

"I stopped off on the way home," said Ali, with a sigh, hefting the shopping bags. "What do you want, rocky road, or raspberry swirl?"

"Rocky road."

Before she could blink, the bag was snatched from her hands, the lids vanished from the top of both pints, and a spoon appeared, quivering in the frozen yogurt. The whole fridge shook on its wheels as its door slammed shut.

"Slow to my speed," growled Ali, prying the spoon free and waving it at the purple blur, "and take it easy with my stuff. You break it, you replace it."

"I'm sorry," said The Purple Lightning, between bites. *His* pint was already half empty. "You know what my metabolism is like. I'm starving."

"Better slow down, my lad, 'cause it looks like you're pushing the boundaries of your Super suit," said Ali, poking him in the stomach, her finger sinking into the second knuckle. "They'll be calling you The Purple Pudge soon."

"Well, thanks loads." P.L.'s expression darkened and he stared unhappily into the carton.

"Sorry," said Ali, leading the way into the living room. "I'm short of sleep and cranky."

"You and the rest of the SS.C.," said P.L. "You, however, are forgiven."

It was no surprise that he managed to get into the living room first. He was dropping into her visitor's chair near the window when Ali spotted the open curtains neatly framing the apartments across the street.

"Hey, be careful,' cried Ali, yanking the curtains shut one-handed. "I don't want my neighbors knowing you're here."

The Purple Lightning vanished. Simply vanished. One moment he was there and the abandoned pint and spoon hovered in mid-air. They had not even been noticed by gravity by the time he returned, now wearing loose green and blue sweatpants and rope sandals. His bare chest was still muscular, but his exposed belly overhung the belt, making him look like a very colorful Buddha.

"Gotta start exercising some portion control there, Oliver, there's more of you than there used to be," said Ali, as she sat down and propped her feet up on the littered coffee table. "What will your fans say?"

"More of me to love?" said Oliver, falling into the matching chair, "Be realistic, girlfriend, when I work I'm using up calories like gangbusters. When I slow down it takes my metabolism a little while to chill out, and by the time I realize I should stop eating I've usually polished off half a dozen pizzas."

"Okay, we should talk about your food choices, as well. Maybe you could limit your post Super-speed pig-outs to salad?"

"Yuck." Oliver rolled his eyes but put the half-finished dessert down. "What am I supposed to do?" he wailed. "It's not like I can take up jogging or anything like that. Run a hundred times around the equator? It'll just make me hungry again."

Ali didn't reply for a few minutes. Poor Oliver's weight was a serious problem, one that had been discussed at more than one high-level S.S.C. meeting. She hoped Oliver didn't know about them. Poor guy would be embarrassed as hell to realize that his weight had been discussed by several serious lawyers, Control, and The Colonel, all sitting around a heavy oak table sipping lattes and eating bagels and croissants.

It'd been an interesting meeting, Ali remembered. They'd consulted flow charts and diagrams. Compared before and after photos of Oliver, and the SS.C. doctors had muttered dire words about P.L.'s health and effectiveness. The Colonel had made a presentation on the physics of the changes in P.L.'s velocity and the diameter of his turning circles resulting from the increase in his 'ballast'. Ali's lips twitched just thinking about it.

No, it was better that he didn't know. He was sensitive enough about his weight and the out-of-control hunger pangs he experienced after a session of using his Super power.

"You could always try my gym," suggested Ali, gently. "I'd been having trouble going three or four times with my crazy schedule, so I signed up at this place that makes you work out really, really slowly. I only have to go once a week for half an hour, and it's supposed to be the equivalent of a weeks' worth of workouts."

"You're joking," said Oliver. "That would never work. Besides, any exercise just makes me hungry."

"Give it a try," said Ali, reaching for her handbag and ruffling through the piles of stuff that accumulated over the years. "Going slow could be just the thing for you. If you don't use your Super Power, there shouldn't be any hunger pangs. Do it the same way a normal person would. I've got a guest trial coupon here. Call them tomorrow."

Oliver regarded the offered square of cardboard without enthusiasm.

"Come on, Oliver," Ali urged, waving the coupon at him. "What would it hurt to try?"

"Well,"

"And I am assuming, since it took you no time at all to get changed, that your latest roomie has thrown you out. Is it, or is it not true that your suitcases are stacked in my closet again?"

Oliver gave her a shamefaced smile, hunched over in the chair and nodded. "Do you mind if I crash here for a few days?"

Mind? thought Ali. *Mind having a Super in my house, eating me out of house and home? Especially since where one was, the others were sure to visit. Particular others.*

She slumped down further in the chair and rested her chin on her chest. She was getting too old for midnight gabfests and the blow-by-blow rehashing of some Super fight. Pizza and beer parties were for college kids, not over-worked and exhausted insurance assessors. Cleaning up in the morning after the Mysterious West had decided to do spell experiments and burned holes in a tablecloth, table, the carpet, and, possibly, the apartment underneath, was not something she wanted to do again. And if she wasn't careful, you-know-who would start behaving as if Oliver sharing her apartment was a good reason for him to drop over at any time of the night or day.

No, having a Super as a roomie was not fun. Most people had ordinary soaps under their kitchen sink. When Oliver was staying with her, Ali's cleaning supplies came in special containers by secure courier, and her trash was removed in the middle of the night by silent men in protective clothing.

Useful, but a little disconcerting.

She preferred to spend her spare time as far away from Supers as possible. But as she studied Oliver's unhappy face she knew that, yet again, she'd let him stay. She reached over and ran a hand over Oliver's shaven scalp. Having him crash at her place between love affairs had gone beyond habit and achieved the rank of Tradition. Besides, when he was living somewhere else she missed him – junk food cravings and all.

"It's fine," she said, "on the condition that you go to the gym."

"You charge a high price for your couch, lady." Oliver took the coupon with a scowl.

Ali ignored the comment. "So, why'd you get tossed this time? I thought you and Harry were doing fine."

"Oh, the usual," Oliver shrugged and picked up the ice cream again. "My unscheduled disappearances and unpredictability - etcetera. What was mysterious and charming when we were dating becomes emotional unavailability when we move in together."

"Ah. Yeah. I'm sorry."

Ali watched him eat for a moment. Of all the Super loonies, Oliver was the sweetest, and the one she'd known the longest. A mix-up in college had made them roommates in her freshman year – during which time she'd spent weeks trying to convince the college administration that she wasn't a guy. Considering she made most of her complaints to the Dean of Housing *in person*, that experience had been more than a little disheartening.

She credited Oliver with the fact that she'd graduated. He'd started working part-time for the S.S.C. somewhere during his last year and loaned her money for some of her tuition. The only thing she held against him was that he'd set her up with her current job.

She knew she should be grateful. There were hundreds, thousands, of people who would love to work anywhere in the Super Support. But security was tight, nepotism rife, and a personal recommendation necessary. Without one, it was near to impossible to get in the door. Ali graduated college forty-seventh in her class, with degrees in math and statistics and three recommendations for S.S.C. employment. Thanks to Oliver, Mysterious West and Ultra Man, Ali was actively recruited into the Super Support SS.C.

"Say, did you catch the news today?" Ali asked. Oliver in a funk was poor SS.C., and if he didn't start thinking about something else soon, he'd just keep eating.

"Yes!" Oliver brightened immediately and put his spoon down. "I got screen credit! The little old couple were so cute. I loved the bit when grandma said she'd get her granddaughter a membership in my fan club for a birthday present."

"It was nice of them."

"Don't think I don't know that you got them to do it, somehow."

"Not guilty," said Ali. "I'm not the one who went back into a crumbling building for a cat and an empty bird cage. If you want air time and credit for your work, you should slow down long enough to be seen, or turn up for the press conferences."

"Was it empty? I didn't notice. Ain't that a kick," Oliver laughed and glanced down at his bare belly. "But I'm not going on screen again until I lose a little weight."

"I *am* sorry about you and Harry."

"Occupational hazard. I should be used to it."

"Maybe you should try something different this time. Instead of looking for a nice person you enjoy spending time with, maybe you get someone who's self-absorbed, selfish and only cares if you're not around when you don't pay the rent on time."

"My kind of guy," said Oliver solemnly, "I'm so desperate that I'll even give that some thought. In the meantime, I heard from West that you turned Ultra Man down for a date again."

"Gossip travels faster than you," she said, keeping her voice steady and face still.

"Always has," Oliver leaned forward and peered up at her, wiggling his eyebrows. "Soooo, no dice?"

"Leave it alone, Oliver," said Ali.

"Come on, Al Pal, he – "

Ali raised her hand and stopped him. "If you're going to pitch him at me, Oliver, then you can start looking for another place to stay. I may have to put up with the insane Supers – present S.S.C. excepted – at work, but there is no way I'm letting one into my social life."

"What social life?"

"Thank you so much for the reminder, *girlfriend*." Ali kept her face carefully blank to cover the hurt. Oliver failed relationships and all got more action than Ali. Hell, there was moldy bread in her kitchen that had more of a life than she did. "Just for that, I'm getting rid of the fold-out sofa and replacing it with something – I dunno – steel pipe modern? Nordic carved wood? Then where will you sleep?"

Oliver considered the options for a moment then gave a fake shudder and changed the subject. "What's on your schedule for tonight? How about we see what's on Pay per View?"

"Not tonight," Ali jerked her thumb toward the paper-filled box on the table. "A thirty-minute fight for you guys results in a month of shuffling paper for me. I've got to get a prelim report ready for Mr. Breakham. He wants it first thing yesterday morning."

"Sorry."

Ali sank back in her chair, rubbing her face. "Ah, it's okay. It's the job, my job, after all. I just get tired sometimes."

"Of being woken in the middle of the night? Hey, we don't pick the fight times, the Villains do."

"Nah," Ali shook her head. "Not so much that. More of going to see people who've just had their houses or livelihoods destroyed in two seconds, usually by something that's entirely preventable."

"Hey!" Oliver's feet hit the floor hard as he stood up to confront her. "That's a bit much. Sometimes we're all that's between someone and painful, messy death."

"And what was this morning's near fatal disaster?" asked Ali, sarcasm dripping from her chill voice.

"Ah. Well." Oliver sank back into his chair. "We were acting on a tip that Nuclear Man was going to be there. We were trying to catch him."

"And ended up trashing a six-story apartment house and a parking garage that serves two apartment complexes and a hospital. Looking for someone who was home with a cold. Some threat!"

Tension stiffened his shoulders and Oliver hunched forward and scraped the last of the chocolate syrup out of his carton. "Yeah. That's about the size of it."

"Good work."

"Thanks."

Silence reigned for a few minutes while Oliver stared at his fingernails and Ali watched her dessert melt to mush.

"I'm sorry, Oliver. I didn't mean it."

"Sure, you did. But it's okay, sweetie. That's how it goes. There are times when I wonder what it is I'm trying to achieve. It seemed so simple when I started. Saving the world from Evil looks good as a headline, but it gets kind of old fast when Evil just keeps coming back. There's always one more Super Villain. One more Powered up, the illegitimate son of some guy you put away years ago." He glanced over at the pile of paper. "Maybe I should try your job."

"You haven't been in the business long enough to worry about sons," said Ali, and waited for Oliver to stop laughing. "Anyway, you don't want to process damage reports and insurance claims. Read contractor-rebuilding assessments and debate the prices of different window treatments? Argue with people about whether the coat they lost was camel hair or polyester? Not your style."

"Sure. C'mon, let me help. It's only fair. I helped make the mess, I should help with the clean-up."

In a blink, he was gone. By the time Ali turned in her chair, Oliver had her computer out of its bag, papers out of their box and neatly arranged in piles over the table. Oliver was seated, hands poised over the keyboard when Ali leapt across the room.

"Listen, you!" she cried, waving her finger under his nose. "If you use Super speed on my computer, melt my keyboard, crash my hard drive, and destroy several years' worth of records, I will personally, with my own hands, break you into teeny, tiny, little pieces and feed your purple ass to my fish."

Oliver glanced across the room to where a nine-inch long fish circled in solitary splendor in its huge tank and came to his feet slowly.

"How about I read while you type?" he suggested, not taking his eyes off the fish.

"Good plan."

Chapter Three

The Northern Star Daily
Ultra Man admits he's terrified of New Super Villainess: The Ice Queen.

Ali woke to the sound of the Flight of the Valkyries playing in the living room. Recognizing it as the tune Oliver had selected for his phone, she pulled her quilt over her head and burrowed back into the warmth. There was a thud, which she guessed was Oliver falling off the couch, followed by swearing, then silence. Ali tossed, trying to find a comfortable position and get a few more hours of sleep, when her own pager starting jangling. Throwing back her bedding, Ali grabbed the phone and tossed it at the wall. Oliver swooped in from the living room and caught it before it reached its destination. Bowing, he held the still-chiming phone out to her.

"Hey, girl. A gracious good morning to you."

"Oliver? I thought you'd be out of here already." Ali read the text, hit the off button and dropped the phone on her bedside table.

"Nah. Got a 'non-urgent' message. The Midwest active teams interrupted a burglary at a bank and are pursuing the Villains. The backup team was called up to continue patrol, and I get to be woken up and asked to go be 'present' at the crime scene since they've no one spare since Wolf Woman is out on maternity leave. They piled on the guilt. You know, be a good guy, and help out the Midwest crew. They're so short-handed. You can get there fastest. Yadda yadda yadda."

"They know how to push the buttons, don't they?" Ali sank back against her pillows and pressed her hands against her face. Her skin felt overheated, brittle, and dry, a testament to how long it had been since she'd had the time and energy to apply any moisturizers, let alone makeup. "Three nights in a row. God, what did I do wrong in a previous life to deserve this?" After a moment she held out her hand for the pager. Oliver held it at eye height. She blinked several times before she could focus on the glowing letters. "Chicago? Oh, for heavens' sake. That's what? Four hours away? With a full site review, I won't get home tonight." She sighed and sagged back against her pillows. "Maybe Norman hasn't left with the Chinook yet."

"On your feet," ordered Oliver, dragging the quilt the rest of the way off her. "I'll take you. I'll even leave a message with Control and arrange for someone to bring you home when you're done. Personal door-to-door, or window-to-window, service. Depends on who's free for transport." At her startled look he laughed, "Hey, you should have some benefits for all the time you spend cleaning up after us."

Ali ran her tongue over her teeth and grimaced. "Do I have time to splash water on my face? Get dressed?"

"You've got five," said Oliver, tugging his tunic into place and pretending to leer down at her. "On your feet, girlfriend, or I'm gonna take you as you are."

Ali looked down at the ancient sweat suit that served as her PJ's. It was tempting to go as she was. Maybe if she looked the way she felt, she'd get some sympathy. Nah. Not likely, she sighed and dragged herself upright.

"What's the weather like today?" asked Ali, as her feet hit the floor.

"In Chicago? Windy!"

"What a mess," Oliver observed.

Resting safely in Oliver's purple-clad arms, Ali craned her neck to look over the edge of the quilt that was wrapped tightly around her body and nodded her agreement. Brilliant white floodlights brought the crime scene into stark, unforgiving focus. The blue and red lights of the police cars chased each other over the shattered walls and windows. From the epicenter of the bank, the damage radiated outward. The pattern of shattered glass and concrete looked like The Shriek's handiwork, a day earlier than his expected recovery time. The Shriek's cry had taken out the windows to the fifth floor on the nearest buildings, scaling down to the ground floor windows as far as four blocks away. And, of course, just to make Ali's morning complete, the site was crawling with people.

When she stepped away from P.L's Super-heated warmth., the chill early morning air hit her and she started to shiver.

"I hope someone did a scan before they let all these civilians in," she said through chattering teeth.

Oliver lowered Ali to her feet and wandered off a few steps, scanning the scene. Unwinding from her quilt, Ali stamped her feet and rubbed her hands together, waiting for sensation to return to her extremities. Her stomach felt as if it was still somewhere over Ohio. She knew she would never get used to traveling *SuperStyle*. What with P.L.'s body pumping out waves of heat, and the air's friction, the only thing that protected her skin and kept the meat on her bone, was one very old and battered quilt.

Yawning until her jaw cracked, she fumbled with the zip on her attaché, searching for her phone. She needed to send a text to get the Super Clean team in contact with local glaziers ASAP. From the look of the site, they were in for a significant windfall.

Oliver tugged at his purple mask and tight belt, then waved to the nearest cluster of police officers.

"I'll leave you here, Ali," he began.

"Actually, you'd better stay put until I show someone my ID. Getting dropped off at a crime scene by a Super, in the presence of cops, might be misunderstood."

Oliver glanced back at the crowd of police officers now heading in their direction, expressions intent, hands resting on weapons.

"I get your point," raising his hand to wave again, he faced the cops and called, "Hey, guys, come on over and meet a friend of mine. She needs coffee, by the way, and I wouldn't mind a spare doughnut. Or ten."

"Wow," whispered the skinniest of the cops as P.L. zipped away toward the damaged bank. "Do they fly you around a lot?"

"Run, not fly, in Purple Lightning's case," Ali snorted and ran her fingers through her tangled hair. "And hardly ever. It's rare for a member of the Super Teams to have any contact with the Clean-Up squad."

She gave the eager officer a puzzled look. He was watching her so intently that she was getting nervous. She'd heard the Supers complaining about being eaten alive by people's eyes. The weight of his gaze was almost palpable, and she found herself babbling.

"It was an exception. Because, um, it's... such an ... important crime scene. Yes. Important. They wanted everyone On-Site as soon as possible."

"Wow," said Officer Ford again, and he seemed to grow two inches taller.

Ali started backing away. "I have to, you know, start working. So, if you'd excuse me?"

"Oh, sure." Officer Ford nodded so briskly that Ali feared he'd concuss himself with his own chin. "Let me know if you want anything. Anything at all."

"Well, I'm fine for now. There will be other S.S.C. team members arriving shortly, so if you could let me know when they get here?"

"Sure. Absolutely. Yes, ma'am." He almost saluted, his hand hovering at shoulder height for a moment before it sank back to the grip of his pistol.

Ali walked a few steps down the splinter-covered street and glanced back at him. The officer was staring up at the sky, watching for whatever else might descend and add to his day. Smothering a grin, Ali searched through her bag for pens and camera and started work.

Glass shards littered the street like sharp, sparkling snow. Ali blessed the impulse that had made her pack her leather gloves when she'd left home and hoped that her new shoes would hold up. The last thing she needed was a trip to the emergency room to have a hundred glass shards pulled out of her feet.

Despite her first impression, there were very few true civilians about, thank goodness, and most of those were huddled around the police barricades waiting for clearance to start salvaging their businesses. None of the affected store owners and only one member of the bank's personnel were permitted past the roadblocks. Through the bank's shattered windows, she could see Oliver trailing along, following the manager and the crime scene team.

Ali sketched a rough grid map on her pad, added as many street names as she could see and started down one side road, her faithful police liaison trailing on her heels, still watching the sky. Ali made a mental note to warn him about irregularities she found in the pavement but otherwise left him to it.

Officer Ford's diligent sky search was rewarded two hours later when a police helicopter preceded the S.S.C. Chinook into the event area. The Super Clean™ logo glowed on the Chinook's belly and sides – and on the small black van dangling beneath it – as it maneuvered delicately through the canyon of high-rise buildings.

"What's that?" shouted Officer Ford over the rattle of helicopter blades.

Ali didn't answer; instead she grabbed the young officer by the collar and ducked into a storefront. With her scarf held over her face to shield herself from airborne glass fragments, she huddled close to a wall. The officer took the hint and pulled his regulation jacket up over his head. Even though *she'd* just pulled him out of harm's way, she had the feeling that he'd barely managed to keep himself from throwing himself on top of her to save her from possible injury. Meeting her steady, calm gaze and raised eyebrows, he settled back on his heels and kept his heroism to himself.

The Chinook descended until the black minivan swinging beneath it settled its wheels on the ground in the middle of the empty four-lane road. The magnetic clips disengaged, and the helicopter rose to hover. A moment later, a bulky figure emerged from the helicopter door and was lowered to the ground. As soon as he released the cable, the Chinook rose and vanished into the sky.

Ali waited until the worst of the noise had faded and glass shards settled before walking over to greet Norman.

Officer Ford had his gun out and was in front of her before she took two steps.

"Put that the heck away and take it easy," Ali soothed. "He's the one I'm waiting for. He's the S.S.C. Site Examiner. No one from our cleaning crew is allowed On-Site until he's determined if it's safe."

The officer gave her a narrow look.

"Including you?" he asked.

Ali laughed, "Oh, no. Well, yes, but I got here first, so he can yell all he wants. Don't get the idea I'm stupid. If we were informed that Nuclear Man had been here, then the Super Team would still be on site, preventing anyone without a Hazmat suit from doing anything until we'd completed containment and clean-up."

"Oh, okay."

Norman settled his protective suit in place and started scanning the nearest pile of wreckage. He glanced up as Ali crunched toward him. Ali assumed his face would be the usual airsick green under his mask, and he placed his feet carefully, as if distrustful of the ground.

"Well, hell, girl. How'd you get here so fast?"

"Purple Lightning carried her," said Officer Ford, before Ali could frame her reply.

Norman's masked face turned to Ali and they both nodded. There might not be many benefits to their jobs, but awing the locals was the most fun.

"Do me a favor," said Ali holding out the trash bag she'd been dragging around all morning. "Can I dump this with you? I'll need it again later."

Without comment, Norman ran a scanner over the outside of the bag, then took it and tossed it onto the passenger seat. Repositioning his re-breather mask, he gave Ali a nod and headed for the ruined bank.

"Wow," Officer Ford said as he watched Norman go by, obviously torn between the tedious job of following Ali around and the lure of all of the mysterious gadgets hanging from Norman's belt and pack.

"You know, I've always wanted to develop a Super Power," he said, before turning hopeful eyes on Ali. "I'm just twenty-five. That's not too late to get one, is it? I read somewhere that a guy down south got his powers when he was in his fifties."

"Yes, that would be Sam Kreptz," said Ali, making a mental note to zap an email off to old Sam. He'd be over the moon to hear that his reputation had spread this far north. "His Power is starting fires."

"You know his name?" Officer Ford's eyes opened wide – a blending of professional concern and awe. "Isn't that supposed to be a secret? What happened to him? Was he too old to join a Super Team?"

"Oh, no," Ali replied, crunching her way to the next storefront. She snapped a couple of photographs of the gaping windows, perforated clothing, and climbed through the door. "Sam's pretty open about his abilities, and never bothered with a secret identity. As far as being part of the Super Teams is concerned, he would love to join up. The problem is that he can only start fires when he's five inches away from his target, which has to be a bone dry, flammable object. Even then, the fire he produces is only this big." She held her thumb and forefinger up, with just enough space between them for light to be seen. "Barely more than a spark, really."

"He must have been disappointed," sighed the officer.

"Ah, he's not so bad off," she told him, taking another couple of snapshots of damaged mannequins before leaving the store again. Pausing to note the name of the store on her sketch, she added, "He's been officially listed as having Super Power, and he's been issued a logo, and a Super name for this little business he's started up. He does kiddie parties, is the guest of honor at fireworksWork displays that sort of thing. I understand he makes a nice living at it."

Leaving Officer Ford to puzzle out his reaction to that information, Ali turned to the next store. This one had clouded white fragments hanging from its windows instead of the usual clear glass. No skinny model figures or piles of shredded clothing filled this room. Instead, rows of uncomfortable seats sat facing a single overturned table. A smashed computer that she assumed belonged on the table lay at the bottom of the wall, its components smeared across the floor. At the far end of the room was a door hanging by its top hinge. Its window was labeled "therapy area."

"What the heck is this place?" asked Ali, freezing in the middle of the debris field.

Officer Ford glanced at the caduceus on the sidewalk. "Oh, this is the St. Michael's Center City Clinic. It opened a couple of years ago. All these business types can't take time out of their busy days for visits to the doctor, cardiac rehab therapy, cholesterol checks, dialysis, chemo, that sort of stuff, so St. Michael's opened a storefront clinic."

"For business men, bankers, and other middle management types?"

"Right."

Ali wandered through the rooms, took her routine photos, and exited the clinic. To her surprise, she found herself standing directly across the street from the devastated bank – the epicenter of The Shriek's destruction. The local police crime scene team was clustered around their own van a few steps down the street. Purple Lightning was leaning against a lamppost, watching as the manager argued with Norman outside the bank. Both of them were waving arms and shouting. Norman's electronically adjusted voice echoed.

"....unstable.....dangerous."

"What's going on?" asked Officer Ford.

"Sounds like the Site Examiner has condemned the building. No one will be allowed back in."

"Really?" said Officer Ford. "What about the crime lab?"

"They're included in the *no one*. The Shriek can do a lot of damage to structures. I've seen him turn all the concrete in a bridge to dust. Mind you, he couldn't talk for a week afterward. His is sort of a one-shot Power."

Ali waited until Purple Lightning's bored gaze traveled her way, then beckoned to him to join her. He crossed the road in a heartbeat, sending glass shards billowing up in his wake.

"Hey, girlfriend. Ready to go home?"

"Actually P.L., I have a problem," Ali told him, her voice calm, casual. "Take a look around the clinic behind me and see if you notice anything."

There was a split second in which the air in front of her was empty, then P.L. was back.

"Uh-oh," he said. "Did you touch anything?"

"Just the floor with my shoes," said Ali jerking her thumb at Officer Ford. "Him, too."

"What's wrong?" the young cop demanded, his hand once more going to his weapon.

"The bank robbery might've been misdirection," Ali said. "The real target could've been this clinic. The medical equipment that should be there is missing. I'd take bets that chemotherapy drugs have vanished, as well. I was wondering why they'd hit such a hole-in-the-wall bank."

"You're kidding! Why?"

Ali turned a pitying smile on him as the Crime Scene techs, alerted by P.L. to the situation, started across the street toward them at a run.

"Nuclear Man is dying," said Ali. "He has cancer, remember?"

Chapter Four.

'Eye on Seattle' P.M. commute radio show.
A candlelight memorial service will be held again tonight at the base of Mt. St. Helen's for The Thump and The Power. The S.S.C. plans to send no representatives. They have merely repeated their official comment regarding these two Supers, not seen since this day two years ago, is that they are still listed as 'Missing In Action.'

By mid-afternoon Ali was wilting. Three nights in a row of interrupted sleep were bad enough, but when you added the time difference and insufficient coffee, no food, and cheap thin-soled shoes, all she wanted to do was find somewhere to curl up and pass out. She reclaimed her quilt and wrapped it around her shoulders as she sat on the rear running board of Norman's van, slumped against the door. If she'd had the strength, she would have crawled through the van to the front seat and passed out. The way she felt right now, she'd be asleep the instant her butt hit the cushion.

Feet crunched their way toward her and Norman arrived. He climbed past her and pulled one door closed to hide from the TV crews and their long-range cameras. Tossing his mask into a basket, he shrugged out of his backpack. After scrabbling around in the van for a moment, he returned with a flask and poured out a cup, handing it to Ali before pouring a larger cup for himself. Ali sipped the 'special' coffee without speaking. Guaranteed to take off the top of your head under normal circumstances, today the blend was barely enough to keep her eyes open.

Officer Ford joined them a few moments later. The crunch of his feet on the broken glass gave Norman enough warning to pull his mask back into place.

"Ma'am? Miss?"

Ali raised bleary eyes to the cop. "Yeah?"

"There's someone, a lawyer, at the south barricade on 3rd street. Says he's supposed to report to the Site Supervisor. Is that you?"

"It is," Ali tossed off her quilt and came to her feet. Every inch of her legs ached. In addition to her usual duties, she'd had her feet and shoes photographed and printed and been questioned by the police. Politely, but questioned, nevertheless. She swallowed her annoyance. If it hadn't been for her, it was likely they wouldn't have noticed the stolen medical equipment for a while. But even though she was a member of Super Support, she'd been questioned as if she'd taken part in the robbery. Now, all she wanted to do was go home, pour herself into a deep bath, and let the world go to hell. Tomorrow, this site would have its own assigned S.S.C. insurance liaison. Today, it had her. Grabbing her attaché, she glanced across at Norman.

"Is the site cleared, by the way?"

Norman barely moved, all of his concentration directed toward getting coffee from cup into his mouth. "Yeah, we're good."

"Can I call a team in?"

"The nearest team is finishing up a site in Ann Arbor. You know, The Blast was in town there a few weeks ago. It's taken this long to do prelim stabilization of the damned bridge, but they're packing right now. Won't be here until tomorrow morning, at the earliest." Norman climbed further back into the van and started searching through the bits and pieces scattered around.

"I'll send an email, let the S.S.C. know the site is officially cleared. The locals can provide security until the team gets here. Are you going to be okay, waiting for them?" asked Ali.

"I will if we don't get another call."

He started connecting the items he'd pulled out of storage, and Ali realized he was assembling a hammock bed. He caught her grin and continued his work.

"I'll tell you what," he said, unfurling the mesh sling, "I'll be happy when they get this region's Clean-Up team on-line again. All this hauling back and forth cross-country has stopped being fun."

"From your lips to Control's ears," said Ali, feeling a little like a toddler as she reclaimed her quilt, still wadded in its plastic sack, and stepped back so he could close the door.

The walk to the barricade on her aching legs seemed to take hours. The police officer in charge pointed out a middle-aged man, briefcase clutched to his chest. Crossing to stand in front of him she held out her site access ID.

"Miss... That is, Site Supervisor, I've been given a commission by the law office of... "

"Never mind names," interrupted Ali. "They would have faxed you a letter. Let's see it, and I'll tell you if it's authentic."

The lawyer almost vibrated with anxiety and eagerness as she read the note. It was from Nigel, of course. If he wouldn't even get out of his car to speak to survivors in his hometown, she shouldn't be surprised that he wouldn't fly cross-country to deliver mere paperwork.

"I need to phone in to verify this," said Ali, taking out her cell and turning away. A few minutes later, she had spoken to Nigel, irritable because she'd interrupted his afternoon tea, (Oolong and raspberry - iced) it seemed, and had his confirmation.

Ali gestured to the officer on duty and they lifted the barrier so the lawyer could join her.

"Howdoyodo?" he stammered, holding out his hand. "I'm –"

"I don't need to know your name," Ali interrupted wearily, "and I am not permitted to give you mine. You had the coded message, and that's all I needed. I've already done a tour of the barricades, with Officer Ford," she waved at her companion. "Most of the shop owners are over there, waiting. I've collected names and insurance information. Here's your copy. The hospital clinic is the only one who didn't have an official rep turn up, but our office has been in touch with their head office and faxed over the necessary forms. All you need to do is go with this officer, and he'll help you find everyone so you can deliver your share of the paperwork."

The arrival of the lawyer meant the official end of her day. Ali went in search of P.L. only to be told he'd received a call and been gone for 'hours,' and none of the Super Team turned up to replace him.

Groaning, she started back toward Norman's van, then stopped and reconsidered. Norman was as short of sleep as she was, if not more so, and wouldn't be pleased to be woken up just to listen to her complain. There was no way she could be confident that P.L. called Control to arrange for her trip back. Daylight was fading, and she had no luggage – unless you counted a quilt, and because she hadn't arranged her travel through the SS.C., she had no transport voucher. God only knew where the Chinook was. She gritted her teeth and reached for her cell phone. A call to the home office would get her the voucher. With luck, she'd get on a flight home tonight. If not, it wouldn't be the first time she'd spent a night in an airport hotel with no luggage and no toothbrush. Perhaps she should call a taxi and book into a hotel. Skip the call. Sort it out in the morning. With luck, she might be 'lost to communication' for a whole night and catch up on her sleep.

Wind slammed into her, past her, through her, sending glass and splinters of concrete flying. She shuddered in the blast of freezing air and turned, her face lighting up with a relieved smile.

"P.L., am I……Oh. It's you."

The smile morphed into a frown so fast she could feel her muscles spasm. Ultra Man – in the over-muscled flesh. That was all she didn't need.

Keeping his own nonchalant smile in place through sheer force of will, Ultra Man took his hands off his hips and relaxed down from Power pose #2.

"Well, that's not the usual reaction to my arrival," he joked; hoping he'd kept the disappointment out of his voice.

Shrugging, she walked away from him, stepping into an open storefront, and rifled through her attaché.

"I wasn't expecting *you*," she told him, in a way he suspected boded very ill for Oliver when she next got her hands on him. "This isn't your district."

"I don't know why not. Didn't P.L. promise that someone would take you home? I was just checking in to see if you were ready to go."

"You! He asked *you* to take me home?"

"I was available," he said, keeping his tone very, very neutral.

Oliver was in enough trouble already, without tipping Ali that his availability was prearranged.

Instead of looking pleased, Ali stared at her shoes, the wall, the broken glass – everywhere but up at his face as she considered her options. He knew her well enough to follow her line of thought: home was miles, hours away by public transport, her entire body ached, and he could get her home to her own bed even faster than Purple Lightning. He knew Ali was both proud and stubborn, but above all, she was practical. He was counting on the practical to win through.

"Ready to go?" he prompted, before she could get past the lure of her own pillow to the drawback of being in his arms.

"I guess so, except, I suppose the police might like to talk to you before you go; to give you an update. You know what it's like. Everyone wants a word with *Ultra Man*."

The way she drawled his name made it seem like an insult.

"Sure," he agreed, moving closer and lowering his voice to murmur in her ear. "But if we go right away, they won't even know that I was here. Ready?"

Ali shivered as his arms reached around her to take the bundled-up quilt she clutched to her chest. He hoped it was arousal or awareness, but knowing Ali, it was more likely to be a shudder of revulsion. With an effort, he kept his expression mild and friendly. He had the entire flight home to change that. At a thousand feet, with no distractions and no way to escape, he'd finally have Ali to himself and, maybe, he'd begin to make some headway with this stubborn woman.

"Can't have you catching cold," he purred.

Or at least he hoped he purred. Purring seemed to be important in the more lurid Ultra Man fan mail and Internet fantasies he'd been reading. It had come as a shock to him to discover just how many Internet sites there were where women shared their daydreams of dates with him, or rather, with Ultra Man. At first he'd been revolted, and considered asking the S.S.C. lawyers to shut them down. Then it occurred to him that they might just provide a clue on how to thaw Ali out enough to at least get the caffeine-addicted woman to go for an espresso.

Before she could protest, he took the quilt out of her hands and wrapped it tight around her. His arms followed an instant later, then the security of ground fell away and they were airborne. He knew he should have waited for her to agree, but he couldn't take the chance that she would decide on the red-eye flight instead of a moonlit cruise above the clouds that the rest of the female population of the world seemed willing to trade their right arms for.

Chicago's towers passed slowly beneath them. Ali watched them retreat and frowned.

"Is something wrong?" she demanded. "Are you tired?"

"Me? No. Fit as the proverbial fiddle. Why?"

"You're flying awfully slow."

Ultra Man chuckled, trying for the deep in-the-chest sound that some women seemed to find so stimulating. Ali's only reaction was to deepen her frown.

"If I go too fast or too high, you'll disappear inside this quilt and we wouldn't be able to talk."

Ali glanced at the ground again and back at him without enthusiasm. "I'm not so sure that I want you to fly slow. It'll lengthen the time I spend up in the air with nothing supporting me."

"What? You're calling *me* nothing?"

Her glare told him that was the least of what she would like to call him, but she didn't trust him enough to begin the list.

"You know what I meant," she growled.

Taking a deep breath, he pulled her closer, following the script he'd compiled from those online erotic fantasies. Instead of carrying her in his arms, as he usually did with rescued children and other survivors, he held her chest to chest. Hip to hip. If she raised her eyes, she'd be staring directly at his lips. Even with the barriers of her quilt and his body armor, she should feel the heat of him and want to burrow closer, away from the chill of high altitude air. God knew, he could feel her softness. Or, at least, imagine her softness. Gritting his teeth, he mentally turned the next page and hoped that this would work. Nothing else had. Not flowers. Not candy. Not silly souvenir gifts. It had to work; he was seriously running out of ideas.

Crossing his toes because his fingers were busy, he flipped them, so that he was flying with his back to the ground with her reclining on him. This always seemed to be the moment where the women in the stories and letters melted: - when they found themselves pressed against him. Gravity pushing them down, only his strong body holding them safe, high above the world seemed to be an amazing turn-on – at least, in theory. He'd never actually done it with anyone before today. He found the position oddly uncomfortable, being forced to stretch his neck to see her. But she was all soft and warm, pressing down on his body in an undeniably arousing manner.

"What the hell are you doing?!" she gasped.

His grin broadened as she wrestled in his grip, trying to find a way to stay up in the air that didn't require full body physical contact. That's what they all said at first. Maybe this could work. If she kept to her side of the script, the next move would be her curling up like a kitten on his chest. Or wiggling her hips. He was in favor of either.

For a moment, she sat astride him, legs dangling. He shifted his hips against her, rubbing against the junction of her legs and watched her eyes widen. Jackpot. Now he'd get the sigh, the glazed eyes, the kisses and the swollen lips.

There was only an instant of warning. Not anywhere near enough for him to take protective action, however. Her eyes narrowed when she smacked him. A good, solid openhanded slap, right on his chin.

"Straighten up and fly right, you moron," she ordered, shaking her hand, "before I do something you'll regret."

Sighing, he angled to the right. Feeling gravity's grip shift, she lowered herself to his chest to keep from falling off him entirely and suffering the ignominy of a mid-air rescue. Her eyes weren't glazed over with pleasure, he noted. Burning hell-fire seemed a more apt description, and the only thing swelling was the palm that she was cradling against her chest.

After an awkward pause, he coughed and said, "By the way, you never did say about Friday. Are we on?"

"No," said Ali, flatly, her face turned away.

He was certain he felt one of her legs twitch, a knee flexing upward and barely restrained.

"Are you certain you want to refuse the person who's carrying you a couple hundred feet off the ground?" he teased. That line turned up in about eighty percent of the online fantasies. Usually followed by a smile and *I can refuse you nothing, Ultra Man.*

Ali, however, gave him a narrow-eyed look and showed him her teeth.

"Man, you stab right through my head when you look at me like that." He let out a heart-rending groan, and they started to pitch from side to side. Ali's hair whipped back and forth across her face and she let out a tiny shriek.

"Help!" he cried. "Oh, no! I don't think I can keep us up much longer."

Relaxing his mental grip on his flight ability, he let gravity take over. The ground charged toward them. Ali let out one more high-pitched 'eeeep,' wound her arms tight around his neck, squeezing as hard as she could. A few moments later, he smoothed the flight out, decreasing speed.

"Are you quite finished playing?" she asked, her eyes still clenched shut.

"Yes," he croaked. "I'll be good. You can let go now."

Ali loosened her grip a bit at a time, then burrowed her chilled arms back under the quilt.

"You never did grow up, did you, Craig?" she said.

"Well, there are days when I think about it."

"About Friday?" he prompted.

She gave a long-suffering sigh and looked up at him with tired eyes. He ran his hand over her hair, brushing it back behind her ears and gently holding it away from her face.

"I'm not interested," she said, moving away from his hand.

"May I ask why?"

Ali snorted and returned to her study of the passing ground.

"Come on, Ali. Why not? I'm a nice guy. I'm one of the good guys, ask anyone!"

She raised an eyebrow at his chin, the part of his face she could best see from her position.

"Do you mean, ask any female member of your fan club? Or those crazy girls who climb up the outside of the Empire State Building in the hope that you'll come to catch them? Or the women who write graphic pornographic letters and mail them to the S.S.C.? They come across my desk; by the way, since the gang-of-four won't let anyone else handle them. Did you know I have this nice little filing system? There is one drawer for the marriage proposals and a whole room for the marriage-not-required proposals. Or –"

Craig blushed. Oh, God. No. She'd read them! She knew about the fans, their fantasies?

"Never mind them," he interrupted hastily. "They don't count. You know I'm a nice guy. Why won't you go out with me?"

"Other than the current sexual harassment that I could sue your ass off for if you were a normal human being, and I had a normal, sane job? Hell, Craig, why should I? I think the only reason you ask me out is that it burns your ass that there's one woman in the world who doesn't melt into a puddle the minute you look in her direction."

He considered her reply, running his gloved fingers over her hair as it whipped in his jet stream, then shook his head. He'd heard that before, but it just didn't ring true. Ali was smart enough to know that he wasn't a Groupie Groper like Captain Fabulous. She should have been smart enough to know that he hadn't really looked at anyone but her since college. Not seriously.

"Nope. That's not it. Try again."

"You really are annoying, Craig Duane. Why don't you just dry up and blow away? I'm not interested. And don't even *think* about letting go and letting me fall. I will throw up all over you when you catch me, and make you sincerely regret it."

"Fair enough," he said, and for a while they flew faster and in silence.

"So, did you catch them?" she asked suddenly as they crossed the Ohio border.

"Who?"

Ali rolled her eyes. "Whoever robbed the bank and the clinic. The Shriek and the rest."

"It's not my patrol area, but no, they got away."

"I sometimes wonder why you even bother," she muttered.

"What?" he asked, not sure if he was meant to hear that comment.

It seemed he was, as Ali turned to face him again, her expression stern. He told himself he was studying her lips for signs of oxygen deprivation, and her stubborn chin for signs of chill. Ali snorted and went straight into the all-too-familiar lecture mode.

"Look at today's damage. How much money was in that little branch bank? If it had a hundred thousand in the vaults, I'd be very surprised. Versus the cost of the damage done when you guys started fighting The Shriek? That's going to add up to tens of millions, if you include the complete destruction of the bank building, the glazier's bill, and the lost equipment from the clinic. Not to mention the jobs and the disrupted lives from all the other stores in that neighborhood. It seems like you're killing the patient to save him."

"Wait a minute!" he protested. "Are you saying that you can't tell the difference between what we do and criminals?"

"I'm saying that sometimes I can't see the benefit. I mean, look at the damage. Look at the losses. The bank could've lost a couple of thousand dollars and the contents of a few security boxes. No problem, the insurance would've paid out. But you guys come waltzing in and the insurance SS.C. still has to pay out, but the bill has gone through the stratosphere."

"In a minute, I am going to drop you and I won't try to catch you after."

"No, you won't," she said, a challenging light in her eyes.

Craig's hands tightened around her upper arms. "Damn right I won't, and the reason is the basic difference between the criminals and us. The *principle* of the thing. Of justice. What they are trying to do is commit crimes. Theft. Blackmail. Environmental destruction."

"Property damage?" she countered.

Craig's fingers tightened until he saw pain flash across her face. "They are criminals," he growled. "*We* are federally appointed marshals."

"You could be the anointed of God, for all I care. I'm just saying some mornings, when I'm picking through the muck the lot of you leave behind, it's hard to tell the difference."

"Fine. Great. Good to know." He flipped a fold of blanket up over her head. "Hold on."

Ali could feel their speed increasing. Random gusts of wind tore through every loose fold, dragging icy cold fingers across her skin. Her hair danced and twisted in the jet stream, tugging and snapping. No matter how she struggled, his grip did not weaken.

Without warning her feet hit the ground. She staggered, struggling to free herself from her blanket. A rush of air told her Ultra Man was gone. Panting, she leaned against the nearest solid object until her breathing calmed. As her vision cleared and arms and legs complained about the return of blood flow, she realized she was standing on the roof of her apartment building. When she could trust her legs, she staggered across the uneven surface of the roof to the emergency entrance. She was not surprised to find it locked. Trailing her battered and faithful quilt, she crossed to the fire escape and looked down. Even to someone who'd just flow cross-country in the arms of a pissed-off Super, the ground looked far away. Drawing in a ragged breath leg over d down the fire escape.

Oliver came to the window at her knock, his eyes widening as he took in her disheveled appearance.

"Hey, girl," he said, opening the window. "That must have been some party."

Ali blinked back tears and looked him up and down. He was back in his sweatpants, with running shoes and matching T-shirt. He pushed up the window and pulled her in, setting her gently on her feet.

"You look as if you've been here for hours. Why didn't you come back for me?" Ali's voice rose to an embarrassing, self-pitying wail.

"Ultra Man said he'd take care of it," said Oliver. "I called and the personal trainer said he had time for an introductory session this afternoon, so I left you for Craig. You could've warned me about that trainer, by the way. He's a torturer. I feel like someone's worked me over with a brick."

"That may yet happen," said Ali.

Oliver collapsed dramatically on the couch. Ali watched him for a moment, then her frozen stomach suddenly realized she was back on solid ground and registered its protest. She barely made it to the bathroom. When the heaving stopped, she rinsed her mouth and stared into the mirror. Her hair was tangled in knots, standing on end in twisted chunks. Ali stumbled back to the living room, pulling at the mess.

"How am I ever going to get this combed out?" she cried at the lump on her sofa.

Oliver opened one eye with a groan. "Why do you think I shaved all mine off?"

Ali glared at him and stomped back to the bathroom to fetch conditioner spray and a comb. She stood in front of the mirror, alternately spraying and tugging at her hair, practicing her swear words as she reviewed the humiliation Craig had just put her through. Where the hell had he gotten the idea that she would put up with that sort of abuse? Had he completely lost his mind, thinking she was like his harem of houris?

She froze, one hand upraised and clutching the comb.

"Pervert from Peoria!" she shrieked, throwing the conditioner at the mirror.

It never struck. P.L. was there in time to catch it and stood, bottle in hand, staring at her as if she'd lost her mind.

"What is your problem?" he demanded. "What happened?"

"Craig goddamn Duane," replied Ali as she pushed past Oliver. "That bastard had me up in the air acting out the fantasy of some pervert from Peoria wrote to him. That bitch. That in-heat bitch. He had me up in the air acting out every word of her fantasy. It's bad enough I have to read that goddamn trash without him acting it out! Oh, when I see him next, I'm gonna rip his head off."

Ali stormed away, disappearing into her bedroom. Various crashes and thuds told Oliver her rampage continued unabated. Oliver lowered the bottle slowly to the ink and stared dully into the distance.

"Craig, you complete and utter *moron*," he whispered. "All you had to do was bring her home."

Chapter Five.

A.M. New York chat show host to his studio audience of rabid fans.

"Yes, we know that several, if not most, of the North American Super Team members will be at this evening's charity fundraiser, but to all you crooks out there... if you're planning on taking advantage of the situation to go on a spree, we have a warning. If you do anything to drag the Supers away from the warm domestic champagne... the rubber chicken, melted asparagus and panting, rabid fans... they'll probably kiss you. So, don't say you weren't warned!"

1:22 A. M. Eastern.
Pentagon. Sublevel 17, room 4 C
Required security clearance: - Word and above.
Meeting of the Paranormal Oversight Committee.
No secretary/no minutes – by order E - 14/BQ 4899.

The White House representative, code-named Mr. White, slammed his hands down on the table and glared around the room.

"I have to tell you that the White House does not appreciate learning that there's another Super-Powered problem from the evening news," he snarled. "What did Ultra Man tell you about this new one? This Ice Queen?"

"Excuse me?" Mr. Bendit, the Super Support Co. representative to the Paranormal Oversight Committee glanced up from where his fingers were tracing the pattern of the wood grain of the table over and over. "To whom are you referring?"

"The Ice Queen." Mr. White threw a photocopy of the front page of The Northern Star Daily onto the table and stabbed a finger at the illustration of a pneumatic Villainess. "She appeared at the Jersey City event site and you have not seen fit to bring this committee, and through me, the President, information regarding this new threat."

"What threat?" cried Mr. Bendit, reaching for a wad of tissues and mopping his perpetually sweating forehead. "The S.S.C. has consistently provided any and all information available regarding both Supers and Villains. I am aware of no new additions to either side since The Lightning Rod was processed last April."

"Read this," Mr. White shoved the photocopy, sending it skittering across the table. "This rag has video. Post-battle video of Ultra Man admitting that there is a Villain, or, rather, a Villainess, that he can't handle. Do you have any idea what will happen once this story gets picked up by the wire service?"

Mr. Bendit did not reply until he had finished reading the text and sat in contemplation of the brightly-colored sketch, his head tilted to e other department reps waited with varying degrees of impatience as Mr. White's assistants distributed copies to

"Well, what does the S.S.C. know about this Ice Queen?"

"Nothing," said Mr. Bendit.

Mr. White's voice dropped another octave, "What do you mean, *nothing?*"

"According to the morning debriefing, the only Villains at the apartment complex and hospital event site were Mr. Ooze and the Mystress of the Night."

"That's it?"

"Yes. I will return to the S.S.C. immediately and have Ultra Man and the rest of the team recalled. I believe they're on-shift, assisting with the investigation of a series of hi-tech robberies across the West Coast and Midwest. We suspect either Major Calamity or Tech Boy is involved. While they're meeting with the other Super Teams to coordinate, they're incommunicado, unless there's a level three disaster."

"You don't think this is a disaster? A Villainess that the public knows has Ultra man quaking in his boots?"

Mr. Bendit dragged his eyes away from the table and glanced around at his colleagues. The FBI, CIA, BFT, and other gathered acronyms refused to meet his eyes.

"It is concerning, certainly," said Mr. Bendit, dabbing at his sweaty face with a handful of tissues. "But, Mr. White, paranormals turn up all the time. Most of them are harmless, innocuous people who desperately want to be included in one of the Super Teams. They just wander up to a cop, a small-town mayor, a reporter, or some other authority figure and say, 'Hey, look at what I can do.'"

"This one didn't," snapped Mr. White. "It's the ones that don't who are the problems."

"With all due respect, we have no proof, as yet, that this alleged Power represents a problem. We have to run a search for anyone with cold powers, just in case it's someone we know about who's had a Power surge. We'll also communicate with our opposite numbers overseas; to see if this is an import. And as soon as I get a chance to talk to Ultra Man, we'll get more information. A description. A Power profile. Something to work with. When we have that, The Colonel can start designing new armor and equipment for Ultra Man. Ultra Man is Resilient. He won't be fearful for long."

Mr. White paced across the room to the constantly updated world map. Gold, red, and green lights marked the locations of known paranormals. Gold for Super Team members, red for suspected locations of known Villains, and green for harmless. Mr. White had argued against that last designation through three administrations - he considered none of the Powers harmless - but was overridden on a regular basis.

Known. That was the thought that weighed on him. The thought that kept him awake nights. Paranormals. People with Powers of various strengths and, for reasons best known only to Mother Nature – that perverse bitch – all of them different. It was as if she was playing some sort of sick game with the human species.

Without warning, Super abilities appeared in otherwise normal people, normal families. Despite all of their research, nothing was showing up in the gene tests surreptitiously performed on all babies. Super Powers couldn't be measured, predicted, stored, taxed or replicated under laboratory situations - and that worried him. It invaded his sleep and occupied his every waking hour. There was no way of knowing when the next Power would manifest or what form it would take.

Everything else in life could be reduced to statistics. Numbers. Predictable, comfortable, numbers.

Except them.

"Get me information about the Ice Queen," ordered Mr. White, not caring how unreasonable his request was. "NOW!"

Friday Evening.

Ali took a left turn at a rubber tree and slipped behind the floor-to-ceiling velvet curtain. She might be required – by employer fiat – to attend the annual fundraiser for Victims of Super-Villains, but no one, not even her *date* was going to force her to socialize.

Last year, she'd been able to hide out in the chair repository behind the curtains for two hours before someone realized she was missing and texted her. This year, she was seriously considering turning off her phone, accidentally forgetting to charge it. If she lined up four chairs, she could pretend that it was a bed, a thin, uncomfortable bed, and catch a catnap. Ali pushed her way under one last length of dusty drapery and halted.

"Good evening, Ms. Brent," rumbled a familiar voice.

"Ah, Mr. Crunch. I was... ah . . . um...." Ali froze as heat climbed into her face.

"Yes," said the fourth member of the firm's *gang-of-four* lawyers, climbing out of a folding chair. "I know exactly what you were *ah um'ing*. I'm retired from active duty, not stupid, Ms. Brent. As a matter of decorum, it's generally expected that my date will stay somewhere in the vicinity of the party, if not me. It's only polite."

"Yes, sir," said Ali.

"And conduct herself appropriately while at the gathering."

"Yes, sir."

"As we now understand each other, we should rejoin the people in the main ballroom."

He turned and Ali meekly followed him through a small doorway and out into the corridor. Mr. Crunch waited until Ali stood at his right hand before stalking off down the hall.

"Now, Ms. Brent, a certain amount of socializing is required of the firm's employees on such occasions. As a senior member of Super Support, you are part of our public face. And don't roll your eyes at me, Ms. Brent."

"No, sir," muttered Ali.

The retired Mr. Crunch was one of the early Super Team members under the name Captain Smash. His only power was invulnerability. He was one of the few Supers going around with a rank in their name who was entitled to it. He'd served as a police officer for fifteen years, rising to the rank of Precinct Captain. Then he'd changed careers and become a prosecution lawyer before deciding he could do more good with his Power than with a badge or law degree. He'd acquired the rest of the name due to his teammate's tendency to pick him up and throw him through windows, through doors, and on one memorable occasion, through the wall of a stone fortress. Despite his invulnerability, Mr. Crunch had acquired what was charitably referred to as a 'rugged face'.

Ali hadn't been feeling particularly charitable a few days previously, when he'd come into the coffee room in time to hear her refer to him as "The Brick." That was how she'd earned tonight's punishment, escorting "the Brick" to the charity dinner/dance. Reminding herself to be more careful in future, she followed Mr. Crunch down the corridor as he continued his lecture.

"I expect you to speak to the attendees, find out their favorite heroes, and if they're present, direct them to the appropriate photo booth. Don't forget to point out the unique items in the silent auction. Tell them you've bid on one or two pieces yourself. *Actually* bid on a piece in front of the guests. Show some enthusiasm, Ms. Brent."

"Yes, sir."

Mr. Crunch turned and regarded her quietly. "Are you interested in any of the offerings in the voice auction?" he asked.

"Do they have Captain Fabulous' boxer shorts on offer again this year?" asked Ali keeping her face completely straight.

Mr. Crunch did not so much as blink. Since the offending underwear was carried out of the auction room by Mr. Crunch himself the previous year, Ali doubted that the shorts in question still existed.

"Ms. Brent, it is very true that I do not have a sense of humor, as well as no sense of pain."

"I see," said Ali, biting the inside of her cheek.

He studied her face for several seconds before sighing and shaking his head.

"Do the best you can, then." Mr. Crunch paused at the ballroom doorway and nodded to the formally attired security guards. "You have your instructions. Off you go – and enjoy your evening."

Ali shot him a disgruntled look over her shoulder. No sense of humor, indeed. How could any sensible person be expected to enjoy themselves, eating mystery meat on crackers and talking to complete strangers in an overheated, overcrowded, hotel ballroom? She struggled to stay upupright and inched forward through the crush. There were thousands of people already in the room and, no doubt, thousands still waiting outside for their chance to join the insanity.

Just because Mr. Crunch had forced her out of her hiding place didn't mean Ali had used up all her ways of protesting this forced attendance. When informed formal attire was 'strongly recommended', she'd gone out and rented a tux. It was far more comfortable than her one and only black dress. And, having chosen trousers longer than her legs, she was able to get away with wearing black P.L. brand trainers instead of *proper* footwear. Her ensemble was completed by a black Armani collarless shirt (borrowed), silver leather tie (found in a thrift shop) and topped off with a black fedora (inherited from her grandfather.). Judging from the way Mr. Crunch had checked her out stem to stern, she was likely to get an email on Monday explaining her sartorial errors to her.

She was better off than the Super Team members being honored tonight. The longest line of fans waiting to be photographed with their hero was for Ultra Man. He had also exercised his sense of humor. Instead of wearing his Super Suit or some other formal gear, he was garbed in a bronze polyester tux, with an emerald green ruffled silk shirt. Ali's lips twitched. To cover her smile, she grabbed a glass of something from a passing waiter and pretended to sip. In his colorful outfit, Ultra Man looked like a cross between a kid waiting to take part in an accordion-playing contest and an escapee from the disco era.

Not to say that the suit didn't fit well. The fabric of his jacket was stretched tight across his chest and shoulders. Despite the strange color scheme, he was still the sexiest Power in the room.

And he was doing his duty. As she watched, he smiled and shook hands, listened to inane remarks and kept the punters moving. At a thousand a photo, he was racking up the dollars. Other Super photo booths were not doing so well. In fact, Urban Renewal, a relatively new Super revealed to the world about two years ago and assigned to the California region, and Flash Heat, a well-known veteran with thirteen years of experience. But with an unfortunate arrogant manner that resulted in his being bounced from one region to another (currently, he was assigned to the Northwest region), had abandoned their booths – and their fans – and were standing just behind Ultra Man. Ali took a closer look at Ultra Man. He wore his professional demeanor, but it was beginning to look strained around the edges. Ali drifted toward them, flashing her ID at the plainclothes security guard who moved to intercept her. Ultra Man was shaking hands with a giggling group of ladies – all wearing matching bronze dresses with green sash belts, but his eyes flicked across, taking note of Ali's arrival.

"I love the color scheme," said Ultra Man, draping his arms over the shoulders of the nearest ladies, "but you'd better remember where you're standing. When this photo comes out, no one's going to be able to tell which one's me!"

The ladies blushed and giggled again, turned to the cameraman and – frankly – glowed as their photo was taken. Duty done, Ultra Man stepped back.

"Down that way, ladies," said Ultra Man, waving toward the waiting cashier. "Mind your step, or I'll have to rescue you."

"Did that well," Flash Heat sneered. "Defeated yet another collection of middle-aged female hearts. You even worked up a sweat doing it. Must be so much harder than defeating Nuclear Man."

Ultra Man didn't even turn his head but smiled a welcome to the next group led toward him.

"But he *hasn't* defeated Nuclear Man," said Urban Renewal. "God help us, it's just plain embarrassing. A Super is judged by the strengths of his enemies, and Ultra *Boy* here can't even catch a guy who looks like a strong breeze will blow him away."

The professional smile froze at the 'boy' dig, Ali noted, but Ultra Man continued to schmooze with the fans

"Our boy here couldn't last ten minutes against a decent villain," continued Flash Heat. "Like The Blast, for example."

"Or Major Calamity," added Urban Renewal, and both nodded.

"The boy's got a cushy district. He's got headquarters and all the trainees as backup, and still can't catch a witch, a gimp and a noisemaker. And then people just gush all over him and can't wait to have their picture taken with him."

"Unlike you gentlemen," said Ali, sliding up behind them and slipping her hands through their elbows, "who haven't got the grace or good manners to pay attention to your own fans. Perhaps we shouldn't wonder that you have so few people waiting to see you, when you treat the few that turn up so badly."

Flash Heat raised a hand to his safety helmet and fiddled with the filters on his visor.

"You lecturing me, lady?" he asked.

"Actually, I'm warning you," Ali replied, making sure both Supers got a glimpse of her ID. Then, tugging on both their arms, she led them down the narrow path between the booths and into the crowd. "You know Mr. Crunch's attitude toward intramural bitchiness," Ali hissed, "So, you boys are going back to your booths and staying there for the rest of the evening like good little Supers, or you'll be explaining why you didn't to Mr. Crunch, up close and personal."

Flash Heat and Urban Renewal made no other protests and were soon reinstalled in their assigned areas. Ali refused to look back at Ultra Man's booth. Her quick check in one of the mirrors scattered around the room – trying and failing to make the room look bigger – showed her that he was still watching her, tracking her through the crowd. She snagged another drink off a passing waiter and retreated to lean against a wall. A few minutes later, Mr. Crunch wandered past with a group of local dignitaries.

Ali caught her boss's glare out of the corner of her eye and left her refuge to join to the nearest group of potential donors. She took a couple of minutes to settle herself into the proper mindset *(note to self - lose 40 IQ points and turn off cynicism)* before entering the conversation.

"Have you seen the silent auction in the next room?" asked Ali, trying her best to imitate a groupie's breathless voice. "It's *overwhelming*."

"I know. I've been trying to tell my husband to put in a bid for the damaged helmet Ultra Man wore when he defeated The Kraken," said one woman, sparing her husband a pouting look. "But he's holding out for the spell that Mysterious West has on offer in the voice auction."

"He's a West fan?" asked Ali, taking a quick glance across at that photo queue. It was fairly long and populated mostly by young women wearing black makeup and far too much silver jewelry.

"Oh, no," said the wife, digging her husband in the ribs with her elbow. "He's having business problems. I think that he thinks he can get The Mysterious West to put a whammy on his competitors."

Ali smothered a laugh and took a deep breath before replying. "I don't know that West would consider that ethical."

The husband shot a glance at Ali's identification, barely visible under her jacket, grabbed his wife by the arm, and disappeared into the crowd. Another woman looked at Ali's ID and moved closer.

"You work for the Super Support? Oh. Only with Super Clean?" Her disappointment was evident, but she labored on. "Do you see the Supers often?"

The familiar hungry look was in her eyes. Ali tried to step back and found her retreat blocked by a small table. "No, not really. The Supers are usually long gone by the time we get on scene, but they're always polite if they're around."

Several heads nearby nodded agreement, although how they'd know was a mystery, while Ali continued with the SS.C. line. Words like conscientious, brave, unselfish fell from her lips until she feared she'd never been able to utter an honest, unscripted sentence again.

A blast of cold air behind her was her only warning. Ali put a hand to her head, catching her hat as it threatened to take flight.

"Hey!" P.L. appeared at her shoulder and smiled at the fans. "Excuse me, please. I have to talk to the Site Supervisor for a minute. Urgent SS.C. business."

Not waiting for a reply, he grabbed Ali and carried her at blurring speed, down several corridors and up the fire stairs. Somehow at the speed he moved, the rooms seemed empty, but even so, Ali kept her eyes closed for most of the trip. Dropping Ali on a balcony, he ran to the edge and peered over.

"What's going on?" demanded a shivering Ali, following him.

"Wait, wait. West will be here in a minute. We've got a problem we need your help with."

"My help? Why? What have you broken this time?"

P.L. laughed and vanished. Seconds later, he reappeared with West in his arms.

The Mysterious West also eschewed her Super suit. When P.L. put her down, she straightened her tall turban, settled the folds of her multicolored caftan back down around her ankles, and smiled up at Ali.

"Hey there, girl. Looking good!" West tugged Ali's shirt front straight. "We can't be away from the photo booths for long. Don't let anyone know, but I have trouble flying if it's only for a few feet. Now I'm getting old, I need a running start ... damn ... kickstart broom."

"No one will hear it from me," promised Ali.

"Good. You know, we all know we can trust you, Ali. You're one of the best. There isn't a single Super in this region who doesn't realize how much he owes you."

Ali frowned, sensing the arrival of deep B.S. "You mean the Clean Up squad?"

"No," said West, "you, girl. Most times, we go back to a place where we've made a mess, the residents are a bit hostile. But you, you calm everyone down, talk us up. It makes a difference."

"Ah huh," said Ali, crossing her arms and tapping one foot impatiently. "And the bullshit is getting so deep in here we could use it to fertilize most of the Midwest. What's going on?"

West ignored the comment while P.L. simply sank onto the nearest bench, hands hanging limp on his knees. Ali's heart took a dip.

"What? What's wrong?"

"Didn't you see?" asked P.L. "The Vice President's here with his wife tonight. I don't know how he did it, but he's talked the SS.C. into putting a date with Ultra Man into the voice auction. Apparently, the V.P.'s sister, or daughter, or someone in the family, is a big fan and wants to go out with him."

"On a *date?* A Super Bachelor auction? They've never allowed that before. Isn't that against the SS.C. rules?" Ali started to laugh. "Poor guy, have they told him yet?"

"Yeah," P.L. scowled and shook his head. "He's stoic about it, but you gotta know it bites. Hell, there's no way this can turn out good," continued P.L. "If they go out and he doesn't put moves on her, she'll be pissed and it'll be bad publicity. If he does, it will be even worse."

"You see her?" added West, raising her eyebrows. "Woman's got gold and green striped hair."

Ali closed her eyes and shuddered. She had seen a woman with particularly vivid hair standing on the other side of the enclosure, watching as Ultra Man greeted his other fans. Unlike the other fans, she'd naturally refused to leave, and she had enough rank-by-association not to be moved on by security. Poor Craig - what a horrible situation Ali could imagine the jokes Flash Heat and Urban Renewal would make once they'd heard. Craig would put on a professional face, but inside the embarrassment would burn.

"What can we do?" asked Ali. "I mean, if the SS.C.'s approved it, they'll have already put it in front of Hackham, Bendit, et al. They'll have contacted the PR department and will be getting ready to spin it no matter how the date turns out. If they send enough press along, nothing is going to happen. There won't be an opportunity!"

"We can't wait for that," said P.L. "It means that Ultra Man would have gone out on the date. It's a terrible precedent to set. And it isn't as if they'd asked for volunteers and he said he'd like to play. They just walked up and announced it was all arranged. Ultra Man's stuck unless you help us. We have a plan." P.L. paused a moment for dramatic effect. "And we need you."

"Me? What can I do?"

P.L. glanced at West again and Ali's heart sank.

"Come on? What?"

"We want you to bid," P.L. blurted, "on Ultra Man. For the date."

"Have you gone completely nuts?" Ali cried. "I've got two dollars and seven cents in my savings account, which isn't going to last long once the bidding gets tense. And you know the charity is not going to accept an IOU against my next paycheck, such as it is."

"No problem," said West with a grin, tapping herself on the chest. "We'll pay."

Ali gaped at them until her brain unfroze and reconnected to her tongue. "You have lost your minds? Completely? Have you any idea how many people will be bidding once the news gets out? We'll be up against whole fan clubs bidding over the Internet. Those women are probably pooling their entire life savings and mortgaging their houses at this very minute, just so that they can share the date in five minutes increments. No way you've got enough money."

"P.L. and I can cover your bid up to half a mil each," said West, her familiar patois vanishing as she calmly folded her hands under her ample chest. "But I don't think it will go that far."

"Where the hell did you get that much cash?" demanded Ali, "I've seen the budget for your salaries, it's pitiful."

"Merchandising, baby," West answered. "You don't think we'd approve all those dolls and stuff without gettin' a cut, do you? And keep that under your fancy hat. It's more of a secret than the flying thing."

"But...." Ali gasped, "I thought that money went to pay for the Super Clean squad salaries, supplies, and stuff. SS.C. expenses."

"Yeah, but...." P.L.'s voice dropped and he moved closer. "We get one percent of the proceeds up front. That adds up fast. Particularly since none of us have much time for spending it."

Ali ran a quick calculation of the number of Super Team dolls, the Mysterious West spell lab candy making sets, P.L. running shoes and other paraphernalia selling each year, and came to an astonishing total. She slipped an arm around Oliver's shoulders and smiled up at him.

"P.L., friend, buddy, pal, could I hit you up for a loan? My car needs some maintenance work."

"Sure," said P.L., giving her a one-armed hug, "I owe you something toward the rent, anyway. But first, you have to rescue Ultra Man."

"Rephrase that, please. I can't imagine rescuing a Super," Ali said, drawing a deep breath and letting it out slowly. "Okay, let me get this straight. I'm authorized to bid up to... oh Heaven help me, what, one million, two million, for this date?" Her voice rose to a squeak. "I'm not sure I could do it with a straight face."

P.L. pulled himself to his full height. "You're authorized by the Super Teams of North America to bid whatever it takes to keep that date out of anyone else's hands. You got it? We have to get back to glad-handing the masses."

"I can't. Truly, I know we have to help him but," Ali rubbed at her temples, wondering if the buzzing she could hear was outside her head, or not. "One big problem. There are cameras set up in the hall. The auction's going to be on the net and TV as a live broadcast. You guys have your masks, but my identity is only secret as long as no one cares. You put me front and center in a bidding war for Ultra Man, and my face is going to be on every news broadcast and fan hate list within the hour."

P.L. nudged West. "Sounds like a job for you. Got any suggestions?"

West scratched at her chin then started rummaging through a colorful silk bag bigger than one Ali would have packed for a two-week vacation – assuming she ever went on another vacation. Soon West was arranging candles, a few packages of powder, and a glass jar on a nearby table.

"A little magic, a little luck." She threw a wink up at P.L. "Go on back before they miss both of us. Mamma will fix."

P.L. nodded and vanished over the balcony. Ali peered after him, then turned her attention to West who how pinching a little of this and a little of that into the glass jar, then stirring it with her little finger. When she was satisfied with the consistency, she waved a hand over it while she chanted. Ali stood, arms folded, and tried to pretend that the sensitive hairs on the back of her arms and neck weren't standing on end. West might be matter-of-fact about her magic. Oliver and Craig didn't even blink when she pulled out her essence of frog or whatever. Ali still didn't know how she felt about Super-level-Magical abilities, and preferred to keep her distance, especially after seeing a couple of West's mixtures burn through tables, carpets and floors (the ground underneath, several layers of rock – you get the idea.)

A change in the quality of the light in the room was the only signal that the spell had taken. West smiled, screwed the lid back on the top of the jar, and handed it to Ali.

"Apply just a dab, on the forehead, the chin," said West, "before the auction starts. It will dazzle the cameras. You might want to put a little under the eyes, just a dab, don't rub. Very good for the tired skin."

Ali's hand shook as she accepted the jar, then she peered more closely and almost screamed. West had just magicked a jar of skin cream that cost more than three hundred dollars an ounce! West laughed at Ali's stunned expression, then sobered.

"Will fool the TV and the cameras, but not the people in the room with you. That's no problem since most people are intentionally blind. Won't see and don't remember. But the spell won't last long. Put it on just before the auction starts. Reapply it if the show lasts long."

Ali nodded and tucked the magic cream into her pocket.

"I don't know why I didn't ask you for this before. It would be useful when I have to go On-Site after an event."

"Spell won't stay in the cream for more than a week," said West. "I don't have the time or Power to keep remagicking it. Sorry, honey."

"Oh well," Ali sighed, but swallowed her disappointment, "it was just an idea."

Both women turned and made their way back down the stairs to the main ballroom. Ali glanced across at West a time or two, wondering why the Super Witch hadn't flown back down – then remembered what she'd said about running starts. They separated just inside the door, West to return to her fans and Ali to find a place to hide from Mr. Crunch until the time came to bid.

Using her ID to ease her way, she pushed through the crush in the corridors until she was just inside the main ballroom. A quick glance around told her Mr. Crunch wasn't immediately visible. The noise level had increased since she'd left the room. Raucous laughter drifted in from the buffet room off to the left, adding to the voices of thousands of people competing with each other for the attention of sixteen Supers.

Ali drifted through the crowds, seeking a corner, somewhere out of the way, where she could do some serious thinking. To her surprise, she found the quietest area of the ballroom was the line for a photo with Captain Fabulous. Given Captain Fabulous' sense of humor – base, gross and anatomical - it was usually the noisiest. Ali studied the faces of those nearby. Men and women who had just experienced their meet-and-greet were walking slowly away, glancing back over their shoulders. The men's faces were stunned and pale. The women's faces were more difficult to read. Some appeared interested and aroused. Other's – frightened, even awed. Ali didn't have to look to know what was going on. She closed her eyes for a second, swallowed a curse, and plunged back into the crowd.

Even though it was safer to have limited contact with Mr. Crunch until after the auction, she threaded through the crowd as fast as she could. Mr. Crunch was the only person she knew who could control Captain Fabulous. A few minutes of frantic searching later, Ali found Mr. Crunch in the center of a cluster of high-ranking law enforcement officers.

Ali slipped up behind Mr. Crunch and tugged at his sleeve.

"Sir?" she whispered.

He tilted his head and raised an eyebrow in her direction.

"Sir, uh… we have a… situation." She jerked her head toward the quiet corner. "Fabulous is at it again."

Mr. Crunch stiffened, sighed, gave the officers and their wives a polite nod, and was off. The crowded room provided no more resistance to Mr. Crunch's passage than the walls he'd traveled through in his heroing days. Those who saw him coming jumped clear. The rest bounced away like Ping-Pong balls. Ali followed close in his wake.

"Fabulous!" shouted Mr. Crunch, his voice echoing across the room, shaking the chandeliers and stunning the guests to silence. "That is enough! Roll yourself up, right this minute, sir, and put yourself away."

Mr. Crunch gripped the stretchable shoulder of Fabulous' Super-suit and twisted, bringing the artificially tall man up onto his toes, his head twisted at an uncomfortable angle.

"You, sir, will do an imitation of a Ken doll for the rest of the evening," hissed Mr. Crunch, "or I will personally string you around a lamp post and tie you into a pretzel."

Under the pressure of Mr. Crunch's hand, Captain Fabulous' suspiciously overlarge groinal bulge shrank down from elephantine to merely human - then vanished. Ali ducked down behind a guest, stuffing both hands into her mouth to muffle her laughter. In the distance, she could hear applause. A quick glance told her that the sound was coming from a few of the Super guests. Ultra Man, however, was leaning against a wall, unashamedly laughing. With Mr.

Crunch distracted delivering his lecture to the hapless Fabulous, Ali decided now would be a good time to hit the auction rooms. No doubt someone would record the lecture for the later enjoyment of the S.S.C. staff. She made a mental note to put in her order for a copy in the morning.

Her ID tucked out of sight in her vest, she walked through the Silent Auction room behind chattering guests.

She noticed one woman strolling down the exhibits, her face thoughtful as she studied one item after another. Eventually, the woman paused beside a baseball cap decorated with the glittery Super Clean logo. Ali wandered over to stand behind her and peered over her shoulder. There wasn't a single bid on the card.

"Super Clean cap," said Ali, "Wow, that looks interesting."

"Don't be ridiculous," said the woman, flicking the cap's brim with one long fingernail. "Why would I want this? I'm a doctor. I don't even clean my own house. Besides, I'm looking for something that we can put in the foyer of our hospital. The Supers stopped Captain Nuclear when he tried to break in last year and we want something to commemorate the event. Something that would look *dignified.*"

"Nuclear Projectile Vomiting Man," corrected Ali, turning to study the surrounding displays until she had her temper under control. "That rules out Captain Fabulous' boxer shorts, I suppose."

She remembered the site and the amount of damage Nuclear Man had done. The Super Clean team had spent months restoring the hospital. Two people had become ill doing the Decontam and were still on medical leave. And now, here was a doctor sneering at them. Mere cleaners, not worth her time or consideration. Looking for a souvenir of the people who'd been on the scene for less than fifteen minutes. Ignoring the work done by those who'd risked their lives, their health, for months. Ali counted to ten, twice, but it didn't help.

"I don't think you realize the contribution of the Super Clean team." Ali said in careful, neutral tones, "When we come to a Super event site, we find damage that needs more than a quick wipe with furniture polish to put right. The Clean Up squad can be there for days, weeks, even months. We rebuild houses; reconstruct hospitals. We remove and dispose of toxic substances, and most people pay no more attention to them, and give them no more credit than they do a …"

"Cleaning lady?" supplied the doctor, in a cool, flat tone. "No, I suppose we don't. I hope you are not saying that cleaning up is as important as solving crimes and defeating villains. That would be like comparing a surgeon to the floor buffer."

"Say that to the guy who invented Usol soap, which, if my history is correct, also saved a few lives. Surgeons wouldn't be able to do much without him," said Ali, but the doctor didn't hear, or she didn't think the comment worthy of a reply.

Ali turned and stalked down the narrow pathway between the display tables, her hands curled into tight fists. Her head was pounding and her teeth gritted, holding back words, vicious, angry words she wanted to shout at a world that valued muscle-bound Supers in tight suits over quiet, dedicated people who did their best every day to make the lives of complete strangers better. No one saw their faces; their own families didn't know what their jobs were. Anonymity was the rule in Super Clean. At work sites, the victims did little other than complain. About the dirt, the debris, the delay. No one blamed the Supers or the Villains – *they* were long gone. The Super Clean team took the flack for both sides.

Ungrateful, ignorant bastards.

Ali halted, drew a deep breath through her clenched teeth, and forced her anger and frustration down into her churning stomach. She'd just insulted a guest at the charity ball, and she knew one insulted civilian complaint – passed on to one eager and hungry reporter – meant bad publicity for the whole SS.C.

Which would mean Ali would be the person making early morning explanations to Mr. Crunch, something she'd do a lot to avoid.

She retraced her steps and found the doctor studying a melted pile of cutlery. All that remained, Ali remembered, from a hotel fire started by either Flash Heat or Major Calamity, she couldn't remember which.

"There are some interesting items here," observed Ali when she had her voice under control.

The doctor honored the ranked tables by casting her attention over them, then sniffed.

"I am looking for something both unique and specific. Something that communicates to the ages the service provided by Ultra Man and his associates to our health care facility."

"Unique? *The ages*?" Ali bit the inside of her cheek and tried to keep her voice level. "I believe I know which landfill the wreckage from your hospital was transported to. Maybe we could go through it, find something with Lightning's footprints. Of course, we'd have to have it decontaminated. Nuclear Man projectile vomited over a considerable part of your facilities."

"Maybe we could get Ultra-Man to autograph it," said the doctor, her eyes lighting up. "The old hospital sign, or something like that. It would be – "

"*Impossible*," said Ali, not for the first time pleased to deliver that piece of bad news, "None of the Supers are permitted to sign autographs."

The Doctor's face fell.

"What a shame. Are you certain an exception couldn't be granted? That would have made a wonderful centerpiece for our main foyer."

"No signatures," Ali said firmly. "Do you wish to have it exhumed?"

The doctor gave the matter a few moments' thought, then shook her head. "No, I hardly think *trash* would be suitable."

"Then I'm sure if you look around, you'll find something dignified," said Ali and started out of the room.

Before she could reach the door, secret service agents appeared and spread out, scanning the room for threats. The Vice President and his wife followed, chatting with Mysterious West and trailing a woman whose spiked yellow and green hair clashed violently with a skin-tight, navy-blue ball gown. Their bodyguard detail herded Ali and the other guests up against the wall, muttering into the microphones on their lapels. Ali growled when her S.S.C. ID was examined, then dismissed. The guard sneered and pushed her closer to the wall. Ali resigned herself to the wait and spent the time watching as the woman who was causing so much trouble for the S.S.C. wandered through the displays. Ultra Man's fan was a tall, striking woman - hair notwithstanding - and didn't appear too dangerous. Even if she had used her political pull to arrange for a date, she didn't look like someone who'd make too much trouble for Ultra Man and the Supers. Maybe she just wanted the thrill of appearing in some public place with her hand on Ultra Man's arm.

Maybe West and P.L. could save their money.

Then the woman picked up Ultra Man's crushed undersea helmet and hugged it to her chest, bestowing a kiss on its crown. Instead of putting it down again, she snatched the bid sheet off the table, waving it at Mysterious West. It took a few minutes for her to be persuaded that no one was about to *gift* her with the helmet, and a few more to get her to put it back on the table.

Ali felt her lip curling.

Maybe. Maybe not.

Ali wasn't able to get a chance to speak with West or P.L. before the auction was announced. Using her bid card as identification, Ali forced her way into the overcrowded room until she found a place to stand up against the back wall, squeezed between an overweight gentleman in a tight purple cummerbund and his equally large companion. There were so many people in the room that Ali wondered how they all expected to breathe. Banks of phone operators lined one side of the room, right behind several computer stations - to collect the bids of those tuning in via the Internet. If the previous year was anything to judge by, they could expect at least two servers to collapse from the strain.

From her position, Ali could see the VP and his party were seated in the first row, and there were two rows of seats behind them – empty. Security again.

If the VP, et al. were so worried, why couldn't they watch the bidding from some secure room, via closed-circuit TV or something, and let ordinary mortals have a chance to sit down?

The first dozen items went quickly, the audience applauding politely each time the auctioneer banged his gavel. Ali caught sight of Mysterious West and Ultra Man standing together to one side of the stage whispering. Ultra Man's professional expression broadened into a smile as West spoke. No doubt West was advising Ultra Man of the planned rescue. Sure enough, an hour later, when Ultra Man was called onto the stage by the auctioneer, he scanned the room until he caught sight of Ali, then he nodded to her. Under the brilliant spotlights, his muscular form was well displayed, even in his funny polyester suit, and Ali could see the curtains on each side of the room ruffling as all the women in the room – herself excluded - sighed.

Ali dropped her eyes and dug through her pockets for the jar of face cream, grumbling to herself. Damn him. He looked too relaxed – complacent, even. That was unacceptable. The man had been asking her out for years. Now he'd been told Ali was bidding for a date with him. Publicly. With his ego, he'd probably decided it was her idea. That she'd volunteered. Well, she would bid, but first, she'd make him suffer a bit. Ali turned her back on the stage and applied the cream generously to her face, remembering to pat a little under her eyes. Who knew when she'd next get a chance to use this quality cream? Then she pulled out her bid card, turned, and with arms folded, watched as the auctioneer started his pitch.

"Ultra Man has consented to escort a lucky lady," the auctioneer paused to cast a broad, suggestive grin around the room, "for one evening. So, if you've ever wanted to have supper on the moon or fly to the top of Mt. Everest for a picnic, then tonight you might get your chance!"

He raised his hand to call for the first bid, but never got the words out. The bidding started, furious from the first, leaping from one thousand to twenty thousand within five seconds. Ali watched as the operatives on the computers frantically entered data and called out bids. It was clear to Ali that the V.P.'s sister was determined to win. Instead of raising her card when she wanted to bid, she simply held the card aloft and nodded to the auctioneer whenever he glanced her way.

The bid rose to seventy thousand before the last of the telephone bidders dropped out. Now it was down to three women in the room, an anonymous bidder on the computer and Ali, who was yet to make a move.

"Excuse me – Hello – Sorry. Watch it!" P.L. shoved his way through the mass of humanity to squeeze in beside Ali.

"What's going on? Ali?" he hissed. "Have you forgotten?"

"No. I'm fine," she replied, her eyes on the stage where Ultra Man was starting to sweat. "I'm enjoying the show."

"What show?" asked P.L.

Ali shrugged. Behind them, the gentleman in the purple vest was goggling at P.L. and nudging his companion. They turned and stared at him. Camera phones appeared in their hands and they started taking turns standing behind P.L. and taking each other's photo. P.L., however, did not notice them. Instead, he took Ali by the arm and turned her back to the stage and gave her a little shake.

"Ali! Bid!" and then he vanished.

Every few seconds Ultra Man would try to make eye contact with Ali and either smile, or wiggle his eyebrows, or shift his shoulders. It made him look as if he was having a bad case of the fidgets. Each time Ali would nod, graciously smile in return, and nothing more. Giggles bubbled up in her, more potent than any sparkling wine. It was the perfect opportunity to pay him back for all those disaster scenes she'd walked over. All those shattered lives. Let him suffer now. It would only serve him right if she didn't bid at all.

Now, there were only two bidders. The green and gold-haired woman, and another lady, who kept consulting with a group of friends standing with her.

"Ladies," called the auctioneer, "I must ask you to decide. It's one hundred and eighty-nine thousand against you."

There was another furious exchange of whispers before the woman turned and shook her head sadly.

The auctioneer scanned the room.

"And we have one hundred and eighty-nine thousand, going once."

Ultra Man glanced across at Ali again, his eyes wide and worried. Ali stayed still.

"Going twice…."

Ali bit her lip as Ultra Man's face started to crumble and P.L. nudged Ali's arm, hard. Finally, she raised her card.

"Two hundred thousand," she cried, her voice cracking on the last syllable.

Voices rose like a wave, and the V.P.'s sister stood and turned, scanning the room for her competition. Ali tried to hide behind the huge man beside her but he dodged away.

"Two hundred thousand," cried the auctioneer, pointing at Ali. "To you, ma'am."

Camera stands whined as their operators spun about, focusing on Ali, cowering against the wall. P.L. had vanished – damn him. She'd never felt so exposed. A lightning storm of photographers struggled to get closer to her. Ali crossed her fingers and prayed that West's spell was working.

Green and gold hair shook as the V.P.'s sister shot her hand into the air and held her bid card high. The auctioneer shot a look to Ali, who gave Ultra Man an assessing glance, from his emerald green shoes up to the top of his helmet and lazily raised her card.

So it went for several minutes. Ali feared she'd have a nosebleed when the bid went above five hundred thousand, but she didn't, and the bidding continued, up and up. She was as light-headed and short of breath as if she were flying, but she stayed on her feet, frozen smile making her face ache.

When they broke a million, the faint murmuring from the audience died to a stunned, respectful silence. The V.P. was on his feet, his hands wrapped around his sister's upper arm, whispering urgently in her ear. Ali chuckled and kept her bid card up. He probably didn't want to see all that money going to charity instead of his campaign chest. or something. It took another twenty thousand dollars before the sister shook herself, cast one venomous look across the room toward Ali, and sat down, burying her face in her hands. The VP patted her on her back and shook his head at the curious auctioneer.

"The bid stands at ..." the auctioneer's voice broke, barely able to say the words. He coughed, swallowed, and tightened his grip on the microphone. "Are there any other bids?"

There were none.

The auctioneer counted her out. When the gravel stuck the podium, the room erupted to cheers. Hands grabbed Ali from all directions and she was half carried, half dragged from her sanctuary to the front of the room. Ultra Man bowed and smiled as he lifted her onto the stage. Not realizing they knew each other, the auctioneer offered to perform introductions. Ali shook her head, kept her eyes down, refusing to give her name, and dodged when Ultra Man tried to retake her hand.

"Miss, where do you want Ultra-Man to take you on your special date?" asked the auctioneer, holding the microphone to her lips.

"Bowling," Ali answered, and as everyone laughed, she ducked away, past Ultra Man and Mysterious West and into the dim security of backstage.

And straight into the arms – metaphorically speaking - of Mr. Crunch.

"Ms. Brent. When I said you were to bid on something this wasn't what I had in mind."

Chapter Six.

A.M. Phoenix radio announcement.
Pet's 'R Everyone announced that a two-million-dollar award will be given to the first person to breed a Guinea Pig with Panda bear markings. Parents and pet shops everywhere brace for a Guinea Pig population explosion.

"I'm very sorry, sir." Ali's heart plummeted, and her hands started to shake.

"It appears that we should talk a look at your salary scale –" continued Mr. Crunch.

"No! No!" Ali cried. "I'm not paid too much. P.L. and West asked me to do it. They said they'd cover the bid."

"That's right, Mr. Crunch," said West, as Ultra Man escorted her down the stairs. "We wanted to be sure that the date situation was dealt with harmlessly. Since the SS.C. couldn't offend the VP by refusing, getting Ali to bid was the easiest way out."

"I see." Mr. Crunch studied them without any expression Ali could read on his face. After a moment, he nodded. "Did it occur to any of you that the SS.C. might have wanted Ultra-Man to go on that date?"

The conspirators stared at Mr. Crunch in stunned silence. Ali wondered if her heart would beat again, it was wrapped so tight in bands of sheer terror. What had they done? What plan had they disrupted?

"No. I see you didn't," continued Mr. Crunch. "Very well. It is too late to correct. In a few days' time, I'll tell the publicity department to put out a press release about a nice innocuous dinner and bowling date that took place between an anonymous young woman and Ultra Man, that was platonically enjoyed by all, and that will be the –"

He fell silent as two men in dark suits pushed past him and took up stations in the corridor, muttering into their lapels.

Mr. Crunch stepped forward as West and Ultra Man moved to stand beside him. Ali found herself trapped between Ultra Man's broad back and the wall. Peering over their shoulders, she watched as the VP and his sister approached. The woman had a predatory look in her eye and, after her brother had stopped a polite distance away, she kept walking toward them.

Ultra Man backed up a few steps. Ali squeaked as he pushed her back against the wall. Ultra Man glanced back at the sound, gave her a reassuring smile, but kept his body between her and the other woman.

"Sorry, Ali," said Craig, but he didn't shift to give her more breathing room.

Ali growled, but before she could punch Craig in his indestructible kidneys, the V.P.'s sister moved even closer.

"Ultra Man, I'm sorry that my trust account gave out before...well, before *her*." The V.P.'s sister gave Ali one scorching look before fastening her bright eyes back on Craig. "But I've had an idea. I'm pretty good at bowling, too. Perhaps, for another donation, you'd be willing to double date. That way we," she flipping sharp bronze tipped fingers at Ali, "wouldn't take up any more of your valuable time."

She took another step forward, forcing Craig's back against Ali's chest. Ali's head bumped against the wall and the heat of his back burned into her breasts. She tried to dodge from behind him, but with Craig and that woman in front, West and Mr. Crunch to the sides, all her escape routes were blocked. Unable to move, Ali folded her arms, leaned against the wall, closed her eyes, and ignored them all. Let them fight until they'd sorted it out. Ali didn't care and she wasn't going to take part.

"Maybe these guys can wake me when they've finished – I dunno – posturing? thought Ali.

There was a stunned silence, followed by the scuffling of feet. For one moment, she was thoroughly crushed against the wall, but she refused to open her eyes.

"Oh, God, did I say that out loud?" whispered Ali.

Dead silence was her only reply, and after a few seconds, the hot weight pressing on her was removed. Ali opened one eye, then the other. The bodyguards were gone, as was the V.P. and his family. Craig was still in front of her, trying to block her view of Mr. Crunch. It wasn't until Mr. Crunch made eye contact with Craig and raised one thick eyebrow that Craig moved aside, leaving Mr. Crunch face to face with Ali. The Mysterious West – abnormally pale – and P.L. hovered behind his shoulders.

"Ms. Brent," said Mr. Crunch, in his soft, deep voice. "Perhaps you would like to tell me why you found it necessary to insult our high-ranking guests?"

"Sir," said Craig, "it's been a difficult night. We ..."

Ali waved away Ultra Man's interruption and glared down at her boss.

"Putting the Supers on the auction block is tantamount to slavery," she snapped. "It's one thing to work for a salary, but this stunt is going too far. What if whoever won the bid wanted Ultra-Man to participate in something unethical or criminal? Or even just a stupid advertisement? Or support for some controversial political stance? Or wanted to set him up some other way? They wouldn't have to say it up front; they could have just arranged to have a TV crew standing by wherever they went for the date. And what if the winner was just an ordinary person, and she'd expected sex? Ultra Man's reputation would be damaged even if he turned her down. If you'd realized how damaging this could have been for Ultra Man's reputation, West and P.L. would not have had to approach me for help, and I wouldn't have had to personally insult the V.P.'s sister."

"Is that your final excuse?" Mr. Crunch mild words surprised her, as did the degree to which her heart was pounding and her hands shaking. She was nowhere near strong enough to go toe to toe with a retired, and still Powerful, Super.

"It's not an excuse," said Ali, her hands tightening into fists. "It's an accusation. We were trying to recover a bad situation that you got Ultra Man into. Why the hell did you give in to them? There was no reason... "

Mr. Crunch sighed and leaned closer.

"Such naiveté is unbecoming a college graduate, my dear Ms. Brent. The local political powers have some influence over the Supers; no matter how hard we pretend that they don't. We have to operate within the laws of this country. That means the law writers have something to say about what we do and don't do. And, that they can occasionally ask us for a favor."

"Then this was something like a bribe? You hand over Ultra Man on a silk-covered platter, and in return, they don't pass awkward legislation? What does that say about the S.S.C.?"

"You have no idea what is involved, the extent of the diplomatic maneuvering required to keep the S.S.C. working, and independent." Mr. Crunch scowled around at them all. "That being said, since you are so concerned with the SS.C.'s reputation, you will be happy to know that I will undertake to speak to the publicity department. This situation must be redeemed. I will be required to spend the evening working on an appropriate story for the publicity department. The White House will have to create their own press releases. This does not, however, excuse you *all* from making your promised payment to the charity."

"Yes, sir," said Ali, her righteous anger fading away, leaving her shaking and weak. "Thank you."

"Because this is a political situation, I am going to be under pressure to discipline you in some way," continued Mr. Crunch, in his mild voice. "As we are already shorthanded, I cannot put you on suspension, Ms. Brent, which is unfortunate, as I can only put this error in judgment on your part down to lack of rest. I am certain you would welcome even forty-eight hours off-call – shame I can't give it to you. If you would be so kind, Ms. Brent, I would appreciate it if you would meet me in my office in half an hour. I must speak with the Supers now."

Ali glanced across at the Supers, then back at her boss. Her gut clenched as anger burned its way through her.

Yet all she could say was - "Yes, sir."

The door to Mr. Crunch's office stood open. Not in welcome, thought Ali as she paused in the corridor to straighten her clothing, but in unspoken command. Ali brushed her hand over her phone, half hoping that some emergency might strike.

Sighing, she tucked the phone back under the jacket and tapped her fingernails on the open door.

"In."

Ali suppressed a shiver and, back straight, walked into Mr. Crunch's playpen.

Nigel Hackham's inner sanctum was decorated after the style of a perfect English Gentleman's club – substantial leather chairs and bookcase upon bookcase of glossy, leather-bound legal tomes. Mr. Bendit's hidey-hole was so cluttered with loose pieces of paper that no decorations could be seen. As far as Ali knew, no one had crossed the threshold into Mr. Breakham's office, except Mr. Breakham. (He even vacuumed his own office to avoid invasion by cleaning crews.)

Mr. Crunch's office, however, was the cause of much, in-house only, discussion. The bookshelves lining the walls bowed under the weight of dolls (from the clunky, solid plastic statues of the first Super Team to the tiny, smoothly articulated models popular today), Super Team jet planes and Super suit sets and weapons. Then there were the stacks of other Super-related merchandise. Captain Fabulous stretchy toys, The Mysterious West's candy making spell lab. Purple Lightning's three different lines of sports shoes and energy drinks.

And, arranged across Mr. Crunch's otherwise bare desk, were the action figures of the current teams. Both the locals and the internationals, clustered by affiliation.

Some people thought that Mr. Crunch's collection of every single piece of Super merchandizing was due to his pride in the success of said merchandising, which was used to finance most of the S.S.C. activities.

Some thought it proof of his truly impressive, anal-retentive, obsessive-compulsive nature.

Ali didn't want to think what it said about Mr. Crunch that he surrounded himself with toys, but she suspected it was a control issue. His way of controlling everyone he met. Reducing everyone into little tiny chess pieces that he manipulated in a complex game, in which only he was privy to the rules.

The only other items on the desk were a small wedding photo in a silver frame and an old, much used and aged World's-Greatest-Daddy coffee mug.

As Ali entered, Mr. Crunch was pulling off his tuxedo jacket and draping it over the back of his battered leather chair. He reached down and picked up the newest Mysterious West doll. Ali could remember the fuss made when West had demanded a 'mature-figure" doll be issued to replace the one first designed when she was a teenager. Despite the publicity departments' reservations, both were selling well. The younger one, to teenage-witch wannabes. The older, to the 35 + married-with-children demographic – who, for some reason, purchased it to give to their teenage daughters.

Mr. Crunch balanced the doll on his palm and lowered himself into his chair.

"We don't have a replacement for her," he said, replacing the doll on the table and adjusting the position of P L. and Ultra man dolls on either side of her. "It's been three decades since a magic user of her level appeared, and that one insisted on staying and serving in India."

Ali remained silent. Mr. Crunch in this mood was unpredictable, and she wasn't going to worsen her current situation if she could avoid it. He didn't seem to notice her silence and continued in the same soft voice.

"Do you, or P.L., or West, or even our own, ever popular Ultra Man, have any idea what I do every day?"

Surprised, Ali just gaped at him.

"No?" The corner of Mr. Crunch's mouth twitched up. "I thought not." He settled back in his chair and steepled his fingers.

Unable to bear the weight of his stare Ali stammered, "Sir, I'm sorry"

"For what?" Mr. Crunch demanded, his voice still soft. "Sorry I'm angry with you? Well, that goes without saying. Sorry for interfering with something you don't understand? A plan that you're not privy to? Certainly, you're sorry now. Ms. Brent, coordinating community support for the Supers, who especially pride themselves on their individuality – is only slightly easier than herding cats. Personally, I prefer cats to this bunch when they decide to be creative. Sometimes it seems they spend their spare time thinking about ways they can drive me insane. They cultivate eccentricities just to raise my blood pressure. Fabulous, for example."

He halted mid-rant and breathed deeply for a moment.

Ali realized she was chewing on her lip, stopped and simply stared at him. She'd expected a cold and scientific ass-chewing – she could deal with that - but being on the receiving end of a contemplative monologue was chilling.

With a sigh, Mr. Crunch sat forward and picked up the Ultra Man doll, cradling it in the palm of his hand.

"Whenever possible I try to warn my Supers when they are going into situations requiring different skills. When I'm going to have to ask them to take on an unusual duty."

"Like gigolo?" asked Ali, very softly.

Mr. Crunch heard her, but his only reaction was another slight smile.

"Whenever possible, I warn them," he repeated. "However, there are times when I want their reaction to be sincere. To come from the essence of who they are. Therefore, I do not warn them."

Ali blinked, wondering what sincere reaction they'd expected from Ultra Man toward that political relative and the bachelor auction setup. Instead, they'd received P.L.'s and West's reaction, which was to defend their friend.

But all she said was, "Oh."

"Mr. Hackham is currently attempting to bring the political situation under control. Although, under the circumstances, we will find the price higher than if the auction had proceeded as planned."

"I am sorry, sir," said Ali, wondering what Ultra Man was supposed to have paid for. And how.

Crunch nodded. "Now I am prepared to accept your apology, Ms. Brent, as it is an informed act of penitence, and you may go."

Ali hesitated and then turned to leave. She paused at the door to glance back. Mr. Crunch had picked up another action figure, she couldn't see which. As she pulled the door closed, it occurred to her to wonder if he kept the dolls as a way to feel connected to the people, the Supers. As if he could, somehow, shelter and protect them.

She shuddered and pushed the thought away.

9:42.P. M. Eastern.
Pentagon. Sublevel 17, room 4 C
Meeting of the Paranormal Strategic Overview Committee.
No minutes/No secretary.

"Somebody has to know! She can't just appear out of nowhere," cried Mr. White.

"Why not? Isn't that the way it usually happens?" asked Mr. FBI, who was retiring in a few months and no longer cared who he offended. That morning, a publishing house had offered him enough money to buy his own small Pacific island as an advance on a tell-all book, and he was seriously considering breaking with years of FBI tradition (and a few small Federal laws) and accepting. At least if he had his own island, he could write his own no-extradition laws.

Mr. White turned slowly and glared down the length of the table at Mr. FBI. The other representatives swayed back, out of the line of fire.

"Are you trying to be funny, or just intentionally obtuse?" demanded Mr. White.

Mr. FBI tightened his grip on his pen and smiled, or, at least, he showed all his teeth. "Mr. White, there are some paranormals who don't want to spend time in the public eye. A small number, given the bounty we offer and the prestige of competing for space on the Super Teams. But as with every other demographic, there are those who stay under cover. They don't want to be known."

"And how many of those who hide turn to crime? Do we know? No, we don't!" spat Mr. White, "and therein lies the danger, gentlemen. You can't tell by looking which represent the danger. They look just like everyone else. They hide in our supermarkets, our banks, our schools. Just like the sociopaths." All the acronyms drew breath to protest that chain of reasoning, but Mr. White plowed on. "We cannot meekly stand by in ignorance. Until those time servers up on the Hill wake up and legislate for a Federal registry or free up for funds for the development of screening tests that work, we have to do the best we can with what we have." Mr. White rounded on Mr. Bendit. "What have you heard from Ultra Man?"

"He's... uh, still on loan to the Midwest, following up on some robberies. I haven't had a chance to talk to him. I have, however, spoken to The Mysterious West. She says that no one new was on scene in New Jersey. She, Purple Lightning and Ultra Man battled Mr. Ooze and the Mystress of the Night. That's all. No Ice Queen. No Ice Princess, or even an Ice Pageboy. And, according to our local and international registry, there are no Supers with ice Powers on record."

Mr. White stared at his hands, then raised his eyes slowly. "That's all she saw? All she said? Or all she knows? Did you confirm that with Purple Lightning? I hesitate to trust Mysterious West unless there's verification. There is something untrustworthy about witches. In fact, I insist you downscale that West woman's security status. While we are waiting to hear from Ultra Man, we have to go all out. Not just for this Ice Queen, wherever she is, but every other one of Them that's still hiding. Self-reporting is not enough."

"We've tried," protested Mr. Bendit, mopping at his face with tissues, "There is no way to test for paranormals."

"Find one," shouted Mr. White, "and get Ultra Man in for a proper debriefing. I insist on being present. Call him. Tell him he's on suspension until we hear his report on the Ice Queen."

It didn't take long for Ultra-Man to receive the summons. He was not pleased to be called off an active investigation to go back to home base to be debriefed about an event site he'd already filled in several reams of reports about. He was also a little embarrassed. As a matter S. S. C. policy, he'd received a report on the damage to the apartment and hospital in New Jersey. The only reason he'd read it was that he knew it'd been written by Ali. But when he reached the end of the report, the number of zeros in the repair estimate had him groaning.

Fortunately, Ali and her skilled team would repair the damage quickly. Even so, it was strangely embarrassing to see the results of his fight with Villains reduced to a price list of replacement parts.

He pulled on his Ultra Man persona and fixed a stiff, stern expression – one that his PR coach told him inspired confidence - on his face and prepared to face the fall-out.

"I'll let them know you've arrived," said the secretary, torn between trying to get Ultra Man's eyes to focus on her cleavage and preventing him from walking in on the meeting. "If you'd like to wait here."

The woman appeared a little too alert and chipper for this hour of the morning, Craig decided, drawing himself up to his full height. This last week had contained several different types of hell – particularly that moment when he'd been informed he was going to be 'sold' to a woman suspected of being an uber-fan of questionable emotional stability – and all he wanted right now was to drag his butt home. Well, that wasn't all. He wanted to find West and P.L. and thank them for increasing the gulf between Ali and himself by using her as their shill. But for now, he'd accept at least six hours of sleep.

"No, thanks," he said, reaching past her for the door. "I don't want to keep them waiting."

Craig pushed through into the conference room. The summons had not been politely phrased. In fact, it had been more of a threat – come back right now or we send the Super Hunters after you – than an invitation. Craig paused on the threshold. Crunch and Bendit, et al., weren't the only ones in the room. Mr. White, the obnoxious head of the Oversight committee, was seated opposite the lawyers at a long, polished table almost completely covered by newspapers. A cluster of unremarkable men in dark suits ranged along the wall behind him.

"I'm sorry, sirs," said the secretary, "I asked him to wait, but who could stop Ultra Man?"

Mr. White glanced up from a pile of newspapers and nodded, slowly. "Indeed, Ms. Hathaway, I have wondered that myself from time to time."

The chill, suspicious tone raised all the hairs on Craig's neck. Before he could respond to that remark, Mr. Crunch pointed at a chair. "Ultra Man, how provident. We were just talking about you."

Craig stalked down the table, picked up one of the newspapers, read the headlines, and stared. "What the hell is this? Who is The Ice Queen?"

There was a moments' silence, then Mr. White spoke. "That, Ultra Man, is why we called you here. We want you to explain why you didn't see fit to inform Control, Oversight and the S.S.C. of the existence of a new Villain. Moreover, why you involved your teammates in a conspiracy to conceal the existence of a new Villain that you, personally, find terrifying?"

"Sir," Craig blinked and turned to Mr. Crunch. "What is this trash?"

"Trash?" Mr. Bendit almost popped out of his chair, his hands folded under his chin, "Terrible situation. Unbelievable that you should take it so casually. Our poll numbers haven't been so low since the Kraken situation. Consumer confidence polled at forty-seven percent this morning. Forty-seven! We were eighty-sixed last Sunday."

Mr. Bendit pulled a tissue out of the box at his elbow, dabbed at his face, then tossed the crushed paper into the trashcan at his feet.

"Stop doing polls," suggested Craig, not inclined to indulge the trembling man, "I don't understand. What is going on? I haven't heard of any new Villain, and the only person who worries me is that IRS auditor who is going after my mother."

"This is no time to be flippant," said Mr. Crunch. "There are reports on the news services that while at the New Jersey event site, you stated that you were afraid of a Villainess named the Ice Queen."

"Why didn't you immediately report her existence?" shouted Mr. White.

"Because there wasn't any Ice Queen there." Craig's voice rose and he took a moment to bring his confusion and growing anger under control. It was gradually sinking in that this was not a normal SS.C. meeting to chastise him for some small issue. He glanced down at the newspaper headlines. He had no idea what they were talking about and, as far as he could tell, they didn't believe him. That spelled trouble in any SS.C., and in the S.S.C. it meant Very Serious Trouble. "I assume you mean that apartment complex event that you've had the team re-debriefed about. We told you. There was no one there but Mr. Ooze and The Mystress of the Night. Who told you otherwise?"

"It's been on the news every day since then," said Mr. Bendit. "You cannot say you haven't heard."

"Yes, I can,' said Craig, bestowing a cold stare on the lawyer. "I've been a little busy. Besides, even when I'm not busy I have better things to do with my spare time than reading my press. Sleeping, eating. Trying to track down Nuclear Man. That sort of thing."

"You are required, by S.S.C. rules, to stay up to date with current events, Ultra Man," said Mr. Crunch, his voice was mild, but the sting of the reprimand was hard.

Craig straightened when he caught his superior's eye.

"Sorry, sir. I can name the current president, my senator, the governor, and the current Miss Universe. Has anything important changed?"

"You found time to go to a party," began Mr. White.

"As is required by my contract," snapped Craig. "And immediately thereafter, I was back on duty. Sadly for me, I am not able to watch TV when I am on a cross-country flight. I have to stay alert for pigeons!"

Mr. Crunch's face didn't twitch. Instead, he picked up a printout of a computer web page. "We are seeing a distressing number of news reports commenting on your fears, Ultra Man. We need to know as much as you do about The Ice Queen."

"I have no idea who you are talking about. My fears are no one's concern but mine. And since The Ice Queen they seem to be wasting so much ink and paper on doesn't exist, you can safely tell everyone to calm down and stop worrying. I've told you. P.L.'s told you. West's told you. There was no one else at the New Jersey site. There is no such thing as the Ice Queen! I don't know where these news services got the idea that she did. She doesn't. Give it a few days and the story will die."

"Your complacency does not inspire confidence," said Mr. White.

Craig frowned but continued to address himself to the SS.C.'s lawyers. "Mr. Ooze and the Mystress were at the hospital getting something for Nuclear Man. There were no other Villains on-site. What is so hard to accept about that?"

"I have reviewed a copy of the film purchased by the Northern Star." Mr. White leaned forward. "How do you account for your own words?" He flipped open a notebook computer and clicked through files. After a moments' work, he spun the computer around. "We have not been able to persuade them to surrender the original, but we will."

"Can't take it again ... she." said the tiny image of Ultra Man. "Freeze me out ... chill ... straight through to the heart ... stops me dead ... kill me ... can't do it."

At the end of the recording, Mr. White settled back in his chair, folding his arms across his chest. "Well, Ultra Man, what is your explanation?"

"Ah," Craig blushed and sank down into the nearest chair. Exposing the details of his failed love life to his Super team members was one thing. He could trust Oliver and Lacey to keep quiet. But to talk about it in front of suits? Complete strangers? "Sir, that's a little embarrassing."

"Embarrassing? Your pride is all very well, Ultra Man, but something that you find frightening is terrifying to the ordinary people you are sworn to protect." Mr. White rose, slammed his hands on the table and glared down at Craig. "Leaving aside the unconscionable action of permitting news reporters to discover your cowardice - inspiring fear and trepidation throughout the country - and mark me, that will not be left aside for long – you failed to immediately report the existence of a Super Villainess capable to scaring you to death!"

"You're overreacting to a little misunderstanding," began Craig, as a blush crept up his neck.

"Overreacting?" shrieked Mr. White. "We've just been discussing the feasibility of canceling all off-duty time for all Super teams and activating second and third string Powers until the disaster is controlled."

"What disaster?" cried Craig, coming to his feet. "There is no Ice Queen. There are no icebergs in New York harbor, no glaciers inching down Main Street, USA. Nothing. And you know why? Because there is no Ice Queen. What happened on that site was that I'd asked a girl for a date. She turned me down. That recording must have been taken when I was telling Mysterious West that I'd struck out. That's all. End of story."

Dead silence settled in the room. Mr. White lowered himself into his chair and folded his hands on the polished table. After a while, Craig shrugged and sat down.

"Embarrassing though it is to admit, I don't take well to being turned down for dates," continued Craig, hoping that the blush he felt staining his face was hidden by his mask. "Mysterious West was giving me some advice."

"I see," said Mr. Bendit. "How interesting."

Craig's eyebrows rose. "Interesting?"

"Surprising, certainly," observed Mr. White, "that you expect us to believe that any woman would decline a date with you. Especially considering that some woman was willing to bid a million dollars for that honor only last Friday."

"Hey, I'm not Fabulous, hitting on groupies at every event site," said Craig and watched as the other men exchanged glances. There was no way he was going to volunteer the information that the woman he'd asked out and the famous anonymous bidder were one and the same. "I asked a girl out and got turned down. It's happened before and I expect, given my luck right now, that it will happen again."

"Unbelievable," said Mr. Bendit, reaching for another tissue.

"Entirely. What is more believable, more likely," said Mr. White, his eyes narrowing, "is that you are protecting someone. And we must ask ourselves who… and why?"

Craig felt his hands curling as if around a scrawny neck. Although Craig had had little to do with him over the years, he'd heard stories from the other Supers about Mr. White. Stories of harassed parents, of medical tests on siblings and offspring, all orchestrated by Mr. White. The general opinion amongst the Supers was that he was crazy, that he hated Supers, and wanted nothing more than to destroy the Super Support SS.C. and anyone possessing a Power. All of this made Craig wonder about the sanity of the politicians who'd assigned him into a position of Oversight over the largest organized group of Supers on the planet. Craig straightened and turned his attention to Crunch and Bendit. They, at least, were sensible people who knew him well enough to listen.

"Mr. Crunch," said Craig, "being a Super does not automatically make you a Casanova. You and I both know that our attentions are not always welcome. I mean, it's legendary how long it took you to get to the altar with your late wife."

"Thank you for reminding me," said Mr. Crunch, distantly. "And, yes, I do know that."

"I'm sorry to remind you of your loss, sir, but there are those here who don't have our understanding of the issue. I was turned down for a date, simply that. The girl involved has turned me down a dozen times before and I was upset. What this all looks like is that I must have been overheard by a reporter more interested in ratings that reality. I mean, look! This whole thing has been blown out of proportion. Just listen to that tape again. There is nothing in that recording about a Villainess."

An odd expression flickered over Mr. Crunch's battered face and he leaned back in his chair. "Possibly." he mused. "Let me see it again."

"Impossible," shouted Mr. White, on his feet again. "What is far more likely is that Ultra Man has been seduced by this Ice Queen and is trying to discourage the search for her."

"Seduced? That's ridiculous," said Craig, "She –"

"Who is she?" demanded Mr. White. "Who is the woman that you would have us believe turned you down? What's her name? We'll bring her in and get to the truth."

Craig stood slowly, unfolding himself from the chair inch by inch, taking the time to pull on his professional face and assume Power posture number one. He stood as tall as his six feet would permit, and even permitted his body to lift off the floor, just to gain a little more of an advantage. His voice was hard and flat when he eventually spoke. "I will not give you that information. You have a reputation, Mr. White, for abuse of authority. Of harassment. Of turning people you don't like over to the IRS. Of sabotaging careers and credit scores. I'm not going to let you loose on a woman whose only crime is that I like her."

Mr. White, however, was not cowed. "So you admit it?" he said.

"Admit what? Liking her? Since when has that been a crime?"

"Any member of a Super team becoming involved with a Villain is committing a moral crime," said Mr. White, his voice crackling across the room. "While it may not yet be on the books as such, it can be interpreted as treason."

Mr. Crunch and Bendit came to their feet protesting, but Craig could barely make out the words for the echo of 'treason' ringing in his ears.

"You are completely out of your mind?" Craig shouted when he could form the words. "There is no Villainess for me to be involved with! There is no Ice Queen."

"You're under arrest, Ultra Man," said Mr. White, gesturing his entourage forward.

"You *have* lost your mind," said Craig, turning to Mr. Crunch. "Sir…?"

The retired Super brought his hand up to neck height and drew his flat fingers, fast, across his throat. Craig hesitated, pulling back, staring at the lawyer.

"That is enough!" shouted Mr. Crunch, freezing everyone in the room.

"Before this gets completely out of hand, Ultra Man, you are on official suspension. You will not wear your armor or appear in public in your Super persona until this matter is settled. And you," he drew himself to his feet and faced Mr. White, "have overstepped your authority here. Accusations without proof are not a basis for arrests. Particularly on such extreme charges. Baseless, unbelievable charges. Not in this country, sir. Unless, and until, you have proof that I will accept, you may not arrest Ultra Man. I have made a lifetime's study of the law, sir, as a cop, a Super and a lawyer. I train the Supers of the S.S.C. in their responsibilities and duties. If any of them were to act in the same manner as you did just now, I would be seriously investigating their sanity and their worthiness to continue to serve."

Craig could feel the Super-Powered heat pumping from Mr. Crunch as he waited for Mr. White's reply. The suits, who had stepped forward at Mr. White's command, quickly withdrew to their places against the wall. They might not know who Mr. Crunch had been in the past, but no one wanted to take any chances. After a moment, Mr. White sank back into his chair, his face still flushed.

"Ultra Man," said Mr. Crunch, "in the interest of our SS.C., the status of the Supers and to keep," he jerked a thumb at Mr. White, "this one placated while we investigate your statements, I'm asking for your Super and Federal Marshall ID."

"Sir?" Craig wilted, the strength leaking out of his posture. His ID? His identity as Ultra Man? To be commanded to remain plain Craig Duane for some unknown time, and for no good reason? Somehow, he couldn't seem to find the strength to be angry. All he was, was shocked. Numb.

Mr. Crunch's granite expression did not change, and his hand remained outstretched and would until the world dissolved under his feet. Craig reached into the special pocket in his suit, drew out his identification and placed it in the lawyer's hand.

"This is a temporary measure only, son," said Mr. Crunch, tucking the small pieces of plastic away in his inside coat pocket and patting it gently. "We'll have you back on duty as soon as we can."

Face numb and ears buzzing, Craig ignored him and stalked from the room.

Craig didn't realize where his feet were taking him until he paused just outside the open door of Mysterious West's storage room, breathing deeply, seeking some sort of calm. As soon as he'd left the conference room, the rage had bubbled up, choking him. How the hell had it happened? How had that interview gotten so far out of hand? This morning he'd been a famous, trusted Super, and now he was skulking through the corridors of the S.S.C, afraid that his suspension was tattooed on his mask. He had no idea what to do next, so he sought out the person who'd been his guide from the first moment he'd arrived in the S.S.C. Mysterious West had been one of the first Supers. She had authority. Years of service. The respect of every person in the S.S.C. Enough magic to turn anyone who irritated her into a walrus. She'd be able to give him an idea of just how much trouble he was in. And, more importantly, tell him what to do next.

West, in full regalia, was supervising the restocking of her magical supplies. The S.S.C. employed three pagans, two alchemists, and one Ph.D. level chemist to keep Mysterious West supplied with the weird, wonderful, and just plain odd stuff she needed for her spells.

As far as Craig was concerned, the room contents just reminded him of a crowded potpourri shop. A potpourri shop whose contents were capable of reducing metal to slag, which was why he never entered without her at his side.

West glanced up and spotted him waiting. With a tilt of her chin, she dismissed her assistants, who filed out in silence.

"Come on in, baby," said West, applying sealing wax to a porcelain jar and setting it on a shelf. "Tell mama all about it."

Craig stepped in and closed the door, activating the security block. "I cannot believe the meeting I just had with those idiots upstairs. They..."

"Before you go any further," said West, glancing up at the flashing security-active light in the ceiling, "you should know that my security classification has been downgraded to level two. You shouldn't be discussing that meeting with me."

Craig gaped at her. If she'd been a Villain and this an event situation, she would have had almost a minute to beat him up before he unfroze.

"Civilians have higher clearance! Lacey? What the hell happened?"

"I have no idea. And don't call me Lacey." A grin flickered over her face. "The way they acted when they questioned me earlier, I don't think they'd trust me with the knowledge of my own secret identity."

"This is insane. I can't believe what is going on. You won't believe it. They've just suspended *me*! What the hell is so important about one apartment building falling down? It isn't as if we haven't done more damage elsewhere fighting the same damn Villains."

"Mind your language, boy,' said West, patting long-nailed fingers against his cheek. "Don't worry. All will come right in the end. We just have to ride it out."

She glanced up at the security light again. It still held green. Craig turned and glared up at the camera.

"They can't treat you, *us* this way, West."

"It seems they think they can."

Ali was contemplating her decimated pantry when the doorbell rang Sunday morning. Cursing the absent Oliver, Ali picked her way through the living room, stepping over scattered chips packets and discarded bedding to open the door.

"Morning, Ali Cat. Ready to go?" Craig stood outside, his hands deep in his denim jacket pockets. With his baseball cap advertising a recent movie and his tight-fitting jeans, he looked just like an ordinary mortal. There wasn't anything remotely green or bronze or Super about his outfit. And his face, instead of the proud, brave expression he affected when working – that Ali secretly thought made him look constipated – appeared cheerful and relaxed. He was not, however, someone Ali expected to see on her doorstep this early in the morning.

"Craig? What the hell are you doing here?"

"Bowling," prompted Craig. "Remember? You said you wanted to go bowling. Go get your ball. I've reserved us a lane at the best alley in town. Well, when I say best, I mean that the lanes are decent, but I can personally testify that the fries at their snack bar are superior."

"I said no such thing," snapped Ali, shifting to block him when he attempted to move past her into the apartment.

Craig stepped back and scanned her, top to toe. His smile broadened. "Looking good."

Ali ran a hand over her hair. Yes, as she feared, she'd neglected to comb the mess this morning. Instead, she had twisted it into a knot and secured it in place with a broken pencil.

"I was planning on spending the day cleaning," she muttered, tugging the pencil free and letting her hair fall across her un-made-up face.

"No, you're not. At the auction, and don't try and say you didn't, you said you wanted to go bowling with me. There are thousands of witnesses – excluding everyone monitoring over the Internet, or the people who watched the televised coverage – who heard you."

"No!" Ali gasped as her hands trembled. She shook her head and started to close the door. "No. Mr. Crunch took care of that. I saw the news reports. He's already got the spin story out. We're off the hook."

"I don't care," said Craig. "There's a date owed. As per your choice, I have my bowling ball right here, and I'm ready to go."

"What I meant was, if I went on a date…. That is…." Ali drew a deep breath and tried to order her thoughts. "The auctioneer was going on about flying to the moon, sipping Mai Tai's on Everest and other nonsense. Why anyone would want to do that is beyond me. Bowling was the most ordinary, boring date option I could think of. That's the only reason I said it."

Craig's grin turned wicked. "Sounds great to me. Better than Everest, for sure. Go comb your hair and we're out of here."

Ali pushed free of the doorjamb and folded her arms. "Okay, what's going on?"

"I'm here to collect my date."

"And I'm not interested in going anywhere with you. I thought I'd made that clear. P.L. and West asked me to do the bidding. This is all their fault. If anything, you owe them the date."

"Uh-uh." Craig leaned one hand on the doorframe and brought his face down level with hers. "You owe me."

"Oh." Ali's heart skittered and she leaned back, damning those Super pheromones as she raised both eyebrows. "How do you figure that?"

"Simple. If you had agreed to come with me on Friday as my date, then when the V.P.'s front person came with his ridiculous demand I could have said, 'Hey, I'm already spoken for. Can't insult my date by going off with someone else.' There was no way they'd ask me to stand on the block if I had a date in the building. No auction, no embarrassment for the SS.C. No huge payout from P.L. and West. No lecture from Mr. Crunch. So, the way I see it," finished Craig, poking her on the shoulder, "you owe me one date."

Ali's dry lips moved as she tried to frame a word, any word, but none came to mind. Craig's smug face only inches from hers did not improve her concentration. Unable to decide if it were better to slap or punch him, she closed her mouth with a snap, spun and headed for her bedroom, leaving the door open behind her. Craig sauntered into the apartment and settled on the couch.

"Are you sure you should be here?" asked Ali. "P.L. left hours ago to go on patrol."

"Yeah. I know. I've some time off." He waited a moment before continuing, "which means I have plenty of spare time for you."

"Great." Ali stood staring into the mirror. Why was she going along with this – stunt? Her list of things to do for today, efficiently taped on the refrigerator door, was long. Some of the tasks, like grocery shopping and laundry, were urgent. Even so, here she was dragging a comb through her hair and wondering if she should change to a tighter, or looser, pair of jeans. It was possible – possible – that she morally owed Craig a date. Half asleep as she was, she couldn't muster the brain cells necessary to argue. Granted, if she'd accepted his invitation, he wouldn't have had to stand up there, in front of the whole world, and be auctioned off like a slab of beefcake.

Also granted, if he'd asked someone else when she turned him down, he still would've been off the hook. So, it was partially his own fault for not asking someone else. That meant, while she did have to go out with him, one game would be enough. Then she could come straight home.

Satisfied with her rationalization, she dropped the comb onto the vanity and headed back to the living room.

"Well, with all my early morning callouts, I need all my spare time for myself." Ali swung out of her bedroom and grabbed her bowling ball and shoes from where they had moldered for, what, months, years? At the bottom of her hall closet. "Let's get this over with, so I can get back to more important things."

"Ouch," Craig pressed a hand to his chest. "I'm wounded. Call the medics."

Ali sniffed and stalked out of the room.

"Maybe I should follow in my car," said Ali, as they left her apartment building. "That way I won't be left stranded if you get called in."

"No, you're good. Told you, I've got plenty of time." Craig led the way to his truck – the same battered vehicle he'd had in college - and held the door open. Judging by the vibrating chassis, she assumed the engine had been upgraded even if the rust on the body was still untreated.

A stray thought hit Ali and she paused, one foot on the running board, staring up at him.

"That's odd. Even if you're not second team this weekend, you should still be on call."

"Just get in, Ali. No one's going to need me."

Ali jerked at the bitter tone in his voice, scrambled up onto the shabby leather seat and watched Craig wrestling the truck into motion.

"What's going on?"

"Nothing." He gave the meager traffic more attention than it warranted, and his hands tightened on the steering wheel.

"Why don't I believe you?"

"Please, Ali, give me a break. I don't want to talk about it. Let's just have some fun. It's been a long time since I've been completely off-duty, and I'm going to take advantage of it."

"Well, I'm still on call even if you aren't," Ali tugged vainly at the seat belt, then remembered it hadn't worked in college, either. Facing the windshield, she ran her fingers over the familiar dusty leather of the dashboard. If it hadn't been for Craig's old truck, she and Oliver would have been pedestrians throughout college – the pair of them too poor even for bus passes.

Ali sat and traffic-watched a few minutes, searching for an innocent subject. It might not have been her idea to go out, and she could think of any number of things she'd rather be doing this morning, but she was here and she hadn't had a chance to talk to Craig for... years? They'd never been friends, but in the political and complicated world of Super Support, he'd been a known face. Not that she'd ever taken advantage of knowing him – or P.L. By the time she turned up on event sites he was long gone, and whenever he visited the offices, sheer pride prevented her from being amongst those clogging the corridor's hoping to catch a glimpse of his famous shoulders. After a long silence, Ali shifted round to face him.

"So, what have you been up to lately?"

Craig spared her a quick glance. "What's your security clearance?"

"Higher than yours," shot back Ali and watched the familiar grin flash across his face.

"Hey yeah, that's right. I keep forgetting, *Senior Regional Supervisor*. Congratulations, if I didn't say it before, I'm proud of you. Well, let's see. For a while now, we've been trying to track down Nuclear Man. His behavior has been becoming stranger and stranger since the rumor about his latest cancer starting circulating."

"Regional Supervisor doesn't mean that much since I don't have that many people to Supervise," said Ali. Besides, who knew what title she'd have come Monday? After her interview with Mr. Crunch, she wished for a tanker of antacids to calm her stomach. She didn't think she'd be fired or even demoted, not after that strange late-night chat, but the uncertainty was enough to grey her hair. More to distract herself than out of real interest in talking shop on her only day off, she asked, "What's Nuclear Man been doing?"

Craig scowled at his hands. "Usually when he hits a hospital it's either to sabotage a research project or to collect meds. Last year, he started taking equipment. Computers. Data files. All sorts of new, even experimental machines. He's even raided a couple of pharmaceutical companies working on gene therapy."

Ali remembered processing pages of insurance documents covered with incomprehensible words. Lists of equipment with their corresponding replacement costs. She'd been so impressed with those price tags and too busy arranging to authorize replacements to worry about what those machines actually did.

"Doesn't anyone have an idea what he's been doing with it?" she asked.

"Not yet. A couple of people think it's just him self-medicating. The rumor is that his cancer's metastasized to hell and back. But I'll tell you, the S.S.C. arranged for me to have a meeting with a couple of geniuses out at Brookhaven Labs. Man, those guys are *weird*. They spend their time sitting around drinking coffee and making up the most outrageous stuff. Space Ships powered by magnetic bottles and ice volcanoes on Jupiter's moons. I gave them the list of what's been taken and asked what they could make out of it and got some answers that - let's say, after that, I've lots of reasons not to sleep well at night. I just have to hope that Nuclear Man isn't as crazy as they are."

Craig turned into the Bowling Lane parking lot, but before he could get out Ali caught his arm.

"What I don't understand how it is he keeps getting away. I mean, how hard is it to catch a guy on crutches, or in a wheelchair? How fast can he shuffle, for heaven's sake?"

Craig's eyes flashed and his knuckles whitened on his bag as he jerked himself free of her grip. Ali remembered the digs Flash Heat and Urban Renewal put in last night and started to stammer out an apology. Craig waved it away.

"Don't start with me. I'm not invulnerable even with my armor on. No one on the team is. And when you're faced with someone projectile vomiting nuclear and chemical waste at you, you'd be distracted, too."

Ali blushed to the roots of her hair and climbed slowly out of the truck.

One largely undocumented advantage of going bowling, Ali observed, was that, for at least half of the time, you got to watch your date's rear elevation while they bent, twisted and bowled. Depending upon your date's physical attributes, this could either be a burden or a blessing. In Craig's case, it was a definite positive benefit of the game. Ali took custody of the chair directly opposite the lane and sipped her soda while Craig demonstrated, for the fifth time, the correct approach to the lane. A smile tugged at the corner of her lips as she nodded solemnly. His Super Suit had been designed, at his request, baggy in the trousers, so most women only got to speculate about Ultra Man's gluteus maximus. Ali could tell them all – should she want to – that when clothed in skin-tight denim, Craig Duane had a Superior Posterior.

"Got it now?" asked Craig still crouched, glancing back over his shoulder.

Ali blushed and dragged her straying attention back above his – and her – waistline.

"Maybe you should show me one more time," said Ali, laughing as Craig stood and put his fists on his hips.

Power Pose #1 suited him even in civilian clothes.

"Uh Huh. No way. Up you come. It's my turn to sit and watch."

Ali stood, smoothed her hands down her jeans and reached for her ball. Heat balled in her stomach. She hadn't realized he'd noticed the direction of her attention. She shot a quick glance over her shoulder as she positioned herself before the lane and spotted Craig sliding into the seat she'd just vacated. He leaned against the plastic back, folded his hands behind his neck and gave her a wicked grin.

Determined not to be put off by his attention, Ali dipped, swung and pitched the ball. It ran straight and true for the first strike of the day. She tossed her hair back over her shoulder as she turned to face him.

"Hmmmmm, very nice," his eyes wandered up and down her body, "technique."

Ali sauntered back to the chairs and reclaimed her drink. "I haven't been in an alley since college," she said

"I'm impressed."

The combination of pounding rock music battling with the sound of falling pins raised the background noise level to deafening. Ali walked over to Craig's chair and leaned closer. His eyes flashed down to the cleavage of her shirt then up.

"Guy's shirts still, Ali? I thought you'd have outgrown that style by now."

"It gets me a cheaper rate at the dry cleaners and keep your mind off my clothes." Before Craig could respond Ali had her hand over his mouth. "And leave that straight line alone."

His lips twitched, but he nodded.

"I've been thinking about," She glanced about, but no one seemed close enough to overhear. "You know, *him.*"

Craig gazed at her blankly for a moment, then blinked. "Oh, okay, him. What about *him*?"

Ali picked up her ball and held it balanced in her hand for a moment before pitching it down the lane. All but two pins fell to her attack. She wandered back to lean on the ball return.

"The files are pretty complete on most of the villains. Everyone knows why The Shriek turned to crime – the idiot. Mysterious West has some decades-old feud with The Mystress. Hackham, Bendit and that lot have gathered a lot of info on the various Villains, but they don't know anything about," her voice dropped to a whisper, "Nuclear Man."

"That's not all they don't know about." Craig's face darkened for a moment and his hands clenched in his lap. After a few seconds, he visibly forced himself to relax. "You don't have to whisper, Ali. People talk about the Supers and the Villains all the time. Considering that there's been a situation involving him in town this last week, it'd be unusual if we weren't talking about him." He stepped up to the line and threw his ball for a three-pin split. "And you're right. We've never been able to do so much as to get his real name. The profilers have had a hard time getting a handle on his motivations. Makes it difficult to predict where he'll be or what he wants. And as that debacle the other night proved, we can't rely on informers to let us know where he's going to turn up." His eyes narrowed and he cast his second ball, missing the remaining pins. "I've been working on him for a year and I'm no nearer to getting him than when I started. And now…"

"Now, what?"

"Never mind," Craig headed back to his chair. "It's your turn."

Ali cast her ball, scattering six pins. Fortunately, the remaining ones were in tight formation. While she waited for the ball, Craig sat rubbing his hands together and staring at his shoes.

"Your head's not here," she said after a pause.

He glanced up and forced a smile. "Sure it is."

"No. You're so far away that I'm going to beat you, extra abilities or not." So saying, she turned and threw the ball, taking out the remaining pins.

"I'm saving my energy," said Craig.

"Oh, yeah? For what? French fries? You've got something on your mind. If you don't want to be here…."

"No!" he was on his feet in an instant. "It took me long enough to get you on a date, I'm not giving up now."

He approached the lane, threw and guttered the ball. Shaking his head, he returned to sit beside Ali. He swore, watching the ball's progress down the lane and the inevitable goose egg score appearing on the overhead scoreboard. "Okay, fair enough. There is something on my mind." He tugged Ali around, positioning her so they sat knee to knee, "I gotta ask, Ali. Did you or Norman put anything special, different, in your report on the apartment complex situation?"

Ali blinked. Whatever she'd expected, this was not it. "Special? The apartment? No. My site reports from that one were pretty much routine. A lot of damage, consistent with an extremely localized F three storm. Rain. Wind. That's all."

Craig did not respond and continued to stare at his hands.

"Craig, what's up?"

He tilted his face up to hers. "Nothing? No comments about large pieces of ice, or excessive water damage?"

"Ice?" Ali gaped at him open-mouthed. "Well, hell, of course, there's water damage. Any time you break six floors worth of water pipes without draining them, you get clean and dirty water damage. Despite the F3 that night, it wasn't cold enough for ice to form. Why?"

"I have no idea what is biting those guys. The whole team has been called in and questioned more over this little event than we were over any other event in the history of the SS.C. I mean, I had all the lawyers, Control and that moron from the Oversight committee questioning me. All over an event that lasted less than twenty minutes."

"What are they so excited about?"

"Ah, that's the thing. It's weird. Have you heard anything around the office? Seen the news?"

"When do I get a chance to listen to gossip? This week has been so busy the only sleep I've been getting is when I pass out at my desk."

Craig stared at his hands folded over his knees. "They've gone and downgraded West's security clearance to the point that she isn't allowed to attend daily briefings. If anything's planned, she doesn't find out about it until we're in the thick of it."

"But that's stupid," cried Ali

"Lower your voice," he hissed as a pair of bowlers wandered past.

Ali shrank back and blushed.

"Sorry. Maybe we should go. We aren't playing and this isn't the place for this conversation."

Craig shrugged.

"Poor Lacey! How's she taking it?"

"Badly." Craig studied the reset pins for a moment, then shook himself and focused on Ali, flashing the charming smile that always seemed to impress the photographers who followed him about. "I shouldn't let it get to me. In a few days it'll all die down. So, how about you finish beating me here and we get lunch? Later, maybe, I could talk you into playing hooky for a week and going fishing, or skiing. Or maybe we could go somewhere with sunshine and sit on a beach?"

"No deal, chum. I'm here under protest, remember, so playing hooky with you is not going to happen. Besides, I really do have to do some laundry, go grocery shopping. Have you any idea what Oliver is like if he comes home and we're out of ice cream?"

"Well, that is really low," said Craig, "Going skiing with me ranks lower than laundry? I may never recover from the blow to my ego. How about I come with you instead? Carry your bags, miss?"

"Forget it, sunshine," Ali told him. "You have things on your mind, even if you aren't on patrol. You should concentrate on them."

"Yeah. Nuclear Man." Craig sighed. "Ah, what a mess."

He jumped, grabbing at the phone on his waistband. Ali's eyebrows rose to her hairline.

"What the heck? I thought you were off-duty?"

"Forgot to turn it off." Craig checked the display. When he glanced up his eyes were dark, intent. "Dammit, I should have turned it off. Major Calamity and The Blast attacked the old cash depository in Maryland. They're heading north now. I gotta go."

"What about the Southeast team?" said Ali, "It's their area."

"P.L. and West are already en-route. The page was from the South East coordinator via Control, sending a general call for assistance with an intercept."

He leapt to his feet, kicked off his old bowling shoes, shoving his feet into his battered trainers. Scooping his ball out of the return, he tossed it into its bag and headed for the door. Ali grabbed her gear and ran after him. Since he wasn't using his Powers, she arrived at his truck only a few steps behind him.

"But Craig," she hissed, "by the time you get there, they'll either be captured or gone."

"Do you think that means anything?" demanded Craig, throwing his bag onto the floor of this truck. "P.L. and West are on their way...without me. Neither of their powers is up to dealing with that pair. The Blast and Calamity rank high on the danger list. Only Nuclear Man is higher, and that's because clean-up is so toxic. I'm not letting them go without my backup."

Flipping up the passenger seat cushion, Craig retrieved a simple blue carrier bag. He glanced quickly around the parking lot and headed toward a line of three huge trash bins, Ali still on his tail.

"Keep watch," he ordered, ducking behind the metal bins.

Ali sighed, turning to scan the parking lot. There was no way she could stand here and not look conspicuous. What reason could she pretend to have for loitering near smelly trash? Fortunately for her, Craig was practiced in turning into Ultra Man, and hissed for her attention only moments later.

"Take this," he said, tossing her the bag and his truck keys, "I'll swing by your place later and pick them up. Now get out of here. I can't take off with you standing about, attracting attention."

With a sniff, Ali turned her back and stalked away. She concentrated on not turning her head when the familiar rush of air overhead told her he had launched. Instead, she walked calmly to his truck and packed the small bag of clothing away beside Craig's bowling equipment. As she dropped her own bag on the floor of the truck, she noticed the top of Craig's bag was not as tall. Not as tightly packed. She pulled the zip back and muttered a curse. The moron had left his shoes behind in the alley.

She could leave them. The odds of anyone ever connecting the Super fool with his bowling shoes were minuscule. And any creature that someone might, hypothetically, clone from Craig's sweaty feet would be pathetic, at best. Nevertheless, Ali sighed and wandered back into the bowling alley to retrieve Craig's shoes. SS.C. policy was SS.C. policy.

Chapter Seven

Boston Evening news, channel 56.
Supervillain, Clive the Pitiless, was arrested yesterday at shopping mall in New Haven when his floor-length black cape became entangled in a revolving door. Clive's lawyer announced his client's intention of suing the mall's management for failure to post warning signs on this dangerous mechanism. Clive is asking for a multimillion-dollar settlement. There has been no comment from the Mall's management as yet, but graffiti on a nearby billboard – signed by Techno Boy – criticized Clive the Pitiless for his antiquated dress code and outdated criminal operations.

When Ali returned to the building, despite the heavy beat of rock music blasting out of the speakers, the alley was remarkably silent. Absent was the familiar thud of balls and crash of pins. Instead of waiting intently, as their partners bowled, the players were clustered around the snack bar watching the TV set suspended above the popcorn machine.

Ali tried to ignore it. She knelt, scrabbled around under the chairs until she retrieved both of Craig's shoes and turned, heading for the door and safety. Out of the corner of her eye, she caught sight of the TV just as it showed two helicopters pass too close together, then swing apart, endangering yet another nearby copter.

"......*ngton's News 3,"* said the commentator over the roar of copter blades and the background music. *"In view of the number of near-collisions so far this morning, the police are requesting that the news helicopters land, leaving the area clear for them and the Supers, but I haven't heard if any of the stations have yet complied with the request."*

"What are you planning on doing?" asked the blonde talking head back at the studio.

The on-air talent didn't even have the grace to blush. He blinked as if the thought that he was included in the order hadn't previously occurred to him. *"Well, as we haven't received any instructions from station management, we are staying in pursuit."*

At that moment, the picture jumped and bucked. Ali heard the pilot swear as he swung the copter out of the path of a colleague and the two flying Villains.

"Moron," muttered Ali, sinking onto one of the high chairs, her eyes not leaving the screen. "Land and get out of the way."

But they didn't. The TV picture jumped again.

The on-site talking head smiled brightly into his camera. *"We're switching to our news van that has just come on scene following police cars and emergency vehicles."*

This time the picture was stationary. No wind shear or last-second dodging to make the viewer nauseated. Filmed from the ground, they could see three police copters jostling for position with four news copters, with several others circling further away. As far as Ali could tell, no one had obeyed the command to land. In between them all sky-danced Major Calamity with The Blast dangling from a thick black cord below him. Ali winced at a particularly sudden change of direction that had The Blast jerking and kicking at the end of his rope. She watched, wondering why Major Calamity hadn't dropped his partner-in-crime and fled.

"Slowing down, Calamity," muttered Ali, "and forgetful with it. Left home without your sharp scissors, did you? Bad planning that."

The other bowlers spared her puzzled glances and Ali bit her lip shut.

On screen, as if hearing her, Calamity snatched at the buckles of the harness binding him to his cohort, but with wearing gloves, having to dodge news copters, and cops, and the struggling weight of the other Villain, he was unable to free himself. The Blast swung helplessly below.

Ali checked her watch. It was far too soon for Ultra-Man to be on-site. Depending on the location, it could take hours for him to make the flight. In the meantime, there didn't seem to be any sign of the other Supers supposed to be serving that area. Where the heck were they?

There was at least one flight-able Super in every district. In this one, she mumbled to herself as she searched her memory. Knight Flight. Right. Never the fastest of Supers, he'd been injured the previous week in another battle with Calamity. No doubt that was one of the factors included in today's Villainous plan. The criminals had hoped to get away before Supers from other districts could be involved. Maybe they'd even committed the previous crime just to get an opportunity to take out Knight. And what with the interference from the news crews, it seemed that the non- Super law enforcement wasn't able to bring this confrontation to any sort of conclusion.

Despite the number of people on-site and those watching TV, the Villains were unlikely to be captured unless something changed. The Villains weren't obeying orders to land – no surprise. They were immune to bullets – thanks to previously stolen S.S.C. armor. Ali held her breath waiting for the Super Team to arrive. Any of the Teams arrive.

Minutes ticked by, and still no one appeared.

Ali wasn't the only one who'd noticed. The little blonde talking head back in the studio was forcing a stern, worried look on her face – while carefully avoiding wrinkling her brow (let's not have any premature wrinkling or was it recent Botox?) – and speculating as to what could be keeping the Supers.

"*What can you see there now?*"

"*Well, Andrea,*" said a movie-star pretty newsman, "*we see a lot of maneuvering by the police copters as they are trying to keep the criminals from flying off, and their work is severely hampered by civilians on the scene, as well as the continuing absence of any Supers.*"

"Moron," muttered Ali, "You're the civilian. You're part of the problem. Get out of the cops' way and they'll ground Calamity fast enough."

"Nah," said the thickset man sitting at her right as he chewed on an unlit cigarette. "I vote to keep some of the TV copters airborne. At least the one with the Channel 6 logo. That pilot looks like the most determined. Getting the best shots too, I bet. Hey, can we switch to Channel 6?"

Ali gasped and spun in her chair to face the speaker. "What the hell do you mean – *vote?* This isn't some idiotic reality game. This is real life! Those news copters are interfering with a police pursuit. The pilots can lose their licenses for this."

The not-quite smoker sniffed. "As far as I can see, the news copters have the better pilots and, until we get a direct video feed from the cop's copters, then they need to be there. How else can we see what's going on? The way I see it, the TV copters are better at getting up close. If the cops got on the TV copters, they'd be able to catch the Villains, no trouble."

"Are you insane?"

"Keep your voice down," commanded the manager, turning to glare at her, "some of us are watching."

"This isn't a game," repeated Ali, "and news copters and other civilians are required to keep out of the way, *by law*. The cops exist to protect them," she paused as, on screen, a single-engine plane flew through the crowded airspace. As it swooped in, scattering three copters, they could see that several people in the plane were armed with small cameras. "God, no. Not more idiots. What are they doing here? The civilians should all leave the area."

"Well, that can be your vote," drawled a woman at the far end of the snack bar. "If anyone asks you."

"This isn't a voting situation. It's life and death. Law and order. Catching criminals. You know, *reality*!"

The manager turned again. "If you can't keep quiet, then you can leave."

"That's my vote," said the man to Ali's right.

"I second it," added the woman.

There was a general mumble of assent from the other watchers.

"Sounds like it's unanimous," said the manager, jerking his thumb toward the door, "You've been voted out of the alley. Leave."

Ali could barely draw breath. She had never been so angry and so helplessly frustrated in her life. How could these people actually think that their opinions – so far away from the action – could have any real impact? Could those opinions matter at all to those who had to fight and risk their lives to protect such idiotic civilians from Villains? Ali snatched Craig's shoes from the counter and glared down the line of smug faces.

"You are all insane," she said, "and I wish you the infinite joy of being yourselves for as long as possible."

There was a moment of silence, while her audience tried to work out the insult.

"*Andrea, I have to report that Major Calamity and The Blast are nowhere to be seen.*"

Everyone spun to face the TV. Ali took in the scene in an instant. Major Calamity and The Blast had taken advantage of the confusion following the stupid maneuver by that small aircraft and managed to hide or leave the scene.

Before the others could work that out, Ali grabbed the shoes, turned tail and fled.

The audience had missed the excitement of the escape.
She didn't want them taking their displeasure out on her.

Not willing to hang around outside the alley and risk being attacked by an irate mob of bowlers, Ali drove Craig's truck back to her apartment. The drive was not anywhere near long enough to cool her temper. How could people be so stupid, so ignorant as to sit and *vote* about a hot police chase?

She'd broken her usual rule about news programs and listened to the radio on her drive home. Apparently, the small aircraft whose interference permitted Calamity and Blast to escape was piloted by a group of soccer moms using their cell phone cameras to try and get a prize-winning photograph for some Internet contest.

Risking their damn lives. Interfering with a police chase. And the odds were good, Ali realized as she stalked through her apartment, slamming into the kitchen to check whether Oliver missed the chocolate bar hidden in the frozen peas package, (he hadn't), that even if the police tried to charge the soccer moms with interference, there'd be a charity fundraiser within an hour to raise money for their court costs. (And agents, fishing for advances for their TV movie rights.)

Lacking chocolate, and someone to shout at, Ali stomped through the apartment.

"Damn them to hell anyway," she muttered, picking up empty cups and putting them down again. "Damn them all."

Her hands clenched around a pillow and slowly, carefully, she tore it in two, scattering stuffing across the floor. After taking several deep breaths, she flicked on the TV and started pacing her living room while the latest updates washed over her.

All the talking heads were enjoying nattering on about the situation. Not only had Major Calamity and The Blast disappeared minutes, seconds, before Ultra Man arrived at the scene, but the news crews had immediately descended on him, preventing him leaving and beginning an effective search.

The cops were giving press conferences, saying – in the politest of terms – that they were angry they'd been prevented from one-upping the Supers by catching the Villains, and mad at the Supers for not providing the service they'd promised.

Back at the S.S.C., the publicity department was expressing their politically correct distress that Supers were being held responsible for the escape. That sound bite was followed by a shot of the hospital where Knight was recovering from his injuries while the on-the-spot reporter speculated – without any validity or S.S.C. confirmation - that the local Supers were upset with the out-of-town Supers for even appearing on the scene.

(Especially given that Ultra Man was on the scene for a full hour answering questions before the local team arrived, P.L. and West having paused en-route to do a kid-trapped-in-a-well rescue.)

And, of course, the news crews, despite being responsible for most of the havoc, were reporting it all with unrestrained glee.

Maybe one day the human race would grow up? Ali sighed and shook her head. Maybe her fish would climb out of his tank, start riding a bicycle and join a circus.

Ali spent the rest of the day doing some long overdue chores. For the first time in months, she went a full weekend with no call-outs. Craig did not turn up to reclaim his truck. Oliver phoned to tell her Purple Lightning was temporarily assigned to the Southeast to assist with the search for Major Calamity and The Blast, but he didn't know where Mysterious West and Ultra Man were.

Apparently, after Ultra Man's interview he'd been summoned back to headquarters and hadn't been seen since.

Ali could have gone into the S.S.C. headquarters. She had sufficient rank to be permitted to hang around with the secretaries in Central Super Coordination up on the fifteenth floor. Those phone jockeys knew everything. Knew everyone. Unfortunately, Ali was famous throughout the SS.C. for mocking those who spent their spare time waiting for the next Super event. Which meant now, when she wanted to know what was going on, she had to rely on the news services just like every other mortal.

As if.

Ali had too much self-respect to spend her life hanging around waiting for the next Super sighting. Craig was a big boy. He could look after himself without her monitoring. As soon as the live report ended, she resumed her usual habit of keeping the TV off.

Ali told herself she didn't need updates. As long as the crimes weren't committed in her area of responsibility, there was nothing for her to be concerned about. No paperwork, therefore, no problem. That comforting thought did not help her sleep or stop her from pacing her apartment.

Monday morning, Ali was through security and up to her office a full hour earlier than usual. She paused at every TV lining the corridors, but there were no updates about Ultra Man, P.L. or West. There didn't seem to be any change in the background buzz of the S.S.C. Perhaps the team was still helping in the Southeast.

Reaching the sanctuary of her office, the first thing Ali saw on her desk was an approval for replacement work boots. She examined the much-anticipated piece of paper and sighed. Retired Army, The Colonel created all the event site related equipment. He was not anti-female. As far as he was concerned, it was the Power, not the gender that was important. Despite that stated opinion, all the equipment he designed was aggressively unisex. It would be too much to ask that he'd design a safety shoe like a nice classic pump, or even boots with feminine styling. The best Ali could hope for was that the new boots weren't the massive things with three-inch tire-tread soles that were too heavy to walk in.

Knowing that she'd regret it if she postponed picking up her new boots, Ali put running down to supply at the top of her to-do list. Taking the staff-only elevator to the basement, she was a little surprised to find Oliver was already in it, leaning against the wall.

"Where the heck have you been?" demanded Ali.

Oliver ignored the question.

"Hey, girlfriend. Wassup?" he said, giving her a tired, one-armed hug.

"I've been approved for three more sets of work boots." Ali waved the requisition clutched in her hand. "I'm not sure whether to be happy or upset about it. On the upside, I need the boots. I can't keep running around event sites in ordinary shoes forever. On the downside, it means I'm still visiting event sites. No matter how high they promote me, I'm still called out. I wish they'd get their thumbs out and hire a few more naked-face Site Supervisors."

"That's not going to happen until you stop being perfect, girlfriend. Why should they get someone else, when they can get you to do it all?"

Ali snorted and examined the requisition again. "Says here they've just installed some new features. Apparently the new boots have radiation detectors in the soles."

Oliver froze, his head tilted to one side and tapped one long finger on his chin.

"What's with you?" asked Ali.

"I'm trying to think why anyone would think it was a good thing for their shoes to tell them they're standing *in* something radioactive," said Oliver, with a grin.

Ali thought for a moment, started to laugh, then stopped, all humor vanishing from her face. "You know, you're right. That is not a happy thought. Still, as long as they hold up better than my last few sets, I don't really care what they've stuck in them."

She looked Oliver up and down. He was wearing his mask, which meant she should address him by his Super title. SS.C. policy being what it was, he should address her in return as Regional Supervisor, or Ms. Brent.

His mask's eyepieces were looking a little frosted - signs of damage from windblown dust. She scanned the rest of his clothing. Instead of his Super suit, he was wearing a loose blue sweat suit, and it seemed that he was standing awkwardly.

"Wassup with you?" she asked.

"I'm here to be fitted for a new Super suit," he whispered.

"Why?"

P.L. blushed under his mask and glanced away. "It's personal."

"Come on, P.L.," said Ali, tugging on his collar, straightening it. "You're talking to the girl who had the infinite joy of washing your boxers this weekend - I'm going to charge you for that if you hide your stuff in my basket again. Why are you keeping secrets from me?"

P.L. seemed to shrink in on himself. "I've just come from the SS.C. doctor's office. I left it a little too long to go on a diet. My suit's gotten tight. Too tight. After all the running around this weekend, well, I have this little chafing problem."

"Chafing?"

Ali's breath hissed out in spurts. She couldn't hold it in. By the time the doors opened on the 9th sub-basement, she was clutching the wall to hold herself up as she laughed. P.L. stalked out of the elevator, head held high. A few seconds later, Ali caught the closing door and followed him. She had to jog to catch up and walk beside him, slipping her arm through his despite his efforts to shake her loose.

"I'm sorry, P.L."

"I'm not talking to you."

"Forgive me?"

"No." But he didn't pull his arm away.

They walked in silence, arm in arm, into the supply department, and stopped dead just inside the door. Before the door could close behind them, a brilliant light flashed through the room, spilling out into the hall. Ali staggered, bent double, fighting nausea and clutching desperately at P.L.'s sleeve. His body was the only certainty in a world cast suddenly upside down and twisting. Writhing light and color danced behind and before her eyes, blurring her mind. Struggling to breathe, she slid toward a floor that was bucking and twisting under her feet.

"Dammit, Tye Dye," shouted P.L., as he grabbed at Ali, slowing her fall. "Shut it off, NOW."

The noxious colored lights ebbed and bled away. The floor straightened and returned to its proper place. With a sigh, Ali slumped against the wall, both hands pressed against her stomach. She felt a thin trickle of moisture over her lips. She licked it and gasped when she tasted blood. She blinked rapidly and tried to focus. She hadn't heard that Tye Dye's power caused nosebleeds. P.L. lowered her to the floor, then charged across the room. Through blurry eyes she could see him running, no faster than an ordinary mortal, snatching a box of tissues off a nearby desk and returning to press a handful against her nose.

"You okay, Al Pal?" he asked, pressing on her shoulders. "Just sit here for a moment while I tear old Tye Dye a new one."

"Hey, take it easy," cried the room's only other standing occupant, holding his hands out to his sides as P.L. advanced toward him. "I was just trying out my new Super Suit. Isn't it fantastic?"

"Fantastic is not the word I would have chosen," P.L. moved fast, grabbing Tye Dye by his multi-colored shirt and lifting him to his toes and shaking him. "Are you aware of regulations, stupid? You're supposed to give warning. I didn't hear a warning." Raising the other Super higher, P.L. shouted, "Anyone hear Tye Dye here announce his intention of activating his Power?"

There were negative sounding groans from scattered places around the huge storeroom, and the distant sound of at least one person throwing up into a trash can. Ali clutched tissues to her nose and risked a glance toward Tye Dye. Despite P.L.'s grip on his throat, he was grinning broadly. She knew him by reputation. A second-string Power, if that, he received a stipend from the S.S.C., and turned up for the occasional photo call, but he was rarely called on to act. The most important reason was that Tye Dye's ability was not directional. Any time he activated his light show, there was a lot of collateral damage. The current state of the supply room was a good example of what his Power could do. The most important other reason he didn't work full time was that he didn't have the sense God gave a walnut.

"That is one seriously nauseating shirt, Tye," said Ali, dragging herself up the wall, her voice muffled by the bloodstained tissues. "You don't have to activate your Power to blind people or make them wish they were blind. All you have to do is walk down the street."

Tye Dye tapped P.L. on the wrist and was lowered to the ground. He brushed his clothing straight and tossed his thigh-length yellow ponytail back over his shoulder. Tight orange leather pants and cross-tied boots of violent green completed his ensemble.

"Good God, that's a revolting outfit," said Ali.

"Good to run into you, Lightning," said Tye Dye, ignoring Ali's remark as he flicked imaginary lint from his sleeve and straightened his suit, "I suppose you've come down to welcome me to the team."

P.L.'s face paled. "What do you mean?"

"While old Ultra Man's taking a well-earned vacation," Tye Dye's grin broadened and he spread his arms wide. "I got 'the call.' They asked me to stand in for him."

"What's going on? What vacation? And they sent for you? To stand in *for Ultra Man*? You? Ultra Man?" said Purple Lightning. "Now I feel sick."

"I'll say. In fact, everyone will," said Ali, looking Tye Dye up and down. "You two are *so* going to clash."

"Hey, Brent, watch where you're going."
Ali lowered her arms and peered over the top of her boxes. The Colonel's new Super Safe Boots were four times heavier than her usual work boots but had only two inches of tire tread soles. Carrying three pairs at once effectively blocked her view. Any normal person seeing another one with that sort of burden would have dodged out of her way. That meant, he'd just bumped into a Super.

Flash Heat stood in Power Pose #4, effectively blocking the corridor. He tilted his head to one side and cast Ali what he obviously thought was a charming smile. Ali thought he looked like an evil toddler.

"Flash Heat? What the heck are you still doing here?"

"Just visiting The Colonel after spending the morning talking to Mr. Hackham," Flash Heat grinned at her, lifted the lid on the topmost box then tutted. "Not exactly stylish, Ali."

Ali ignored the fashion criticism and raised her eyebrows. "I thought Mr. Crunch took care of the new "A" hole tearing for the SS.C., not Hackham."

"Ah, but that's where you're wrong, Ali dear. I requested the interview with Mr. Hackham. Poor Urban Renewal went home again, nice and well behaved little toy soldier that he is, before the shit hit the fan about Ultra Boy. Me, I was still here, so I'll get to put myself at the head of the line."

"Ultra Man?" Ali froze, her heart thudding in her throat. She'd tried to ignore the worry that had arisen when Tye Dye announced he was standing in for Ultra Man. It was entirely possible that the third-string Super was being self-aggrandizing. But if he wasn't, if something had happened to Craig, a first-string Super was more likely to know. Ali swallowed against her rising fear. What if Craig hadn't come to reclaim his truck because of some injury? "What happened? The line for what?"

"Ultra Man's really screwed his career this time," said Flash Heat with a chuckle. "Disobeying a direct command. I've heard he's been arguing with Oversight, and with Mr. Crunch, in front of witnesses. That's insubordination, that is. He's on suspension. With Ultra Man out, the Northeast region is short of a Level One Super. I just put in for a transfer. Smile dear, you haven't thought it all the way through."

Ali paled. She hadn't paid that much attention to Tye Dye, no one did. But this? Flash Heat might be an arrogant son of a bitch, but he wasn't prone to exaggeration. Well, yes, he was, but not to telling outright lies. If he was saying Craig was suspended, then something had to have happened. Still, until she knew what was going on, she wasn't going to give Flash Heat the satisfaction of believing him.

"Rumors. Gossip. This place thrives on it. You should know better than to listen, and I'm too busy to play with you right now." Ali tried to dodge past. Flash Heat stepped sideways and blocked the corridor. She held her ground as best she could, but she could feel the temperature of the air around her rising. Using Powers to intimidate SS.C. personnel was a major no-no, but there was no one nearby to act as her witness. It was possible that Flash Heat wasn't doing it intentionally. She could just be feeling her own panic, her own fear. But the fear wasn't just for herself. If Flash Heat had permission to hang around instead of heading back to his assigned area, then Ultra Man might be in more trouble than she'd realized. And the only source of information she had was Flash Heat.

"Cheer up," laughed Flash Heat. "It's good news all around. You'll be cleaning up my sites now. With my Power all that's left is ash. Loads easier."

"You're happy that Ultra Man's having a bad week?" said Ali. "How very kindergarten of you."

"Don't be snippy. We may be working together soon. Closely." He reached out a gloved finger, as if to stroke her face, but pulled back fast enough when she snapped her teeth at him. Invulnerability was not one of his Powers, either.

"Not while I still have a heartbeat," muttered Ali. "I'll transfer to Midwest the day they move you to head office."

"But we'd make such a great team. I've always thought it was a crying shame that you never developed a decent Power. I can just imagine you in a skin-tight Super Suit." Flash Heat's smile did not waver. "I told old Hackham that P.L. can stay. He'd do as a sidekick for a while, but he'd have to work on his patter. I'll have my scriptwriters talk to his. But I told him; I'll have to get a sexy female on the team, just to round it out. Mysterious West would have to go. Much, much too old." Ali's low growl caught his attention, and he laughed. "It's not as if I don't have incentive to make the transfer. Northeast is prime real estate for a Super. New York. Boston. Washington. The S.S.C. headquarters. The home of the real movers and shakers. The Southwest sector is too quiet. The East Coast is where the real action is."

Ali bridled at the slur on Purple Lightning – sidekick, indeed! There were no sidekicks in the S.S.C. You were either a Power or you weren't - and scowled at the arrogant Super. "Too quiet? What, has someone captured all the Villains on the West Coast over the weekend and no one told me?"

Flash Heat waved a dismissive hand. "Villains are villains, no matter where they are. I'd rather handle them here."

"That isn't what you were saying Friday night," said Ali, her eyes narrowing.

She was determined not to let Flash Heat go swaggering around S.S.C. headquarters as if he owned the place already. Someone had to keep an Ultra Man-sized hole waiting for Craig to step back into. Whatever was going on was sure to be sorted out soon, and she didn't want him reassigned ... her thoughts skidded to a halt. What did it matter to her where he worked?

Flash Heat had not noticed her inattention.

"You heard us chatting with Ultra Boy? Hell, that was just guy talk. But with Ultra Boy on the way out, his territory is up for grabs and I intend to be the one first in line."

"Don't pack your bags yet, Flash Heat. Ultra Man's on suspension; not fired. He'll be back at work within the week. You might be a level one, but you are nowhere near as talented as Ultra Man, and not in the same ballpark when it comes to popularity. No way you'd be given his place."

Flash Heat stepped around her, patting her on the shoulder as he walked past.

"That's not what I hear. I never thought you were a Bronze and Green fan. Not the colors for your complexion. You'd look much better in Red and Gold. Still, you can go ahead and keep the faith if you want to, but don't go making long-term plans about Ultra Boy. From what I hear, he's gone. Permanently. If they do let him back in, he's likely going to be assigned to

Alaska, and it couldn't happen to a nicer boy scout."

"You can't change your color, P.L. It simply isn't feasible."

Nigel Hackham stalked across his office to flip open a photo album resting in solitary splendor on an oak pedestal. "Here you are, in your first Super suit. Ah, don't you look handsome? So young. So idealistic. I remember vividly the day you accepted an active position in the S.S.C. You *insisted* on purple being your color."

"That was before you decided to team me up with that toxic sunrise," said P.L. "Clothing choices aside, Tye Dye is dangerous. Hey, we all are if we lose control, I'll admit that, but he's pathological. He never considers collateral damage. Did you hear about the stunt he pulled down in Supply? Today? Six staffers are still in sickbay because they're too weak to go home. That new suit of his has upped his Powers to the point where he is truly dangerous. He gave Ali a nosebleed and instead of apologizing, he laughed at her. Laughed about injuring a civilian!"

"Ms. Brent," corrected Mr. Hackham, absently. "Tye Dye's little exercise can be put down to understandable exuberance about being activated and put in a Super team,"

"Not from what I saw. He simply did not *think*. There are people down there going to be sick for a week. And another thing, with me in purple and him every color of the rainbow and a couple that doesn't exist in nature, no one is going to take us seriously. If you must have him activated, you should assign him to another group. A less visible group. Somewhere with limited Villain activity. Somewhere he can cause less trouble."

"If the criminals taking time to laugh at you gives you an advantage, I hope you'll take them down before they recover." All signs of amusement faded from Mr. Hackham's face and he frowned at P.L. "The S.S.C. is a business, *Purple* Lightning, don't ever forget it. We provide a service to the community. Everyone within the SS.C. is a member of the greater team, so we don't have time for superstars and divas. You *will* go where you're told, and work with whichever Super you're assigned to, and I don't want to hear any complaints."

"But Tye Dye doesn't have flight or speed powers," protested P.L. "How are we supposed to get him to event sites? How's he supposed to go on patrol?"

"You and West will just have to take turns carrying him," said Mr. Hackham, ignoring P.L.'s shudder.

"I can't believe it!" P.L. paced back and forth across Ali's living room, plucking at the loose folds of his new suit.

He'd been at it for a while before Ali made it home, and there was a significant dent in her carpet to prove it. Knowing what she did about his merchandising income, Ali made a mental note to ask for her carpet to be replaced and held out a carton of ice cream as he turned to make another circuit. His rant had gone beyond amusing and was rapidly approaching frightening. She'd never seen the easy-going Super so worked up.

"I'm serious Ali, this is a disaster. We're going from being the number one Super team to a joke." P.L. took a mouthful of ice cream, then made a disgusted face and dropped the carton on a table. "I've been trying to contact Craig all day. He's not answering his phone. Just wait until he hears who've they've replaced him with. He'll ..." He slumped down in a chair. "God knows what he'll do."

"Are you feeling okay?" she asked, crossing to rest a hand on his forehead.

"I'm fine," said P.L., jumping up to resume his relentless pacing.

Ali picked up the carton and held it out to him. When P.L. focused on her hand he shook his head.

"Oh, that? No. I'm on a diet. Can you believe it? When I was in with the SS.C. doc *Control* was there, God help me, *in person*. She just stood there the entire time and watched them weigh me. Measure me. With me wearing just my BVD's and my mask. Now that was truly embarrassing. Hackham even lectured me about my *professional image*. Bottom line - I have to lose twenty pounds, at least, or I'll be losing *my* active status "

"You'll do it. In the meantime, I like the new threads," said Ali, ran her fingers down the front of his deep purple Nehru jacket as he stalked past her. Underneath, he wore a mauve turtleneck emblazoned with a silver lightning bolt, slightly flared pants and his signature running shoes. The jacket did a good job of minimizing his extra poundage.

"Yeah, they're okay. But Hackham..."

"Enough rant," interrupted Ali. "Ride it out. Tye Dye will cause a PR nightmare at his first fight scene and will be reassigned to, I don't know, Alaska before the week is out. I hear the Aurora Borealis could use a little freshen up."

"From your lips to Control's ears." P.L. seemed prepared to continue his complaints but was interrupted by the doorbell. He jumped, glancing up at the wall clock. "Oh no. I'm late. Cover for me," he hissed, heading for the door to the bedroom.

"Late for what?"

"A date!"

"Date? Since when?"

"Since this afternoon."

There were sounds of fabric flying and the shuffling of feet from her bedroom while Oliver shed his super-suit for ordinary clothing.

"Who is it?" said Ali, peering through the security hole.

A tall, skinny black man, wearing a bulky leather jacket and jeans was outside. Ali spun and followed P.L. into the bedroom. "Whoever he is, he's cute."

Oliver glanced up from one of his suitcases and waggled his eyebrows at her. "Very cute," he said, wrestling with his new belt. "It's Steven. Steven Holtzman. I met him at the gym. We're going out for dinner."

"I'm glad for you, but why the hell's he meeting you here?"

"Cause when I told him I was between apartments and I was staying with a girl he just wanted confirmation that *we* weren't dating. That I'm not sneaking around behind someone."

"He said that?" Ali's eyebrow disappeared into her bangs.

"No. He hinted it, and since that's what I'd be thinking, I asked him to pick me up here. Told him my car's in the shop. Go on. Let him in. Talk to him while I get changed."

"You don't own a car," whispered Ali. "And you could get changed at Super speed. You answer the door."

Oliver's eyes widened and his chin trembled. "Talk to him. Please! I want your take on him."

"Okay. Okay," Ali groaned and turned away. "Just for that, I'm going to warn him that you use Bambi eyes to get your own way."

Ignoring Oliver's sputtering, she plastered a welcoming smile on her face and unbolted the door.

"Hey there," Steve straightened and gave Ali a broad smile. "Ali, isn't it?"

"Yeah. Oliver's just getting ready," said Ali, beckoning Steven in. She stared at his heavy jaw and sideburns and frowned. "You look a little familiar."

Her visitor's smile didn't falter.

"Gordon's Slow Gym Fits, I've seen you coming in when I'm heading out." When Ali nodded slowly, he continued. "Oliver tells me you nagged him into starting exercising again. He says as a flight attendant he doesn't get to exercise regularly."

Ali blinked at this interesting new lie that Oliver had chosen as a Super cover story but recovered fast.

"That's right. He complains that he never knows what city he's going to be in or if he's going to have enough energy left to work out. And he's always on call. I never know if he's going to be here or out on a flight."

"Yeah, he warned me. That was the major issue of his last breakup. I'm afraid that I'm in the same boat. Things aren't much better with my job. I'm the regional coordinator for a sales team and can get called out of town with no notice at all. That's why I'm so glad that we were able to make this date. I worried all day that I'd get a call and have to run."

"Yeah," said Ali, "but when it comes to having things in common - being absent without warning isn't usually what people look for in a relationship."

"Gotta point there," said Oliver, emerging from the bedroom pulling on a leather jacket. "I'm glad Ali lets me stay here. I'm dreading the thought of apartment shopping. I never have the time."

"So, don't," said Steven, giving the room a quick once-over, nodding to himself at the clean floor, neat flower arrangements and algae-free fish tank. "I've got a place that's empty most of the time, I wouldn't mind sharing expenses. How about to take the stress off this date we treat it like a time-share interview? What do you say Ali, is Oliver a good roommate?"

Ali swallowed a grin. Steven had no idea that she'd spent all Sunday picking up Oliver's empty junk food bags. Let him find out for himself how messy Oliver was. Ali folded her arms and studied Steven, taking time to scan him from top to toe. Her first impression was based on the physical – tall, dark, thin and fit – but now she looked closer. His posture was confident and relaxed. His clothes were expensive. If the shirt he wore so casually under his soft leather jacket didn't cost more than her entire wardrobe, she was going blind.

"Well, I think first dates aren't as stressful as finding a good apartment and that first dates are the wrong time to make long-term decisions or commitments. Rental or emotional."

Both Steven and Oliver nodded.

"On the other hand," continued Ali, glancing sidelong at Oliver, "a good roommate is hard to find. How much will you pay me, Oliver, not to answer that question honestly when the time comes?"

"We'll talk," said Oliver, giving her a peck on the cheek.

Apparently satisfied that there was only friendship between Ali and

Oliver, Steven shook her hand before preceding Oliver out through the door. After the boys left, Ali leaned against the wall and just let her body sag. She felt – just a little – like she'd just pushed her baby bird out of the nest. And a lot jealous. There went Oliver, only a few days out of his latest relationship and off on a date, and she couldn't remember the last time she'd seen the inside of a restaurant or movie theater with another person. Not counting the aborted bowling trip with Craig. That had never risen to the level of a date.

    The door had barely closed behind Oliver and Steven when a blast of cold air filled the apartment. She turned just in time to see Craig fly in through her bedroom window.

    "What the hell is your problem?" she hissed. "Have you forgotten everything you were ever told about personal security? Flying in my window – and in civilian clothes. What were you thinking?"

    "You'd rather I flew in wearing my Super suit?" snapped Craig.

    "I'd rather there was no flying in my apartment at all." Ali drew a deep breath, knowing that her first impulse, picking him up and throwing him back out that same window, would also attract attention, and forced herself to calm down. "Why are you here?"

Chapter Eight.

The Sail and Hull Weekly.
"The Life Guard rescues Titanic passengers trapped on an iceberg since 1912."
The survivors are believed to be in good shape and spirits, although it is reported that one of them attacked a rescue worker last night when he was apparently offered an iced tea.

Craig clenched and unclenched his fists, gazing everywhere in the apartment except at her.

"If you can't answer a simple question, after putting my privacy and security at risk, then you can hit the road, chum." She pulled the door open. "Go."

"You let Oliver come and go as he pleases," muttered Craig.

"What has that to do with anything?" demanded Ali. "Besides, he goes so fast that no one sees him unless he wants them to."

"Whatever you say. I needed to speak to you tonight. I need someone's help, and you're elected."

"Me? Why do you need me? Why not Oliver, or Lacey, or anyone else in S.S.C.?"

Craig fidgeted for a moment longer before staggering back across the room, heading for the couch. Slumping down on a pile of purple and silver pillows, he grimaced when the sofa crunched, pulled out an empty candy package and tossed it on the coffee table.

"Give me a break, Ali. I can't ask Oliver or Lacey, because I don't want them in any more trouble than they already are. If the S.S.C. finds out they're helping me, they'll get suspended, or worse. And I know you and trust you. You're the only other person I can ask."

"So, you'll risk my job instead?" said Ali, pressing her fingers against her chest. "I've got news for you. My job's my only income. I don't have anywhere near the nest egg you guys must have. There aren't any Site Supervisor or Super Clean dolls out there with my face on them. If I don't work, I don't eat."

"Are you pissed with me because of the dolls? Give me a break Ali; those things are more embarrassing than all the other stupid PR stunts they make us do. Do you think I like the idea that I'm in every toyshop in the country? With accessory sets? Get your kid the Ultra Man suit for Halloween! I feel like a goddamn Sesame Street character."

"That's not the only reason,' said Ali through clenched teeth, then folded her arms and sighed. "Don't worry. They'll stop riding you about the Major Calamity escape soon. It's not as if a Villain hasn't escaped before."

"I can handle the fall-out from Calamity. No. That's not the problem." He sighed and dropped his head into his hands. "God, this is insane. Have you seen the press recently? There is a story going around that there was a new Villainess called the *Ice Queen* at that apartment event site, and that I'm scared to death of her. It's ridiculous. It'd even be funny, except that I got called into a top-level meeting and suspended because of it. No matter who I speak to, I can't get it through anyone's thick head that she doesn't exist." He let out a low growl, "I don't know what's wrong with everyone! It's like some contagious madness. They're so used to strange Powers popping into existence that the possibility that they've over-reacted, jumped the gun, simply doesn't register."

"You know I don't watch the news, SS.C. policy notwithstanding, I can't stand it," said Ali, then heard the chill in her own voice and forced herself to speak in warmer, kinder tones. "But you should relax. Sooner or later, they'll start wondering why they haven't heard anything more about her and they'll forget about it."

"In this case, silence is not going to help. They'll just decide that she's gone undercover."

"Don't worry so much. Really." Ali considered mentioning Tye Dye and Flash Heat and decided Craig did not need more things to go ballistic about. "Give it time, the story will die on its own."

"That's what I thought at first, but now, I don't think it will. That idiot from Oversight is involved and you know anything he gets excited about just gets worse. No. I've been thinking about it since they suspended me. The way things are going, until I make the Ice Queen go away, I'm stuck. Ultra Man may as well retire and start the kiddie party circuit, because my career is over."

"Hang on a minute. You really are suspended? I thought Flash Heat was just blowing smoke."

"No. It's true, all right."

"This is crazy," said Ali. "Are you sure there's nothing behind it?"

Craig gave her a long cold stare and shook his head.

"I'll go over my site report," said Ali. "I know I didn't put anything in to support the idea of a new Villainess. And I'll talk to Hackham in the morning. See what we can do about getting the story killed before it goes too far."

"Wouldn't help, Ali. Too late. The story has been picked up. Front-page news all around the world. Despite there being no S.S.C. announcement, the news services are going all out, ranting about a new Villainess that has me running scared. I've just left the S.S.C. Hackham tells me there'll be a limited, 'we don't know much, but we're pretending we do' sort of PR spin going out for the next news cycle. They're still working on the language. This despite my telling him there was *no new Villainess*." He growled as he tunneled his hands through his hair.

Ali shook her head and settled onto the couch at Craig's side. "I still don't see how I can help?"

"The only way I can think of getting back to work is to make the Ice Queen unimportant," said Craig, "It's not as if they'll let the story die if she disappears. They'll think she's hiding. You know how much the news services love paranoia. A 'here one minute, gone the next' Super Powered Villainess is just the thing to fill in slow news days. I'll never hear the end of it. Bendit says the score on my polls shows my trust level dropping. Bottom line is, I'm going to have to do something special. Something no one else has been able to do. If I do something stunning, then maybe they'll listen to me when I say the Villainess doesn't exist!"

"What?" Ali thought for a moment, then paled. "No. Craig, you can't."

Craig grinned. Anyone looking through the window at that moment would have recognized the confident Ultra Man expression on his face immediately. "Exactly. I have to find someone who's been all but unreachable, un-catchable."

"Nuclear Man," gasped Ali, her hands clenching. "Oh, my God. You can't be serious. If you're going after Nuclear Man, then you're going to need someone strong as a backup. You've got to take Oliver and Lacey. Even they may not be enough."

"Not really. As everyone keeps saying, Nuclear Man is ill. I should be okay if I can sneak up on him. I've been tracking him for months. It's tough going, but I think I can do it. The question is, how long is it going to take? The longer the Ice Queen story is out there, the stronger it will get."

"How are you going to track him down? You've never had any training for that. How you can expect to act like a detective when you've had no training, no experience, is beyond me."

"Well, thank you very much for that!" Craig's eyes narrowed and he straightened on the couch. "Can I help it if they didn't give me the training I asked for? They've told me they don't want me to detect. Whenever I ask questions and try to get involved in evidence follow-up, or something like that, they pat me on the head and tell me to leave it to the experts. They've got whole teams of profilers and data crunchers on staff to do my thinking for me, so I should just sit on my hands like a good boy and wait. They'll just calculate the most likely location of a crime and send me out to bash heads." Craig stared down at his hands, clenching his fingers into heavy fists. "This isn't what I imagined when I joined up. I don't just want to be a hired hammer. I want to, hell; I want to be more than a Superweapon. A threat to scare baby Villains with. Be good or Ultra Man will pound your face into dust! I want to *deserve* my Federal Marshall's badge."

Ali's hand hovered over his bent shoulder but did not touch. Craig kept his face down, so she wouldn't see the gleam that came to his eye. It was a first, the first time she'd reached out to him. It might have been just pity, but it was a start. Like with any fire, the first spark had to be nurtured, coaxed and fed, but slowly, so as not to smother it. Choosing his determined *but concerned* expression he faced Ali, putting his hand on her arm and moved closer, but not too close.

"Even if they don't want me to grow professionally, too damn bad. I know the Super that I want to be and I won't let them box me into some old-fashioned idea. I've been gathering information on Nuclear Man, but since I've been put on suspension, they've restricted my access to the files. They took my ID, so I can't get back into the building, and by now they've changed all the codes, so I can't hack in."

"What good will it do you to catch him if you haven't got your ID?"

"Citizen's arrest?" suggested Craig with a grin; "anybody can hold a known criminal until the legitimate authorities arrive. Of course, if I happen to hold him in front of a news crew or two, that would only be a bonus."

"This help you need, that only I can give you, is getting some papers out of the S.S.C.?"

"It's not just *some* papers. I need every report of every Nuclear Man sighting. All the crimes he's committed or been associated with. I've been working on it for months, and I thought I was starting to see patterns. The profilers won't discuss patterns with me. Won't even confirm the ones I've tried to point out. The powers-that-be didn't make it easy for me. They always insisted that I couldn't take the reports out of the secure file room, and I couldn't make copies. Do you have any idea how hard it is to keep everything in my head? You have higher security clearance than me, that's why I need you. I know where the stuff I need is kept and whom you'd have to fool to get to it. By the time I've finished prepping you, it'll be easy."

Ali leaned back in her chair. She seemed to be having trouble breathing. If she panicked, he'd be lost before he even got started. Before Craig could reach for her, try to reassure her that he had everything planned, she waved him away.

"Let me get this clear," said Ali. "You need every piece of paper we've ever processed on Nuclear Man. Accident reports, locations, insurance evaluations of the equipment and medications stolen. Damage to buildings, times, colleagues, villains. All that? Do you have any idea how much stuff that is? How big a pile?"

Craig took her hand, holding it tightly between both of his. Ali suppressed a start at the tingle that seemed to leap from his fingers to hers. The kick in her chest, just under her heart. Perhaps there was some residual static electricity from his flight, or his recent use of Powers. She dragged her gaze up from their clasped hands.

"I know it seems like a lot," he said, his voice a soft croon as he stroked her fingers. "But if you do it a bit at a time, in a couple of weeks I'll have what I need."

"Yeah, sure." Ali shook her hand free and stood. "In a couple of weeks, this Ice Queen thing might be a permanent feature of the public consciousness."

"Ali, please," Craig came to his feet in an instant. "I know it's a risk. To you. To me. If they catch you, us, yeah, it could even mean jail time, but we have to do it. I need your help. It's the only way for me to get my career back. To make the Ice Queen less important. Please, help me. I'll do everything I can to protect you, teach you what you need to get the stuff."

While Craig was speaking, Ali hauled her laptop out of her bag and placed it on the table between them.

"There's a reason I have a high-security clearance, Craig. Everything crosses my desk. Police reports, insurance reports, everything for every event site in the northeast and central region. Every quarter, as I am the *Senior* Regional Supervisor located at the S.S.C. headquarters, the other Regional Supervisors send me summaries of their events. In here," she said, tapping the plastic cover, "I have all the data right down to the cost of the light bulbs used in the bathrooms, for every event involving both the Supers and the Villains, for the last three years."

Craig stared at her, open-mouthed.

"What the heck did you think I did all day?" asked Ali. "I process insurance claims! You'd be surprised at what I need to see."

"Well, hell," said Craig and started to laugh. "Here I was getting ready to teach you how to lie convincingly to security guards, open safes, fool electronic sensors and smuggle out data."

Ali drew herself up to her full height, intending to address him with ponderous dignity, but collapsed into the nearest chair laughing instead.

"Your face," she cried. "Oh, man. I thought you were going to fall over."

Craig gave her a disgusted look. "Hey, I've been trying to think of a good reason why you shouldn't turn me into the gang-of-four – and I couldn't, by the way– only to find out you have what I needed in your handbag. Typically female, by the way. What else do you carry in there? The map to El Dorado? The secret of life, the universe and everything?"

"Didn't you get into enough trouble with adolescent jokes?" asked Ali.

"Laughter is the best medicine," he sighed, reaching for the laptop. "But for now, I'll take this ho—" He stopped as Ali snatched the laptop away from him.

"You take this nowhere, chum. Absolutely, nowhere. This computer is not leaving my sight."

"Ali! There's tons of stuff I need to read. What do you want me to do, print it out? How many trees will that kill?"

"You can't print it out or move the files. Anything. The Colonel put in a very effective security program in place to prevent the data getting out of S.S.C. control. It's impossible to remove data from this unit unless it's docked into one of the stations at S.S.C. I can input and review all I want, but that's it. To get it out again I have to be at headquarters."

"Well, hell. This doesn't help as much as I'd hoped. The info's in here, but I can't use it?"

"You can read it here. I'll even set you up with some coffee. You'll have to come up with an excuse for Oliver, when he gets home and finds you here. Now, if you'll excuse me, I haven't eaten."

"I could use some food," said Craig.

Ali opened the computer lid and watched it go through its booting up routine, tapping in a succession of passwords. "If you're standing there waiting for me to come over all domestic and start bringing you finger sandwiches and beer while you work, *honey,* then you're doomed to disappointment."

"That's okay." Craig didn't miss the warning note in her voice and turned toward the kitchen, "How about take out?"

"Menus are on the fridge," said Ali.

She turned the now-active computer toward him and headed toward the bedroom.

That, Craig thought, was a less than subtle hint.

But he was a Super with several powers, one of which was catching hints, if someone tossed them slow enough and highlighted them in neon yellow. Ordering food was, obviously, his job tonight. He wandered into the neat little kitchen and found three stained and battered menus held on the fridge with the magnets the S.S.C. gave kids at charity events. He pulled the Chinese take away menu out from under the Mysterious West's cauldron magnet and scanned the rest of the fridge. She had two of the rare *The Thump* magnets which, considering their age, she could only have received as gifts. Several P.L.s, which was no surprise. She even had a few of the colorful Villain magnets that The Colonel had given out as gag gifts the previous April 1st. He scowled and starting lifting the other stray notes and reminders. There was a magnet on her fridge for every Super, local and international – except *his*.

It shouldn't hurt, but it did. Yet another rejection. Yet another sign that, despite his hard work, she was totally unimpressed, uninterested and unmoved by him. Kings and Presidents competed to give him awards. He had one of the most recognizable faces in the world – when he had that suit and mask on. He'd worked hard for years and not only wouldn't she date him, she wouldn't even put his magnet on her fridge.

There were many ways a woman could put a man in his place. That one hurt the most.

Ali, now dressed in comfortable sweats joined him in the kitchen.

"When did they say they'd get here?"

"I haven't ordered yet," said Craig.

"Something wrong with your dialing finger?" she asked, pulling her hair back into a bright green scrunchie.

"I wasn't sure if you still ordered the same thing. Could be that you've developed... I don't know.... adult tastes? People do change from the people they were in college when they go out into the real world."

"What's with you?" asked Ali, startled.

"Nothing...."

"Craig, that's an odd thing to say. Especially, since there's nothing weird about what I order. Oliver, now, he'd – "

"I'm not talking about Oliver. Except to say that you seem to have different standards when it comes to what you tolerate from him and me. He can do Super speed loops around the block while he lives in your apartment, and I can't even come in the fire escape without getting yelled at."

Ali's hands froze in her hair, then lowered slowly to her sides. "Well, in the mundane world, people do not usually enter through the fire escape unless they're criminals. Outside of situation comedies, that is."

"That's not the point. Any of the Supers can come here, and do. You hosted a bridal shower for Black Lace last year, and she doesn't even work in this region. You're nice to all of them, except *me!* Why do you hate me?"

"I don't hate you."

"You do a pretty good imitation of it."

"I am...." Ali gazed at the ceiling as if the word she needed would be written there, "indifferent to you."

"And that's supposed to be better?" growled Craig.

"Well, hell, Craig. Oliver's a friend of mine. West and the others are nice enough – in small doses. But you're all part of my job, and I'd like to have some time away from it. It's annoying to have it follow me home. I'm on call every night as it is. My time off is precious."

"And you don't want to spend it with me."

"In a word. No."

"But Oliver lives here."

"When he's homeless, yes."

"Why?"

"What do you mean?"

"Why me? You don't object to Oliver. You've known me as long as him. We were all in college together! Why can he infringe on your precious time off and not me?"

"Because he doesn't annoy me."

"Annoy you?"

"Yeah. You get on my last nerve and tap dance. It's one of your more Powerful abilities."

"What the hell? Ali, what have I ever done to you?"

Ali folded her arms and regarded him intently, scanning from P.L. trainer-shod feet to deep, angry eyes and unruly hair. Strange. He was one of the most powerful Supers, but she had never been afraid of him. Probably because she'd known him too long. Didn't like him then, didn't like him now. But he'd never been scary.

"Let me think. You're right, Craig. You've never done anything. You're completely innocent. It must have been someone else who saran wrapped all the girl's toilets in the dorms. Someone else who took all the trash cans on campus and reshaped them into a phallic symbol on the top of the library. And who do you think stripped the assistant coach naked and stranded him on the clock tower?"

Craig gaped at her.

"Hey, that all happened the year before you came to college."

"Not all of it. But that doesn't mean I didn't hear about it. Your stupid stunts became legends at college. I expect they'll be talking about you a hundred years from now. With a little luck, no one will ever associate those stupid practical jokes with *Ultra Man*."

"And you're holding *jokes* I played as a teenager against me? I was having fun."

"You were bad enough, from what I heard, when you were an ordinary mortal, but when your Powers came in you turned into a *Super bully*. If you pulled any of those stunts now, you'd be on the Villain list. I'm surprised the S.S.C. recruited you." She thought about that for a moment, "Actually, no I'm not. They took you in because you were so Powerful, and they put up with your other stunts for the same reason."

"What stunts?"

"I know you, Craig Duane. I can recognize one of your practical jokes from ten miles away, blindfolded, backward through a brick wall. Six months after you were recruited, it *snowed* indoors during a Lakers game."

Craig caught the look in her eye and cut his chuckle off fast.

"Ali, please. It was a joke. An adolescent stunt, yeah, maybe, but a joke. And I cleaned up later."

Ali poked him hard in the chest. "*You* took Super credit and got front page of the newspaper praise for cleaning up. But you never admitted you'd caused the mess in the first place."

"I was a kid. Being in the Super Teams was still new and stressful, and I was letting off steam. Perfectly harmless steam."

"The Lakers lost. And I'm supposed to believe that, magically, it all stopped? Your bullying? Your stupid stunts?"

"I wouldn't call it bullying, but yeah, Ali, I grew up. I saw the error of my ways. I put the things of childhood behind me. Etc. Etc. However you want to put it, I stopped." He gazed at her sadly. "I guess this means that all the things I did since then, trying to impress you, missed the mark?"

"Right," said Ali, derisively. "Since I've never been fond of the 'frog down the back of the dress' school of getting someone's attention."

Then she heard the rest of what he'd said, blinked and refocused. *Impress her?* Since when, and why?

"I don't know why I try with you, Ali. You've obviously made up your mind to hate me forever. I'll be thirty in a few weeks, and you'll still think of me as an eleven-year-old."

"If that's the way you act, then yes."

"That is *not* how I behave now! I've put those things so far behind me that you're the only person who remembers. It may come as a shock to you, but I've got a responsible job and people who rely on me. I do things that other people simply cannot do. Every day, I rescue people. Face it, without me people would die."

"Sometimes you act like an overgrown kid with your mother's tablecloth tied around your neck!" Ali shouted.

"Guess I'll stop wasting my time, then." Craig pushed the crumpled menu into her hands and headed for the living room. He snatched the computer up from the table and tucked it under his arm. Ali ran after him.

"Hey, you can't take that. I need it."

"You can't do without it for one night?" said Craig. "Think of it as getting some precious time away from work."

He took one step toward the window, threw a narrow-eyed look at her, then turned and left through the front door. Ali shuddered as the slam echoed through the apartment and sank down on the nearest chair.

"Oh, perfect. That was just perfect."

Oliver peered out of the restaurant's panoramic window. Beneath the balcony, the lit ribbon of the north New Jersey Turnpike undulated under the brilliant display of the New York City sky-scape. At this time of year, the skyscrapers had added to their usual luminosity with competing holiday light displays. Oliver watched one building's laser-light display of dancing reindeer and grinned.

"I'm sorry, I had to deal with these messages." Steve glanced up from the phone that had occupied his attention since they'd been shown to their table and caught the direction of his gaze. "So, you're a child-at-heart sort of person?"

Oliver nodded, "You're not going to hold that against me, are you?"

"No, but I am going make a note of it." He raised one eyebrow, a skill that Oliver envied. "Just so I know, will you pout if I don't remember anniversaries and holidays?"

"Of course. And I expect a big pile of glittery boxes under the tree, even if there's nothing in them."

"Okay." Steve tapped a few lines more into his phone before snapping the metal cover closed and tucking it back into his breast pocket. "I've just made a note on the calendar for our first date and I've turned the phone off."

Oliver refused to blush, not that it would show with his complexion, and tried not to get too hopeful. The date was not even an hour old, far too soon to be planning anniversaries. Maybe he should be worried about Steve turning stalker.

"Who were the emails from?"

"Change of subject?" inquired Steve, exercising his eyebrow again.

"Absolutely."

"Okay, change of subject it is. They were from my business partner. Don't worry, she's a girl. A friend, just like your friend, Ali. Actually, she was just updating me about the health of a mutual friend."

"Bad?" asked Oliver.

"As bad as it gets," Steve sighed and fiddled with his wineglass. "He's sick, getting fragile. The chemo doesn't help, just seems to take everything out of him. She just sent me a note saying that he was climbing out of the bath this afternoon, grabbed the safety rail and a bone in his hand just broke."

"Oh, man," Oliver closed his eyes briefly, "Was he alone?"

"No. She and I take turns looking after him. He lives in my house down south, and when I have to go out of town, she looks in on him."

"I thought you lived near here?"

"Yeah, I do. I commute between Phoenix and Jersey City. I maintain a house in Arizona and an apartment here. Of course, I travel so much I'm rarely in either."

Oliver nodded. "I know the feeling. It never seems to make much sense to me to have a place of my own. I'm never home. Sometimes I think it would be better to talk Ali into getting a bigger apartment and share it full time. Then I'd know I'd have somewhere to crash when I'm in town."

"Crash? That's not a term I thought a flight attendant would use."

"I'm not superstitious," laughed Oliver, "It is nice of you to look after your friend."

"I haven't got much choice," Steve's expression went distant. "You know, there are times, situations, when your family doesn't stand by you. You turn to friends for help, and sometimes those friends become more to you than family. I made some stupid mistakes when I was young. Really stupid. And for a while, I thought I'd never recover. I couldn't be what I'd always planned to be and I thought my life was over. Thought I might as well give up and become what everyone said I was. But Doug, he was like a father to me. What my father should have been. He supported me. Listened to me and helped me find a new path. And now, when I want to change my life again, he's supporting me with that, too. It seems only fair that I should help him. I suppose you think I'm over-sentimental."

"No. No, I think that's great. I have friends who, I admit, I care more about than my family. That I think of as family."

"Like Ali?"

Oliver grinned. "Oh, yeah. Ali's my sister. Would you believe that the dean put her in the men's dorm her first year of college?"

"What? No! A looker like her?"

"Of course, with Craig and me looking after her, she didn't get hit on. We both made it clear she was off-limits."

"Craig?" There was a note in Steve's voice that Oliver recognized and acknowledged.

"Craig is a friend. A brother by another mother, if you know what I mean. He'd risk his life for mine and has. He and Ali are an item, or they would be if Ali would pay attention and Craig would stop trying so hard."

Steve considered this while he broke bread sticks into dust. "I don't get it."

"They're meant for each other. Everyone who knows both of them knows it. It's just that Craig pissed Ali off ages ago, and she hasn't forgiven him. I keep trying to bring them together, giving Craig advice, and he keeps," Oliver waved his arms expansively, "improving on my ideas, and manages to piss her off again. I keep telling him, keep it simple, stupid."

The waiter finally appeared at their table with a bottle of the house wine. Steve nodded to him to pour and lifted his glass as soon as it was filled.

"Here's to the simple life."

The phone rang the next morning while Ali was in the shower, trying to persuade her body that spending ten minutes under boiling hot water was an adequate substitute for sleep. She'd replayed the argument with Craig over and over in her head until the echoes of the words threatened to drive her insane. She'd wanted – dreamed – about telling Craig exactly what she thought of him for years, and when the moment finally came, it didn't turn out as satisfying as she'd expected. Somehow in her dreams, she'd ended up feeling vindicated, empowered and righteous. Not nauseated and guilty.

She had to admit she hadn't heard about him engaging in any silly stunts for a year or so. Okay, more than a year or two. And it did come as a shock to her to realize how old they'd both become. She closed her eyes, leaning into the spray. She could see his face clearly. The adolescent softness had disappeared, along with the silly soul patch be'd affected for about six months. There was a bone-deep strength to him now, a solidity that she hadn't noticed building. She felt like a mother, realizing that her child had grown up.

When had he become an adult, and why hadn't she noticed?

"Ali?" Oliver tapped on the bathroom door and leaned in, one hand over his eyes. "Craig's on the phone. He says, 'sorry, but is there any way you can do without what he borrowed for another day?' What's he talking about?"

She leaned her head against the tiled wall and wiped soaking hair off her face.

"Sure, Oliver. Sure, he might as well keep it. Tell him tomorrow morning's soon enough, but not one minute more."

"Great."

Even after she turned off the water, she remained in the shower stall, water draining down her face and body. She knocked her forehead gently against the tiles once, twice, then resumed leaning.

To hell with him, anyway. When had he tried to impress her? She barely saw him. The only time she heard about him was those damn event sites, which generated those endless piles of paperwork. Was she supposed to be grateful that he'd torn a hole in train tracks while fighting Major Calamity? Was she supposed to be turned on when he pushed over buildings? Did he think that she gained some vicarious thrill from processing his disaster recovery data?

She slammed open the shower door, grabbed a towel, and wiped the steam from the mirror. What the hell had he been saying? Sure, they'd known each other for years, but they'd barely spoken in college. He'd been a visitor to the rooms she'd shared with Oliver. The guys had recognized each other as Powers-to-be pretty quickly, and since Craig had never been a scared, homophobic moron, he'd spent hours talking with Oliver about the future. About the rescues they'd do. About well, everything, and they hadn't tried to keep her out. They'd trusted her. Insisted she stay, just to provide the balance of a normal point of view.

But whenever he'd visited, she'd stayed in her room studying. Ignored them. Given them their privacy to talk over Super things. When they'd gone places together, the three of them, it was because Oliver had asked her to tag along with them.

Hadn't it?

Why the hell was he so bent out of shape?

She pushed her hair back off her face and stared at her reflection. Unfortunately, it had no answers for her.

Being unable to control her thoughts she turned her attention to something she could control. Clothes. She pulled one pair of her new work boots out of its box and set it on the floor beside her feet. The Colonel would not be on her December Holy Day card list this year. His boots were getting worse. Solid black leather overlaid with green-grey mesh, two-inch thick soles and, for some reason – she still hadn't read the thick instruction manual that came with them – a line of seven green, red and yellow flashing lights along the instep.

Her work wardrobe was chosen for long-wearing, indestructible characteristics, instead of warm, gentle or feminine attributes. It was pointless trying to be fashionable when she spent half her professional life climbing through collapsed buildings. She'd drawn the line at denim overalls and ruined quite a few business style suits in the process before approaching the Colonel for specially treated trousers and shirts. Of course, the Colonel, being busy with other more important matters, gave her clothing he'd designed as daywear for male Supers. There was nothing feminine or fashionable about them. (And the buttons were on the wrong side.)

Nothing, however, in her wardrobe was anywhere near compatible with those goddamn boots. She tried on three pairs of trousers, finding that the tops of the boots were so thick that she couldn't pull anything less than wide flares down over them. There was a line of elastic on the inside of the tops that prevented her tucking her pencil trousers in, which left her with fabric bunched up around her calves all the way to her knees.

Swearing, she dug into the back of the closet and emerged with a bright blue and green striped sweater and black skirt so old she couldn't remember purchasing them. They weren't really suited for the cool weather, and she'd probably regret the skirt by lunchtime. But as there was no way she could conceal or even draw attention away from the great, huge clodhopper boots, she might as well flaunt them.

Growling, she stared at herself in the mirror. Instead of drawing her hair back off her face in her usual ponytail, she left it falling over her shoulders. There was no way she was going to be able to pass this skirt/giant boot look off as an intentional style. She had no style. No fashion. No femininity. Nothing. Over the last few years, she'd used her hectic work schedule as an excuse not to think about anything outside her work. She glared at the discarded clothing spread across her bed. She'd accepted the dull clothes The Colonel passed on to her. Accepted the increasingly ugly, ungainly boots.

Accepted her position as the dogsbody, run around, hard-working *victim* of the S.S.C. Any job the powers-that-be wanted to be done, but didn't want to do themselves, they tried to pass on to Ali.

The only thing she'd managed to dodge was the committee for the annual charity bash, but only since she'd made it clear she'd insult anyone she was forced to deal with.

Ali settled her feet firmly into the heavy boots, straightened her spine and smiled.

Today, that changed. She was going to march into S.S.C. headquarters and stir things up. Demand another person to do the call-outs. If she had to wear the SS.C. work boots, she was going to demand that they weigh less and look better.

And if, in the course of the morning, she found something that might help Ultra Man get back to work and stop diving in her bedroom window, that was good, too.

Sauntering down the corridors of the S.S.C. and facing the puzzled good mornings from the staff an hour later, she fought to keep an evil grin off her face. Between the garage and her office, one messenger turned completely around and collided with a wall while staring at her. Another had tripped over furniture and performed a perfect Van Dyke dive into a secretary's lap. Head high, Ali ignored the chaos and kept walking. Unfortunately for her plan to stir things up, all the lawyers, The Colonel, even Control, were unavailable that morning. Their secretaries were all apologetic, but firm. Until further notice, the S.S.C. senior management was too busy to see anyone without an appointment. Sorry, we aren't making any appointments.

Ali received her order to 'deal with the routine stuff as you see fit' with an evil smile.

If they wouldn't see her to tell her the SS.C. plan, she'd have to improvise.

Chapter Nine.

S.S.C. Villain File:
Name: The Shriek
AKA: not known
Characteristics:
Strength/Dexterity: normal human scale 10/10
Powers: vocal energy blast.
Limitation: may only use approximately once every seven days.
Range: limited. Less than 500 feet.
Cone of destruction. Area of maximum effect: 15 feet, decreases exponentially with distance.
Extent of destruction: at full power can reduce concrete to powder.
Disadvantages: substance abuse: alcohol
　Enraged when drunk.
　Poor impulse control when drunk.
History: Arrived anonymously at S.S.C. and applied for admission as Super at age approx. 17 – 20. In testing it was discovered that his abilities had the above listed severe limitations. As it can only be used once – at full power – approximately every seven days, and as he has no associated Powers, such as strength or flight, and no maximal or meta-human abilities/intellect, he was classified as Third string. When offered the standard stipend and entry into S.S.C. relocation, The Shriek declined. Later that day in Atlantic City, The Shriek became drunk, utilized his Powers and destroyed a karaoke bar. Several people were hospitalized and treated for varying degrees of hearing loss, some permanent. The Shriek resisted capture by the local police and, due to his abilities, was referred to the S.S.C. for apprehension
Known associates: Nuclear Man. Mystress of the Night. Mr. Ooze.
Outstanding warrants: Vandalism. Theft. Grand theft. Grand larceny. Breaking and Entering. Destruction of Property. Performing Cher hits in public without a permit.

　　　Later that morning Ali stood, staring out of the third-floor conference room window at distant Ellis Island, coffee cup in hand.
　　　Behind her, Eliza and her assistants were packing up the last of the papers from the Buffalo event. The four of them worked with the smooth coordination of long practice, and soon had the central conference table and all four walls' worth of bookcases and credenzas cleared. Ali watched as the last of the labeled and cataloged boxes were loaded into a secure traveling document case and escorted from the room under the bored gaze of a team of S.S.C. security guards.
　　　Ali had claimed the conference room after the Vermont incident, years ago. With over a thousand homes, and four times that number of individuals

affected by the Vermont disaster, the paperwork had been truly overwhelming. She'd needed a decent-sized flat surface to spread out the paperwork and get it organized – or at least, that was what she'd told the SS.C. lawyers. Three years later, whenever someone requested she surrender the room, all she did was point to the piles of paper still waiting to be completed, sorted and boxed, and ask for their help to move it, pack it or process it. It was surprising how quickly they'd fled, leaving her standing triumphant. Admittedly, she was standing triumphant in the middle of a huge, unending mess, but still in possession of the conference room, and that was what counted.

Drawing a breath, she turned away from the window and drew a finger down the length of the empty table.

"Eliza? Call document holding in South Jersey. Tell them I want everything with Nuclear Man's name on it in this room by two. Not just our area. Everything they have."

Eliza paled, and the other assistants pretended to have heart attacks, clutching at their throats and staggering.

"Are you insane?" demanded Eliza, her voice rising to a squeak, "*All* of it?"

"I have a project. A cost review of the impact Nuclear Man has had on our SS.C. and the insurance industry," lied Ali, ignoring the dramatics. "We keep saying he's more expensive to clean up after than any other Villain, and now they want numbers." She paused long enough to watch identical expressions of horror pass over their faces, then smiled. "This is *my* project. You guys have enough going on with following up on the collapsed apartment building and garage. I think six insurance companies haven't called back with go-aheads for their share of the repairs, and they represent thirty percent of the total costs. And I'm sure you have things to clear up with the mid-region events."

"On it," said Eliza, and shooed the others out of the room before Ali could change her mind about the assignments.

Ali chuckled as the sound of their running feet disappeared down the corridor, then she took herself off for a long lunch. Returning at two, she found that the efficient Eliza had worked her magic. Most of the records had been delivered, with the promise from the document facility manager that the remainder would be there by morning. Ali stared at the boxes stacked five high and three deep around the perimeter of the room, clenched and opened her fingers, loosening them. Poor Craig. He'd been planning on teaching her all sorts of stealthy, twisted, tricky ways of overcoming security and baffling guards. If only he'd known that all she had to do was ask her secretary to fetch, and all that he needed would be delivered. If not on a silver platter, at least efficiently.

The pile was intimidating. She held her tiny Exacta knife in one hand, poised over the security seal on the first box and hesitated. Then her hands dropped.

Why was she doing this? Craig had her computer. All this data was on it. She should let him sort out his own problems. It would teach him a lesson. She sighed and sank against the wall. She needed some sort of motivation to go through this mess. If she were smart, she'd send the whole lot back to storage, unopened. It wasn't as if this were her job. Her responsibility. Craig, after all, was *Ultra Man.* Capable of feats of strength and derring-do unimaginable by normal men.

Her lip curled and she sniffed, shaking her head. There had been an air of desperation about him, and she wasn't used to seeing that. Craig, even normal, pre-Power onset Craig was a person of confidence, of strength, and if he was worried she should trust his instincts. Even though the madness currently infecting the bosses of the S.S.C. must surely pass soon – with an apology being given to Ultra Man and everything returning to normal – she couldn't count on it. Like any sensible, paranoid employee of a large multinational SS.C., she knew she couldn't leave it to the bosses to be sane.

Still, she hesitated.

Telling herself that this pile of work was all self-inflicted didn't help. It wasn't. It was all Craig's fault.

Telling herself that she'd take it out of Ultra Man's hide helped a little. Revenge, after all, was a great motivator.

She counted the boxes, estimated the hours she'd be putting in on this and smiled. Submitting a bill, privately, to Ultra Man for overtime when he was back in the SS.C. and could afford it - that was a plan! At her usual hourly rate, she could charge him enough to replace her ailing car and put some cash into her buy-a-house fund.

Breaking the seal on the first box, she lifted out a handful of paper and settled down to read. It wasn't long before she was on her feet arranging and rearranging piles on the long table.

Quitting time passed, and still she didn't look up. Around midnight, she staggered to the women's locker room to collapse unconscious on the couch. The next morning, after a quick shower, she changed into a Super Clean sweat suit she kept under her desk for emergencies and returned to stacking.

She ignored lunch, two scheduled meetings, the three times she was overhead-paged and all cell phone calls. Neither did she remember to drink the cups of coffee she poured. Hours passed, and still there were boxes she hadn't touched.

Eliza poked her head around the door close to end of business day and stared at the complicated mess. With the air of someone who feared that if they drew attention to themselves they would find a pile of work landing on their head, Eliza maneuvered her way past a stack of empty boxes and tapped Ali on the shoulder.

"What?" Ali jumped, knocking the nearest swaying pile into its neighbor. Both Eliza and Ali dove to prevent a table-wide domino collapse.

"Sorry," said Eliza, "but you were in such a trance, I haven't been able to get your attention all day."

Ali waved a dusty hand at the table. "I've had a lot on my mind."

"No kidding." Eliza shuddered theatrically, then plunged on. "Listen, you have someone at the main desk asking to see you. She hasn't an appointment, and we closed her site file ages ago. She says she won't talk to anyone else."

"Who is it?"

"Dr. Audrey Wilks. She says it was her hospital Nuclear Man totaled last year."

"Which one?" Ali rubbed a hand over her face, leaving streaks of dust across her chin. "They all start to run together after a while."

"Out in Westchester. Big lab, snooty neighborhood hospital with a high-octane reputation and fancy decorations. They gave us a whole pile of..." Eliza coughed, "joy about needing to get the clean-up finished ahead of schedule."

"I think I remember that one. Saw it just a little while ago," Ali scanned the piles, picked up one midway down the table and started leafing through it. "What's her problem?"

"She says you promised to find her something for the hospital foyer."

"Oh, God," Ali cringed, wincing as the scene in the Charity auction came flooding back. "I remember her She wants something dignified and spectacular so everyone will remember Ultra Man and his team's hard work."

Eliza poked out her tongue and blew a spectacular raspberry. "Why's she after you?"

"Because I got pissed at her attitude and let her know it. Then, to avoid bad public relations, said I'd go through what is left of the hospital, find something with Ultra Man's footprint on it and have it bronzed."

Eliza couldn't keep the laugh from bubbling out. "God, and she didn't realize you were being sarcastic?"

"As she's here looking for me, apparently not. I guess I expected her to choose something at the auction. I completely forgot about her after," Ali stared at the papers in front of her and sighed. "Send her up and have a quick look through inventory. See if we've got something big, with glitter. If we don't, add some glitter."

"On it," said Eliza and climbed out of the room. "But it's not likely. All the good stuff's already gone in the auction."

"I know. Still, we have to make an attempt."

A few minutes later, the door squeezed open and the dark-eyed blonde Ali remembered wiggled into the room. She spared a horrified glance at the masses of paper before granting Ali a professionally emotionless smile.

"Ms. Brent, thank you for seeing me without an appointment. I know how disruptive it is when people call on me… unexpectedly."

Ali refrained from rolling her eyes, gritted her teeth and pretended to herself that she was smiling. The obvious – My time is more important than Your time – snub had not gone unnoticed, but Ali was too tired to play that game today. Instead, she said, "Don't worry, Doctor. We're pretty loose here. If it wasn't you, I might just as easily get a call telling me to copter over down to Delaware, or up to Connecticut to evaluate another disaster site." Ali watched as the Doctor processed and dismissed the comment as a low-level-flunky exaggeration, "What can I do for you? I'm sorry I can't offer you a seat, or coffee. Paper seems to have overtaken this room, and I've lost the coffee machine somewhere under it."

The doctor shuffled her feet to clear a space and chose a pile of boxes to lean against.

"Oh, no problem. I just dropped in to see if you've given any thought to the memorial we want to create at my hospital. We're almost at the decorating stage, and the architect and designer want to know what we're going to be getting so they can, you know, change things around if necessary to enhance it."

"Ah, yes." Ali gave herself a few seconds to swallow all the synonyms for chutzpah she could remember before opening her mouth again. It wasn't enough that the Super teams saved them, and the S.S.C. cleaned up? Now they had to decorate? "But you realize, Dr. Wilks, that the S.S.C. isn't in the business of making monuments, and most of our souvenir-quality pieces went in the auction a few days ago. We really don't have anything for you. You should have taken the opportunity and bid on something that night."

Dr. Wilks waved a dismissive hand. "There was nothing that really seemed appropriate. Nothing sufficiently dignified. Awe-inspiring. I was hoping that something could be... created?"

Ali gave her own professional smile and waited.

"For a fee," added the doctor, with a sigh.

"What do you have in mind?" The S.S.C. was a profit-making SS.C. after all, thought Ali. Before Dr. Wilks could let her imagination soar too far Ali listed – twice – the standard prohibitions – no DNA, fingerprints, signatures, or other identifying items – the doctor pulled out an artist's rendition of her dream foyer and tried to unroll it on top of a few piles.

"Take it easy," said Ali, hurrying to shore up a stack.

Dr. Wilks lifted her drawing again and read the topmost sheet on the pile.

"Nuclear Man? *Him!* My lab had to be condemned after he got through with it. I had to relocate to some new facility miles up the road, which is very inconvenient." She gave Ali a severe look, as if she were personally responsible. "They said some of the debris would be radioactive for thousands of years. What did you do with it?"

"We have a special storage facility," said Ali, mildly. "The location's top secret."

"He really hates doctors. And don't get me started on his attitude toward the AMA," observed the doctor, letting her sketch roll up again as she skimmed a finger down the police report. "Nuclear Man completely destroyed last year's AMA convention hotel the day before our annual meeting. I've often wondered if Nuclear Man is the same person as the 'med student with the Radioactive Spine.'"

"What? Who?" gasped Ali, "What are you talking about?"

Dr. Wilks shrugged. "Nuclear Man's been writing hate letters to the American Medical Weekly, and Cancer Monthly, for years. At first we printed them, but when they got more abusive, well, there's no reason for us to give a forum to someone who just wants to call us names, so we stopped. Before that we used to get the same sort of letters from a medical student. One who said he never graduated because he got sick and it was his doctor's fault."

Ali snatched an armful of paper off a nearby chair and dumped it on the floor.

"Sit," she ordered, stabbing her finger at the chair. "And talk. What the hell are you going on about?"

The doctor seemed startled by the sudden change in tone, in focus, but she sat and held her drawing in her clenched fist, as if ready to be used as a club if Ali's strange behavior made it necessary to defend herself.

"American Medical Weekly and Cancer Monthly are peer review journals. I'm on the committee that does the actual reviewing of all the materials we receive. We decide which articles get published. I did it because it looked good on my resume until I got some of my own work published. We read all the submitted articles for accuracy and relevancy, and proper research protocol and techniques, of course. Since I was a friend of the editor, I also heard about the more interesting letters that got sent in. A few years ago, Cancer started getting letters from a person signing himself 'a med student with spinal cancer, or radioactive spine,' something like that. Initially, it was a whistleblower type letter, complaining about a researcher who contaminated a few students helping in his lab, all of whom turned up a year or so later with very aggressive cancers." The doctor's hands twisted around each other and she gave Ali her first sincere smile. A little frightened, hesitant twitch of her lips. "It's been on my mind ever since Nuclear Man attacked my lab. Wondering if he's the same person."

"Why?"

"Because I'm one of the people who responded to his letters, both in the CM and the AMA. My name, title and hospital affiliations are printed after my replies. I said I'd talked to the researcher he'd complained about and verified that the protocols and procedures were within Federal guidelines. I called him a petulant and selfish child and said that research was important to the development of medicine, even if people got hurt in the process. He kept writing back. One time, he wrote in complaining that the Cancer research protocol he was enrolled with had not put him in the treatment group. That wasn't what bothered him. He understood that there had to be control subjects. It's just that they were giving him a drug to simulate the side effects of chemotherapy, without giving him the beneficial drugs. He said that was wrong - making people who were dying suffer unnecessarily. I wrote back that it increased the validity of the study."

"Wrote back," said Ali, leaning forward. "You have his name? His address? And why the hell didn't you mention this to someone when we came to your hospital? Why hasn't anyone sent these letters on to the police? To *us*?"

"At the time, I didn't make the connection. And I didn't write to him personally. My replies were printed in the journals."

"Damn it," said Ali. "Did you keep the envelopes his letters came in?"

Dr. Wilks found a haughty look in her repertoire and showed it to Ali. "After all these years? Don't be ridiculous. Besides, they weren't sent to me personally, they were sent to the journal. All I ever saw were the letters. The secretaries opened them"

"What about the letters?"

"The text of the ones we printed, you could find in any decent sized medical library. Of course, they'd be a little hard to find. Sometimes when you do a subject search, they don't pick up on *all* the letters section. And, of course, I don't know if he wrote to any other journals."

"Does he still write to you? To the journals?"

Dr. Wilks shrugged. "Every so often. Not so much recently. The AMA sent a letter out to the physicians who were supposed to attend the convention that got canceled, saying they'd received a message from Nuclear Man claiming responsibility. Had some rant about how until doctors cleaned up their act he'd continue to punish them. That's the only one I've heard about this year."

"And they didn't tell us?" demanded Ali, her voice going shrill. "What's wrong with those guys? How are we supposed to find and stop these Villains if people don't tell us when they're threatened? When they get goddamn evidence?"

"I wasn't involved in the decision-making process. Then again, I suppose they didn't want to give Nuclear Man the idea that we take him seriously. Do you have any idea how many patient complaint letters the AMA get in any given week? Besides, I suppose they thought your SS.C. already knew."

"How could they be that stupid?" Ali groaned, pushing the heels of her palms into her face and rocking back and forth. "This wasn't an ordinary patient complaint letter. This was from a known Super Villain." She took a deep breath and tried to regain some professional composure. "Do you have any of the letters?

Copies? Anything?"

"Some were printed, as I've said, in journals."

"Do you have them? Could you send me copies?"

"Of course not. I haven't room for that sort of clutter." The doctor gave the untidy room a sweeping glance, which was the only sweeping this crowded room was likely to get this week.

Ali gritted her teeth and reminded herself that murder was a momentary pleasure bound to get her talked about and kept her clenched fists in her pockets. Unfurling her fists one finger at a time, she tried again.

"You don't have a scrapbook? Something you are planning to use when you get ready to write the collected published works of Dr. Wilks?"

"Really, Ms. Brent, how unprofessional do you think I am? You may collect records of all your media appearances, but I know my own worth. I have no need for something like that."

Yeah, right, thought Ali. This woman probably had photographs of herself with celebrities plastered all over her office wall. But saying so would not persuade her to be helpful. "Okay. Will you help me track down as many of these published letters as you can?"

"I doubt I'd have the time. I do have other commitments," said Dr. Wilks rising and handing Ali the rolled-up drawing. "and I have to return to them now. Perhaps you could take a little look at this and get back to me with an idea of when it will be ready."

"I haven't agreed – that is, the S.S.C...." Ali stuttered at her.

"If you can't be bothered searching through medical journals for the information you obviously need, then you'll have to pay someone to do it for you. You have my number. I do have a schedule to keep to for the refurbishing of the foyer, so don't take too long." With that smug exit line, Dr. Wilks kicked a box out of her way and left.

Ali clenched both hands in her hair, tugged hard and let out a low whistling scream. There was not enough room on the floor to pace, so she threw herself into the vacated chair and stared up at the ceiling. Damn the woman and her preoccupation with her precious, useless monument. If she was so turned on by statues and souvenirs and such, maybe she should have joined the national park service. In the meantime, the S.S.C. and the police needed those letters. Ali paused and reconsidered. The S.S.C. had survived without this information for this long and Craig are necessary to find Nuclear Man in order for Ultra-Man to get his life back.

She balled up the monument drawing and threw it across the room. Several piles of paper, knocked off balance by her throw, began a slow and stately cascade, sending towers of paper to the floor. Ali ignored them.

Stupid, arrogant doctors, keeping all those letters from Nuclear Man near secret. And why hasn't anyone picked up on it, if it'd been going on for years? Surely a reporter, or someone, would have noticed. Then again, who reads the *letter to the editor* page of a medical journal? Probably only people who wrote to the editor. Ali climbed out of her chair and started searching for a phone, then stopped. Under normal circumstances, all Ali would need to do was phone Control and pass on the tip. But she couldn't. Once she gave that piece of information away, she lost control of it, and with Craig on suspension it was unlikely he'd hear through official channels in time to do anything useful with it.

She couldn't tell Control. Not yet. Instead she pulled out her phone and searched for a number she'd had for years and never used.

Craig's home phone rang forever, then the answering machine picked up. Ali could barely contain her impatience as the standard greeting started to play. Snarling, she hit redial.

"Craig. Craig? Are you there? Pick up!"

T "I'm here. What?"

"Craig…"

"Ali, wassup?" His voice sounded foggier than usual, deeper, husky … and sexy.

Ali's heartbeat accelerated, which she told herself was anger, and her grip on the phone tightened. "What were you doing sleeping? Hell, I've been working here until my back is a pretzel."

"I was reading all night," interrupted Craig, "and just passed out … oh… about an hour ago."

"Never mind, listen. I've just had a fascinating conversation with a doctor." Quickly Ali outlined what she'd learned, interrupted, from time to time, by Craig's swearing.

"Now what?" demanded Craig. "I've no idea how to read a medical journal and find this stuff. My degree is in economics."

"Mine's statistics and math," replied Ali, "Oliver's is in Chemistry and teaching. He may have a better idea of what keywords to use."

"I'd rather not bring him in."

"Well, if you'll take a suggestion?"

"Go," snapped Craig, the sharp ring in his voice reminding Ali that until days ago he'd led a first rank Superteam.

"Visit the hospital. Go see this doctor. Wear your Super Suit. She'll be so all over you that she'll personally dig up everything you want just to keep you near."

"I'm not supposed to be doing public appearances," muttered Craig. "And I don't have my ID."

"Do you think *she* knows that? Or that she's going to call the press and share you with anyone? This is Doctor Uber Fan that we're talking about. Go on. Fly in her office window and she won't ask for your ID. She'll be too busy salivating on you. Talk to her. Just remember, don't kiss her or sign anything."

"Kiss her?" Craig's voice took on a different, still urgent note. "Well, now. Why don't you want me to kiss her?

"Moron," said Ali, flushing. "DNA transfer. She's a research scientist. You don't want to be in a clone situation, do you? That's all I meant."

"Suuuuuure. If you say so," his voice was warm, teasing, and heat spread over the back of her neck. "Bye now, Ali. I'll tell you *all* about it when I get home."

"Moron," repeated Ali, but she was talking to a dead phone. Cursing, she dropped the phone and sat. Why the hell had she said that kissing stuff, anyway? On the upside, that annoying woman might be so happy with Ultra Man's personal visit she'd give up the idea of the grand monument. Or she'd decide she wanted a marble version of Rodan's 'The Kiss,' starring her and Ultra Man, smack dab in the center of the hospital foyer. Ali was certain that the good doctor would find all the time necessary for the modeling any sculptor could require.

Chapter Ten.
The Scientific Belgian.
Investigations are still ongoing into the origin of the Super-powered Rat who saved six preschool children and their teacher from a fire last month. Local authorities are alleging illegal genome research.

Ali left the conference room awash in paper, locked the door and headed home. To her disgust, Craig did not appear or call her that evening. Nor the next day. While she was just as glad not to see his famous face, frustration at being excluded from the search when she'd found him such an important fount of information, made her snippy with Oliver and short-tempered at work. Nevertheless, life went on. Two days passed without any Super-Villain activity, leaving Ali free to process paperwork, visit and sign off on four completed work sites and petition her bosses, yet again, for the hiring of a replacement Site Supervisor for the Midwest region (decision postponed), and more assistants (declined).

And worry.

For the first time, she surrendered to the SS.C. policy on TV's and arranged to have a small set installed in her office. There she sat and chewed the ends of a pile of pencils watching news commentaries about Ultra Man's prolonged absence from action. Most of them were speculating that he'd been injured by the Ice Queen and was off recuperating in some secret location. Others, worse yet, thought he had run off and was currently in hiding. Every time she heard the term 'Ice Queen' Ali's head pounded.

The more time passed without hearing from him, the more worried she became. Not about him, personally, but about his career and his reputation.

Strange to think that he'd become so devoted to his work. She had to admit, at least to herself, she felt less safe as time passed and he remained on suspension. Not that there weren't a dozen or so Supers on duty at any time, countrywide. And granted, some of them had individual Powers equal to, or stronger than, Ultra Man's. It was just his combination of Powers that was rare. TV commentators reminded her, and their audience, that people had become accustomed to Ultra Man's protective presence. He couldn't be everywhere and he wasn't all-powerful, but he had an air of competence, of determination, that made you feel better to know he could be called on. And now he wasn't there.

Ali watched the talking heads mouthing their scripts, wondering how she'd managed not to notice the change. She could barely recognize Craig from their descriptions. Of course, they weren't talking about Craig. They were, practically, worshiping *Ultra Man*.

Mid-afternoon on Thursday, the hated artist's rendition of the Ice Queen flashed across the screen, then the view changed to a collapsed wooden building in the middle of an empty field. Ali dove across the room to scrabble through the piles on her desk for the remote. She jabbed at the volume button until the reporter's voice came through, clear and excited.

"...horror in a community this small, but today has proven that is not the case. In the small hours this morning, Mr. Jason Quinn and his family were awoken by a tremendous crash as this barn, only yards from where they slept, crumbled near to dust."

The barn didn't look all that dust-like to Ali. It was more like a half-capsized wooden kite. Kneeling beside the TV she studied the scene, then reached for her phone and hit the speed dial.

"Central Super Coordination, operator twenty-seven," said an artificial, genderless voice seconds later. "What is your Super emergency?"

"This is Ali Brent, regional supervisor. Turn to channel four! What's going on?"

She heard her order echoed at the other end. Shortly she could hear the same reporter chatter echoing through the phone. There was a click when her call was transferred.

"Ms. Brent," Mr. Crunch's voice crackled down the line. "What is this?"

"I was just asking you. I had the TV on and the next thing I know I'm watching a news report on a Villain event. Television crews are crawling all over the site and not a police officer or Super team member to be seen. What happened? Where is this?"

"We were unaware of this event site until this very minute. I have people scanning for the location and type of attack as we speak," said Mr. Crunch, and Ali distinctly heard him snap his fingers. "We are also investigating *why* we were not notified."

"Who calls TV crews before the police – or the S.S.C.?" demanded Ali.

"Apparently," came Mr. Crunch's chill voice, as the TV reporter turned his microphone and camera toward the grinning, weather-beaten face of the farmer, "someone more interested in publicity than public safety. We are trying to find out where this farm is, and I'm certain we'll have the location before you reach the Chinook."

"The Chinook? Me?" repeated Ali. "But it may not be in my sector."

"Irrelevant! Get airborne, Ms. Brent. We're sending you down with Norman. You'll be met by the police, I guarantee it. As soon as we find out where this disaster is taking place, we'll be sure to mobilize them."

Ali was no longer listening, her attention caught by the reporter.

"Ice Queen?" she echoed, and a smile spread across her face. "They're saying the Ice Queen was there?"

"Roger that," said Mr. Crunch. "Be very careful to preserve as much evidence of this," he paused as on screen a reporter pulled a length of wood out from the collapsed building behind him and showed it to the camera. In the background they could see people dismantling the barn and carrying pieces away, "well, as much as remains. Get to the airport as quickly as possible. You're already very late."

Ali grabbed her attaché case, coat and hit the door running, her grin still firmly in place. She even took a moment on the way to the door to do a happy-me quick step.

Perfect. It was just perfect. She was surprised it had taken as long as it had for someone to try this con. Half of her site visits, under ordinary circumstances, were to fake Villain sites. This was her opportunity to start undermining the damn media. Start casting doubt on the very existence of the Ice Queen. If she managed it right, and found some evidence of fraud, then, with luck, by the week's end the Ice Queen would be dead, Craig would be back at work and everything would be back to merely abnormal.

Norman ran a finger around his collar and swallowed. Five minutes of flight and he was already feeling green. To distract himself, he studied Ali. They'd traveled together by Chinook before and usually she was as nauseated as he by the vibrations, the odd movements, and sudden lurches. This trip, however, she was completely unaffected. If anything he would describe her as bubbly… chipper, even.

"Are you wearing feather underwear, Ali?" he asked, as a broad smile spread across Ali's face.

Ali's eyes snapped back into focus and locked on Norman's. "Excuse me? What?"

"You," said Norman. "You're almost giggling. What's got into you?"

"Ah. Yes." Ali leaned forward to watch the pilot, then shifted to sit close beside her old friend, "I wonder how long it's gonna take us to get there."

"Stop avoiding the question. What's with you?"

"Nothing much. I was just thinking how much easier my job is when I know from the get-go that the case I'm investigating is a fraud."

"Fraud?" Norman dropped his voice below the sound of the propellers. "You know that?"

Ali nodded. "All we have to do when we get on the ground is find the proof that this farmer, whoever he is, set this up as a media fraud and insurance scam. I've just got a text message from my secretary," she said, waving her phone. "The ink isn't even dry on this farmer's Super insurance rider. I'm going to tell the pilot, when we land, that he's to find somewhere nearby to wait. I don't think we'll be there long."

"Well, that's good news," Norman settled back against the padded seat. "But how do you know?"

Ali glanced around. There was no one else in the belly of the Chinook, and the pilot and co-pilot were too far away to overhear. "Ultra Man told me," she whispered. "The Ice Queen doesn't exist."

A familiar, devoted fan expression crossed Norman's face and for once Ali welcomed it.

"Good enough," was all he said.

Norman settled his respirator into place as the helicopter thundered its way back into the sky. Ali settled her boots thankfully into the churned soil and looked around. As the helicopter circled for a landing, she'd seen police cars were in position at last, but they didn't seem to be doing any good. Camera crews and reporters were still climbing all over every structure in sight, as were any number of civilians.

She identified the person in charge by looking for the biggest hat and greatest amount of tin glitter. She spotted a sheriff's car front and center of the rutted driveway leading to the farm, and the sheriff himself was in the same position in front of the TV crews. He'd turned to watch Norm's van being lowered, and Ali and Norm's descent from the Chinook with one hand resting on his broad, braid-covered hat. Now he beckoned to both of them to join him.

"Whaddayathink, Ali?" asked Norm, his voice muffled by his mask as he adjusted the fit of his overloaded tool-belt.

"I'm not going anywhere near a camera until I'm good and ready," said Ali, rifling through her attaché. "Why don't you start your scan? We may as well do this by the book."

"Gotcha."

Norman pulled a device from his belt and started towards the wrecked barn. Ali pulled out her digital camera and checked its settings. When she'd finished fiddling with that, she started making notes in her PDA. It didn't take the sheriff long to realize that waving his arms at someone who was not looking in his direction lacked dignity. A few minutes later, a very young-looking deputy was hurrying across the uneven ground toward Ali.

"Sheriff needs to speak to you, miss," said the deputy, when he finally came alongside her. "He's waiting for ya over there."

"And I am waiting for him over here," replied Ali, barely moving her lips. "Away from the camera crews, reporters, civilians and any other person who may be waving a camera and microphone about. Please inform the sheriff that when he is finished posing, I would be grateful for a moment of his time."

Ali didn't hear what the deputy actually said, she was certain that he'd paraphrased it a little, since the sheriff was smiling when he sauntered toward her.

"Sheriff," said Ali, holding up her identification and ignoring his outstretched hand. "Are you acquainted with the Federal guidelines for the securing of a suspected Paranormal crime scene?"

The sheriff's sunburned face paled a little, but his grin didn't falter. He took his hand back and tucked his thumbs into his belt. "Why, yes surely, ma'am, but we can hardly be held to that directive when the landowner doesn't notify us before the TV crews."

Ali gazed at the nearest crew – the ones who'd tagged along with the sheriff. They'd positioned themselves only a few feet away and were surreptitiously trying to focus a long-range mike and camera on Ali and the Sheriff's conversation. She glanced across to where Norman was loitering, gave him a quick nod and a jerk of her thumb. Norman pulled a sound suppressor out of his pocket and aimed it at the crew. Creative swearing filled the air as the TV equipment stopped functioning.

"This is a private conversation," called Ali. "You will be notified when and if a press conference is called."

Grumbling, the camera crew gathered their stuff and retreated.

"Interfering with the freedom of the press, Ma'am?" The sheriff's face settled in a scowl, which, considering the pattern of pale lines and sunburn crisscrossing his face, was probably his usual expression.

"Definitely, sheriff, when it comes to my work. Right now, you should be in favor of it, or are you happy to have a reprimand transmitted around the world before you get back to your office? In case you've forgotten, let me remind you - all, and that means *all,* suspected paranormal crime scenes are to be secured for the purposes of public safety. These people should have been rounded up and placed behind police lines as soon as you arrived, not only to maintain the integrity of a crime scene, but for their own safety. Now, I know exactly when you arrived here. I may have been in transit, but I was updated about activity on the ground. You've been on-site for more than an hour. In that time, what action have you taken to pull the camera crews off the site? To reclaim potential evidence? To keep the survivors safe?"

The Sheriff's mouth worked for a moment, but no sound came out.

Ali plowed on. "Acting as you have, I must assume that you share our suspicions that this is a fake scene and have spent your time, not entertaining reporters with your war stories, but investigating the alleged victims. Examining the affected barn?" She raised her eyebrows and allowed a faint smile to cross her lips. "If not, what, exactly, have you been doing?"

The sheriff rocked back on his heels. "Uh…. Well, ma'am, I had no reason to think that this here was not for real."

"That's interesting," replied Ali keeping her expression neutral, she still managed to convey the message 'you thought this was real and still putzed around for an hour?'

The sheriff cast a worried glance toward the gathered press, leaving Ali to wonder just what he'd said before her arrival. She dismissed that train of thought. The sheriff's re-election was not her concern.

"I mean, we've heard so much about the Ice Queen,' continued the Sheriff. "No one knows what sort of crimes she's like to commit. She's as likely to come here as a big city…."

Ali choked back a laugh. "You thought that a paranormal Villainess – whose existence has not yet been confirmed by the S.S.C. – bypassed several large towns, roadside diners, large cities, banks, rivers, power plants and political whatever – to come *here* and cause an empty barn to fall down?" Ali pulled herself to her full height, such as it was. "That didn't seem odd to you. Not in the smallest degree?"

Now the Sheriff's color came flooding back. He shifted forward, going into full intimidation mode, stepping close to glare down at her, nose to nose. "Like I said, *ma'am,* no one knows anything about the Ice Queen."

"But we do know some things about the owners of this farm," said Ali, reaching into her attaché to pull out a thin folder.

The Sheriff's threatening behavior did not worry her. Since she knew her car insurance was paid up and her car safely locked away in a secure garage back in New Jersey, she remained calm and unconcerned.

"Here is a copy of this farm's insurance forms. I had it transmitted to me on the way here. This family added a Super rider to their policy three days ago." She handed the flimsy page to the sheriff and reached for the next sheet, "and this is a copy of the photo that the farmer claims to have shot of the Ice Queen. The same one that he sold to the AP news service two hours ago for five hundred dollars."

"Well, wow. Sounds like he doesn't need that insurance money after all." The sheriff focused on the picture and whistled. "That Ice Queen is quite a looker."

Ali's eyes narrowed and her jaw started to ache with the pressure of holding back words she wanted to scream but couldn't. Wouldn't. Not and keep her job. She took a deep breath and continued in a steady tone. "And I think it looks like a kid's doll painted silver. If you would be so kind as to begin securing this site – as per the Federal protocol – while you're doing that, I would appreciate it if you would ask your deputies to keep watch for signs of spray painting, and an odd-colored doll of the Barbie variety." When the sheriff didn't move, but continued to glance between Ali, the press, and the damaged farm buildings Ali continued, politely. "Beginning *now,* please."

Not waiting for the Sheriff to respond, Ali nodded to Norman, and they trudged across the uneven ground to the remains of the collapsed barn. At Ali's gesture, a few deputies trotted across to them and she set them to clear the site of scavenging press.

"We can expect a few lumps of wood to be offered on the online auctions tonight," observed Norman as he watched the police and press wrestle for ownership of termite eaten wood.

Ali's only response was a grunt.

When the barn was cleared, Ali and Norman paced carefully around and over the splintered wood. Norman scanned back and forth with various pieces of equipment.

"No radiation," he muttered. "No sign of the usual toxins, nothing of Mr. Ooze, or Nuclear Man…. Thank goodness."

"No surprise, since we know this isn't for real."

"Just being thorough," said Norman, taking a few steps back and studying the scene. "From the pattern of collapse, the initial damage was inside the building." He frowned. "Over there, where all the wood's gone."

"Dammit to hell," Ali flashed a glance over toward the barn door, through which the cluster of news vans could be seen, "Well, we know where it is, don't we? What do you think of our chances of getting it back?"

Norman watched the people behind the hastily erected barrier swarm back and forth, trying to get a better shot of what they were doing. "I'd say… zero to negative none."

Ali nodded, "Especially since I expect the local law enforcement have copped one or two pieces as well."

"Yeaaaaassss," said Norman. 'For evidence, only, I'm sure. And, there's also the possibility, considering the farmer's already proven he's computer savvy – and interested in profit - that he's kept a few pieces to offer online."

"We get it off him, and we'll have evidence. Let's see what we can do about getting the cops moving, collecting it back. We need to examine as much as we can get our hands on."

"How we going to get it back?"

An evil grin bloomed across Ali's face. "Let's start with the farmer. Trust me, I have a cunning plan."

Getting the police moving took all of Ali's authority, persuasion, and one or two creative threats. But after another half an hour, officers were moving through the house and surrounding buildings. The press crews had invoked every right in the constitution and a few more that Ali was convinced they'd made up and refused to give up anything they'd stuffed into their vans. With the Sheriff backing them up, Ali had no authority to make demands. Still, she tried not to care. As soon as she got some proof that the site was a con, all that wood would be valueless anyway.

"I don't understand what's going on," said the farmer, a Mr. Jason Quinn, watching reluctant deputies poking at piles of rusting trash with sticks.

"We're investigating this site for possible insurance fraud," said Ali, focusing her camera on another section of damaged wood. "The police are collecting evidence of that crime."

Mr. Quinn gasped and his eyes darted back and forth. His mouth worked for a few seconds before he was able to frame words. "Fraud? What do you mean? Me and mine are the victims here. That Ice Queen flew in here, spat at my barn and crashed it down. If it weren't for my son coming out here with his shotgun, she'd've come after the main house."

"Interesting assumption," Ali tilted her head just a little to gaze up at him. Mr. Quinn was a person who talked with his hands. If you tied him up or cut off his arms, he'd be voiceless. To keep him off balance, Ali kept her movements small, her voice soft.

"Flew? Did you actually see her fly? I was under the impression from the news report that you and your family were asleep."

"We saw her fly away," declared Mr. Quinn, the loose skin on his neck quivering. "That's when I took that there photo."

"And she *spat* at the barn?" Ali raised a disbelieving eyebrow.

"Yeah."

"Spat. You saw that?" Ali came fully upright an inch at a time. "I've seen transcripts of the news reports. You stated that the noise of the barn collapsing woke you up. All the flying and spitting would've already taken place." She studied the farmer for a moment, taking in his twisting hands and restlessly shuffling feet. "Keeping in mind all the sound bites you've been handing out this morning, the ones that I can collect from various news sources later, would you care to reconsider your recent statements?"

Mr. Quinn stuttered for a moment, watching Ali focus her camera on another area of the farm, then reached into his pocket to pull out a glossy sheet.

"I got a photo," he said, waving it under Ali's nose. "As she flew away. We didn't get out of the house in time to stop her, but we saw her leave. I had my camera and took a shot."

"Interesting," said Ali again. "In the middle of the night, when a strange noise woke you up, your first thought was to grab a camera. Your son's was to grab a gun."

"Yeah," Mr. Quinn stuck out his chin and the extra skin under it quivered. "So what?"

"I've looked in your house," said Ali, in scathing tones. "Your front room is so messy that you make a pile of cooked spaghetti look organized. Now you expect me to believe you went outside, saw a fallen down barn and a Super Villainess and then, panicked and afraid, you went inside, grabbed a fully powered, ready and loaded camera and came back outside just in time for a perfectly framed profile shot. Nothing blurred. Nothing over or underexposed. Close enough and clear enough to see the 'I. Q.' painted on her anatomically unbelievable chest. That's your story?"

Mr. Quinn folded his arms across his chest, his jaw working. "That's what happened. Take it or leave it."

"Since you give me a choice, thank you, I'll leave it," said Ali. "I don't believe a word. And with those vultures over there taking every piece of affected wood, there is no way you can prove that anything happened other than someone taking an ax to the barn's supports. It will say so in my report to the insurance SS.C.. Once that report has been processed, the news services will be after you to get the money they paid for that photo back."

Mr. Quinn's trembling increased, until he was almost vibrating in place. With a curse he turned, charged into his house, swearing at his wife when she reached toward him as he passed.

The sheriff had been loitering nearby, listening to one of his deputies, and now hurried over to stand beside Ali.

"We've got some traffic problems building up," said the Sheriff. "Those news reports have brought tourists out by the hundreds. These ones driving up now are just the ones who live close by. By this evening, they'll be here in the thousands."

"Yeah," muttered Norman, 'that happens all the time. People coming out to see a Super battleground. I don't know what it is about someone else's suffering that brings out the tourists, but you can expect them for days. Maybe even a week. This far out into the country, you'll have some pretty nasty traffic control problems for a while. Better call in the state troopers for help."

The sheriff bridled at this implied slur on the abilities of his small police department.

"No offense intended," said Ali. "Even when we notify the news services that this is a con, you're still going to get tourists. You can either set up roadblocks – that won't work, people are stubborn – or give directions, make it a one-way system and keep 'em moving."

"Whatever you might think of us non-city folk," said the sheriff, his voice growling with barely concealed anger, "we do know how to manage a little traffic."

"Suit yourself."

Ali turned away, grinning across at Norman as Mr. Quinn came out of his house at a run, a long length of wood clutched in his arms.

"Here, this is a main upright, or what's left of it." Mr. Quinn shoved it at Ali and Norman. "See. Look at this end of the wood. Ice Queen spat at it and it just shattered."

Ali pulled on a set of latex gloves before running a finger down the length of the dirty, dark wood. There were a scattering of pale spots clustered near the broken end of the four by four. Norman caught Ali's eye, and nodded. They lowered the piece of wood to the ground between them. Norman took out his scanner and Ali reached for her camera and took shots from several angles while Mr. Quinn watched.

"Well. Do you see?" said Mr. Quinn, after a few minutes impatient waiting. "It's what I said,"

"This style of stud is from the inside of that barn, isn't it?" said Ali. "Are you saying the Ice Queen went *inside* the barn to find the supporting beams?"

"I don't have to explain why she did it," declared Mr. Quinn. "It's what happened."

"Your story is not supported by evidence," said Ali, nodding to Norman. She turned, catching sight of a deputy hurrying around the corner of the house.

"Sheriff," the deputy shouted. "I found it. In a ditch in the back. What the Site Supervisor said. A patch of grass covered with silver paint and this." He held up a grey canister.

"Liquid Nitrogen," cried Norman, recognizing the canister color code. "Knew it. I use it all the time, cleaning up after Mr. Ooze. I'm the world expert at recognizing liquid nitrogen splatter pattern."

"And the silver grass?" asked the Sheriff.

"That's where Mr. Quinn painted what looks like a Barbie doll clone." Ali waved at the glossy photo sticking out of Mr. Quinn's pocket. "Sheriff, as I said from the beginning, this looks like a fake attack site. A setup for insurance fraud."

"What the hell?" cried Mr. Quinn. "You can't –"

The Sheriff's eyes narrowed and he raised his hand, cutting off the flow of words. "Isn't fraud until he files a claim, and that hasn't happened yet."

"Granted, but he has sold a faked photo to news services," Ali bared her teeth at the farmer. "They will be after you for their money back. They may even sue you for the damage you've caused to their reputations. By now, they'll have transmitted that damn photo around the world. You've deceived them. And while news companies may like to spin the news, they don't like someone spinning them."

Mr. Quinn paled under his deep tan, and his hands started to shake.

"And calling in a fake police report is a crime," continued Ali.

"Then the Super Support better watch out," broke in the Sheriff. "Mr. Quinn didn't call us. You did. Your SS.C.."

Ali stared at him, stunned. The Sheriff grinned at her, but she didn't think he was feeling cheerful. His next words confirmed it. "Quinn. This here's your private property. These *cleaners* don't have no right to demand entry. You didn't invite them, you can send them on their way whenever you want."

"In that case," said Mr. Quinn, spitting at the ground between Norman and Ali, "You'all can get the hell off mah property. Now!"

Back aboard the Chinook, Ali typed up her report and emailed it to the home office, then she settled back, eyes closed. Beside her, she could hear Norman tapping out his own report.

"What's another word for clumsy," asked Norman.

"Gauche, inept, maladroit… klutzy," recited Ali, and smiled when she heard Norman chuckle.

"Yeah, that'll work."

Unfortunately, they didn't.

Ali sauntered into S.S.C. building intending to go to her office and add a few more delicate touches to her report. She really wanted to skewer that sheriff. Not that she wanted to interfere with his eventual re-election, just make him work a bit harder. Instead, she found Nigel's secretary standing in the foyer, waiting for her.

"Mr. Hackham's office. Now," was all she said before jogging back down the corridor.

Diffuse guilt had Ali's face blushing dull red by the time she faced her boss across his mile-wide desk. She'd given Ultra Man unlimited access to her secure laptop as well as feeding him the information about Nuclear Man's letter writing hobby instead of talking to the data crunchers. If any of the lawyers, or worse, Control, learned that, she'd be in several yards of trouble.

"Ms. Brent. I find myself wondering where you've been this afternoon," said Mr. Hackham, steepling his fingers and regarding her over their tips.

"Sir?" Ali blinked then swallowed, "I was sent down to the fraudulent Super event site. Mr. Crunch authorized the out of sector assignment."

"Yes, I do know where Mr. Crunch ordered you to go, but did you actually go there?"

The sarcastic tone in his voice bit deep. Her back straightened and she glared down her nose at the seated lawyer. "As I'm not the pilot, and as far as I know we weren't hijacked, yes, we went where *they* were told to go."

A brief smile flickered over one corner of Mr. Hackham's mouth, then his usual superior expression reasserted itself. "Then could you tell me why your, and Norman's, reports vary so much with what has subsequently been reported from the scene?"

"Excuse me?" Ali's mouth went dry and she remembered the smug, sneering expression on the sheriff's face as she'd re-boarded the Chinook.

"The Sheriff - what is his name – Halliburton, has been on the news almost continuously since you went off-scene talking about the – and I quote – 'famous site of the Ice Queen's first defeat.' Saying that where the Supers have failed, one lone man – Mr. Quinn – equipped with a mere shotgun, drove her away."

"His story has changed again; isn't anyone paying attention to that?" cried Ali, reaching into her case and pulling out her file. "First time through, it was him with a camera and his son with a gun as Ice Queen was flying away."

"I've read your report," said Mr. Hackham, "Now validate it. Before you were evicted from the scene, you'd declared it fraudulent. What was your proof?"

Ali consulted her folder. "First the ink on the insurance rider was fresh, and, according to the insurance risk data assessment, the odds of a Super event in that neighborhood registered statistically as less than zero. Secondly, the story changed. Every time we challenged an aspect of that guy's tall tale he twisted it. I recorded all the permutations of that story in my email. Third, Norman agrees with me that the splatter pattern – on a piece of wood from the *inside* of that damn barn – was exactly like liquid nitrogen. The damaged end was completely shattered, again, exactly what you'd expect from liquid nitrogen. Add to that one of the deputies said he found silver paint on the grass outside the house. The same color as that stupid photograph the farmer's circulating. The same deputy found a canister of liquid nitrogen. I was not able to obtain samples, or a photograph, before we were ordered off-scene. *And,* to top it all, Ultra Man, P.L. and West all say that Ice Queen doesn't exist."

Mr. Hackham shook his head and waved away the papers Ali thrust at him. "Leaving aside that last aspect of the issue, which one of these pieces of damning evidence did you bring back with you?"

Ali's mouth worked for a moment then she settled back on her heels. "I have some photos of the liquid nitrogen splatter on wood, but the local police kept the actual piece. If we really want it, we should look for in an online auction this evening. Besides, it's S.S.C. policy that the Supers catch 'em and hand them off to the cops with the evidence. The same policy covers my responsibilities. When I find anything significant on-site, I'm supposed to hand it over. I do insurance investigations, not criminal."

"Indeed," Nigel placed his hands palm down on the desk, framing a web newspaper front page. "I received this from the editor of, well, shall we say not one of the more serious and intellectual of the daily bloggers? Nevertheless, this site receives a significant number of hits every day." With a single push he sent the page skidding across the desk. "As you see, this side is your report, which we released as per protocol in fraud cases, side by side with interviews with the Sheriff, the alleged fraudulent farmer and some witnesses who claim they saw the

Ice Queen flying across the state last night. You do not come off well in this, my dear Ms. Brent. Sheriff Halliburton accuses you of conducting, and I quote, a *superficial, lumbering, uninformed review of the site*, and of, *leaving precipitously when the Sheriff refused to assist you in fabricating evidence to support your preconceived and unjustified suspicion of fraud.*"

All the air fled Ali's lungs and for a moment it was all she could do to stay standing.

"The goddamn bastard. He threw me off-site. Or, actually, he told the farmer to throw me off. He's probably got a shit load of wood in his car that he'll be auctioning off to pay for his election campaign." Ali's grip on her attaché tightened and she wished she could throw it at that sunburned face. "Just wait. Keep an eye on the Internet tonight and you'll see the sales."

"Language," murmured Nigel.

"To hell with that," cried Ali, "This is a con. A setup. That farmer's story didn't match the evidence. For heaven's sake, why would any Super-Villain tear down a barn? Just one barn, in the middle of nowhere. From the *inside?* Why are people having such a hard time seeing this for what it is? How dumb can they be?"

"That attitude is one of the things that the sheriff, the farmer, and the lawyer they've each retained, have objected to." Nigel gestured her to a chair and waited until she sat before continuing. "Ms. Brent, I'm accustomed to fielding spurious lawsuits directed toward the Supers we represent, but *this* is a first. An insurance assessor is being sued. One of our highlyy trained Site Supervisors is the subject of a defamation suit. No, Ms. Brent, that is not what we expect when you are sent out to represent us."

Ali slumped back and put both hands over her face.

"I don't understand what happened," she said. "What went wrong? It was such a clumsy, obvious, *amateurish* setup. Are you saying he's getting away with it?"

"With the apparent assistance of the police and several local businesses," said Mr. Hackham, "Yes."

"Businesses?"

"The tourists visiting this site need to eat, apparently. Port-a-potty rental companies are already putting in bids, that sort of thing."

"Before they finish, they'll have cotton candy franchises and a Ferris wheel," muttered Ali, then groaned. She'd failed. The perfect opportunity to put a halt to the Ice Queen madness, and it escaped.

"Paid for by insurance, as we are unable, in the absence of evidence and police support, to establish fraud," said Mr. Hackham, wearily. "Next time, if you are going to declare something a crime, please remember to bring home proof."

"I could go directly to the companies. Tell them what I saw. They won't pay out."

"Ms. Brent, you will not step out of S.S.C. guidelines."

Ali opened her fingers and peered at her boss. "What happens now? Am I on suspension? Do I need a lawyer?"

"Hardly. We are so short staffed at the moment that you cannot be spared. But, as a personal favor, please refrain from offending anyone else for a month or so. I would appreciate it."

Eliza saw Ali coming, got a good look at the expression on her face and wisely ran for cover, taking the other assistants with her. Ali slammed into her office, threw her case across the room, sank down to the carpet and crawled under her desk. She'd requested the huge desk – instead of some other token of the SS.C.'s respect, claiming she needed the surface area to spread out her work. But in reality it was for times like this. Hidden between the drawer and the back of the desk, a large chocolate bar was duct-taped to the wood. Ali pulled it free, curled into a ball with her arms wrapped tight around her legs, and, safely hidden from sight, broke the chocolate in half and started chewing. Above her head, her phone started ringing and the fax machine continued to throw paper onto her floor. Ali ignored it all. She had more important matters to ponder.

By the time the chocolate was gone, she had reached a decision. She'd gotten involved in the Ice Queen battle, so to speak, as a favor to Craig.

But now it was personal.

There was no other option.

The Ice Queen had to die.

How the hell was she going to arrange it?

"What the hell? Has it been raining paper in here?" Ali stood at the door and stared around her living room. All flat surfaces – including chairs, couches and the top of her fish tank – were covered. Drifts of white curled under her coffee table and slid across the carpet and onto the kitchen linoleum. "I thought I'd left all this at work."

"Hey, Ali." Craig levered himself off the floor and picked his way across the floor toward her. He gave her a lopsided smile that somehow lifted her spirits and made the aggravations of the day start to fade. "Sorry. It kind of got out of hand."

"What 'it'? What is all this?" asked, Ali trying to find a place to put down her bag.

She moved too fast and the nearest table shook and paper cascaded to the floor. Craig dove to catch them, releasing another flood. He ended up kneeling on the floor, thigh deep, as paper rained down on his head.

Ali laughed, for the first time in a long time, and leaned down to brush a few pieces off his face.

"Thanks," Craig shook like a dog scattering paper across the floor and grinned up at her, "Dr. Wilks, she and I – or at least, one of her medical students and I, killed quite a few trees photocopying the hell out of dozens of medical journals."

"What?" Ali's eyes widened and she scanned the room again. "All these are letters from Nuclear Man?"

"Yeah. I think. Pretty much every letter he wrote until they stopped printing them."

"But she told me that it would be difficult to get them at all. How'd you get them so fast?"

"She had most of her replies referenced in her résumé. Have you ever met someone with a forty-three-page long résumé?" Craig climbed to his feet, letting the papers fall where it may.

"Ah." Ali considered for a moment. Her own résumé took up about half of one page. "No."

"Me neither. Apparently, it's normal for a doctor. Or so I'm told. They list everywhere their name's appeared in professional publications. Anyway, she gave me a copy, along with her home phone number, cell number, six different email addresses and an invitation to dinner, Friday. Oh, and a med student. We took her resume to the university medical center library and made copies of everything. Now, I'm trying to sort them out."

"What did it cost you?" asked Ali suspiciously, the home phone number line ringing in her ears.

"Nothing much," Craig grinned at her. "Dr. Wilks had some pretty extreme ideas of what she wanted in that damn foyer of hers. Eventually I talked her down, over a long and cozy lunch in a very expensive restaurant, to the jersey I wore in the charity baseball game a couple of years ago."

Relief left Ali limp. She told herself it was just because she wouldn't have to pass on the doctor's gaudy request. And that it hadn't been anything embarrassingly personal from Ultra Man.

"That's hardly what I'd call dignified," said Ali.

Craig granted her one what she called his 'humble servant' bows. "It was what she wanted once I'd gotten through with her."

Ali ignored the strange pang that struck her heart and suppressed the sudden urge she had to strangle doctors. The woman had annoyed her. She should be pleased that the snob MD had ended up with such a plebeian display in her precious foyer. She took a deep breath and reminded herself that murder was a momentary pleasure bound to get you talked about and tried to let her anger go. It was surprisingly difficult.

"Just have it properly dry cleaned down in Decontam before you send it to her, okay? Now, what have you got," said Ali, turning over a couple of pages? "Is med student with spinal cancer the same as Nuclear Man?"

"I was reading while I was copying. I'm not a stylistic expert, but the subject matter's pretty close. A few of the word choices, phrases and ideas recur under both names."

"Prolific little fellow, isn't he?" said Ali, as she looked around her living room.

"Yeah. Beats me why he took the risk. One thing I've found already is that he's written letters from two places. The journals don't print the full address, just the author and town. I've called the editors; they don't keep the originals. The 'med student with spinal cancer' used to live in Brooklyn. Nuclear Man wrote from Brooklyn for about a year and then...." Craig's smile broadened. "He moved to Arizona."

"That's great," said Ali. "That's more than we've been able to find out about him before. Now I've got something for you."

Craig raised his head suddenly, his eyes widening, and shifted closer to her. Ali pushed at his shoulder with a snarl.

"Get your mind out of the gutter. I went through thousands of documents in the last two days - just skimming - and I've noticed a pattern in his attacks. We've always classified his attacks as in hospital, or out of hospital. But it's more complicated than that. We know he hits research institutions. According to the reports from those sites, he's either collecting data, raiding the computer files, or..."

"On what?"

Ali rolled her eyes. "On cancer therapies."

"Of course," said Craig. "Silly me. What for?"

"Or he breaks in to steal the actual therapies. Chemotherapy.

Radioactive wafers. Needles. Syringes. Things like that. But when he does, he's always careful not to break or contaminate anything he leaves behind. And he never takes all the drug, just takes a few weeks' supply. Same as when he intercepts shipments of medications. He only takes what he needs."

"Okay, so we have a considerate thief."

"Ah, then we have the research sites that he tears to little pieces and contaminates to hell and back with his radioactive - ah - emesis." She reached into her bag and pulled out a list.

"Just to make the records complete, we've asked the researchers to give us copies of their protocols. I did an online search. All – and I mean *all* of the research studies that he disrupted were later shut down, had the grants pulled, or something, because the protocol or implementation was flawed, unethical or dangerous. Apparently having Nuclear Man attack them brought enough attention to those studies that some bright spark would look at them and say – 'Hell, no, you can't do that! It's not ethical, moral or safe.'"

"So he did some research subjects a favor," Craig rubbed at his chin and rose to pace, carefully, across the room. "You know, that's what a lot of his letters were about. Complaining about unethical research studies. Dangerous ones."

"Yeah. Well, it looks like he went from complaining to doing something about it."

"Looks like," agreed Craig. "But he does do a fair amount of other damage. I mean, look at the convention center that he and the Shriek took apart last year. Millions of dollars' worth of damage."

"Which was just before the AMA's annual convention was held there. He's gone after their headquarters, their lawyer's offices, the office of their pitchmen down in Washington." Ali waved at the piles of photocopies. "Anything in here about that?"

Craig stared thoughtfully at the piles, then started picking through, searching.

"A couple of rants about how some doctors have God complexes and think that they're above the law. No names named. Poor bedside manner – which seems a pretty poor reason to tear down a convention center. Indifference to the suffering of their patients. Big surprise. A lot of the same sort of complaints you get in any hospital or clinic when someone feels that their doctor is not paying them enough attention."

"How do you know that?"

"Because," said Craig, "that's what all the doctors who replied to the letters said. Actually, some of them went further and accused the letter writer, med-student back then, of having delusions and a persecution complex."

"Oh, that would've gone down well," said Ali. "Do you really want to be insulting someone with delusions *and* Super Powers?"

Craig chuckled, but sobered quickly. "No kidding. But they had a good reason. In one of his earlier letters.. " He started burrowing through the piles. "He wrote that some doctors who shouldn't be allowed to operate a scalpel are off hunting in the woods – with no training and less skill than they used in the practice of medicine, and one of them shot his pet Jackalope."

"Excuse me?" Ali blinked at him.

Craig started laughing. "Yeah. This is where we find out that the doctors were right about his mental status. He's complaining about a Jackalope being shot by some MDs from New York out on holiday."

"What the hell's a Jackalope?"

"It's this urban legend animal." Craig dropped to his knees to go through a pile leaning against the leg of a chair. "A cross between a jackrabbit and an antelope. A rabbit with a rack of horns."

"That's ridiculous," said Ali, smothering a laugh.

"Yeah. All the doctors agreed. No one but the med-student-with-radioactive spine was surprised when the lawsuit that he brought against the shooter was thrown out. Got it." Craig scanned the pages he'd unearthed then held them out to Ali. "Actually, I'm wrong. It didn't get thrown out. The med student brought suit for the shooting of a family pet, the Jackalope, but according to this letter to the AMA, when he and his lawyer were waiting for a pre-trial deposition, they heard the doctor and *his* lawyer talking. And the doctor said, "It's not necessary to talk settlement. He's got cancer. Draw out the discovery process as long as you want and he'll die before it comes to trial."

"Oh, that's cold."

"Yeah. But the Wall of White formed up behind that MD. He never got punished. Not even a slap on the wrist. No settlement for the Med Student. No apology for the unfeeling attitude. Nothing."

Ali skimmed the letter. The journal had called on a medical ethicist to reply. The ethicist had taken two pages to say that the doctor had done nothing wrong challenging a delusion, and that the med student was just jealous of someone who'd managed to pass and graduate.

"Do we know which doctor was involved in this? It could give us Nuclear Man's name."

"I tried, but since it didn't go to court there's no record I can find so far. Not with my current lack of Federal ID."

"Did he send another letter after this?" asked Ali.

"Yeah. The med student wrote to say he'd dropped out of medical school when they started treating him for a particularly aggressive form of spinal cancer. Too weak to continue his studies. Said he'd been given less than six months to live."

Ali blinked and calculated. "Then it can't be the same guy. Nuclear Man's been around for years."

"Yeah," said Craig, "If it is Nuclear man, and I think it is, it seems there were some unexpected side effects from all the radiation and chemotherapy he received. When he first started complaining, he was an ordinary person. But something must have happened. He developed a Superpower - projectile vomiting of radioactive and toxic liquids, and somehow, he's exceeded his expected lifespan."

"Hell of a side effect," muttered Ali, her lip curling.

"Tell me about it. We've got a lot more info on this guy now, even if we don't have a name. We've got his motivations, all three of them, his favorite targets, and a place to start looking."

"You're going to Arizona?"

Craig considered for a moment, staring at the papers at his feet. "Not yet, no. But soon."

"Alone?" She waited, but he didn't answer. Didn't appear to have even heard her. "Well, I'm exhausted," said Ali. "And hungry. You're going to have to put this away before P.L. gets back from patrol."

"We've got time. He phoned. He's out for the evening. Went straight from patrol out on a heavy date."

Craig sneaked a quick glance at Ali's weary face. He'd come back to her apartment deliberately, to get her opinion on the letters, sure, but also to see her. He'd heard, through the grapevine, about her dressing down. Even though he was out of the usual gossip loop, there were still people willing to call him and tell him about the criticisms, the public insults and humiliation raining down on her after that Ice Queen site visit. He'd even sent flowers to her office, in support, only to be told by Eliza that Ali had left before they arrived and hadn't seen them.

Now he could see what the last few days had done to her. Pale, thinner than he remembered, she didn't appear to have much strength left. Knowing her as well as he did, he knew better than to try to attract her attention, to flirt, when she was this tired. Even trying to take care of her would not be welcomed. The girl's temper was too close to the surface on a good day, let alone when she was exhausted. Better to keep it light, professional and friendly.

f course, it wasn't fair. It seemed that she was never in the mood for flirtation. For seduction. For just plain fun. Sometime soon, he'd have to make the effort. Get her away from both their jobs and try to get those intent brown eyes to focus on him and get that brilliant mind to think about something other than work. Again, preferably about him. He moved behind her, reaching to rub her shoulders. He worked his fingers into the tight muscles and smirked when she leaned into his hands.

"Cooking's too much effort," said Craig. "You up for pizza?"

"Whatever. The local parlor's number is on the fridge." Her phone went off just as Craig lifted his hands from her neck to reach for the phone.

"Damn it," Ali snapped, scanning the display. "Another damned Ice Queen sighting."

"Again?"

"You have no idea. While you've been hiding in libraries, the Ice Queen has been spotted tearing down a poor defenseless farmer's barn." Ali grabbed her case and headed for the door "Now, it seems, she is attacking diners in Delaware. I've got to go. Have this mess cleaned up before Oliver gets home."

She headed for the door at a run. Behind her, Craig returned the phone to its rest and watched the door swing shut.

The Chinook landed them in a school football field a few blocks away from the latest event site. Ali climbed into Norman's van while the helicopter took off to find somewhere nice and quiet to wait.

"Evidence," said Ali, for the fifth time that trip. "This time we need to bring back evidence."

"Got it," said the ever-patient Norman.

He maneuvered his van through the crowds clogging the littered streets. TV crews aimed cameras at them as they inched their way closer to the police barricade. Ali waited as the township cops scanned their IDs. To her surprise, the cop who checked her ID, instead of passing them through, retreated to talk to his superior. A few moments later they both returned.

"You the same Site Supervisor as was down in Virginia a few days ago?"

"There is only one *Senior* Site Supervisor for the Northeast and Midwest regions. That's me," said Ali. "I take first pass through all Super event sites, then pass it on to my assistants."

Ali forced herself to smile at them, when what she wanted to do was scream that the farmer had run a con and that the local cops there had gone along with it. She'd ignored much of the press coverage of the Virginia disaster. Listening to the false information being reported as truth had her stomach churning. Now it seemed that something had been said that upset police departments several states away, and Ali started to wonder what she'd missed.

"Wait here a minute," said the senior cop, and the two retreated again.

"What the hell's that all about?" said Norman, leaning forward to peer after them. "We've never been kept waiting at a site before."

"Things have changed," whispered Ali.

Fifteen minutes ticked slowly past before the police returned and lifted the barricade. Norman obeyed the cop's hand signals and parked the van in the middle of the street, in plain view of all the gathered TV crews. Norman kept his face turned away from the cameras and, before anyone else approached the van, dived between the seats into the back.

"Where the hell's he going?" demanded the cop.

"To finish getting suited up," said Ali. "He's going to assess the site for hazardous material."

"The site's already been cleared by our hazmat team," said the cop. "He can stay in the van while we walk you through the site. Get him. Tell him to sit, hands on the steering wheel."

Shock ran through her like lightning, leaving her shaken and barely able to speak. Hands on the wheel? They were treating them like criminals!

"Ah, yes." Ali turned her head a little. "Hey, Site Examiner, they want you to come back to the front of the van."

Chapter Eleven.

The Conspiracy Theorist Weekly.
After answering questions regarding the rapidly approaching End Of Days, as predicted by the steadily increasing number of moldy slices of bread bearing the face of Elvis, Senior Research Fellow Dr. Joyce Peabody, of the Conspiracy Institute of Wyoming was asked to address issues surrounding the development of Super Powers.

"There are no such things as Super Powers," she retorted. "How gullible are you?"

There was a rumble from the back of the van, then Norman returned, pulling his baseball cap down low over his face he slid back into the driver's seat.

"Get that thing off," demanded the officer.

Norman turned his head toward Ali, who nodded slowly.

"Yes, I know the SS.C. rules about anonymity. Do it anyway. Oblige the nice police officer, please. I'll take care of the paperwork when we get back home."

Norman removed his respirator and dropped it on his lap. For the first time in a couple of decades, he was barefaced in a public place. He met Ali's eye, blushed and inclined his head. Ali tried to stay calm even under the crushing weight of guilt. She was responsible for this. It had been decades since an S.S.C. employee had been treated with suspicion. Since a person in authority had challenged the S.S.C. policy of secrecy and anonymity. She forced down the raging butterflies in her stomach, smiled and started fussing around in her attaché while the officer outside waited impatiently. No doubt she'd have to report to Mr. Hackham in the morning. And what a joyous interview that was going to be.

"You coming out?" asked the officer as the minutes ticked by, and Ali made no move to emerge.

"Yes. Presently," said Ali. "I'm just waiting for someone."

"Who?" asked the cop, then staggered as a blast of cold air swept past.

"For him," said Ali and reached for the door release. Then she blinked and sat back when she saw Ultra Man's masked face smiling in at her. Relief and anxiety warred as they swept through her, leaving her weak. He shouldn't be here. She'd left him safely at her apartment. He was suspended. Banned from all event sites. If Control found out he was here, there'd be hell to pay. Not to mention that he'd gotten here far too fast. To arrive so soon after Norman activated the emergency signal, he'd have to have already been on his way! What was he thinking? Didn't he realize the danger? He was suspended, for crud's sake.

After nodding to the speechless Ali, Craig turned his intent Ultra Man stare on the nearest cop, bending slightly to check his ID badge.

"Well, hi, Officer Jacques, glad to meet you. If you'll excuse me a minute, I need to confer with the Super Clean team."

"Sure. Sure." The cop backed up a few steps, looking around for his superior.

"What the hell are you doing here?" demanded Ali as Craig held out his hand to help her climb down. Craig ignored her question and peered past her at Norman.

"Hey man, what's up?"

Flustered to be talking to his hero, Norman blushed bright red and couldn't speak.

"The cops told him to sit there, with his hands on the wheel and not move," said Ali, when seconds passed and she realized Norman was not going to recover any time soon. "Without his face mask."

A frown passed across Craig's broad face, then came back and settled.

"Don't they know the danger? Exactly since when do Super Support teams get treated this way?" demanded Craig, his voice pitched to carry. "What the hell's going on here?"

"The first question they asked me was if I was on-site down in Virginia," said Ali with a sigh. "Something must have happened. Usually people don't ask questions like that. They forget the clean-up squad and me. I've never had anything from one event site carry over to another before."

Craig rolled his eyes. "Oh. Okay. Wait here. I'll see what's up. And Norm, better suit up. It'll be okay. I'll tell them it was a direct order from me."

He stalked across the street to where the cops waited beside police vehicles positioned to block access further up the street. Ali settled back in the van.

"I don't feel too friendly right now, Norm," she said, nudging him to the ribs to shake him out of his trance. "And it wouldn't be good PR to have shots of Ultra Man yelling at cops on the evening news. Do me a favor and block the TV crew equipment."

"Sooooo against the rules," said Norman, at the same time reaching under the dash. "And the second time this week. Once more, and we're going to be explaining this to Control."

"I'll take the heat," Ali assured him.

It wasn't as if she wasn't already taking the heat. It was doubtful if she'd feel it if they added any more. She was already past pain to numb. Not being believed, supported by the SS.C. after that fraud fiasco had left her doubting her place in the SS.C. Anything more, just one little thing, and she'd tell them where to put the job and all the hassles that went with it.

After a few seconds of fiddling, Norman emerged to watch the show. Unfortunately, there wasn't much to see. Craig managed to maneuver the cops so that they were facing away from the TV cameras, and for the most part, didn't raise his voice or display any angry body language. After a moment, he turned and waved to the Super Clean van. Ali nodded and turned to Norman.

"Time to go," said Ali, "looks like Ultra Man's gotten them to calm down a bit. Even so, we're going to do this site review by the book. Nothing can be even the slightest bit questionable." At Norman's nod, she smiled and added, "Okay, let's be obsessive-compulsive out there."

Ignoring the swarm of reporters, who had not yet realized that their equipment had stopped working, Ali and Norm joined Craig and the police. Having any of the Supers turn up in answer to the signal would have been welcome, but Craig, as Ultra Man, impressed the local cops. She could tell by the stunned expressions on the police officers' faces that there was more than one member of his fan club here tonight.

"Are we ready?" asked Ali, all bright, professional innocence.

"I'm sure everyone here is ready to help you," said Craig, looking back at the police. "Aren't you?"

There was a general affirmative mutter and a senior officer gestured through the narrow gap between two cars. Just off to one side was an opening leading into an unpaved parking lot that could have held no more than ten cars. Crime scene lights surrounded an ancient roadside diner. The aluminum siding sagged. The paint was peeling and faded. Ali tugged at Craig's sleeve and pulled him to one side.

"What the heck were you thinking, coming here?" she said, her lips barely moving. "Control is going to go postal on your ass and there'll be nothing left but –"

"Calm down," said Craig, resting his hand on her shoulder and guiding her further away from the crime scene lights. "I had to come. Had to clear up your place first, but here I am."

They watched as Norman, escorted by an officer in a hazmat suit, thumped toward the diner.

"Going to talk to the survivors, Ali?" asked Craig as he scanned the site.

Ali shook her head, "Not alone and not yet. The Site Examiner's got a video cam, I want to get the interviews on record. You can go in if you want."

"No. I know it's fake. If I pay too much attention to it, it will only add validity to the claim. We'll wait for proof, then go get a confession."

"Just by being here, you add validity."

"I'm here because the police were impolite. They know it. I know they know it. If they make a fuss, I'll make sure the press know it. Meantime, I'll just pose for the cameras and look bored." He gave Ali a warm smile, "Bodyguard duty, Site Supervisor, just for you. A little moral support between friends."

Ali's face burned and she was grateful for the odd shadows the crime scene lights cast. Damn him. She half turned away and pulled out her clipboard. He was standing close, just behind her. She stole a quick glance over her shoulder. Ultra Man had his stern father expression on. Judging by the fact that the local cops weren't approaching them, they were finding his attitude more than a little intimidating. Ali could barely keep giggles from bubbling up. She'd been ignored and insulted during her work, but this was the first time she'd been – by association – intimidating.

Half an hour later, Norman clumped down the steps and across to Ali. The cops nudged each other and trotted after him. Norman gestured to his mask and ear. Ali nodded and pulled her phone out of her belt and dialed Norman's in-helmet phone.

"Site Examiner, report," said Ali.

"Hey, girl," said Norman. "You would not believe the mess in there. They shouldn't have called for us. They should have called the health department."

"Yes?" Ali kept a smile off her face with an effort. If Norman had found anything questionable, he wouldn't have sounded so happy. She hadn't been the only one to get lectured about Virginia.

"Tell me," continued Norman, "What do you get when you throw a lot of dry ice and water into a small, airtight container?"

"A big explosion?" said Ali, and watched the cops near her jump to attention. Craig's face remained impassive, but he leaned closer to listen.

"Exactly," Norman raised his hand, showing her a clear evidence bag containing fragments of blue plastic. "Most of the damage seems to have been done with a high-pressure hose and water. Probably the fire hose. The air in there is cold and misty, but that's from the dry ice."

"Can you confirm? Chemically?"

"Sure!" Joy fairly rippled from the phone. "There's elevated CO2 level in there, and if you give me a few minutes I'll finish the test on these chips and confirm they were part of a container that exploded from internal pressure from expanding CO_2 gas. Extreme cold changes the nature of cheap plastic in a, fortunately, predictable and testable manner."

"Go. Do it."

Ali closed her phone and smiled at Craig and the waiting police.

"What's up?" the detective demanded, "What did he tell you? What explosion?"

"The area is clear of most of the hazards we usually see," said Ali, "No nuclear or toxic materials. But the analysis does show elevated levels of CO2. Prolonged exposure is not advisable. I think we should limit the time unprotected people spend inside."

"The Ice Queen sprays CO2 at people?" asked the cop. "Wow. Early reports from Quinn farm were that she sprayed liquid nitrogen around. How many weapons does this woman have?"

The last question was directed to Craig, and Ali was just as happy to let him deal with the denial. Instead, she borrowed Norman's shielded video camera and made her way inside the diner, a young officer following close on her heels. Leaving the door open wide, she stepped into the filthy interior. Her shoes skidded and squeaked on the wet linoleum. There were a dozen booths with cracked plastic seats and stained tables along one side of the narrow building. The Formica on the service bar was darkened and twisted in patches. A thin drift of white fog hovering over the floor curled around her legs, chilling her skin even through her heavy boots. Ali moved carefully, sliding her feet across the floor, checking for any holes or cracks hidden by the mist. Ali allowed one corner of her mouth to turn upwards. Dry ice fog on the floor, burns on the plastic and Formica. All pretty conclusive – if you were willing to believe the truth. For everyone else, she needed more evidence. She continued through to the kitchen, opened cupboards and the fridge, recording the contents.

Very little in the way of supplies, she thought, old and damaged equipment, dirty floor. All signs of a failed or failing business, making the little diner a prime site for destruction in a property insurance fraud.

She put the video on the counter and pulled her little camera out of her bag. She snapped photos of the damage, fog, the generally dirty and neglected appearance of the diner and its equipment before turning to the officer who accompanied her.

"Are you having trouble breathing?"

"Me?" he paused, raising one hand to his mouth. "No. Well, yeah, I'm breathless. Sort of panting."

Ali nodded. "Don't forget to document that," she said. "Those are symptoms of CO_2 poisoning. This other damage was caused by ordinary water. But that...." She pointed to the cracked Formica. "You put a little piece of dry ice on a table like this one, and it'll buckle up and crack from the cold. Same with the fog. That's evaporating dry ice."

She pulled a ruler out of her bag and laid it next to a particularly picturesque twist of Formica.

"Put your hand next to the ruler, please," said Ali, and took a few more photos, framing a second shot to get the officer's ID as well as the time showing on his wristwatch. "That's enough. Time for us to get out of here. I need to speak to the owners."

"The survivors are in the back," said the cop. "They have a trailer behind the diner."

"Sure they do. Okay, let's go."

Norman was back out of his van by the time Ali emerged from the diner. He was showing Craig a printout but turned as soon as he spotted Ali. She beckoned to them and waited as they trotted over.

"I think you should stay with the cops," said Ali to Craig. "I don't want the owners here to think I'm taking them seriously. You being there will just increase their status."

"Cops want to be with you while you're interviewing them," said Craig. "They don't trust you. Or me, now, for that matter. I told them that The Ice Queen doesn't exist. That I've never met a Villain by that title or with Ice powers, and they don't believe me. Anyway, my being there might just unsettle the 'survivors' enough to make them tell more truth than they intend."

Ali raised an eyebrow.

"I've been beating myself to death out here trying to get them to believe me," whispered Craig, frustration in the set of his mouth and jaw, "let's try and get these guys to give us the proof we need."

"Oh, for heaven's sake. What do they say about the dry ice damage Norman's reported? Did you mention that evidence to them?"

"Oh yeah, we told them," Craig sighed. "Apparently they're amazed that Ice Queen carries that with her in addition to the liquid nitrogen. Hell of a handbag they must think this woman carries."

"That is just great. Even your fans don't believe you."

Ali muttered a few choice profanities then turned toward the back of the diner. Several officers jogged ahead, and by the time she reached the steps of the trailer a tall thin man wearing a logging jacket and dirty jeans, and a similarly dressed short, thin woman, clutching a burning cigarette in her fist, were emerging.

"'bout time," muttered the woman, heading back into the trailer. The man remained on the top step and, when Ali made no attempt to follow his wife into the trailer, he came down to talk to her.

"You saw inside," said the diner's owner. "That Ice Queen ripped the place up pretty good."

"Looks to me like the place was in bad shape to begin with," said Ali, reaching into her attaché. "Is this an accurate copy of your Super insurance rider? The application you filed two days ago?"

He gave the fax copy a careful look then nodded. "Yeah. That's the SS.C.."

"I am sorry to inform you," said Ali, "that, as the required inspection to assess the value of the property has not taken place, the policy is not in force."

"What?" shrieked the woman, charging back down the steps. "You thief! You're gonna try and keep our money from us 'cause the paperwork's not finished? The hell with you."

Craig caught the woman mid-air as she launched herself at Ali, turned her around and deposited her back in the trailer before she'd finished her rant. The woman blinked in confusion, clutching the door for support.

Her husband gave Craig a worried look, but took a risk, moving closer to tower over Ali. Craig raised an eyebrow and he stepped back.

"That bitch stole ten thousand –" the owner began.

"Fifteen," screamed his wife.

"Fifteen thousand out of our till," echoed the husband. "I paid my first premium. I say the policy's in effect."

"Fifteen thousand? Interesting," said Ali, making a note. "And that would represent, what, three – four years income?"

"One week," declared the husband.

One of the cops snorted at that and Ali smiled at him but continued to talk to the owners.

"If your diner generated that much money at any time in its history, I would be very surprised," she said.

"Don't you be insulting my business. I've been in this same spot for ten years and –"

"Not cleaned it even once from the look of the stove," said Ali. "From the appearance of the interior, I don't believe you were actually running this as a business. Certainly, you would never pass a health inspection and most of the burners on the stove don't work. I could check with the local police, since most of them seem to be here tonight, and find out if any of them ever noticed this was, at any time, a functioning business. However, your time here is not the question. I am informing you that you're not eligible to claim on this policy. If you persist and try to put in a claim, we will assist the police and local authorities to assemble a case for attempted fraud."

The word "Fraud!" echoed across the parking lot, coming from the diner owners and the police.

"Do you have anything you'd like to say," asked Ali. "Any statement you'd like to revise about tonight's events?"

"I've heard about your S.S.C., bitch," cried the woman. "The S.S.C. claims fraud 'cause you can't be bothered helping people. The insurance companies pay you more when they don't have to pay out to policyholders. You can go to hell. If we can't file with the insurance S.S.C. for our money, then we'll sue the S.S.C.!"

The second suit in as many days. Nigel would kill her. Before Ali could defend her S.S.C.'s record, the woman had slammed the door of her trailer shut.

"She was here," shouted the husband. "Looking just like she did in her photo. She was here, and you don't want to admit it. What are you afraid of?" he glared at Ultra Man. "And this coward, he must have been off somewhere hiding. He didn't want to lift a hand to help us then, and he's no damn use now."

With that he dragged open his door and disappeared to join his wife.

Ali turned to the police officers who stood in a circle, scowling at her. So *that* was what she'd missed. The Virginia Sheriff and that farmer were spreading rumors: the big, bad S.S.C. against the poor, defenseless, little guy. She couldn't defend the S.S.C. to the diner owner's but she could try with the local police.

"Detective. Officers. The S.S.C. isn't paid unless the site is a Super

Villain event site. We don't get any kickbacks or any such payments from anyone for not helping those affected by Supers or Villains. We have provided good service to the community for decades. It is our," she jerked her thumb at Norman and Craig, "opinion, based on years of experience, that this is not a Villain site. Therefore S.S.C.'s involvement is ended, unless you call us later to provide expert testimony in a fraud case."

"You can't leave," said the detective, moving between Ali and the van. "This here is a Super crime scene. Otherwise he wouldn't be here."

"I'm here because you were behaving inappropriately toward the staff of the S.S.C. A threatening manner," said Craig, leaning toward the detective and scowling. "We don't like it when our staff is threatened, by anyone. There's a panic button in the van and they pressed it when you started behaving as if our staff were criminals."

"The damage inside was caused by application of dry ice and ordinary water," added Norman, in his electronically altered voice. "Your own crime scene investigators will be able to confirm this. You should check the local party equipment outlets. You'll find these two made a purchase of dry ice sometime in the last two days. It shouldn't be hard to find where they got it from. That stuff doesn't last long."

"You may count on it," finished Ali, "that the S.S.C. will be making those inquiries, and when we find the SS.C. who sold them the dry ice we will forward that information to you and to all the other relevant authorities *and* the press. In the meantime, the Super Support SS.C. is only required to clean up Super/Villain event sites, and in my judgment, this is not one. Good night."

With Craig guarding their retreat they walked through the line of silent police officers toward the van. They hadn't made it halfway before Ali and Norman's phones sounded.

Ali unclipped her phone and swore softly as she read the message.

"What's up?" asked Craig.

"Call the copter," said Ali to Norman. "Tell them to warm up, we'll meet them at the football field in a few minutes."

When Norman trotted away, Ali turned to Craig. He moved closer, wishing he could pick her up, carry her. Take her somewhere, anywhere else. Fatigue was gouging deep lines down her face and the battle light had faded from her eyes, leaving her appearing small and fragile. Ignoring the camera crews and reporters, he put a hand under her elbow and supported her as they walked the last few yards to the van.

"I can't stand it," said Ali, "The message said there have been three other Ice Queen sites reported in our sector tonight. Plus two more in Florida, and one in Nova Scotia."

"Hell's bells," whispered Craig. "But maybe this is what we need. These will help to prove fraud. There's no way any one person – Villain or not - could do all that."

"Wanna bet?" sighed Norman, dropping his pack into the rear of the van and slumping against the door. "By tomorrow they'll be saying that Ice Queen flies faster than Purple Lightning can run."

"It'll take a couple of hours to get to the next site," said Craig, supporting Ali as she climbed up the metal steps into the Chinook's passenger bay. "You should try to get some sleep."

"No. No." Ali staggered as she made her way over the equipment crowded floor to her seat, "I've got reports to write. Photos to upload. We've got to get the information on this site back to Control before those cops and that couple gets their version of the story out."

"Bit late for that," said Norman, turning up the volume on his portable TV. "That pair have probably been on air since we left the site. The news crews started transmitting just as soon as I turned off the block. They're on now, telling the whole world that the S.S.C. stands for Screwed up, Stupid and Corrupt. Right now, the on-air talent is competing with the diner owners to find more insulting wordplay."

"Wonderful," groaned Ali. "A PR nightmare. Just what I needed. Now I'm going to be called in by Mr. Bendit to listen to him recite polling data until my hair falls out."

"I'll try and keep him off you," said Craig.

"You!" cried Ali, slamming her hand into his chest, then shaking it until the stinging faded. "You're not even supposed to be here. You're on suspension. Are you trying to upgrade to fired?"

Craig backed off, his hands raised, just as the co-pilot poked his head around the cockpit door.

"Get secured," said the co-pilot. "Taking off as soon as you're in your seats."

Craig buckled himself in, meeting Ali's still furious glare.

"Why are you traveling with us?" she demanded.

"Well, for one thing, I don't know where the next site is. For the other, hey, I'm tired, too. I thought I'd catch twenty on the way. I suggest you get some sleep. Exhaustion is making your usual sunny disposition just a little cloudy."

Ali sniffed and turned her back on him – as far as her seat belt would allow and sat, laptop balanced on her knees while the Chinook sought altitude. Her fingers tapped out a restless beat as she waited. As soon as the electronics' warning sign clicked off, she opened her computer and resumed working. Norman's fingers danced over his own keyboard and he muttered to himself as he reviewed data.

Craig watched for a while, then pulled himself out of his seat to search for something to drink. There were a few bottles of water in the fridge and a box of cheese crackers so old that their expiration date was from another century. Craig tore open the package anyway, popped one into his mouth, and chased it with a swallow of water. He was leaning against the trembling wall while he drank when Norman joined him in the tiny galley.

"Want something stronger than that?" asked Norman, plugging a device into the only DC socket.

"I should try to sleep," said Craig, "but I'm too wound up. What have you got?"

"Coffee." Norman's smile became smug.

Craig leaned out into the corridor. Ali was still seated, fingers curled over her keyboard, but she was watching Norman's TV. The sound was down low, so Craig couldn't tell what was being said, but from Ali's expression, it wasn't good.

Craig went back into the galley, meeting Norman's curious look.

"I don't know what Ali's told you about all this," Craig began.

"Nothing," said Norman. "Our Ali is good at keeping secrets. So am I, for that matter."

Craig nodded and smiled. The adoring fan stunned fish look had left Norman's face and Craig welcomed the change. He preferred to associate with people who had most of their neurons firing. "This thing with the Ice Queen," said Craig. "They're saying I started it. As far as I'm concerned, it's a media fabrication. At this point, it doesn't really matter who started it. We have to shut the Ice Queen down."

"News services don't usually just make things all the way up," Norman paused in the act of pouring powder into his machine and subjected Craig to a penetrating stare. Not since he'd been caught setting up a stunt in his high school science lab had Craig felt quite such a disappointment. "Are you sure you didn't do anything to set this off?"

Supers shouldn't blush, Craig told himself. For a moment, he used anger to keep the embarrassment away. After all, he was a first ranked Super, he shouldn't have to explain himself to anyone. That thought was closely followed by the one that if Ali ever found out he'd acquired that superior attitude, she'd strip him naked, coat him with chocolate and turn him over to a group of his more rabid fans. He shuddered at the turn his thoughts had taken, straightened his shoulders and faced Norman.

"There is this news clip that The Northern Star is showing everyone, claiming it's evidence I'm admitting I'm scared of a new Villainess, which was recorded when I was having a private conversation with Mysterious West."

"About?"

"About how Ali had just turned me down for a date. Fortunately, or unfortunately, the recording is pretty broken up – West's magical field effect – and Ali's name doesn't show up, otherwise I would be in a lot more trouble than I am right now. Could you imagine what Ali would do to me if it got out that the Ice Queen everyone's talking about is her?"

Norman snorted, then his face flushed. "You called Ali an Ice Queen? I should kick your ass!"

"I didn't. I swear, I didn't say anything like that. How suicidal do you think I am? I..." Craig tunneled his hands through his hair. "God, this is so mixed up."

"Now we've got to fix it," said Norman, after a pause, his voice expressionless.

"Yeah. Well. I keep hoping that a simple, easy solution will present itself. I've even considered calling the press and telling them it's some kind of joke I was playing on them. I keep thinking that maybe I should ask Ali to do a press conference with me and say that she'd turned me down for a date. Except I don't want to expose her to that sort of embarrassment – she'd never speak to me again. And there's that idiot from Oversight. I want to keep Ali off *his* radar."

"That wouldn't be a good idea for a couple of reasons," said Norman, pouring Craig a cup of coffee. "For one, the press would not take well to being the butt of a prank of that nature. Not now. It's far too late. The time for that was about thirty seconds after all this started. For another, it would undermine your reputation, and that would be a very bad idea. Do you remember that silly, campy kid's show years ago that had a Super Team taking on a new Villain every week? It was in re-runs a while back, and I was winning major money guessing which episode had been shown the night before just by looking at Ali's face in the morning. She hates, and I mean hates 'The Practical Joker.' Whenever he was An,

Ali was fit to be tied."

Craig sipped a little coffee, choked and gasped as the high-octane caffeine tore down his throat and fizzled along his nerves. He ran his hand over his hair, just to check it hadn't burned off.

"God, what do you put in this?"

Norman shrugged modestly, ducking his head to hide his smile.

"My own recipe," he said. "A few beans of this, a few beans of that. Roast them myself in a machine I designed to really pull out the caffeine. Anyway, you did know that Ali's dad was a practical joker, didn't you? When her mother got divorced, she cited his jokes as a form of emotional and physical abuse."

"Uh oh," said Craig, adding several sweeteners and half a cup of cream to the coffee and taking another cautious sip. Then he stopped, focusing on what Norman had just said. "Oh, God, no. That can't be it!"

"Uh huh. I know you went through a stage of putting criminals up trees and chimneys and upside down in trash cans, and leaving them interesting places, with witty notes stuck on them, to wait for the cops. Ali was furious. She said being arrested and beaten up was bad enough, without being publicly humiliated."

"Oh," Craig stared into his cup. "I got called in by Mr. Crunch and Mr. Hackham pretty quickly. They said that someone in the SS.C. complained about me, I never found out who."

"If anyone, I think it was Mr. Bendit, not Ali. She wasn't with us then. Bendit's the one who's always preoccupied about the SS.C.'s public image."

Craig stared at the vibrating ceiling, "They were right to stop me. I was getting full of myself and needed to be reminded that my job was to arrest the bad guys, not try out for the world's funniest video awards. But I don't believe that Ali thinks I'm like The Practical Joker. Sure, I pulled a few tricks at school and college, but they were routine stuff. Standard adolescent pranks."

"Ah, but Ali is hypersensitive to pranks of any sort. Remember? Her dad elevated tricks and pranks to the level of *abuse*. She couldn't go to bed at night without checking her pajamas for booby traps. The one time she stayed at a friend's house overnight to avoid whatever April Fool's day trick he'd planned, he called her school and told her teacher she had a contagious GI bug and fleas. They practically threw her out of the classroom, embarrassing her in front of all the other students. And when he was called to collect her, he laughed at her all the way home because his stunt had worked so well. But the worst part of his stunts, she told me, was if she or her mother got upset, he'd just walk away, saying they had no sense of humor. If they were mad or upset, it was all their own fault."

"Oh, man," groaned Craig, remembering how many times he had chided Ali to lighten up. "No wonder she hates me."

"Maybe," Norman topped up his coffee. "I'd be careful if I were you. Ali got some revenge later."

"What?"

Norman chuckled. "When she got recruited for the S.S.C., she tracked down her dad and told him. Just that she was recruited, nothing about Super Powers, or only working in the Super Clean division. Just that she'd been hired by the S.S.C. Despite the security warning, like an idiot, her dad boasted all over town that his daughter was the new Super, and then he waited. But there was no announcement on CNN, no news reports and no hometown visit. And, to really rub it in, Ali made sure the SS.C. didn't relocate him. He had to continue working at the same place, with everyone in town laughing at him."

"Ah, revenge," Craig grinned, then straightened "Uh, does she go for revenge often?"

"You mean, if you offend Ali can you expect spiders in your boots, things like that?"

Craig nodded.

"Not to worry. She doesn't go in for that sort of stuff." Norman waited until Craig let out a sigh of relief before adding. "Usually she finds other ways to make you regret your sins."

Distinctly unsettled, Craig took his cup, "Uh, Norman, can we keep this conversation just between us guys?"

Norman poured a couple of cups full, set them on a tray and turned toward the cockpit. "Maybe."

Please, Norman, buddy. You may not believe it, but Ali is important to me. This last week is the first time in ages that she's spoken more than two words to me that weren't work-related. I can't let some newspaper's intentional misinterpretation of my words screw that up."

After a moment, Norman grinned and nodded. "Sure. And in exchange you make a surprise appearance at my sister's kid's birthday party this year."

"Norm, that's against the rules. It would put your identity at risk."

"Nah, I'm not going to tell her you're coming. I'll be as surprised as anyone. Just drop in, say you'd been flying over on patrol and spotted the birthday cake. Say hi to the kids, eat a slice of cake and leave. You don't have to be on the ground for more than five minutes. Please, it would make my niece's day."

"Deal," said Craig with a sigh. "But if Bendit finds out about it, I'm telling him it was your idea."

The two men shook hands, then Craig made his way back to the seats, sliding in beside Ali. She sniffed his cup and wrinkled her nose.

"I should warn you about Norman's special blend coffee. Too much of that and your hair starts picking up FM radio."

"I can take it," laughed Craig. "I'm tough. Resilience is one of my Powers. How about you? Do you want coffee, or sleep?"

Ali bit back a yawn, then gave in and stretched her jaw muscles. "Sleep, apparently," she said, closing her computer down and tilting back her chair. "Do we have an ETA?"

"No one's said yet," said Craig. "Relax. We'll wake you in plenty of time."

Ali nodded, pulled her coat tight around her shoulders and closed her eyes.

Craig tilted back his own chair, coffee held carefully in his left hand and waited. After only a few minutes Ali's breathing slowed and her body lost that tension that marked an awake and active mind. He reached out his right arm and eased her body towards his until her head rested on his shoulder. He curled his arm around her body, holding her tight where she belonged. Now, if he could only turn back time, undo most of his adolescence and persuade her of that fact.

Chapter Twelve.

The Northern Star special Ice Queen edition.
Super Speedy Ice Queen in orgy of destruction!
Details page 1, 2 - 7, 14 - 17 and 26 - 30.

Ali was staggering by the time she made it into the S.S.C. office the next afternoon. Norman was still at the last site, as the chemicals that had been used to simulate the Ice Queen's attack had not yet been identified, and he'd chosen to stay and supervise the clean-up.

Craig, thank heaven, had stayed with her through the whole ordeal – ignoring two messages summoning him home. If he hadn't been there, it was likely she'd have been arrested outside the destroyed gas station in the Bronx. On reflection, arguing with a man who was claiming the serious burns on his hand were due to trying to hold onto the Ice Queen's arm, instead of holding dry ice too long, wasn't the wisest thing she'd ever done. Not when said man outweighed her by forty pounds – all Nordic tattooed muscle.

The brief naps between sites hadn't been enough. She was up, moving and still coherent, yes. Tolerant of flagrant stupidity, no.

Homicidal? If things didn't improve that likelihood was increasing.

But Craig could not stay with her here at headquarters. Now that it was common knowledge that he'd spent the night helping her, he'd been called in to explain. By now, Control had his ass slow cooking over an open flame.

Still, despite the fatigue, she had her reports typed and emailed in. Norman had sent the evidence back with her, all gathered in neat little bags and ready for the forensic department. The gas station was, of course, a dry ice event. At the Farmington, Connecticut site she'd suggested to the affected family that their young son needed behavioral counseling (and that he would probably be recruited by a chemical SS.C. before he'd even graduated from high school). Norman had been unable to identify the chemical mess he'd used to dissolve his sister's bedroom furniture.

The half-finished hotel in New Jersey, whose builder had run out of funds according to the S.S.C. night duty researcher, was significantly damaged by the now traditional liquid nitrogen.

There'd been a fourth call about mid-morning that she was putting - haha – on ice until she'd gotten some sleep. What really had her hair standing on end and was twisting in her gut was that, despite everything she'd seen last night, and everything she'd tried to do, not one of the police departments she was required to deal with was prepared to admit that *their* site was not a true and legitimate Ice Queen crime scene.

It was enough to make her wish she carried a flamethrower, or something similarly powerful, to hold against their throats until they all acknowledged that she was right and they were all dead wrong. She wanted the Ice Queen problem to go away. More than she wanted to sleep, more than she wanted food, she wanted this roller coaster to stop and let her off. She slumped against the elevator wall as it carried her up to the Legal department.

When the doors opened to reveal Nigel's secretary waiting for her, Ali's first impulse was to hit the close door button and go right back down again. Before she could act, Lena had grabbed the doors and held them open.

"They're waiting for you in the conference room," she said.

"They who?" asked Ali, not moving from her place against the wall.

"The senior partners, Control, the Colonel and the head of Oversight," said Lena leading the way down the corridor. "Emergency meeting called to address the Ice Queen crisis."

It took Lena a few steps to realize Ali was not following her. Instead Ali was staring up at the ceiling, hands raised above her head.

"Why me? Why me?" Ali's voice echoed plaintively across the foyer.

The receptionists glanced up and around. Those waiting for their attention turned to stare.

"Come on, you," said Lena, catching Ali by the arm and dragging her away from her audience.

The fifth-floor conference room was larger and more opulent than the third-floor room Ali had taken over. Currently each of the room's leather chairs was occupied by every one of the SS.C.'s lawyers, with their secretaries and assistants ranked, tall, straight and looking well-rested, along the wall. Control, her china-doll pale face glowing in the mid-afternoon light, sat at the head of the table, her attention focused on the computer at her elbow, did not even twitch as Ali entered. That was nothing new. Control rarely gave warning before she struck. Ali had never received a reprimand from Control, although she had heard chilling rumors.

Beside her sat The Colonel, his sharp-planed, narrow face impassive. Since retiring from the military to work for the S.S.C., The Colonel had let his black hair grow long, and wore it unbound, straight down his back. His attention had been on the sketch pad before him as he doodled a design for yet another super tool, but he glanced up to watch as Ali walked in. He wrote a few words on a scrap of paper and passed it and the doodle to one of his assistants, without taking his gaze from Ali.

On the other side of the table sat several men in suits. Ali recognized a few who haunted the corridors of the S.S.C., including the unpopular representative of Oversight and Mr. White. No one else met her eyes or otherwise acknowledged her arrival. She was not invited to take a seat. Instead, she walked to the end of the table and rested her fingers on the polished wood. Mr. Bendit came to his feet and slid a folder across the table to her.

"Ms. Brent. Please examine the documents in that file. Will you confirm the contents to be your work?"

It took Ali a moment to read through and realize that it was everything she'd written about the Ice Queen, including an email she'd transmitted less than ten minutes ago during the taxi ride in from the airport. She closed the folder and pushed it back across the table. "I wrote these reports," she said, trying and failing to keep her voice from trembling.

Mr. White started to speak, but Mr. Bendit held up his hand. "Ms. Brent, can you explain why your reports are inconsistent with data that has come from other sources?"

"Inconsistent in what way, and to what other sources?" demanded Ali.

Mr. Bendit pointed to a mixture of newspapers, police reports and some pieces printed on S.S.C. letterhead scattered across the table. Ali scanned the first few pages and bit back a groan. Each one was a report on a site that she'd declared an Ice Queen fraud, and all of them directly contradicted her. There were S.S.C. reports from other regions - Site Supervisor reports from Nova Scotia and Florida all saying they'd declared their sites genuine Villain event sites. Ali raised her eyes to Mr. Bendit's and swallowed hard before speaking.

"Where are Norman's reports?"

"I am asking the questions. Please confine your replies to the matter before us."

Ali pressed one hand against her churning stomach and breathed deeply to calm her pounding heart.

"With all due respect, Mr. Bendit, but no, I won't. I have been to site after site since all this began, and gathered sufficient evidence, that if it had been any other occasion, or Villain, no one would have questioned my conclusions. But as the alleged victims claimed these are Ice Queen events, no one believes the evidence."

"Ms. Brent –" began Mr. Bendit.

"No,' cried Ali, her voice growing shrill. Her vision was growing fuzzy around the edges and her feet burned. A few minutes more of this, and she'd either cry or go looking for a sharp knife – or a flamethrower. "I've been to these sites. Me, the person you trained to look for fraud. I've done the reviews and examined the evidence. Norman Jones, one of the most experienced of our Site Examiners, agrees with me all down the line. The sites I visited were all clumsy attempts to simulate a Super Villain attack utilizing commonly available tools. Frauds. They are all, every blessed one of them, *frauds!*"

"Ms. Brent. Ali." Mr. Hackham shifted in his armchair. "Your tone is inappropriate."

"I don't care what you think about my tone, my attitude or my shoes, *Nigel*. I've been bounced around like a pinball for the last few days, chasing after a *non-existent* Villainess and frankly I'm tired of everyone else's attitude. The Ice Queen doesn't exist. What is it going to take to get you all to acknowledge the truth?"

"Sit down," said Mr. Crunch, softly.

"I'm tired of not being believed," said Ali, ignoring the invitation even though her feet and legs ached. "Tired of meeting with police officers who act as if I'm out to steal money from helpless little old ladies, instead of them doing their jobs and investigating crimes. They've become so accustomed to Villains dropping out of the sky and the S.S.C. coming in and cleaning up that if there is the slightest hint of a Super Power, they turn into traffic cones. I'm especially tired of people who think that they can pull the stupidest cons and get me to believe them. And the worst of it is coming back *here* and having my skills and my assessments disregarded by the people who trained me to be on the lookout for these exact cons."

She leaned against the table, struggling to stay upright. Those at the table watched her as if she were some curious form of mold they'd found on their breakfast bagels.

"Ms. Brent, we are not challenging your professionalism," said Mr. Bendit. "Certainly, you have put in a great number of hours on this project. Perhaps, once you have had some rest and reviewed the situation in your own mind, you might find yourself reaching other conclusions. I recommend that you be given this opportunity. Go home. Get some sleep. When you come back tomorrow you can look at this data with fresh eyes. Mature reflection, yes, will help us all."

"And if during this mature reflection I should suddenly realize that the Ice Queen has managed to fly from Nova Scotia to Florida to Boston in one night and perform all these acts of petty vandalism along the way, then you'll get out the *good* champagne and we'll all celebrate?"

"Ms. Brent," said Mr. White, leaning forward. "You do understand, I hope, how important it is that the community trust the Supers. There are significant problems, not the least of which are Powered criminals, out there that could not be dealt with without the help of the Super Teams. For there to be uncertainty, contradictions, coming from those who are supposed to be in the know regarding those threats, then people become distressed and worried. It is necessary that we speak with one voice and one opinion. It is the view of the Oversight committee and administration here at S.S.C. that the Ice Queen represents a significant public safety risk. We are asking you, as a Site Supervisor of many years' experience, for your support and assistance."

They might think her mold on their bread, but Ali regarded Mr. White as if he were something smelly decaying on the side of the road. "Bullshit! You're saying that all I have to do is give you the reports you want to see and you'll, what, *like* me? Really, really *like* me? We'll be *best buddies forever*? To say that the Ice Queen spits liquid nitrogen and shits dry ice bricks? I say that, and I'm the star, the teacher's pet. Then we'll all go out and tell the civilians that we're sworn to protect that they should worry about a Villain that doesn't exist. Shall we tell them to check under their beds for The Boogieman as well? I hear he's been seen in these parts. Ask any two-year-old. Tell them to watch out for the tooth fairy? There's a rumor going around that she's stopped waiting for teeth to fall out and she's going in after them armed with really, really big pliers. Well, I've got news for you bozos, I'm not going to add to the hysteria. I'm going to continue reviewing sites and record, accurately, the evidence I uncover until I'm fired. If you don't like it, learn to live with the pain. I'm not changing the truth to make you happy."

"Ms. Brent," said Mr. Bendit, mildly. "Has it occurred to you that you may be incorrect? There must be some doubt in your mind, as everyone else disagrees with your conclusions. Have you forgotten that there are certain sorts of madness in which total conviction in your own beliefs despite proofs, is the major symptom?"

Ali let out a shaky laugh. "Oh, sure. Except for one or two things. First, I'm not alone. A Site Examiner with more experience than anyone else in the SS.C. agrees with me. Norman Jones was doing Crime Scene analysis for the Florida police for twenty years before S.S.C. recruited him. Two, I may not be the only one who's crazy, since you absolutely believe in the existence of this Ice Queen in the *absence* of any reliable proof. And by reliable, I don't mean some farmer from the back of nowhere. I mean someone who is at least impartial. But no. There is no independent verification of the existence of the Ice Queen. And, finally, *none* of the Super Team members have reported contact with her."

"Ultra Man –" said several voices.

"No!" shouted Ali, slamming her hand on the table. At their shocked looks, she took a deep breath and lowered her voice. "No. I've spoken to Ultra

Man, Mysterious West and Purple Lightning. They all state, quite unequivocally, that there was no new Villain at the apartment event site last week. Norman and I, and the Site Manager assigned to clean up the scene have evaluated the damage, which was no different from any other building collapse. Water damage was consistent with broken pipes. There was no ice!"

"Ms. Brent – Ali," said Mr. White. "You aren't helping your case by quoting Ultra Man as your evidence. Suspicions have been raised regarding his, shall we say, his reliability in this regard."

"According to whom? You? The people who want to believe that Ice Queen exists? I think he can live quite happily without your *regard*."

Mr. White turned several shades of red at the sneer in her voice, and his neck swelled to strain against his starched shirt.

"Keep in mind, Ms. Brent," he said, "many people would advise you that keeping my good opinion is vitally important."

"And I think I could find one or two people who think you are a complete moron," shot back Ali, shaking with rage.

Control raised her hand. There was instant silence and everyone turned to face her.

"This is getting us nowhere," said Control in her soft measured tones. "Ms. Brent, do you hold to your reports? You state that they contain a complete and accurate record of the sites you have reviewed to the best of your ability, training and knowledge?"

"Yes, ma'am."

"And you will not change, alter, amend or add to these reports?"

"No, ma'am."

"That is unfortunate, Ms. Brent." Control sat back, returned her attention to the screen beside her and seemed to lose interest in the proceedings.

"It is unacceptable," said Mr. White, and reached for Ali's reports. "Assign someone else to do a secondary review of these reports. You have enough personnel in this building to find a competent –"

"If you alter one word of those files, then take my name off them," said Ali, clenching her fists to stop her hands from shaking. "I will not be a party to a fraud. If one comma is moved, one adjective erased, then it's not my work."

"I'm certain we can find someone who'd be delighted to sign," said Mr. White. "Many, in fact."

"Getting a lot of people to go along with a crime isn't a virtue, *Mr.* White," said Ali. "But if that's what you want, go get them and put them to work. I quit."

"Wonderful," said Mr. White and drew his pen across the outside of the folder, striking through Ali's name.

"Ms. Brent, I should advise you to reconsider your actions," said Mr. Crunch.

Ali shook her head and regretted it instantly as the movement almost had her on the floor. "Frankly, sir, if this SS.C. is condoning insurance fraud and ignoring the evidence that's been presented, then it isn't the SS.C. I signed on to work for. So, again, I quit."

"I am sorry to hear that," said Mr. Hackham, rising, "Lena? Please escort Ms. Brent to her office. She may take her purse and personal items with her. Anything else belonging to her will be mailed later, along with her final paycheck."

Ali gave him one sharp nod of acknowledgment, turned her back on Mr. White and followed Lena from the room. Halfway down the corridor, the reality of what she'd done hit her and she slumped against the wall, shaking.

She'd quit. Quit. The only job she'd ever had, and she'd quit. With all its demands and midnight callouts, it had been the most interesting, challenging job she could imagine. Even if the gang-of-four gave her a halfway reasonable reference, there was no way she'd work anywhere in the insurance business again, and she didn't know anything else. She'd lived, breathed the Supers for years, and had no other life. She ran a hand over her face, imagining Oliver's furious reaction when he heard. Then it occurred to her that Oliver might not be allowed to visit anymore, and she started to cry. Lena wrapped an arm around her shoulders and half carried, half pulled Ali into her ex-office. Eliza jumped up from the table and ran to help.

"Ali! What happened? You look like death."

"She quit," said Lena, her voice trembling. "She called Mr. White a moron, to his face, and she quit."

"Oh, my God. Ali, you didn't! Who's going to do your job? I can't."

"You'll have to," said Lena.

"Of course, she can't," said Ali, crossly. The crisis facing those she was leaving behind scattered the fog that threatened to take over her brain. She rose, rubbed the back of her hand across her wet face and crossed to her desk, grabbing a notebook and pen. "Eliza's the single mother of a two-year-old. She can't be taking night calls. The overtime payments to the babysitter would bankrupt her. Besides, with a kid, I can't see her taking the risk of being one of the SS.C.'s *naked faces*," Ali pressed her fingers against her aching eyes and breathed deep ... once ... twice, then she reached into her drawer for the caffeine pills. Not waiting for the chemicals to hit her system she focused on the other women. "Okay, Eliza, get in touch with the Texas office. Ask for Johnson to be transferred up here ASAP. Tomorrow if possible. He's a complete jackass when it comes to interpersonal skills, but he's got a good eye and he's obsessive about details. He's been a naked face for the SS.C. before, and he's got enough experience that he can take over from me without too much ramp up time. Send James from the San Francisco office down to Texas to replace Johnson as Supervisor, along with an apology. You know what James can be like. But he's a warm body and he'll fill in there, short-term. That mustache of his is so ugly that no one is going to believe *that* is his real face. San Fran hasn't had much action since The Hammer Head was arrested, so they won't miss him much. Call Lee in Boston and tell him he's taking first call for the Tri-state area, whether he wants it or not. Arrange with Control's office for his security. Get hold of Albert, tell him fun's over, retirement can wait, and get him back on the job in the Midwest Region. We can't wait for them to hire someone. When they do, Albert can train him then go back to his fly fishing."

"You don't have the authority to order this," protested Lena. "Even if you hadn't quit."

"To hell with that," said Ali, grabbing a few photos and ornaments off the table and stuffing them into her attaché. Then she stared down at the ugly, horrible, heavy boots The Colonel had issued her and stepped out of them with a sigh. She rubbed her feet on the carpet and glanced around. Her cheap trainers were still under her desk, and she sat down to pull them on her swollen feet. "Do you think I care? They've called me a *Senior* Supervisor for a year and never permitted me to make a single decision for this department. Consider this my parting gift to the SS.C., doing what I should have done when I accepted the promotion. And now you, Lena."

The secretary shrank back, her eyes flashing back and forth as she sought an exit.

"Dig out that list of relocated family members," said Ali, "See if there are any on it with more than one functioning brain cell and something resembling insurance experience. Pull them in ASAP. Eliza can arrange for their training. She'll need about seventeen to bring all the US districts up to minimal staffing levels."

"They're not going to like this," warned Lena.

"As if I care at this point," said Ali, kneeling to reach under the desk for the remains of her candy stash. "Besides, they can fire and relocate them as soon as the relatives they've been holding these positions for graduate high school or get out of jail. You never know, we might show them that hiring people with functioning brains and people skills to do the job is an interesting innovation."

Eliza shared a glance with Lena and then they started to laugh.

"What do you think, Crunch?" Mr. Hackham waited until the door closed behind Ali and Lena, opened his leatherbound diary and held his silver fountain pen poised over the page. "Will two days be enough for our Ali, or shall I wait a week?"

"A week for what?" demanded Mr. White, pausing in his note writing. The pages in Ali's folder were already liberally covered with crossings and scribbled notes.

Mr. Crunch raised one gray eyebrow. "Before we approach Ms. Brent and offer to rehire her, of course. She is, after all, a trained Super Event Site Supervisor. A woman with sufficient courage to represent the S.S.C. in the face of a devastated public. And if you think it is easy to identify and train one of those, sir, you are sadly mistaken."

"Any reasonably competent insurance assessor could do her job," sneered Mr. White.

"Hardly,' said Mr. Hackham. "It requires the balance of a tightrope walker, the courage of a lion tamer, and the backbone of, well, an elephant, I suppose, to deal with the many and varied challenges of walking onto a Super event site before the dust has finished settling. The general public, bless their hearts, tend to get a little tetchy once the Supers leave the scene and they get a glimpse of what remains of their homes and businesses."

"Three days, I think," said Mr. Breakham, glancing up from his book for the first time that meeting. "Given our current situation and workload, I don't think we can afford to be without her longer. There is still the matter of the Midwest region. She has to continue covering for us there until my nephew finishes college, and then he will need to be trained. I cannot think of anyone else who will be able to make him understand his duties."

"Agreed," said Mr. Crunch. "Three days is sufficient to cool her temper, and for her to consider her lack of options. I would suggest a personal visit to drop off her final paycheck. That, properly handled, will serve to bring the desired regret to the appropriate level. Who would be best for that visit? Mr. Hackham? You are her direct Supervisor. Can you handle this assignment?"

"Are you insane?!" demanded Mr. White. "That woman is insolent and uncooperative. She took Ultra Man's side in an argument with you, her employers. You can't possibly want to keep her on, no matter how serious the temporary inconvenience. S.S.C. needs employees who are completely loyal to the SS.C., and she rejected a simple request she demonstrate that virtue."

"We do not need you to tell us how to run our SS.C.," said Control, straightening in her chair as the lawyers nodded. "You are here in an advisory capacity only. Additionally, we have no doubts about Ms. Brent's loyalty. She was under our observation for years prior to her recruitment. No one has ever reported any suggestion that she has flaunted her association with us. Despite being one of our public faces, it has not been necessary, in three years, for her to be relocated. She comports herself well, maintains security and has proven herself worthy of being entrusted with the secret identities of at least three of our Supers. It is entirely possible she knows more than that, but even *I* do not know how many, because she keeps the secrets so well."

"You're joking," gasped Mr. White. "You've let someone with that information just walk out? She's angry as hell, and angry people have been known to make mistakes. Change loyalties. *Go to the press!*"

"We have no concerns regarding Ms. Brent's loyalty," repeated Mr. Hackham, calmly, "and, given her attitude toward the press, can safely count on her silence."

"I cannot share your complacent attitude," said Mr. White, beckoning to one of his associates. "How much does she know about the S.S.C.? How dangerous could she be?"

Control, The Colonel and the lawyers all stiffened.

"Know? I imagine she knows a great deal, Mr. White," said Mr. Crunch, "but while she is currently peeved with us, she is still aware of the implications of any revelations. She knows very well how many people will suffer if she releases a single secret identity. I know she will not –"

"We simply cannot take the risk," said Mr. White, and whispered for a moment to his lackey. The man nodded and left the room at a run. Mr. White sat back in his chair and regarded the room's occupants over the tips of his folded fingers. "You may be willing to take her back, but until she's cooled down, it'd be better to keep her in protective custody, just so she isn't tempted to do something foolish. Something damaging, like taking her irresponsible ideas about the Ice Queen to the press."

"It is not S.S.C. policy to take ex-employees prisoner," said Control, anger raising a faint blush on her porcelain skin.

"How fortunate that I am here to do that for you." With that, Mr. White rose, gathered his papers together and left.

All eyes tracked the exit of Mr. White and his entourage. Control's fingers flickered over her keyboard for several minutes before she glanced up to face the others.

"I have notified Security that they are to ensure that no one offers Ms. Brent any discourtesy as she leaves the building."

Control paused, then scanned the room as a sound similar to a badly balanced load of gravel in a cement mixer filled the room. She finally tracked the source of the sound.

Mr. Crunch.

Grinding his teeth.

He was staring at the closed door with an intensity that chilled. His teeth were visible, but no one looking at him would mistake his expression for a smile.

"I agree with you, Mr. Crunch," said Control, after a moment, "Mr. White has far exceeded any imagined usefulness." She turned to regard the perpetually perspiring Mr. Bendit, who tossed another handful of damp tissues into the trash.

"Mr. White is a political appointee," Mr. Bendit reminded her.

"Then," said Control, her voice deepening as she came to her feet, "it is past time that he was pointed in another direction."

Chapter Thirteen.

The Morning Star.

The Church of The End is Nigh has issued a statement that the world will end at 6:23 PM, Friday next, unless 63 million dollars is raised and given to God. When asked how the transfer of funds was going to take place, Arch Deacon Alexander Wilson said that the world not ending would be the first miracle of the Third Age. The collection of the funds by God would be the second.

Eliza shifted uncomfortably from one foot to another, glancing up and down the street. Up at the sky. Everywhere, to avoid looking directly at Ali.

"The taxi should be along in a minute," she said, for the third time in five minutes.

Ali smiled at her ex-secretary and resettled her attaché strap on her shoulder. Poor Eliza was almost bouncing in place as she wrung her hands and tore tissues into confetti. Either she liked Ali more than Ali had realized, or, maybe, she was imagining trying to deal with the piles and piles of paperwork once Ali was gone.

"Relax, Eliza, I'll be fine," said Ali, balancing a box on one arm and resting her other hand on Eliza's shoulder. She tightened the grip until Eliza stopped fidgeting. "You go back inside, and I'll call you when I get home."

"No really, it's – ." Eliza began then gasped.

A white van skidded to a halt in front of them. The sliding door facing the pavement slammed open and two men in grey suits leaped out. Eliza screamed as she was pushed to the ground by a third man and lay sprawled on the pavement. Ali froze, gaping at Eliza. Before her mind could resume control of her body, two men seized Ali, sending her belongings flying out of her hands, and started dragging her toward the van.

Alarms sounded within the S.S.C. building. Shouting security guards charged toward them. Ali threw herself toward one of the men holding her, hoping to push him off balance. S.S.C. security would be beside her in seconds; if she could only stay out of the van she'd be safe. Her attacker sagged, but recovered, throwing her off toward his partner. She kicked, her feet sliding down the side of his leg – and for a moment, Ali regretted kicking off her work boots. Instead of releasing her, the man's grip only tightened. She tried to dig in with her heels, but they slipped on the pavement, sending one leg between the legs of the man carrying her. He stumbled, swearing as he tried to untangle their legs. Before Ali could take advantage of him, he seized her arms and threw her toward the open van.

Her hands came up and she braced for an impact that didn't come. At least, not in the way she expected. Over-heated arms grabbed her around the waist and her stomach sank to her feet. Icy cold air tore across her exposed skin. After a few seconds, she blinked and raised one hand to shield her eyes. The ground was rapidly falling away. Already the rushing air was chilling her to her bones. Her hair whipped across her face bringing tears to her eyes. The attaché slung over her shoulder bumped rhythmically against her back.

"So," shouted Ali. The buffeting wind made it difficult for her keep her eyes open, something she was grateful for when she saw how high and how fast they were flying. "If I ask what's going on, will I regret it?"

"Congratulations," said Craig, grinning at her. "We are now fugitives from the law."

Craig flew too high and fast for conversation. Several breathless, freezing miles later, he descended, landing them on the uneven ground at the back of an abandoned gas station beside a busy highway. Ali staggered, rubbing her arms frantically, trying to restore circulation to her numbed body. Craig scanned the sky above them, then drew her under the dubious protection of an overhang and started rubbing his Power heated hands over her arms and back. Ali stamped her feet and shivered, struggling to keep her teeth from chattering themselves to splinters.

He wrapped his arms around her, pulling her close to his Super-heated body. Ali sighed and let his warmth leak in. She sagged as the sleepless night and stress caught up with her. She would move away from him, stand on her own two feet, just as soon as her brain and body started talking to each other again. Right now, it was easier to just let him take care of the remaining upright problem.

"You want to explain what happened?" asked Ali, when she had some control over her voice.

"I was waiting for you to head home. I didn't know where you'd left your car, but I thought I'd watch the main exit, catch you when you left. I figured we have a lot to talk about. While I was waiting, I saw that van and those guys. Well, I couldn't let them take you, so I rescued you."

"Do you know who they were?" asked Ali.

"Near as I can tell from the earpieces, severe haircuts and the lack of uniforms, I figure National Security, maybe FBI, or one of the other acronyms. I don't think any crook would be stupid enough to attack an S.S.C. employee right outside SS.C. headquarters."

"What? Why would they try and grab me?"

"I have no idea," said Craig. "What happened after you reported in?"

"I got dragged into a high-level meeting. All the Powers-That-Be, and the annoying moron, White. I couldn't believe it. They've just decided they don't want to hear or see anything other than more proof that the Ice Queen is an evil vandal, with nothing better to do with her time than fly around the countryside destroying failed businesses, empty buildings and, and," Ali grabbed her hair and let out a long whistling scream. "I can't believe it. Why do they want to believe so much? It was like looking at the Three Dumb Monkeys. See no truth, hear no logic, agree with stupid."

"Oh, yeah," Craig laughed, tightened his grip and pressed his face to her tangled hair. "I suppose it's like that situation you get with detectives when they're working a case. Sometimes they get so fixated on their theory of the crime that they ignore all contradictory evidence and twist all the rest into fitting their theory. It's been documented over and over again. WSon we go to the S.S.C. with our evidence, they just can't accept it. Things have gone so far that we can't win with simple evidence, simple logic anymore. They've got too much invested in this Ice Queen scenario."

"What can we do?" Ali shook herself free of Craig's grip. The shivering in her blood was from residual cold, she told herself, forcing her still numb body to move.

"We keep to the original plan," said Craig. "We change where their attention is directed. Give them the dramatic capture of Nuclear Man. Are you up for it?"

"I guess so," said Ali. "Tell me, where are we going to start?"

"Right here," said Craig, waving at the mini-mall behind them.

"A closed computer store?" asked Ali.

"It's the best computer repair store on the East *or* West coast."

"Why are we here?"

"To get help. I can't fly us everywhere. By now, I'm sure Control will have satellites searching for us. It is possible to dodge them, but I don't want to risk it. Not with a passenger. We can't get caught until we either can prove Ice Queen doesn't exist, or we catch Nuclear Man."

Ali regarded the empty parking lot with the boarded-up stores without enthusiasm. The only functioning store in the mini-mall appeared to be the computer repair store. Despite the 'open' sign hanging in the door, its windows were inches thick with dust, so it was barely possible to make out the interior. Craig pushed open the door and led Ali in.

A bell attached to the inside of the door gave one anemic 'ding' then hung limply on a frayed string. The scent of aged dust filled the air. Piles of computer equipment were stacked to the ceiling. Cases leaking cables, wires, and other debris spread across the room. Ali scanned the interior, giving it the same concentrated attention she gave to an event site. Mixed in with the gutted computer towers and the fractured remains of old Ataris were a few high end, modern systems, blade servers and piles of multi-gig hard-drives. While Ali was distracted, Craig vanished between the shelves.

"Hey, there!" A woman emerged from the back room brushing dust off her hands with a paper towel. She focused on Ali with difficulty, blinking her eyes rapidly behind thick glasses. "Can I help you?"

Craig jumped out from behind a leaning tower of towers and covered the woman's eyes with his hands.

"Guess who," he growled.

The woman squealed and clutched at his hands. Alarmed, Ali leaped to her rescue.

"Hey Craig, cut it out. Put her down."

"Craig?" repeated the woman, gripping the Super's wrists. "Craig Duane, you let me go right now."

When he released her she spun, flinging her arms around him, shrieking with joy. He lifted her in both arms, swinging her as effortlessly as if she were a mere child.

"I haven't seen you for a dog's age," cried the woman when her feet were back on the ground. "Where've you been hiding?"

Ali watched as Craig hugged her back and wondered at the urge to pull them apart that gripped her. "If I could interrupt....," said Ali, "and ask for an introduction?"

Laughing, the two separated. Craig kept his arm draped over the shoulder of the tall, square-faced woman, whose dark blonde hair was held off her face by a backward baseball cap – bearing the Super Clean logo!

"Sure. Ali, this is Delia Cobb. Although you probably know her better as *Computer Destructo Woman.*"

Ali gaped at them for a moment, then walked over, grabbed Craig by his shirt front and started pulling.

"Could I have a word? Excuse us," she said to the woman before drawing Craig across the room. When she had him alone, she slapped him sharply across the back of his skull. "Are you completely nuts? We're trying to get back into the good graces of the S.S.C., and you go to see a known criminal? Do you know what they'll do to you if they find out you've known where she's been hiding, and you didn't bring her in?"

"I did bring her in," said Craig, smoothly turning her to face Delia. "A few years ago. Now, come on over, say 'Hi' like a good girl, and we'll explain."

Dragging her heels didn't help as Craig pushed Ali across the room. Face to face with the smiling Delia, Ali reluctantly held out her hand.

"Hi."

"Hey, Ali," said Delia, giving the offered hand a firm shake. "Take a weight off your brain, kid. I have to say it's nice to meet you in person. I've seen you on TV so often I feel like I know you."

"Excuse me?" said Ali, "I'm not on TV, you've got me mixed up with someone else."

"Oh, no?" Delia led the way between stacks of computer parts to her workroom. "Mostly, it's been long camera zooms of you climbing over event sites. But the last couple of days, there've been some very interesting shots. You arguing with cops. Getting thrown off crime scenes. Things like that." She threw a smile over her shoulder. "All very entertaining."

"Aw, hell," said Ali, sinking into an old office chair.

So much for her precious anonymity. She'd made the decision to go barefaced knowing the risks, but if a stranger could identify her, how long before her old friends made the connection? Old enemies?

"Still," continued Delia, "I think today's shots are much more dramatic."

She clicked on a TV set and started channel flipping. It didn't take long for her to find a news channel showing film of Craig – in Ultra Man uniform – diving down out of the sky and snatching Ali out of the hands of the dark-suited goons.

"Hell and damn," cried Ali, dropping her face down into her hands. "How'd they get that? It was over in seconds."

"There are always stalk-aratzi outside the S.S.C.," said Craig. "Someone just got lucky, I guess."

"Yeah, you've got yourself a fair amount of trouble brewing there," said Delia.

"No. Really? How can you tell?" Ali threw her a disgruntled look. It was bad enough to have a criminal stating the obvious without her enjoying it so much.

"And we're going to need your help," said Craig.

"How?" demanded Ali. "And why? Why ask a known criminal to help? When we try to get back into S.S.C., will you honestly be able to say that you've never committed a crime? Once they know about this, they'll never trust you, or me, again."

To Ali's complete surprise, Delia did not appear offended by her outburst. Instead she settled back at her workbench and resumed taking a hard-drive apart. Craig perched on the arm of Ali's chair and ran his hand over her tight shoulders.

"Relax, Ali," said Craig. "As West is so fond of saying, 'nothing is as it appears.'"

"What are you going on about?"

Delia glanced up from her work. "What he means is, I'm not a criminal."

"You are listed on the S.S.C. database as a dangerous 'person of interest,'" said Ali.

Delia shrugged.

"They found out about Delia's powers when she first started working in a hospital –" began Craig.

"Just graduated as a nurse," added Delia, waving her very thin-tipped pliers at the diploma on the wall.

"The trouble started when, despite going to the computer training classes time after time," continued Craig, "she never could get the hospital computer system to work. When she started working on the wards, people started noticing that on Delia's days off the computers worked better than when she was on."

"Oh," said Ali. "Uh oh."

"Hell of an interview I had with the tech support guys," Delia's smile did not waver. "They accused me of introducing a virus into the system. They couldn't find one, but as far as they were concerned, that didn't mean I wasn't putting one in."

"But you weren't?"

"No," said Delia. "*I* didn't know what was going on. I thought that I was just unlucky. I had a hard time with technology my entire life. Waste of time trying to call me on the phone. I've never had a call that stayed connected. And I don't want to talk about static on the radio. Never could keep a hair dryer working for more than a week. Every computer I ever owned stopped working after a few months, when I was younger, but it got to be weeks by the time I graduated. I had three computers at one time, two out being repaired and the one I was currently using. Expensive hobby, that."

"Anyway," continued Craig, "the hospital couldn't prove that she was sabotaging the computers but, since she was still in the probationary period as a nurse, they fired her."

"There I was, all my student loans coming due and no job. Do you know how hard it is to get a job with a nurse's degree that doesn't also involve computers?"

"So, you turned to crime?" asked Ali.

Delia's face screwed up as if a bad smell had entered the room and shook her head, "No! I never turned to crime. I was *accused* of lots of things that simply happened before I realized what my power was. Like the time I went into a bank to renegotiate my student loans. Since I wasn't working, I wanted to apply for forbearance. As I walked past the tellers, their computers just blanked out. I wasn't doing anything intentionally. It just happened. Of course, the effect was worse when I was stressed."

"A few strange occurrences like that," added Craig, "and they started banning Delia from banks, from shopping malls, from airports."

"Could you imagine what would happen if I went near JFK?" sighed Delia. "I have *never* been in an airplane. They can't shield against me."

"Oh, yeah," said Ali, "but how, when, did you start blackmailing people?"

"She never did," said Craig, patiently, before Delia could reply. "The stories about a woman sabotaging computers just by looking at them got around and The Colonel sent a team to investigate. They tracked Delia down, she was living with her folks again, and The Colonel gave her a laptop computer to hold. Just hold in her hands. The Colonel's techs turned it on and Delia didn't even hit one key."

"Took half an hour for me to fry its circuits," said Delia, removing the hard drive disc and placing it on a spindle. She lowered a clear plastic lid and activated the device. "It was a hell of a shock, I can tell you, to discover I had a Super Power that meant that I could break computers just by being near them. The guys at S.S.C. were pretty good about it. They said I didn't qualify for a Super Team position because I was too dangerous to bystanders, and my ability didn't add anything to the team. Now, if there were some Super Villain 'Computer Man' or the 'Mechanical Monster,' then, hey, I'd be their girl. Someone would fly me up and just drop me on his head. But until then, they'd give me the third string stipend and I had to keep them updated if I ever left my house. Of course, that was all *strictly* voluntary. Can you imagine what would happen if they put an electric bracelet on me?" She snickered.

"But everyone says that you're a blackmailer. Wasn't the stipend enough?"

Both Craig and Delia gave her a look usually given to a puppy who won't learn what the newspaper was for.

"Ali, you and I both know you can't trust what 'everyone' says," said Craig. "Delia has a reputation for breaking computers – even the built-in tracking devices, which is one reason why I brought us here today because as soon as I walked in here my trackers were fried. Yours too. Anyway, as per SS.C. policy, they announced Delia's powers and the next thing you know, there are people blaming their system crashes on her. All those accusations were unproven. Unfounded. Wrong. Sound familiar?"

"Oh." Ali's heart sank and she blushed and nodded to Delia. "Sorry."

"It's true," said Delia, most of her attention still on her work, "that there are some companies in California and Japan who pay me a great deal of money not to say their names out loud. But I never asked them to. It's not blackmailed if you never ask. They've offered me a great deal more to sit around chanting their competitors' names. Those jobs I report to the authorities and turn down."

"Then why are you listed as a 'person of interest' in the S.S.C. files?" asked Ali.

Delia and Craig laughed.

"Hunting for Computer Destructo Woman is a training exercise," said Craig. "A psychological test for new recruits. My first year working for S.S.C., I was an overeager little pain in the butt. No doubt you remember. While I was in the 'save the world' phase, Mr. Crunch called me into his office and said that, in my spare time, I was to keep a lookout for Computer Destructo Woman. She was wanted for questioning. All I had to do was bring her into the S.S.C. head office. Of course, I had to find her first."

"It isn't that hard to find me," offered Delia, with a condescending smile. "I do have a website."

"Website?" repeated Ali. "I thought you couldn't get computers to work."

Delia dismissed that issue with a wave of her hand. "My boyfriend says that the only person who breaks more computers than me is some dumb performance artist down in Arkansas who uses computers to drive nails into wooden floorboards. However, since I wanted to be part of the world and enjoy the benefits of technology, I got really good at repairing computers. So now it's my business. *Computer Destructo Woman's Data Recovery and Repair*. I'm very good – and very expensive. Of course, I spend most of my time repairing my repair equipment, but that's a small price to pay for access to the world wide web."

"It took me six months to find her," admitted Craig, with a laugh, "and I never saw the website."

"But when he did find me, he came flying in through the front window," said Delia. "Did a fair amount of damage and tried to drag me back to Jersey City."

"Then she started testing me, only I didn't know it. She sat me down and told me the whole story. How her powers were accidental. That she didn't choose to have a Power that was better suited for a Villain. That she'd never deliberately hurt anyone or anything. If I'd met Delia in my first few months as a Super, I would probably have thrown her over my shoulder and flown back to S.S.C. no matter what she said. But I'd hurt a couple of bystanders and made a few mistakes by then." Craig rubbed Ali's shoulders and grinned at her. "And you'd lectured me about jumping to conclusions and acting precipitously only a few days before when I visited you. I listened to Delia and made up my own mind. I politely asked Delia to aSS.C. me to see Mr. Crunch, escorted her upstairs so she could dress for the trip, and flew low and slow so she wouldn't get upset. When I got her to Mr. Crunch's office I was asked to wait outside for a while, then they called me in and gave me my evaluation."

"You passed," said Delia. "Did the job. Used your head. Treated me with courtesy, but never allowed me to get away with anything. If I had been lying to you, I still wouldn't have gotten away. Mr. Crunch was impressed. That doesn't happen often."

"So am I," said Ali, "but why are they were using Computer Destructo Woman that way?"

"It's a necessary test," said Delia. "The Super Teams are sent out hunting people. Psychologically, there's a risk that the Supers will start getting arrogant and cruel, even vicious. The police and FBI have all these tough psychological exams that they put their recruits through, but the S.S.C., they have to take those random people who develop powers and can make use of them. The S.S.C. doesn't get to choose. They're stuck with Bozos like Tye Dye and Captain Fabulous." She paused and stared at the ceiling. "Oh, God, the pathology those guys represent. If I hadn't signed the S.S.C. secrecy agreement, I could write one hell of a book."

"Oh, no," said Ali, smothering a chuckle. "What did those nit-wits do?"

"I'm not going to say," said Delia, with considerable dignity. "However, Mr. Crunch enforces my recommendation that those two have weekly visits to a shrink. Me, I went back to school for another degree – got a doctorate in psychology on the S.S.C. dime - and now I'm the S.S.C. counselor – in my copious spare time."

"Tye Dye has just been activated," said Ali. "First string. He's working with P.L. and West."

"Yeah, Mr. Crunch called to update me a few days ago," said Delia. "That activation won't last long. Tye Dye likes to strut. First time he blasts a bunch of civilians into seizures, he'll be out on his multicolored ass. I called Control and told her that. We have a bet. I'm saying he'll be back, third stringing it within a week. She says a month. Loser buys the winner lunch. Which brings us to why you two are here. What's up?"

"Have you heard about the Ice Queen?" asked Ali, and when Delia nodded she continued. "There's no such person. Trouble is, no one believes us."

"Obviously, I have been seduced by an evil Villainess and can no longer be trusted. Which explains my refusal to talk about her," said Craig. "And Ali here is letting her loyalty to an individual Super fog her mind. Now I've been suspended, and no matter how much evidence Ali collected at alleged crime scenes, they didn't believe her."

Faced with Delia's confusion, Ali was forced to explain the last few days, and wasn't all that surprised when Delia spent most of the time laughing. If it weren't for her own close personal involvement she would have been able to appreciate how ridiculous the whole situation sounded.

"This sounds oh, so familiar," said Delia, when she got her breath back. "When I first came into my powers, there was this guy with a security detail from Hell who wouldn't believe that my powers were unintentional. Unidirectional."

"Mr. White. We've met. That moron's still there," said Craig

"And still causing trouble," said Ali. "He was at the meeting just this afternoon. A couple of times, I thought things were calming down, but he stirred them up again." She blushed and fidgeted. "Of course, my yelling at everyone and quitting didn't help."

"Being an idiot must be his Superpower," joked Delia. "What can I do to help?"

"We need money, IDs and plane tickets to Arizona," said Craig, "The rest we can take care of ourselves."

"Why Arizona?" asked Delia. "That isn't the traditional home of hideaways."

"Funny girl," said Craig. "We're going after Nuclear Man."

"On your own?" cried Delia.

Craig waggled his hand back and forth. "Well, the jury's still out on that," he said. "Still, it's our best bet for getting people to forget about the Ice Queen. A big, splashy arrest of a high-profile villain will bury her deep. A few weeks with Nuclear Man in the headlines, and the Ice Queen will fade away."

"I suppose," said Delia, uncertainly. "I think you're a little optimistic. Still, I'll help all I can. Do you have some money stashed somewhere? I'd rather transfer from one account to another than create it out of sheer Ethernet."

"My accounts are blocked," said Craig. "Have been for days. Something to do with my suspension. But they probably haven't gotten to Ali's yet."

"That's not going to help," said Ali, startled, "I haven't any money."

"Have you paid the charity auction yet?" asked Craig.

"I never had the money for that," Ali blinked and shook her head. "P.L.

and West were backing me. They were going to pay."

"To keep the charity and everyone else from knowing about us pulling a fast one, P.L. and West were supposed to transfer the money to you. West told me she'd transferred her share of the payment to your account days ago."

"You know an awful lot about that setup," said Ali, leaning forward to press her fingers against his chest. "If I find out you had anything to do with getting me involved with that, I will personally feed you to my fish."

"I'll keep that in mind," said Craig, but Ali took careful note of the fact that he didn't deny anything.

"I'll need your driver's licenses and credit cards," said Delia, wiggling her fingers at them. "Better yet, give me the wallets. I'll transfer the money to an account under a new name, and I'll tweak a few things with your driver's licenses. In an hour or so you'll have a whole new life."

"I'm not really finished with this one, so don't do anything permanent," said Ali, shifting her wallet back and forth between her hands, then taking out the last of her cash. "While you're doing that, I'm going shopping."

"Women!" said Craig. "What is it with you and shopping?"

"Well," said Ali, pulling herself up to her full height and treating him to one of her chilling stares. "For one thing, I've been wearing the same underwear and socks for two days, and that's unpleasant. On top of that, there's no way I'd be able to get through airport security. All of my clothing is from The Colonel, I have no idea how much stuff he might have stashed in the lining."

Craig stared at her, then his own civilian clothing, and up at Delia. "Hell, all my clothes come from the Colonel."

"You know that under my influence those devices are fried," said Delia. "Still, just to be cautious you should strip. Get rid of everything from The Colonel."

"What will I wear?" cried Craig. "I even get my underwear from The Colonel."

Delia and Ali exchanged a quick glance and a slow smile.

"Reeeeeeeeally?" asked Delia.

"We'll find you a towel or something," said Ali, after a pause to scan Craig from booted toes to tousled hair. "Don't go far. I'll get you some clothes. It might just take a little while."

Ali shuffled a few inches forward and halted, watching the bored security guard ahead talking another passenger out of their shoes. Craig was standing in front of her, his arms folded tight across his chest, scowling at his feet. He was wearing a baseball cap over his distinctive curly hair and dead average, boring denim clothing.

"Where are we going when we hit Arizona?" asked Ali, leaning forward to whisper into Craig's ear.

Craig shrugged, "I'm not sure yet. We've never been able to track Nuclear Man down to one state before. If I had access to resources of the S.S.C., I could ask for a radiation scan of the state."

"Would he show up?"

They shuffled a few inches further forward.

"I've no idea," muttered Craig, hunching his shoulders and taking another tiny step. "Hell's teeth, I hate to admit it, but I've no idea how we're gonna find him. I guess I'm hoping something will come to me when we get there. If you think about it logically, where would a radioactive man live?"

"Depends," said Ali. "If he doesn't care about anyone else, wherever he wants. If he doesn't want to hurt anyone, he will go for somewhere isolated."

"In your opinion, what kind of criminal is Nuclear Man?"

Ali gave that question a moment's thought. "I know what I feel from hearing about his letters. He's angry, but he has a social conscience. My guess would be he'd have a place out of town."

"There's a hell of a lot of area 'out of town' in Arizona," muttered Craig.

They were separated briefly to be mauled by security guards. Ali was worried that her name and face had been on the news too much lately and expected at any moment to be taken aside for questioning. But it seemed that the guards were mainly concerned with keeping the flow of traffic going, and no one looked twice at her.

Several minutes later, she was sinking into an uncomfortable plastic seat in the pre-boarding area watching a sea of humanity washing back and forth trailing suitcases. Craig slumped in the chair beside her.

"The last letter published is more than a year ago," he said, reaching into his backpack for a file. It was a risk carrying hard copies of these letters, but he had his excuse all ready. Computer Destructo Woman had created a Ph.D. student ID for him and his story was he was doing his thesis on Villains. A perfectly reasonable, if uncommon, subject. He'd selected what he considered the most interesting of Nuclear Man's letters, and left the rest buried in the bottom of Ali's clothes closet. Given the public abduction someone, would've been at Ali's house within an hour of her disappearance. By now the remainder of his research would be in the hands of one of the S.S.C. lawyers. What they'd make of it he could only speculate. Hopefully, they wouldn't put all the information together too fast. He didn't want them charging down to Arizona and messing up his plan – should he ever create one. "The AMA rep I spoke to said they'd just trashed his most recent letter. They don't remember how long ago they got it, what it was about, and no one can remember anything about his address."

"Why they ignored the threats and didn't call police completely escapes me," said Ali. "Even after Nuclear Man started attacking their meetings and buildings, they didn't let the S.S.C. know they were getting letters? How dumb is that?"

"As far as we know," said Craig, darkly, pulling out Ali's laptop and flipping it open. "I'm beginning to suspect they told someone, but it didn't get passed on to us. As you well know, there is a bit of interdepartmental tension. Local cops can get bent out of shape when the Supers fly in, save the day and grab the glory. The state cops and Feds aren't that fond of us, either. And heaven spare us from Oversight!"

"Hey, what are you doing with that?" hissed Ali, reaching for the computer. "That's S.S.C. property. I should have given it back when I quit. And the trackers…"

"You didn't get a chance. I had it. You can give it back when we catch Nuclear Man. Or not, if we get rehired."

"Rehired? You mean you quit, too?"

"No." Craig pointed to one of the dozen TV screens facing the waiting passengers. "I expect they've fired me sometime in the last few hours."

Ali watched for a moment, then clutched at his sleeve. The picture showed Ultra Man flying down and snatching her from the street. The sound was off, but the teletype across the bottom of the screen read: *Ultra Man, fugitive! Sought by Federal authorities!*

"Craig?" Ali scanned the room, but no one was paying them any attention. Nevertheless, Ali shrank back and tugged at the collar of her jacket. "What if someone recognizes you? Or me?"

"Relax," said Craig, tapping at the keyboard, "No one ever has. You're drawing more attention to yourself by getting worked up. Sit back, read a book and act bored."

She relaxed her grip on Craig's sleeve one finger at a time and continued to study the faces of those passing their waiting area. "Are you sure?"

"Take it easy. My chin is all that shows in that outfit, and besides, who would expect Ultra-Man to travel by plane like an ordinary person? I do it all the time and no one notices. Because I'm in the last place they'd expect to see me, no one *sees* me."

Ali twisted to face him. "You travel by plane?" she whispered. "Why?"

"Flying by myself is boring." Craig grinned, "Besides, you can't read a book when you have to watch out for low flying pigeons and tall cell towers." She stared at him for a moment before settling back into her chair. A laugh bubbled up despite her worry. "Makes sense, I suppose. I guess I never thought about it. I expect everyone who dreams about flying would think they'd fly everywhere."

"Exactly. Except it's boring, cold, and you can get lost. When I first started working for the S.S.C., I was supposed to be going from New Jersey up to some town in Vermont. I ended up landing at some 7/11 in Connecticut to buy a map. The cashier is probably still eating out on that story."

This time Ali didn't bother trying to smother a laugh, although she'd heard the story before. The event had entered S.S.C. folklore, and she'd never been sure if it really had been Craig, or one of the older fliers. Craig's answering grin was strangely reassuring. It was good to know he could laugh at himself. Warmth surrounded the worry that had built in her chest over the last few days, and it started to unravel. Craig – Ultra Man – was on the job, the problem was as good as fixed. The thought might not be logical, given Craig's concern about finding Nuclear Man, but still, she did feel better that she was with him. That she had his help. She wasn't alone.

"It's not as if roads have numbers visible from above painted on them for the use and convenience of Supers," said Ali.

"Well, now I have a GPS gadget that feeds me so-far-at-this-speed-then-turn-left information. It was built into my suit, so I'm on my own now."

Ali sat and people watched for a while, as Craig paged through the information stored on her computer. There was nothing to do for the moment. Nowhere to go or plan. In fact, just sitting here was the most time off she'd had – awake – for months. It was almost a vacation. If she wasn't so worried about her future and Craig's Super reputation, she'd almost be enjoying herself. Scanning the shops lining the gate area she noticed a small spa, and an idea came to her.

"The flight's not for another three hours. I'll be back before then," she said, rising and grabbing her purse.

"Where are you going?" said Craig, his hands resting on the keyboard.

"To have my hair cut."

It had been months since the last time she'd relaxed in a salon and had a soothing scalp massage or a hot oil treatment. Getting a haircut had the added virtue of being the last thing someone sensible would expect a fugitive to do, as well as changing her appearance. Unfortunately, her hairdresser was a Super fan and kept the small TV positioned near the chair on the news channel.

Somewhere between her hair being dipped in oil and wrapped in a hot hood and having her nails painted, the TV news anchor came on with an update, his frosted grey hair quivering with excitement.

"The woman Ultra Man is seen kidnapping has been identified as S.S.C. employee, Ali Brent..."

They flashed Ali's employee photo on the screen. Ali stiffened, then relaxed muscle by muscle, forcing herself to put on an unconcerned air. The photo they were showing had been taken years ago at the end of a week-long, grueling indoctrination. Back then, Ali had affected a scraped back pony-tail, eschewed all makeup, and had yet to lose her college twenty pounds. Consequently, the Ali on screen looked more like a *male* East German weightlifter than the woman in the stylist's chair.

"Ms. Brent," continued the anchor, "has been making news recently with her repeated claims that victims attempting to file for relief after Ice Queen attacks are part of a conspiracy to defraud insurance companies. The S.S.C. spokesperson, Mr. Breakham, has declined to comment on the circumstances of Ms. Brent's abduction, or on the ongoing investigation into the Ice Queen's origins and criminal intentions. Claims that the Ice Queen is an ex-employee of Creamy Whip, injured and emPowered in an ice machine accident, has been denied by that SS.C. through their lawyers."

The manicurist grinned up at Ali. "I wouldn't mind being *abducted* by Ultra Man, if you know what I mean. He's hot! They'd have to drag me kicking and screaming back to my husband and kids."

"Why, sure," Ali gave the girl a bright smile and fluttered her newly painted eyelashes. "He's too cute to boot out of bed for eating cookies. Not like that Fabulous scuzz-bag."

The girl gave this serious thought as she painted Ali's nails silver blue. "I dunno about buying the whole package," she said, "but after what I heard about Captain Fabulous's *special* selective stretching abilities I sure wouldn't mind taking him for a drive around the block, if you know what I mean?"

Ali's nod managed to communicate that she knew what she meant, just didn't want to go on that drive herself. An hour later, on her way back to the waiting area, Ali stopped and bought every newspaper she could find. She staggered over to where Craig worked and collapsed into the chair beside him. Craig jumped and looked up, his eyes widening. The intensity of his gaze warmed and chilled Ali at the same time. It was nice, better than nice, to have someone admire her so openly. She tossed most of the papers onto the floor and flipped the remaining one open to the front page. Craig ignored the computer and continued to stare at her.

"Don't take this the wrong way, Ali, but you should have your hair cut more often. You look great."

Ali ran a nervous hand over the head. After the new cut and perm, her hair now curled randomly over her forehead and flowed down to dance around her shoulders. The makeup she usually didn't have time to apply brought out the gold lights in her eyes. She looked good and knew it, but that didn't mean that

Craig needed to think it was for his benefit.

"Think of it as a disguise," whispered Ali, shaking the newspaper. "They're showing photos of me on TV now and this is as different as it gets to the usual me, short of major surgery."

"You don't need surgery. You always look good, but now you look…" His eyes unfocused as he sought for the right word "Tasty."

Ali blushed to the roots of her hair as Craig's eyes passed over her again. Heat ran over her skin, as if he were brushing his Super-heated hands across her body. She struggled to remain calm, poised, under the pressure of his intent gaze. Seconds passed and his attention didn't waver. Unable to control her traitorous body's reaction to his practiced smile she chose the familiar protection of an attack.

"Pervert," drawled Ali. "We should feed you before takeoff, I don't think they have a meal service on this flight."

Craig chuckled and the intent stare faded.

"I'll survive on peanuts. What are you doing with all those?" he waved at the papers. "Starting your own recycling business?"

"Hell, no," said Ali. "I've been ignoring the news and learned that's something I can't afford to do. I've got to catch up with what they've been saying about me, and about the Ice Queen."

"Don't beat yourself up about it. You've been working the clock round. There was no way you could keep up."

"I should have," said Ali, with a disgusted grimace. Yet again, the front page showed that over-inflated image someone had created of the Ice Queen. "When we get to Phoenix, I'm going to get every local paper and start checking for any hints of Nuclear Man activity."

"It's an idea," said Craig. "But you're not expecting *him* to have put an ad in the personals, are you?"

Ali sniffed. "There might be some pattern of robberies in hospitals or something that no one's put together with Nuclear Man attacks. Minor things like syringes and alcohol wipes."

"I suppose, although those things are easy enough to pick up in pharmacies," Craig closed the notebook lid and rubbed his eyes. "It's hard to get a handle on the guy. Our profilers have been working on him for years, and with the full resources of S.S.C. we've still never understood him."

"I'm surprised no one twigged to his different levels of crime before."

"No one's had the same amount of information as you," he tapped the laptop. "There's so much stuff in here. How can you keep up with it?"

"I don't sleep much," said Ali. "And when I do, I get nightmares."

Chapter Fourteen.

Jersey City Morning News.
Captain Fabulous's fifth wife started divorce proceedings this morning, citing alien affection. Captain Fabulous's North America Fan Club declared a day of celebration and issued a press release offering to pay her court costs.

"This," said Ali, as the outdoor metal staircase of the motel they'd checked into squeaked and shook under her tired feet, "is a dump."

"But it's a dump at the intersection of five roads with a giant golfer statue across the road," Craig said, indicating the advertisement for a miniature golf course with his chin. "When I go flying, I need to have a choice of known roads to follow and a decent sized landmark, or I won't find my way back."

Aside from its location, the motel could claim no other virtues, being old, poorly maintained, and located under the airport's final approach. Even though they'd passed several newer, cleaner and swankier hotels that seemed to have the same virtues so important to Craig, Ali didn't protest the choice. At this point, she was approaching four days without proper sleep – the nap on the airplane didn't count - and right now she would, if given a chance, fall asleep on a picket fence. She followed Craig into the room they were assigned. Two beds, shower and a light that could be turned off. At this moment, she needed nothing more.

Craig dropped his case on the bed nearest the door and flipped it open. He pulled out a thick sweater, dragged it over his head, then tugged on a pair of gloves.

"Where the heck are you going at this hour?" asked Ali, stepping out of her shoes and trying to decide if she had the strength to shower, or if she'd just crawl into bed as she was.

"I'm going take a look around."

Ali studied his preparations for a moment, then realized he intended to go flying.

"You can't," Ali grabbed his arm. "You can't draw attention to our presence. Don't you realize that by now all the Super Teams will have been told to keep an eye out for you? For us?"

"Sure, I know. I just want to take a look around and get an idea of the shape of the problem. Flying is the fastest way to search, especially when you're searching an area the size of this state. I need to familiarize myself with the landmarks."

Ali rocked back on her heels. "Are you completely out of your mind? Stupid question. Of course you are. There is no way you can search a state effectively. Not on your own. If you start flying randomly over the place, in a few days you'll be seen and it will be all over."

"Dammit Ali, I have to. We can't be just knocking on doors and asking people if they've ever met a guy who blows toxic chunks. That'd take forever. Nuclear Man will die of boredom waiting for us."

"Yes, I agreed, we have to do something, but not right now. And not without a plan. A good plan. And not in the middle of the night!" Ali tightened her grip on his arm and pushed him toward the second bed. "Craig, we've been on the move all day. We spent all last night at event sites. I don't know about you, but I can't remember the last time I slept the night through. We need to crash. Sleep. Tomorrow is soon enough to figure out our next step."

Craig stumbled over the uneven carpet as he permitted her to nudge him toward the bed.

"We can't afford to let this go on," he mumbled. "The longer we take to fix it, the harder it will be to bury it."

"I agree," Ali pulled back the blankets, pressed on Craig's shoulder until he sank onto the bed. "But if we go wandering around exhausted, we'll make crappy decisions and, even if we are lucky enough to fall over Nuclear Man, you won't have the strength to do more than point at him as he hobbles away. We need sleep."

Craig groaned and nodded, toed off his boots while Ali tugged off his gloves and threw them at the narrow chest of drawers. "I've been staring at the computer screen for so long that every time I close my eyes I see glowing letters on my eyelids."

He curled up on his side as Ali pulled the blankets up over his shoulders and smoothed his hair off his forehead. He reached out to capture her hand. Before he could touch her, or say anything, she spun, grabbing her gear off her bed and disappeared into the shower. Craig rolled onto his back, gave the room another critical examination and snorted. He'd been fantasizing having Ali alone somewhere for years. Those fantasies had included five-star hotel accommodations, room service, champagne breakfasts and deep, bubbly, heart-shaped Jacuzzis for two. Not cheap plywood furniture, hard mattresses and bubbling paisley wallpaper. And certainly not hard, narrow, twin beds.

Somehow, these threadbare surroundings seemed more domestic, more intimate, than the ones he'd imagined. In the bathroom he heard the shower start. Confident she was busy for the next few minutes, and trying not to imagine her naked, he climbed back out of bed. Rummaging through the clothing Delia had hastily purchased for him, he realized he didn't have anything resembling pajamas. Not that he'd worn anything like that since he'd left his mother's house. With luck, Ali wouldn't get bent out of shape if he slept in T-shirt and boxers. Then again, she'd shared student housing with Oliver. It was unlikely that there was anything left that would shock her. By the time Ali crept out of the bathroom, he'd stripped down to his underwear and was back under the blankets.

"Do you prefer the bed near the door?" he asked and grinned when she jumped and blushed. "We could switch if you want."

"I'll be fine with either," she said, not even glancing in his direction.

"Of course, if you think you're going to get lonely...?"

"Get your mind out of the gutter, Mr. Duane. I sleep just fine on my own."

She climbed into her bed and turned off the light. Beside her in the dark, Craig stared at the ceiling and mustered the strength to smile.

Time alone with Ali. Just the two of them. An unexpected side benefit

of being on the run from the law.
    Who'd've thought it?

    Ali waited until almost one a.m. before pushing aside the thin blankets and climbing out of bed. Since she'd gone to bed in an oversized T-shirt and undies, dressing consisted of putting on a pair of jeans and tucking her feet into shoes. She lifted her handbag from the bedside table and tip-toed to the door.
    As she turned the lock, Craig jerked and his head lifted from the pillow.
    "What? What?"
    "Take it easy," said Ali in the hushed voice people used after lights-out. "It's only me. I'm thirsty. I'm going to raid the soda machine and pick up some ice."
    "Soda's okay," mumbled Craig, his head dropping back down on the pillow, "but I wouldn't trust the ice if it's made from local water. Did you see the color of the stains in the sink?"
    Ali waited for a moment, but he didn't say anything more. A few seconds later and a soft snore told her he was asleep. She left the door a little open, certain that Craig could deal with anyone foolish enough to try and take advantage of an unlocked door. Aside from their rental car, the parking lot outside their room was empty. Nevertheless, she did a perimeter search before retreating to the furthest corner to pull out her cell phone and dial a well-remembered number.

    Craig left early the next morning, sent by Ali to round up the most diverse collection of local newspapers he could find. Considering that he left without any protest, Ali assumed he had tasks of his own planned. Even though she was worried about what he'd do, she hoped that he wouldn't hurry back. She had no idea when her guests would arrive.
    The air conditioner trembled and spat rusty droplets on the floor. Ali sniffed as she stood in the middle of the room. Somehow, roadside motels all smelled the same - mix of equal parts boredom, desperation, loneliness, industrial strength pine scent, and body fluids.
    She checked her wristwatch for the third time in three minutes, then jumped when there was a knock at the door. She was across the room in a heartbeat, swinging open the door. The Purple Lightning paused to permit The Mysterious West to duck in ahead of him.
    "Were you seen?" asked Ali.
    "Nope," said Oliver, pulling the curtain aside about an inch and scanning the buckled parking lot. "Wouldn't matter if we were. West cast an 'ignore me' spell on us when we were outside Baltimore. But since we're supposed to be patrolling on the other side of the country, we'd better make this fast. We've got to leave for home within the hour. What the hell is going on?"
    Ali hugged him. She couldn't help it. She was so relieved to see them both. They were a link to the life she'd lost and hoped to get back. For both herself and Craig. Oliver patted her on the back and pushed her gently away so he could study her face.
    "Looking good, Ali," he said, running his hand over her tangled hair, fluffing up the curls. "If the bursar could see you now he wouldn't argue about you being a girl."

Ali laughed and hugged him again.

"Tell me what's up, girlfriend," Oliver continued, "You didn't give us much to go on last night."

Ali drew a deep breath and forced herself not to cling to Oliver and concentrated. "Craig got this idea that if we made a really public capture of Nuclear Man, then the Ice Queen would be pushed off the front page. If she could be forgotten for a few days, then maybe things would calm down and we could get the powers-that-be to listen to sense."

Oliver and Lacey exchanged a long look then nodded.

"Possibly. I suppose it's better than shouting," said Oliver. "Although I would've paid good money to see you going up against the gang-of-four yesterday. Is it true that you threw a chair at White?"

"Heavens, no," cried Ali, going pale. What gossip was circulating around the SS.C. coffee machines? What were they saying about her, and how would she ever get them to stop?

"Capturing Nuclear Man as a distraction? Do you truly think it's that easy?" Lacey caught Ali's hand in her own. Her deep brown eyes locked onto Ali's and held. Ali couldn't have looked away to save her life. "You think people who pride themselves on their authority, *their* power - will accept it when you tell them they've made a silly mistake. A very public mistake. They, who take themselves seriously, would rather believe a lie, continue spreading a lie, than be embarrassed by a truth."

"That's Craig's plan. But the Ice Queen doesn't exist," cried Ali. "They have to accept that fact eventually."

"You know that, baby. I know it. Oliver and Craig know it. But everyone else *believes*. It's tough to battle belief. Facts are not enough."

Ali stared helplessly at Lacey. It was one of the fears that had kept her from sleeping last night. That after all their work, they might continue to drown in the same, horrible situation.

"How did you find out he was here?" asked Oliver, as he searched through Ali's handbag. She always carried his P.L. Instant Power bars.

"Would you believe he's been writing threatening letters to the AMA for years and no one told us?" said Ali. "The last one they printed was mailed from Arizona. We haven't gotten any closer than that. For all we know, he just had them mailed from here as a cover. Or he could have moved. He could be living the high life in Hawaii, for all we know. Finding him is going to be next to impossible without help. I know Craig hasn't got a plan more than flying across the country and hoping for the best."

"That's my cue," announced Lacey, as she started rifling through her many pockets. "I can help. Do we have any tokens of Nuclear Man?"

"Not with me," Oliver shook his head as Ali grabbed her bag from him.

"All I've got," said Ali, holding out a scrap of paper, "is a photocopy of a letter he wrote about a year ago."

Lacey ran her fingers over the paper, her expression distant.

"Not the best, but this will do," she declared after a moment's meditation. "He put a lot of pain and anger into these words." She pulled a length of red silk from a pocket, laid it over the bedside table and positioned the page in the center. A miniature cauldron was produced from another pocket, followed by envelope after envelope of leaves. "I'm going to do an 'events conspire' spell. It's dangerous magic, very dangerous. The universe will reshape itself so that you will find yourself – seemingly by accident – in the presence of Nuclear Man. I don't like to do this. I've known it to cause traffic accidents, or worse, trying to bring two people together. And since we want this finished soon, I'll have to add a boost. That increases the risks."

"*We* can take the risk," said Ali. "Can you do anything to protect innocent bystanders?"

Lacey waggled her hand back and forth.

"Not a good idea to put too many qualifiers on a spell like this. I'll do my best to make it so that Nuclear Man and our Craig are face to face within, let's say, two, no, three days. That gives the universe a little time to prepare. Any sooner, any more power, and accidents *will* happen. Very bad *juju*. Ordinarily, I wouldn't do this spell at all. It's a bad idea to tell the universe that you want something this bad. It gets offended easily. But we need to take the risk. Things are getting crazy back at S.S.C."

"What's happening?" asked Ali, her hands formed into fists as she watched Lacey's preparations with an intensity that breaking little leaves into smaller pieces did not deserve.

"We're not sure what's happening in the upper levels," said Oliver, "but every single Super in the country has been called in and practically interrogated about their Powers, their families, and about every criminal they've ever been in contact with by Mr. White. If there's the slightest difference between their post-battle reports back then, and what they say now, their security rating is downgraded. There've been wholesale benchings of first-string Supers. Anyone who protests the questions, or the changes, gets put on suspension and is replaced by second or even third-string Powers. And you can be sure that lot are so delighted to be activated that they don't question anything."

"What about you guys? Last I heard you were already in trouble."

"Oh, now that's a fun question," said Lacey, lighting three white candles with one green match, which promptly vanished in a puff of smoke.

"No kidding," said Oliver with a shudder. "First, we get Tye Dye as a team member, and then we get the message that he's our team *leader*."

"Come again?" said Ali, sinking onto the nearest bed.

"He's enjoying it, too," continued Oliver. "Swaggering around the place, you'd think he was king of the world. He's telling everyone that he always knew Ultra Man was unstable and dangerous. That *he* wasn't really second-string all these years. It's just that he was lying low, waiting for Ultra-Man to reveal his true nature so Tye Dye could step in and save-the-day. At least, that was the theme of the press conference he called."

"He called a conference? When? I didn't see anything on TV. Oh, tell me it wasn't sanctioned by Control – she'll slit his throat."

"You had to be lucky to see it the first time it aired. Control managed to block most of the repeats," Oliver gave a one-shoulder shrug. "With all the anti-Ultra Man lead news stories already out there, well it's too soon to hear if there's going to be any fallout. Unfortunately, I don't think it's enough, with everything else that's going on, to get Tye Dye kicked back to where he belongs."

"This is terrible," whispered Ali. "Even if we do catch Nuclear Man, Craig's reputation is permanently damaged. No one will ever trust him again."

"Now, don't go borrowing trouble, girl," said Lacey, laying a hand on Ali's knee. "It's not that bad yet. The good news is, no one's resigned from Ultra Man's fan club. In fact, children and adults are signing up in record numbers.

They're saying that if Ultra Man snatched a woman off the street in broad daylight, then there must have been a good reason for it."

"Yeah," muttered Ali. "I wish I knew what was going on. I have no idea who was after me or what they wanted. Either way, I'm just as glad Craig got to me first. And I'm glad you guys are willing to help us. Craig told me that he wanted to do this alone, but I know it's too dangerous. He trusts you. If this works out, you'll all be back on top together. You're his team. The best Super Team."

"And you're his woman," said Lacey, scooping the crushed leaves and a few other unidentifiable items into the cauldron. "We'll help you both."

"I am not!" said Ali, momentarily confused by the non-sequitur.

"Okay, then," Lacey shrugged. "He's your Man."

"He's not."

Lacey cast her a sympathetic look, put the cauldron on the silk and took Ali's hand in hers. She turned it over to run a blood-red painted fingernail over Ali's palm, tracing the lines and creases. "He's been your guy for years, girl. Just, you didn't know it."

"That's ridiculous."

"You say. You even believe," said Lacey, with a crooked grin and a wink, "but it's not true."

"Lacey," began Oliver, "This isn't the time –!"

Lacey waved his protest away without turning her head. "No, we've got time enough. It will help Ali to understand." Lacey gave her a penetrating look, and Ali wondered if the rumors of Lacey's mind reading talent were true. "Do you know why Craig finished college?"

"College? No. Did he? I had no idea."

Lacey let loose a long-suffering sigh and tightened her grip on Ali's hand. "Do you remember when he and Oliver were first identified as Supers? When Craig was recruited, he still had a year to go for his degree. The gang-of-four were so overjoyed to have someone with Super strength, and resilience, and flight powers, they were on him like fleas on a dead cat. They offered him the choice of area, salary, merchandising, everything, all so he'd start working right away. The S.S.C. recruiters told Craig he didn't need any damn degree. Do you know what he said?"

Ali blinked and shook her head.

"He said he had to ask his girl what she thought. Find out what she wanted. Where she wanted to live. Couldn't make any decisions without talking it over with her first."

Ali's jaw dropped with a click audible across the room. Oliver laughed.

"His girl? Me? He wanted to ask *me*? But I'm not his girl," gasped Ali. "I never was. He hit on me, sure, but that was testosterone. All the guys in the athletic department behaved as if the female half of the student body were just waiting, panting, to be noticed. He was annoying." Ali's eyes narrowed and she glared across at Oliver. "And I know that he was the one who talked you into running top speed across the campus, making all the girls' skirts fly up."

"We've told you and told you," Oliver groaned. "We heard a fire truck go past and were responding. Amateur Super Heroes to the rescue. It was our big break. We'd been waiting for something to do, a chance to let the S.S.C. know we were out there. Do something to catch their attention, instead of just turning up to one of their cattle-calls."

"There was no fire," said Ali. "I checked.

"It was a false alarm!" cried Oliver.

"Enough! Children, please. Chewing over old arguments is not helping." Lacey shook out her braids and folded her hands neatly under her ample bosom. "Ali, when Craig came back to show you his new Super Suit and tell you he'd been accepted, he was also going to tell you about me, the offer from S.S.C., and invite you to come to Jamaica to meet my family. We had a whole celebration planned. A weekend spent on the beach, dancing, eating, talking - all sorts of good times. But instead he called me, said you weren't coming. Neither of you. Him, because he had to talk to his teachers, arrange to become an online student. Make plans for finishing his degree."

Ali sank back against the cushions. "Why?"

"Because you shouted at him," said Lacey. "Took me a while to get the whole story out of him. He said you yelled at him and called him a Superfool. Told him he's as bad as football and baseball hopefuls – bailing out of school expecting to hit it big in the professional leagues. You told him he was going to grow old one day. Maybe get hurt badly by some Villain. Then he'd spend the rest of his life staring at the ceiling in some hospital or mopping floors and flipping burgers because he didn't get his degree and his Powers burned out."

"Are you sure it wasn't his mother that said that?" muttered Ali, although she did remember the scene. The brand new – just announced on CNN – Ultra Man had dived down on her as she'd walked out of the library, snatched her off her feet and flown her to the top of the highest building in town to tell her his news. The remembered fear and anger rose up in her – along with remembered nausea. It had been the first time she'd gone flying with a Super. She'd been helpless, dangling in his arms, knowing that all that was between her and falling to her death was the college practical joker.

"Oh, no," said Oliver. "I remember his mother was over the moon. Couldn't wait for him to start saving-the-day. Man, she was a pest. The SS.C. had to relocate her three times before she settled down and kept quiet. My mom was more sensible," He flicked a smile at Lacey. "They only had to move her twice."

"But you," Lacey poked a long, pointed the finger at Ali, "you told him to stay in school. That he wasn't old enough, or responsible enough, to be a hero. He listened. Didn't like it, but he listened. Did what *you* told him to do. Every few months, I'd see he was unhappy about something and it'd turn out he'd gone to see you. He'd tell you about his work and you'd read him a list of his shortcomings. How he'd been too careless of frightened children in a bus, or how he hadn't thought through the consequences when he'd broken a dam to stop a forest fire."

"He'd come swaggering up to me," Ali's hands twisted in her lap. "Expecting me to tell him how wonderful he was. Just like all the other girls going to event sites and waving 'we heart you, Ultra Man' signs. Hanging off of skyscrapers trying to get him to rescue them. If he was in his Super suit, you could see all the women's heads turning, watching him. Panting after him. I heard women talking all over town about how they wanted to have him. How he was so wonderful. He wanted me to throw myself at him, just like them."

"No, girl," Lacey covered Ali's hands with her own. "You saw all those other women, but you never *saw* him. Never saw he was trying to impress you. Just you. He didn't want you to be like them, he wanted you to be you."

"No. No," said Ali "It wasn't like that."

"You think? Or you believe?" Lacey exchanged a glance with Oliver.

"You've met Captain Fabulous?"

Ali nodded, startled by the change of subject. "Him? Of course. Sure."

"He's been married, what, five times now?"

"Yes, and had more girlfriends than anyone can count," sneered Ali.

"Who does he date? Who does he marry?"

Ali paused to think. She'd seen them haunting the corridors of the S.S.C., hanging off Fabulous's arm on TV. Skinny, tiny women clinging to his stretchable arms, sometimes half a dozen at a time. "Women he's rescued. Groupies. Fans."

"Yes," Lacey sighed. "He's a silly little man and he keeps making the same sad mistake. When he marries, he marries someone who worships him. The girl, she's thinks she's getting married to *Captain Fabulous*. Not to ordinary Fred Morton. You see, *I* still remember the name he had before he had it officially changed. For the first few weeks, marriage is wonderful. Then comes a time when Fred starts to get tired. After all, he can't be 'Captain Fabulous' all the time, no matter how hard he tries. Too much work. He'll get up cranky one morning. Leave his socks in the living room. Cut his toenails on the coffee table. Something ordinary. Then the girl, she gets upset. She married Captain Fabulous, but, you see, she's living with Fred."

"And she gets divorced," muttered Ali.

"No. First she tries to force him to be Fabulous all the time. When that fails, she feels unhappy, angry, hurt, and betrayed. Fred gets unhappy for much the same reasons. Goes looking for someone who loves him, looks at him the same way she did when they first met. He gets caught, of course. Shame and scandal. Then they get divorced, and the whole mess goes around again."

"However," broke in Oliver, "Craig is a sensible guy. He knows what's important. He wants a girl who knows that under the uncomfortable Super suits is Craig Duane. A guy with a temper and a sense of humor. Who gets tired and has bad days. Who likes bowling and extra cheese pizzas and going to comedy clubs. He wants someone who understands the job. You've gotta say, Ali, you know the job better than anyone, 'cause you see the survivors. Look after them. Help them get their lives back." Oliver pulled Ali to him in a gentle hug. "At the end of the day, he wants a real life with someone who won't let him get away with anything. He thinks you two will make the perfect team. He'll knock 'em down, you'll pick 'em up."

Ali said nothing, leaning her head against Oliver's chest. She'd never considered Craig anything other than an annoyance. In her mind, he'd never grown up. Stayed the hormone-driven just-out-of-teenage boy she despised. But while her attention had been on other matters, he had grown. Not just in the physical sense, though the Super suit had been refitted four times. But his actions, his heroing, was more thoughtful now. The accidents and incidents of his early days had disappeared, and he deserved his reputation as the most powerful, most admired of the Supers.

Maybe it was just when he was with her that he was silly. Perhaps what she'd thought was foolishness, or jokes, was *play*? When he was with her, he relaxed and let his insecurities, his worries be seen? Maybe he trusted her enough to show her the real him. Had he really been courting her for all these years?

She thrust both hands through her hair and tugged. No, not possible! The news had been full of his exploits. The women. The fans. The one night stands. Her breath caught and she sat, staring at the wallpaper. With what she knew about the Ice Queen situation, maybe, just maybe, not all those reported events were real.

"You remember," asked Oliver, "when I got recruited, I started sending you money. I said I didn't like the idea of you working all the time. I wanted you to have more time to study."

"Wouldn't let me pay you back," whispered Ali. "I wouldn't have made it without you. I was drowning between work and school."

"It was Craig's idea. His money. I never thought of it. He just knew you wouldn't accept it from him."

"Oh, damn the man!" Ali released Oliver and started wandering around the room. "Why didn't he say?"

"Because he didn't want 'thanks for the money' sex," said Oliver. "Not that he would turn down 'just for fun' sex."

Ali sat down again, stunned, staring at Oliver.

"I'm surprised he put up with me," she said when the bands of guilt around her chest had loosened enough for her to draw breath, "I honestly never thought of him that way. Couldn't he have found someone," Ali gestured helplessly and grimaced, "nicer? I've said some horrible things to him."

"Yeah," said Oliver with a laugh, "what a blow to the ego it must be for him to know you didn't notice him beating himself to death trying to flirt with you. But every now and then you'd say something nice, to a survivor, or in one of your reports about him, and he'd hear about it and be walking on air for days."

"He had hope, child," said Lacey, "which is not to say that he didn't look, once in a while, for someone else A girl a little less of a problem. Little less hard work. Just he never found one he liked half so much as you."

"So, what do we do?" asked Ali.

"We do what he's planned." Lacey turned her attention to the set up on the table and started chanting. After a few minutes, she clapped her hands, sharply, three times. A puff of smoke rose from the cauldron. Ali waved at it, dispersing it before it could set off the fire alarms.

"There," said Lacey. "In three days, four at the outside, Ultra Man and Nuclear Man will stand face to face. What happens next depends on luck and skill. Meantime, you look after Craig, and yourself, the universe will take care of everything else."

"How will I get in touch with you? Let you know it's happened. Craig left all his stuff, his armor, everything with Comp....somewhere safe."

"Let's see," Oliver pulled at the lining of his new suit, finally tearing a hole under the sleeve and pulling out a small ball of electronics. "This is my emergency beacon. I'll apply for a new one once all this is over. If I apply for it now, someone might ask questions. Hit it when you're ready and we'll come."

"Everyone in the region will come," said Ali. "Things could get out of control and Ultra Man won't get the credit. Remember, we need a flashy capture for this to work."

"Hey, who do you think you're talking to? No one's going to get there before me, I guarantee it. Meantime, stay out of sight, and keep in touch with us, if you get the chance. Things are so crazy now that if you're arrested, you might never be able to clear yourselves. Especially, stay away from the Feds. I don't trust that guy, White. The rumors are he's out for your blood."

"Ah," said Ali. "Incentive. Just what I needed."

Hours passed after Oliver and West left, and still Craig didn't return. Ali kept the TV on but couldn't keep her mind focused on the jabbering. She ran through all her memories of Craig. The tall, stick thin teenager, who had filled out quite nicely into a powerful, square-shouldered Super Hero. Now that she allowed herself to look at the memories, she could recall the flowers he had brought with him to her room in student housing. They certainly hadn't been for Oliver. He'd never exactly offered them to her, simply placed them on the nearest clear space on a table. She recalled the unbelievable number of times he just 'happened' to be walking past her lecture room doors just as she came out. And then there was the number of times that Oliver suggested going to the movies, only to discover at the last minute that he had assignments due, but Ali might as well use the already purchased two tickets. And who would be standing by, waiting to go inside with her? Craig. All those triple dates bowling, driving out to see fall leaves – her, Oliver and Craig crammed onto the front seat of his disreputable truck. More often than not, Oliver would claim he had to "run" and he'd bail at some point. Had she really been that blind? Oblivious to the setups? The almost dates?

She swore under her breath and flopped down on the unmade bed. Craig had been the one who kept saying that he and Oliver didn't need to keep their Powers secret from her, so she could stay in the shared living room and listen when he visited. It occurred to her now that Craig hadn't been all that interested in talking with Oliver. It wouldn't have taken so many conversations to discuss each other's Superpowers. The subsequent visits might just have been to see her. She covered her eyes and groaned.

Now that Oliver and Lacey had dropped this particular bombshell, she'd no idea what she was supposed to do with the information. Indecision and confusion had her up and pacing the room again. It wasn't until she found herself restlessly tidying up his scattered clothing and straightening his hairbrush and razor in the bathroom that she realized that, if she truly wanted Craig out of her life, it would be easy to do. All she'd have to do would be tell him everything Oliver and Lacey had said and let him know his feelings, his interest, was not reciprocated.

Knowing him she'd be standing alone in the middle of the Sahara Desert ten minutes after she'd finished speaking.

Or not.

No, definitely not.

He hadn't abused his Powers for years. The last time she'd offended him, he'd still taken her safely home. Just made it so she had to work a little to get down to her apartment. A little twist to let her know his feelings were hurt. But if she didn't want him out of her life? She leaned on the bathroom sink, her hand clenched around his razor.

Did she only want a nice, calm, controlled, professional relationship with him? Polite nods to each other when they ran across each other at event sites? Emails and memos being the only way they communicated?

Was that all?

Ali had finished chewing her newly polished fingernails and was seriously thinking about chewing the walls when Craig returned.

"Where the heck have you been?" she demanded, as he pushed the door open with his shoulder.

"Shouldn't we be married for a year or two before you start with that line?" Craig joked as he maneuvered past her, his arms filled with loosely folded paper.

Ali blushed. Damn him. Why did he have to say things like that so soon after she'd had the world dumped on her by Oliver and Lacey? She hadn't had time to let what they'd said settle in her mind. Did she stay with him, or run? Right now, the impulse to run was ahead and its lead was lengthening.

"Don't take that attitude with me, Craig Duane," she said, unconsciously falling into Power Pose #1. "It isn't funny. I've been worried sick that you've gone off solo to face Nuclear Man, and he'd melted you like a snowman in July."

"I'm sorry, Ali, really." He dumped the paper on his bed and ran his hand down the side of her face, leaving a smear of printer's ink. "I knew you'd be worried, but I didn't have the hotel number with me and didn't want to risk using the cell. I found the local library. It occurred to me that Nuclear Man, being a letter writing guy, might have sent a few letters to local newspapers over the years."

"Did you find anything?"

"Depends on what you mean. Did I find a letter from Nuclear Man or his favorite alternative, med student? No."

Ali gripped him by his shirt front and lifted. There was something about his expression. His inability to meet her eyes that had her mouth drying and heart racing.

"Come on Craig, give. What did you find?"

"Two things. First," he grimaced and held up a photocopied page, "there's been a rash of Jackalope sightings."

Ali dropped Craig and grabbed the page. The headline was, predictably, playing the story for laughs with a photo of a small bunny with a tiny rack of horns between its ears under a scant two lines of text.

"Oh my god. Jackalopes. Nuclear Man, or the Med Student, complained someone shot his pet Jackalope."

"Exactly. It occurred to me while I was reading that radiation is mutagenic," said Craig, "Think about it. Can you think of anyone else who could have a pet like that? And what if Nuclear Man did have a pet bunny? What would happen to one in constant contact with him? The change could be unintentional, maybe, but what if he really had a pet Jackalope? Considering what rabbits are like, wouldn't he have more than one?"

"Why not?" said Ali, running a finger over the photograph, "If we grant that he could have one, is it unrealistic that he'd have more?"

"That's what I thought, and it could be a clue to where he's hiding. If a couple of his Jackalopes escaped, chewed their way out of the bunny hatches or something then, logically, Nuclear Man should be living where the highest concentration of Jackalope sightings are. I photocopied all the references I could find and figured we'd plot them out. Maybe we'll find some hint of where the Jackalopes came from. Look for statistical clusters, that sort of thing."

"Good idea," said Ali, being careful not to say that it was their *only* idea. "What was the other thing?"

"Pardon?"

"You said 'firstly.' What's the secondly?"

Craig glanced over at the muted TV. "I take it you haven't been following the news while I was out."

"Not listening closely. I figured if anything interesting happened they'd do that Special Super Report logo. I have limited tolerance to being lied to by someone with more hair than personality and got burned out on the news industry yesterday at the airport. Why? Oh, God, what did I miss now?"

Craig picked up the topmost paper and held it against his chest. "Before you look, I've got to tell you. It's not as bad as it looks. We can still fix this."

"Gimmie, Ultra Pest." Ali snatched the paper out of his hand and stared open-mouthed at the headline.

"Ali Brent Is The Ice Queen," screamed the Phoenix Morning News headline, in red letters, two inches tall.

Chapter Fifteen.

Phoenix Morning News.
"Ali Brent is the Ice Queen," said Ms. Waltern-Jones, sister of the Vice President, in an interview at her brother's east Washington home today. "I recognized her immediately when I saw the news report and put it together with the video footage from The Northern Star. I was suspicious of her behavior at the time of the charity auction. She was just so determined to win the date with Ultra Man that I just knew that something had to be wrong. I just wish that I'd hung in there and won the bid, then maybe this horrible situation with Ultra Man becoming a fugitive might not have developed. I just know that she must have some sort of evil hold on him. Ultra Man just isn't the sort of person to give up years of dedicated service to the community for some whor... sorry ... Villainess.
I can only hope that Ultra Man returns soon to hand her over to the proper authorities. Ultra Man, if you hear this, I still believe in you."

"That bimbo! I'm going to kill her," shrieked Ali, twisting the remains of the paper into a knot and throwing the mass against the nearest wall. "I am going to kill her dead. I'm going to pound her botoxed butt into the ground, and then I'm going to –"
"Don't hold back, Ali," said Craig, from behind the barricade he'd made out of the room's small couch and chair set. "Tell me how you really feel."
"Bitch," Ali hissed, her fists raised to an enemy who wasn't in the room. She glared across at Craig and straightened. "And you! You're enjoying this too much."
Craig held out his hands, palms up. "Hey, I'm a guy, and you're talking about a girl-on-girl fight. I can only hope to see the two of you wrestling in a pool of jello."
A pillow ricocheted off his head while Ali growled, low and harsh. Despite the threat in her voice, Craig gathered his courage, stood and walked across to her, brushing her new curls back off her face before drawing her into a hug. Under ordinary circumstances, she wouldn't let him hold her like this. Not without trying to remove his head from his shoulders. But right now, he was not the enemy. The V.P.'s sister, now, she was in trouble.
"Don't let it get to you," he said running his hand down her spine, risking a brush of fingers over the curve of her butt and closing his eyes when heat started to build in his groin. Wrong time, wrong place. Dammit, when was it going to be the right time? His hand returned to her waist. "She's a bitch, sure, but we're dealing with it. It will all go away soon."
"I don't understand. Why is she saying this? Why is the S.S.C. letting them get away with all this publicity? I mean, someone in-house had to give them my old photo." Ali twisted out of his grip and climbed onto the bed, drawing her

knees up to her chest and hugging them tightly.

"I have no idea who's responsible for the photo thing, although I'm certain Mr. Crunch is investigating."

"But why? Why me? Why could they possibly think I'm a fake Super Villainess? I've never manifested so much as a twitch of a Super Power."

"Ah." Craig's hands tightened on hers for an instant.

"Ah? What do you mean 'ah'?" Ali pulled back, a familiar glare in her eyes. "What do you know, Ultra Pain?"

"Listen, Ali. It's not what it sounds like."

"I'm not hearing anything. Talk fast, or I'll get my answers out of your steaming entrails."

Craig scooted back up the bed and raised his hands. "Ali, please. Give me a few minutes to get the words out before you grab a knife."

"Talk!"

Craig drew a deep breath and tried to organize his thoughts. "To be honest, I'd hoped we'd be able to bury the Ice Queen story without you ever finding out where it had originated."

"Because?" The growl was back in her voice.

"The video she's talking about was recorded after you left that apartment complex event site. I don't know how she got to view it, the editor of The Northern Star has been sitting on it like a mother hen, but it shows me talking to Mysterious West."

Ali's eyes narrowed and she crossed her arms over her chest, waiting.

"You know the effect West has on recordings. They didn't get both sides of the conversation. Hell, they didn't even get all of mine. But the recording was sold to that trash Northern Star newspaper, and the next thing I hear, they're using the recording as proof that I said I was afraid of this Villainess, The Ice Queen."

Ali's hand lashed out, slapping him hard across the face. "You called me an Ice Queen?"

"No! No! I swear, I didn't. I didn't say anything like that. I've seen a copy of the recording. If I could, I'd show it to you. I'd never say anything like that about you, Ali. Never."

"That so?"

"God," Craig dragged his hands over his face, "Ali, please believe me. I wasn't mad when you turned me down. I was *sad*! I told Mysterious West that I was ready to give up on trying to get you to go out with me, because you always were so cold to me. That being turned down all the time was like being stabbed in the heart."

"Oh," said Ali, staring down at her hands. "I'm sorry. But you could have stopped asking anytime."

"It would've been easier to stop breathing." Craig risked getting his hand ripped off, and brushed fingertips down the side of her face. "Straight up, Ali Cat. I couldn't stop. I had to keep hoping."

"Oh."

Craig watched as Ali continued her study of her now battered nail polish. As the moment stretched and she didn't fling herself into his arms, his heart sank into his churning stomach.

She didn't love him. She sincerely didn't love him.

Here was the perfect opportunity for her to declare herself to have been pretending to hate him all these years, and she was letting it go. He wasn't going to swallow his pride and let her know how much her silence hurt him. Unrequited love tasted foul.

"I am sorry, Ali," he whispered. "I never thought that you'd be sucked into something like this. I'd do anything to take that five minutes back. I'm sure it can still be fixed."

"We can't be sure of that," Ali started to cry, rocking back and forth. "Things are getting out of control. The Ice Queen was bad enough when she didn't exist, but now she's real. She's me, for heaven's sake. I'm the criminal. Just you wait. A few more hours, and they'll be saying the reason I kept saying that those sites were frauds was that I was trying to protect myself. Protect my goddamn secret identity."

Craig considered keeping quiet but knew that wouldn't work. Not once she recovered enough to read the papers or turn up the sound on the TV.

"They're already there, Ali. Have been for hours."

Ali dropped her forehead down on her knees and covered her head with her hands.

"I'm not myself anymore," she wailed. "They've made me into someone else. No one is ever going to believe this. I'll never be free."

"Don't worry so much," said Craig, stroking her hair. "It's going to be all right."

"No, it's not," Ali's head came up and she snarled at him. "Do you even realize what this means?! We're losing our jobs, our friends, everything! We're going to become fugitives for the rest of our lives. We're going to be on the run, not just for some crime we didn't commit, but for a crime that didn't even happen!"

Craig started to laugh at that. Quick as lightning, Ali slapped him across the shoulder. Not as hard as before. Craig took some comfort from that. Either her hand was getting weaker, or she wasn't as mad as she seemed.

"A lot you care."

"I do care, Ali, and you should relax. Even if we don't fix this, you're not going to be alone or helpless. I'm going to stick with you and look out for you. So what if we have to start over? It's not as if we're that old, or that we're leaving that much behind. I mean, besides your fish and Oliver, who have you spoken to outside the S.S.C. building in the last few months? The guy who delivers pizza? That's all, isn't it? Together, we'll be okay. We'll get jobs that don't involve getting woken up at two a.m. and live somewhere we can have conversations with our next-door neighbors without watching every word we say. Come on, think about it. It'll be fun."

Ali stared at him open-mouthed. Craig's ears finally caught up with his mouth.

"Anyway," he muttered, subsiding, "that's just one option. You shouldn't think the worst. We haven't failed yet."

Ali snapped her mouth shut and reached out to straighten his shirt collar.

"It's true, isn't it," she whispered. "You've been carrying a torch for me since college."

"I wouldn't say that, exactly," said Craig, painfully aware of heat spreading over the back of his neck. He shifted away, moving to the other bed.

"What would you say?" said Ali.

"That, I guess, if you'd ever said yes to me any of the times I asked you for a date then, perhaps, we might have had some fun."

"I see," said Ali, pushing her hair back off her face. "That's it?"

Craig studied her, watching for some sign of sorrow, or disappointment. But there was nothing but the usual calm, professional face that she'd shown him for so long. He was tempted to say something more, just to see if he could get another, any other reaction from her. Instead he simply said, "Yes."

"Lacey and Oliver were wrong, and they shouldn't have set us up with that auction nonsense."

"What?"

It was Ali's turn to laugh. "Thinking back over the last few months, they've tried a few times to get us together. Remember that trip back from Chicago? That was Oliver's idea."

Craig put on his own professional face and avoided eye contact. He'd been well aware of that setup. The plan had been in place for ages, waiting for the right event site to occur to put it into action.

"Not the auction, no, they're not responsible for that. I had a long talk from Mr. Crunch. That one did come down as a special request from the White House. For some strange reason, the S.S.C. really did want me to go on a date with – uh, that botoxed bitch."

"Too bad," said Ali. "They've got no right to complain. It was an auction, which means there was a risk that she wouldn't win. There was no reason why we, or anyone else, couldn't bid against her. For all S.S.C. knew, one of your fan clubs could have won the bid."

"I'm just as glad it was you," said Craig.

Ali's color heightened. "I am sorry I was so mean to you, Craig. Even not being interested, I could have been... politer about turning you down. I suppose I deserved the ice queen dig for the way I treated you."

"I never actually said 'Ice Queen,' Ali. I hope you believe me."

Craig watched Ali trace the enormous cabbage rose pattern on the quilt with her finger. The rage seemed to have faded, for which he was grateful, replaced with a strange stillness. He wasn't sure how long it would last, or what it meant, but he had to keep her from letting the latest news overwhelm her. He knew from his own Super training that once you gave up, once your spirit yielded, you might as well lie down and die. The other guy had won.

He might be biased, but he wanted the team of Craig and Ali to be the winners here. He wanted to stay on the Super teams, and he wanted Ali to be happy, which seemed to mean getting back the job she claimed to hate. In the meantime, she was so preoccupied, he might get some straight answers out of her.

"Yeah. I guess I believe you," said Ali, "It wasn't your style. Not really."

"Just out of idle curiosity, what was I doing wrong all these years? I can't believe it's because you weren't interested."

"It isn't important," said Ali, letting the tangled curls fall over her face.

Craig kept from brushing them gently back again only by sitting on his hands. When he'd tried to touch her in the past, she had kept dodging away. A stray touch may be all that was needed to send her back inside that shell. Patience was required here. Patience and a slow, careful absence of hand.

"It is to me," he said, trying out the Bambi-eye look that seemed to work so well for Oliver. "I'm the one who keeps striking out. For a guy, I'll have you know, that's no fun. Let me off the hook and tell me it's some deep childhood trauma and not my hair cut or aftershave."

"It was a deep childhood trauma," echoed Ali. "Your aftershave could make the S.S.C. a million bucks."

"No? Seriously? And I don't mean the aftershave, I don't wear any."

A grin flickered over Ali's face and Craig relaxed. The fight light was there in her eye. Faint, but there. She straightened, and her spirit seemed to settle firmly back in her body. The confident, competent Ali was back, and he would bet major bucks on the outcome of any mud wrestling match between a certain politician's relative and Ali would find Ali the victor.

"Oh, yeah? Talk to The Colonel about testing your pheromones. As for dating me, you were fighting a battle you couldn't possibly win. My dad, may he find fire ants in his jockey shorts for all eternity, was a practical joker. My earliest memories are of him putting toothpicks in my pancakes and giving me rubber knives and forks to eat with."

"Oh," Craig rubbed a hand over his face. "Ah. That's why you, uh...."

"Went ballistic whenever you pulled a stunt in the residences? Oh yeah. I hate that sort of so-called humor. I'd suffered through years of my dad's jokes before I left home. The worst part of it was even when mom and I were soaking wet and bruised because he'd put buckets over the doors or trying to wash some trick soap off our hands, he wouldn't let us get angry with him. Absolutely refused. He'd shout and glare at us. Or he'd just waltz off, saying it was our fault for having no sense of humor. Do you have any idea how much frustration hurts when it gets down in your stomach and sits there, day after day? It burns like acid. Like hate." She folded her hands over her belly. "I couldn't stop him. I couldn't avoid him. He was my dad, and I couldn't escape. Not for years. Every day, I'd stand on the street outside our house, or go to friends' homes, anything to avoid going home. Knowing that the longer I put off going inside, the worse he would get. I couldn't escape him. Not 'til college. Have you any idea what it's like living with someone like that? Home is supposed to be where you feel safe. And then, when I thought I was safe, that I was away from him, what do I find in college? You!"

Norman's comments had warned him, but he hadn't wanted to believe her anger went this deep.

"Ali, look. My stunts weren't like that and –"

Ali leaned forward and poked him in the chest. "Did you, or did you not saran wrap the girls' bathroom in the gym? Humiliating the girls who thought it was safe to take a pee?"

"Um. Yeah...."

"Put the coach, complete with reclining chair, on the top of the library? When he thought it was safe to go to sleep?"

"Well...."

"The leaning tower of trash cans? The groundskeepers almost got squashed when it collapsed."

"No one got hurt. Seriously hurt...."

"The mysterious gales through the quad that sent skirts up and trash flying everywhere?"

"We've explained about that one, Ali. I've lost count of the number of times I've explained we were responding to a fire engine siren."

"But the others, all those stunts. That was you?"

Craig raised his eyes and hands to heaven. "Yes! Yes. It was me. I'm guilty. Strike me down dead now for my sins!"

Ali slapped at his arms and shifted away. "You did things that humiliated people. Stood around encouraging other people to laugh at them. And you never, ever apologized. You never took responsibility."

All amusement fled Craig's face. "Okay, if that's what it takes, fine. I apologize. I'm sorry."

Ali regarded him quietly, her face set and stern. "Exactly what are you apologizing for?"

"Um," Craig stared at her in confusion. "For the jokes?"

"You don't even know what you're sorry for! That invalidates your apology. Until you fully understand, there's no way you can be sincere."

Craig fell back on the bed his arms outflung. "Tell me!" he demanded of the ceiling. "What do I have to do?"

Ali bounced off her bed and turned to face him, standing in Power Pose #2. "You've got the idea that if you say a generic 'I'm sorry,' then I can't be angry anymore and the whole problem goes away. You've probably got some hope stuffed away not too deep that when I forgive you then there might be some sex in your future. Well, tough, I'm not buying. That's not the solution. You don't get sex."

Craig groaned, covering his face with a pillow. "I am so tired of this."

"Well, it should be a comfort to you that it is all self-inflicted," said Ali, grabbing a newspaper and started flipping through. "It can stop at any time. Go hit on someone else."

"Ali – "

"No," Ali interrupted, "enough. I'm – no, I don't want to talk about this. It's not something we can resolve."

Craig rolled over and watched her in silence. Her movements were jerky and sharp as she flipped through the paper in her hands. She was so angry, he was surprised that the paper didn't burst into flames. But there it was. The familiar dance. The same frustrating damn argument. He didn't know what frustrated him most. That he wasn't able to get through to her. Explain to her. Convince her of his sweet disposition and responsible nature.

Ha.

No, the worst part was that he couldn't give her up. Couldn't give up hope. Couldn't go find someone lower maintenance. Someone who'd accept him. Some hero he was, accepting this abuse and standing outside her door, in the rain, metaphorically speaking, waiting vainly to be invited in.

He shook his head and gathered his scattered thoughts. All this was not helping solve the immediate problem. He still needed Ali's support and help.

"Well, we've got a lot of work to do to get our lives back," he said, slowly, extending the words as carefully as a turtle. Was it safe outside his shell?

"Exactly," said Ali, without raising her eyes from the paper, "And sitting around here rehashing our past is not helping."

Reaching for the pile of newspapers, Craig started turning pages himself. "I've got the map of Arizona. Let's start plotting the Jackalope sightings. It's the only lead we have."

"I wish we had a computer."

"It isn't safe for either of us to use one. We'd be tempted to use special codes, and they'd find us in seconds."

"Fine."

"I think that's enough," said Craig, a couple of hours later as he shook out the map. "The sightings are all south and east of here. Of all the Jackalope reports, this one's the most recent and it's inside the cluster. Let's hit the road. If we can't find anyone near the sighting to tell us anything, we'll move on."

"Exactly how are we supposed to do this?" asked Ali impatiently. "Go up to random people and ask them if they've ever heard of a Jackalope? They'll laugh us out of town."

"Hey, why should they? As far as they know we're some yellow sheet newspaper reporters doing a follow-up."

"You're kidding, right. Two reporters for a Jackalope story?" said Ali. "No one will buy that."

"Well, that's my cover story," said Craig, irritably. "Come up with one of your own if you don't like it."

It didn't take long to get them packed and on the road. Ali gave the matter thought for most of the afternoon as they drove south and resolved her problem by buying a complicated-looking digital camera when they stopped for dinner. Both a reporter *and* a photographer chasing Jackalopes might be more than any reasonable person would expect, but as long as she and Craig bullshitted with style and grace, no one would protest too much.

They arrived in the first town too late to do any serious Jackalope hunting, but established their cover by questioning the hotel receptionist, the maid and the waiter in the hotel's spectacular one-star late night diner. In reply, they received similar blank stares followed by sneers and giggles. The reactions were no less annoying for being expected but following the Jackalope trail was their only current hope. Unless they found another clue, or Lacey's spell worked faster than expected, they were stuck asking silly questions.

Leaving the diner, Ali kept her hand on her abdomen, trying by continuous pressure to still the razor-blade winged butterflies dancing in her stomach. She trailed behind Craig, watching his tight, muscular butt moving under the denim. She tried and failed to convince herself she was just another girl admiring the scenery as her blood heated and pulse raced. All the time knowing when they made it back to their room they'd be alone.

Craig's declaration that morning had taken her by surprise. Craig liked her. She was not prepared to give his feelings the more frightening or weightier word – love. All those years since college was a long time for it not to be a serious attachment. Without any reciprocation any sensible heart would have wandered off, found someone easier, less trouble to love.

He was loyal enough to stay with her, even if he didn't love her. If it did turn out to be necessary to create a new life, then she'd be sure to do it solo. She wouldn't hold onto him just because he was the last familiar face from her old life.

Her heart thundered as he put the key card into the slot – drowning out the rainstorm outside - and opened the door. Now, they had to get through the trauma of getting ready for bed.

Last night she'd had trouble sleeping, thinking about how to get her life back, and too stressed to worry about sharing a room with a reasonably healthy man. But today, yes, she was tired, but not so much that she wasn't aware that on the other side of the room was a man, a strong young man whose Superpowers included resilience. A man who thought he wanted her. Whatever it was he was thinking about was triggering one or another of his Powers; she could feel the heat of his body from across the room. Crowding her. Making the already tiny hotel room seem claustrophobic.

Craig stalked across the room, tossing his overnight bag carelessly onto the room's only easy chair and rooted through the piles inside until he found his toothbrush and a plastic package of clean underwear. Then he dove into the bathroom, not even bothering to ask if she wanted to use it first.

Irritated, Ali thumped down on the nearest bed to wait. She twisted her newly purchased cartoon character pajamas into knots while she studied the closed bathroom door.

Damn him, and the Super Power he rode in on.

The problem was, the longer she was away from the insanity of the Super Support SS.C., the less she wanted to go back. Who in their right mind would want the stress of keeping those secrets? Who would want to be woken at 3 am to pick their way over Ooze covered remains of homes and businesses?

Not her!

She hadn't applied for the job. Mr. Hackham had appeared at her dormitory door the day after exams. She'd been packed to go... nowhere, really. Mr. Hackham announced that, since she knew the new Purple Lightning's and Ultra Man's secret identities, she had a choice. She could work for the S.S.C. or go into Super witness protection. Since he'd described the protection program as something that sounded like a cross between a high-security insane asylum and a pathological Fantasy Island-type resort – one from which she would never be permitted to escape - she'd elected to take the job. She'd discovered later that the moving crew she'd hired were secretly paid off and replaced by an S.S.C. crew. It hadn't mattered to them which life she'd chosen, she was not going to escape being absorbed into the S.S.C. machine.

But now, with all the Ice Queen b.s. and being on the run from the law – and the S.S.C. – she was free for the first time in years. They'd thrown her out, or they'd let her quit – the end result was the same thing, she was out. It was her chance. If she ducked deep undercover now, took the money Delia had shuffled into a fake credit account, she could make herself a new life, far away from the Supers.

Free.

That assumed she would be able to escape Craig. The more she thought about it, the better the idea seemed. She knew enough to make creating a new identity possible and, heaven knew, if the only job she could get was waiting on tables in some diner, it still wouldn't wear her out the same way as her old job did. The only downside was giving up her old friends. Eliza. Norman. Oliver. Lacey. Her chest tightened and she turned to study the closed door again.

Craig.

She had one last responsibility to fulfill before she escaped – to the world and to Craig. She had to help return Ultra-Man to the side of right and light and get him back on the job.

Ultra Man was too important, too strong, too *Super* not to be working for the greater good.

Ali winced at her own thoughts.

When had she started thinking like a cliché greeting card writer? She sighed, swallowed to try and force down the pain in her chest.

No matter how cliché it sounded it was the truth – the world needed Ultra Man.

And Craig needed to *be* Ultra Man.

Life wouldn't, however, come to a crashing halt if Ali Brent disappeared. Which meant Ali could have her own life, far away from the noise and stress of the Super world. The T-shirt fabric between Ali's fingers tore and she glanced down – surprised. She'd expected to feel happy having come to a decision. Instead a heavyweight continued to hang in her chest.

Not long afterward, Craig emerged from the bathroom followed by a mass of steam. Ali tried to keep her eyes on the pattern of her quilt as he passed, but she couldn't help noticing the mist of moisture clinging to his bare legs. The scent of the generic hotel soap. The very short cotton boxers that he favored as nightwear. Craig halted only inches away from the end of her bed, fiddling with the TV, which put the curve of his butt within her reach. Her hands lifted, almost of their own accord, itching to cup that firm muscle. Instead, blushing to the roots of her hair, she grabbed for her toiletries bag and dove for the bathroom, banging her head on the door on her way past. Turning the water on hard, which didn't help to drown out his laughter, she stripped quickly.

The shower head seemed to prefer spraying the walls and the thick plastic curtain rather than the person in the tub, but by swaying from side to side Ali managed to wash most of the dust and sweat of the day off her skin. But she wasn't able to hose out the uncomfortable thoughts that kept the heat returning to her face.

Sooner or later, she was going to have to get out and face Craig. Nagging at the back of her mind was the realization that Craig deserved something for his years of... loyal courtship? Unrequited lust?

What had Oliver said? Craig wouldn't say no to just-for-fun sex. Well, right now, she wouldn't say no to thanks for not-hanging-me-out-to-dry sex. She might even mix in a little 'it was good to know you and you're good looking even if you're annoying' sex. She rested her head against the cool tile and let the water run. She had to admit to herself that most of her motivation to let Craig seduce her was that it was a good a way as any to say good-bye. She felt a little guilty that after all these years, she hadn't noticed his flirting. That she hadn't realized his flirting was serious. Before she took off to find her new life, she and Craig could, well, *do* something.

Who was she kidding? A deep blush spread across her face and headed south, heating her breasts.

She did not want to take the risk, but she wanted to give Craig – and herself – a goodbye party. And the best way to do that, she thought, grinning, was horizontal. She dragged the shower curtain back and picked up the tiny square of hotel soap and sniffed it. None of the soaps a hotel provided was even remotely sexy.

Ali reached across the toilet to her little bag. She'd picked up a fruit scented body wash at the airport spa -- that would be a whole lot better.

Craig was off the bed and tearing the bathroom door off its hinges before Ali's scream faded.

"Ali!"

"Don't come in," Ali shouted back. "Stay out."

Craig stopped, door still clutched in his hands. "What happened?"

"Never mind," Ali's voice echoed strangely and there was a sound like a dozen junk food packets being crushed. "Just stay the hell out."

He waited a moment longer listening to the shower being turned off and a few muffled thumps and curses. He leaned forward and peered around the door.

A low-flying, soggy washcloth splattered against the door he still held. "I said, Stay Out," shrieked Ali.

Chuckling, Craig propped the door against the wall and retreated. He'd gotten a good look at the wrecked bathroom. Poor Ali was sprawled in the tub under a twisted curtain rail in a pose that would never have made the centerfold but was pretty good as far as Craig was concerned. The opaque crumpled plastic shower curtain covered most of Ali's essential details, but he had a good imagination.

"Are you hurt?" called Craig.

There was a long pause before Ali replied.

"I have a bruise on my dignity," she said.

Craig chuckled and turned away. "Yep, that would describe it."

Ali emerged ten minutes later moving stiffly, her hair straggling down her face. She glared across at Craig as she scuttled across the room in her pretty t-shirt and dove under the blankets without making eye contact with him.

"Ali Brent," Craig glanced up from the paper just long enough to see her eyes darken and brows draw threateningly together. If she were a weather system, right now he'd be warning ships at sea to get ready for a perfect storm. Instead, he returned his attention to the paper. "You have a high opinion of yourself, don't you? Are you expecting me to leap across the room and ravish your unwilling body?" When she didn't reply, he casually crossed his legs, tenting the blankets up to conceal his building erection and kept his gaze focused on the newsprint. "Sorry to disappoint, dear, but if I remember correctly, that's illegal in this state, so I'll take a pass."

Ali blinked at him. "Illegal? What?"

"Ravishing a girl in a Powerpuff T-shirt." He pointed at the cartoon characters on her chest, "It'll get you five to ten in maximum security lock-up."

"Comedian," said Ali, pulling the covers up to her shoulders.

Resolutely, she turned her back on him and wiggled about under the blankets trying to find a position that didn't put pressure on her new bruises. A few minutes later, Craig clicked off the light and the only sound in the room was the rustling of sheets. Ali was almost asleep when she heard a strange, strangled cough from the other bed. She came upright prepared to perform the Heimlich maneuver if necessary when she realized that Craig had a pillow stuffed in his mouth to smother his laughter.

Chapter Sixteen.

Québec Times
The Sasquatch was inducted into the Washington state Super Team today. Canadian authorities immediately protested on the grounds of nationality, stating that The Sasquatch should serve in Canada. When it was pointed out that The Sasquatch had signed a three-year contract, the lawyers retained by Canada responded saying that a creature that is not literate, numerate and incapable of intelligible speech cannot participate in legal contracts.
He was immediately approached by representatives of several political parties to run for Premier.
Litigation is expected to be ongoing.

Ali leaned against the side of the rental car and watched Craig attempt to drag information out of the gas station attendant who'd – they'd heard that morning from the cook at a diner - bragged about shooting at a Jackalope. The guy had missed, which was why he didn't have a trophy to prove his claim. Craig emerging from the pay kiosk, the frustration written plainly on his tired face was a far too familiar sight, this being their third stop today. Ali let her attention wander. Arizona did not measure up to her expectations so far. Granted, it was warmer than New Jersey this time of year. But all she'd known about the state before arrival was that the Grand Canyon was somewhere in it. The road they'd been on this morning was flat and straight, the car had four wheels, and the roadside diners served the same pancakes and bacon as back home.

She smiled, watching Craig make his way across the dry asphalt. It surprised her how quickly she had gotten used to seeing him in civilian clothing. Out of the Bronze and Green, he seemed real in a way Ultra Man never achieved. Ultra Man was magical. He entered the room, spoke to you and you felt like you were in the presence of an Archetype, an Avatar... her lips curved, a pop star? In his Super Suit he had incredible presence. In blue jeans and a button-down shirt he was still handsome, still strong, but approachable.

She could tell Craig was finding their journey a trial. He'd been Ultra Man for so long that he'd forgotten how most folks reacted around ordinary people. He was experiencing delays for the first time since he'd put on his Super Suit. The waiter at the diner hadn't fallen over himself to bring Craig's meal fast, or first – after all, a Superhero must always be on his way to some important crime scene and needed expedited service. The motel receptionist had been bored and paid more attention to the music coming from the headphones hanging around her neck than Craig's attempt at conversation.

Craig stalked back to the car, his feet kicking up dust. He passed Ali a six-pack of cold sodas and climbed into the driver's seat.

"Anything?" asked Ali, settling back into the passenger seat.

"He offered to sell me the local equivalent of the Brooklyn Bridge, since I was gullible enough to believe in Jackalopes."

Ali nodded solemnly. "Well, I could do with a nice bridge. Is it wood or steel? Did you ask what the price was? Payment plan?"

"Funny girl," growled Craig. "Why couldn't the Jackalopes be sighted in one of those Hollywood small towns? Then we'd have half a dozen dozy locals lining up to tell us about this here house down a dirt road where *strange things have been happening, ya'all*. We'd go take a look, and there would be Nuclear Man. All nice and iconic."

"Ah, isn't it a real shame life is so hard," Ali sighed and rubbed the cold soda can against her face.

"Got a better idea?" Craig gripped the wheel hard and glared at her. "Going to use your feminine wiles on someone to get an answer?"

"I was thinking of checking in with the local news-rag and see if someone will extend a little professional courtesy."

"It's a plan," said Craig, grudgingly. "Where do we start?"

Ali extended one finger and pointed across the street. The local newspaper office was a neat storefront in a well populated mini-mall, right next to a chain grocery store and a pizzeria. They parked the car in front of the grocery, choosing not to advertise which store they were patronizing. This time, Ali chose to start the questioning. Knowing that her dour S.S.C. employment photo was still on the front page of papers all across the country she freshened her makeup, fluffed her new do and fixed a brilliant smile on her face. It occurred to her, briefly, to wonder why no one at S.S.C. had come forward with a better photo. Surely someone back there had to have a shot of her smiling. Who had released the damn photo anyway?

The receptionist looked up from her computer long enough to measure Ali from toe to top, then let her eyes slide pass to repeat the assessment on Craig. She smiled and nodded to him but flicked her gaze back to Ali when she spoke.

"I hope you can help us," said Ali, moving closer to the desk. "We've been sent down to do a follow up on a story that seems to have originated near here, but we're not certain if it actually started with your paper. The Jackalope story."

"Your editor sent you out chasing Jackalopes?" the receptionist asked, laughing. "Man, what did you do? Pass on an interview with Mr. Ooze? Refuse to go on a date with his ugly son?"

"It's a nature story," lied Ali. "My editor has a bug up his ass about the Supers. There're more of them every year, he says. He's wondering if Jackalopes were signs that whatever's wrong with the human race is spilling out over to the rest of the animal kingdom." Ali winked at the girl, "His words, not mine."

The receptionist sat up straighter and appeared to give that news slant serious thought. "Could be. You know, that's a nice spin. I'd like to help you," said the girl, again letting her eyes drift over Craig. "In fact, this paper's *official* stance on Jackalopes is that they don't exist. We may be small, but we have some pride. We usually don't do that sort of human interest story."

"But you do know about it," said Craig, moving closer and blessing her with his famous smile. "Can you direct us to the person responsible?"

The girl sighed and shook her head, now directing her answers to Craig, no matter who questioned her. Ali stepped back and left them to it. Although not officially one of his Powers, when Craig turned on the charm, most women melted. It was nauseating to watch.

"Don't tell my dad, but the truth is, it was my stupid brother who put that photo and story on the wire. Jimmy was so pissed when he didn't get credit when it got picked up that he told me about it. When he calmed down he told me it was only fair, since he'd filched the story from a kid he met."

"What about the photo?" asked Ali. "Was it real or a photoshop job?"

"Real, *he says*. He got it from the kid."

"Which kid? Can you find who and where?" asked Ali.

"Nah," said the girl. "Dad found out about one of Jim's other stunts and sent him off on a shit job. I'm not sure when he'll be back. Sometimes when he gets these assignments he just doesn't come back for days. Just to show Dad that he's an independent spirit and stuff."

"Terrific," muttered Craig, then raised his voice again, "Are you certain you have no way to get in contact with him?"

"Not when he wants to hide."

Craig nodded, turned on his heel and stalked out of the room.

Ali said goodbye to the disappointed receptionist and restrained the urge to slap Craig over the head with her purse. He'd turned the charm off so suddenly it was surprising that the girl hadn't collapsed in a puddle. Ali gave the receptionist a sympathetic smile and got a jealous glare in return. Sighing, Ali followed Craig from the building.

She was beginning to get worried. It was almost two days since Lacey had activated her spell, and something should have happened. The universe should have reshaped itself to get them going on the path to Nuclear Man. They should be getting some sort of hint that it was working. Instead… nothing. Or could it be that Ali suddenly deciding to ask someone at a paper about Jackalopes, just when she was standing outside the newspaper where the latest round of stories originated, was a result of the spell?

She chewed at what remained of her nail polish. Maybe they should stay here, let Nuclear Man come to them. Lacey had said they should just move, do whatever seemed right and the universe would catch up with them.

She walked beside Craig as he stumped down the street. Maybe she should tell him about the spell. He'd had years of experience of working with The Mysterious West. He might have an idea of what they could do to increase the spell's effectiveness.

Whatever's going to happen has to happen soon, she thought, crossing her fingers by reflex.

The more time passed without clearing their names, the harder it was going to be to get people to believe them. As it was, there was certain to be some permanent damage to Ultra Man's reputation. She glanced across at Craig. His face was set. Stern. If he wasn't careful, someone would comment on his similarities to the photos of an angry Ultra Man.

"Do you want me to drive for a while?" asked Ali, leaning against the car.

Craig shook out the map and spread it over the roof. "Nah, I'll be fine." He grinned and put on his sunglasses. "I need to feel I'm doing something."

"Ah," said Ali, closing her eyes and turning her face toward the sun. "Testosterone."

Craig snorted. "I think it'd be a waste of time to just go randomly questioning all the teenagers in town, trying to find the person Jimmy stole that photo from. Which leaves us with the question, what now?"

"We could wander around for days and not find him," agreed Ali. "Maybe we should go to the next sighting and see what we can find."

"Okay." Craig nodded and folded up the map. "So, what do you want to do? Hit the diner for lunch?"

"Nah." Ali thought about it for a moment, staring at the faded grey and pink painted building. It didn't feel right. Instead she pointed to the grocery store. "Let's just pick up some junk and hit the road."

The air conditioning hit them like a wall just inside the doors. Ali sighed and lifted her hair, letting the cool air brush across the back of her neck. The other customers glanced around at the new arrivals, then returned to their shopping. Craig stepped up close and scanned the room from over Ali's shoulder. Ali's lips twitched and she kept herself from patting him on the head and saying "down, good boy," with difficulty.

"Let's just grab a hot dog and some drinks and hit the road," said Craig, cupping her elbow and guiding her further into the store. He stopped as they passed the smokers' section and tossed a box of Magic Lights (Mysterious West brand) matches into her basket.

"For luck," he said.

Ali tried unsuccessfully to ignore the pressure of his fingers on her skin. Craig's protective gene kicked in at the oddest times, and her reaction to it baffled her. Last night's embarrassment still burned, but she found she liked the touch on her arm, the warm presence at her back. Independence was all very well, but it got tiring after a while. Every now and then, it felt good to be protected. Sort of cherished. Sometimes it felt good to just know she could take it easy and let someone else take out the trash – metaphorically speaking.

She threw a smile over her shoulder and rested her hand over Craig's fingers. Craig stopped scowling around the room and focused on her.

"What?" he asked.

"Nothing," said Ali, taking her hand away.

"No. Come on, Ali, there's something on your mind."

Ali backed away, still grinning, a little inhibited in her maneuvering by the narrow aisle and bumped into the shopper behind her. She turned, an apology on her lips, then gasped.

"Steve?! Heavens above, what are you doing down here?"

Craig was beside her in an instant, maneuvering himself between Ali and the new arrival.

"Who's Steve?" he demanded, not taking his attention from the tall black man.

Ali laughed, resting her fingers on his shoulder.

"Relax, Craig. I don't suppose you got a chance to be introduced, things have been so crazy this last week. Steve is dating Oliver." She cast a worried glance at Steve. "It is still present tense, isn't it? I'd hate to think you'd broken up already."

"No." Steven closed his mouth with a snap and seemed to struggle to gather his wits. "I mean, yes, we're still dating. Ali, isn't it? I didn't expect to see you here."

"We're on vacation," lied Ali, glancing down to where Craig's grip on her arm had increased. "Steven Holtzman, this is Craig Duane. Craig, this is the guy Oliver's been dating for about a week. They met at the gym."

The two men exchanged stiff nods and a brief handshake. Aware of a tension she didn't understand, Ali chatted on.

"Of course, I don't expect you've seen much of Oliver the last few days. Last time I spoke to him, he said he had to do a lot of overtime. Some staffing problems with the airline, I think."

"Yeah," said Steve, keeping his attention mostly on Craig. "I had to go out of town, so it worked out okay for us. I call him every evening, and we exchange messages on answering machines."

"What are you doing here?" asked Craig.

Ali caught the warning tone in his voice and bit back a protest. Steven didn't appear to notice and lifted a bag of chips off the display.

"I'm covering for a salesperson who had a family emergency. One of the disadvantages of being a sales manager."

"Of course," agreed Ali.

"But I expect to be back in New Jersey soon," said Steve. "Perhaps we could get together. Double date?"

"I'd like that," said Ali, ignoring Craig's scowl. "We should be going home soon. I'll mention it to Oliver when I next speak to him. I think you're likely to call him first. Remind him to feed my fish."

"Sure. Look forward to it." Steve smiled at them both, waved and headed away toward the checkout.

Ali watched him go then, pressing her hand hard on Craig's chest pushed him further back in the store. She tried not to think about the warmth that spread up her hand from his chest. His skin was heating up, a sure sign that he was angry or preparing to use his Super abilities. Not wanting to see him pound on Oliver's current sweetie, Ali concentrated on blocking Craig's efforts to watch Steve leave the store.

"What's wrong with you?!" she hissed when she had him pinned against the freezers.

"Who is that guy?" demanded Craig, still glaring at the exit. "What happened to Harry?"

"Where have you been? Boy, are you out of the loop. Harry kicked Oliver out a couple of weeks ago. Why did you think he was bunking at my place?"

"Oh." Craig blinked and settled back on his heels, tension leaking from his face. "I guess I didn't think about it. You're right, I do remember Lacey saying something about a breakup, but isn't it too soon for Oliver to be dating again?"

"Who are you?" demanded Ali. "His father? I don't think it's been more than two dinners and a movie, so far."

A strange look passed over Craig's face, and he refocused his gaze on Ali. "Then they're ahead of us, aren't they," he said. "Dating wise."

"Well, yes," Ali blushed and stepped away, pulling her hand off his chest as if stung. "Actually, we've had breakfast, lunch and dinner together for the past two days. I suppose you could say we've caught up."

Craig's grin broadened and he ran a hand over her hair.

"All we need is a movie. We'll have to see what's available at the motel tonight."

Flustered, all Ali could think of saying was, "Okay."

Turning, she snatched a few bags of chocolate chip cookies off the shelf. A moment later she halted and smiled, batting her eyelashes at him.

"But Craig," she said, sweetly, her head tilted to one side. "You didn't have to go to all this trouble just to get a date with me. The being chased by the Feds is just a little over the top, don't you think? For a first date, that is."

He didn't reply immediately, and Ali's smile started to fade. Then he wrapped an arm around her shoulders and kissed her cheek.

"Nothing's too good for you, Ali girl. And here I was thinking you didn't appreciate all my hard work."

Ali sat in the passenger seat, a pile of empty food wrappers on her lap, trying to persuade her shivery stomach and nerves to calm down. It had been a simple peck on the cheek. Barely half a second long, in the junk food section of a grocery store, for heaven's sake. Hardly the sort of thing to appear on America's Most Romantic Moments.

Mr. Bendit had kissed her in the just the same spot last December when she'd caught him under the mistletoe down at the Supply department bash, but that kiss hadn't left her insides bouncing around like the only ice cube in the blender. She held the map in hands that clenched and trembled whenever she remembered the heat passing from his body to hers and the light, casual kiss. It meant nothing. She was hypersensitive, that was all. If Lacey and Oliver hadn't told her about Craig, she wouldn't even have noticed.

To clear her mind and try to give herself time to escape from her thoughts she considered the strange meeting with Steve. Had something gone wrong with Lacey's spell? Ali reached into her handbag, searching for the photocopied letter she'd given Lacey as a focus. She unfolded the paper and examined both sides. She couldn't see anything that might refocus the spell onto Oliver's current squeeze, except maybe the fact that Oliver had handled the paper.

"What's up?" asked Craig, having watched her antics for several minutes in silence.

"I'm not sure…. That is, I don't know if I can discuss it with you."

"What do you want me to say? 'Darling, you can trust me with anything'?" Craig rolled his eyes. "Hell, as long as it's nothing to do with personal hygiene, I'll listen."

Ali crinkled her nose at him and smoothed the crushed corners of the photocopy. "Oh, gross. No, I was just wondering … hypothetical situation, you understand… does talking about one of Mysterious West's spells make it less effective?"

"Oh hell," groaned Craig, slapping his forehead. "Did you ask her for something?"

"Yes. I mean, running into Steve here, out the wrong side of nowhere, is odd. I was wondering if something had gone wrong."

The car slowed down as Craig gave her a long, intent look. "What, pray tell, did you ask her?"

"I'm not sure if I can tell you," said Ali, ashamed of the wail in her voice.

"Ali, don't tease. Either tell me, or…. Hell's bells, just tell me!"

She twisted the paper in her hands into a knot then unrolled it and smoothed it out on her knee.

"Um. Well…. I guess I should tell you I've been in contact with P.L. and The Mysterious West since we left New Jersey."

"Damn," Craig slapped the steering wheel. The car swerved across the lane and he pulled it straight with a curse. "Didn't I tell you I didn't want them involved? I wanted them to retain deniability." He huffed out a breath and concentrated on the road for a few seconds. "Okay, you spoke to them. Then what happened?"

Ali decided that there were certain parts of that conversation she didn't think Craig needed to know about and stuck to the highlights.

"I called them to talk about providing backup when the time came. I told West that I was worried that we could wander out here for months and never find Nuclear Man. She did something she called an 'event's conspired' sp –"

Craig cursed again and tightened his grip on the wheel, shaking it.

"Dammit Ali, do you have any idea how dangerous that spell is? We never use it."

Ali shrank back in her chair and gave one weak nod.

"She told me. She said it could cause accidents, crashes, goodness knows what, trying to bring two people together. But she agreed with me, we had to do something to make it possible for you and he to meet, and soon. The thing that worries me is that it might have gone wrong. The only out-of-place person we've run into is Steve."

Craig stared thoughtfully through the windscreen.

"No. Actually, Ali, this could be a good sign. You didn't have any reason to expect to run into this Steve person, so it could be an early indication that the universe is reshaping itself. How much time did West put into that spell?"

"No sooner than three days, I think, and we did it two days ago."

Craig nodded, the worried air that surrounded him fading.

"Good. I'd say we were on schedule. Sometime tomorrow we'll see Nuclear Man."

"But, how? And what do we do in the meantime?"

He turned and flashed her a smile before returning his attention to the almost empty road.

"Nothing. Anything. Relax. Everything we do will bring us closer to the meeting. Once the spell takes hold, and this meeting with Steve makes me think that it has, then the spell's resolution is inevitable."

"And that's good, is it?"

"You're the one who started it." He chuckled. "Don't play with Powers you don't understand. You could end up burned, oh Ice Queen."

"Huh." Ali folded her arms and settled back in her seat staring out of her window at the dull scenery. "You're the one who's got to face Nuclear Man, Oh Ultra Guy. Have you given any thought to how you're going to do it without your armor?"

"I could ask Oliver to bring down my spare suit, since you've already told them what we're doing. Except there is the risk that they have activated the tracking unit in it. Even if Oliver disables it, they'll know immediately and he could get into a ton of trouble."

"If they catch him," said Ali, but Craig shook his head.

"It's too dangerous, Ali. I have no idea how much technology they've stuffed into my damn suit. For all I know, it's got triple redundancy global positioning backup systems, and I'll never be able to disable all of it before the Super Hunter squad arrives. And since I don't want to punch any friends in the face, I think I'd like to avoid having them joining the party."

Ali chuckled. "What if they promised to send Flash Heat and Urban Renewal instead of the Hunters?"

"Ah," said Craig, smiling broadly. "Now that would be a punch in the face of a different color."

Chapter Seventeen.

New York evening news radio.
Captain Fabulous was admitted to hospital this afternoon after he over-extended himself during a bridge rescue. A team comprising 4 orthopedic surgeons and 16 chiropractors have been working on the injured Super since his admission. A hospital spokesperson stated that they cannot comment on Captain Fabulous's prognosis at this time, as they do not yet know if they have all his bits in their correct order.

Now that Craig knew about the spell he was cheerful, almost relaxed. No doubt with all his exposure to Mysterious West's spells over the years, he'd learned to rely on her magic. Ali, however, continued to worry, something that seemed faintly ridiculous in the face of Craig's new confidence and complacent good humor.

"Have you given any thought to what you're going to do when we get back?" asked Craig.

"Back?" Ali swallowed as heat spread up from her chest to stain her face red. "…To the hotel?"

Fortunately, Craig was not paying attention. "No, to work. To the S.S.C. Have you decided if you're gonna make them beg before you go back? Or are you going to forgive them if they promise to give you a raise? The way I figure it, they owe you at least a title bump for the hell they've put you through the last week."

Ali twisted in the car seat to face him. "Are you nuts? There is no going back for me. I've known since the moment they used my real name on TV that I'll never have my life back. I may go out with a naked face at event sites, but I was never supposed to be identified. You know SS.C. policy! *Protect your secret identity at all costs* applies to me as much as to you."

Craig's smile vanished. "Ali, we're going to –"

"Don't tell me we can fix this," growled Ali. "It's not going to work. The most we can hope for right now, is for you to get back to work with your reputation mostly intact. With what they've been saying in the press, there'll always be people who don't trust you anymore."

Craig gritted his teeth and tightened his grip on the wheel. "I can earn it back. I'm going to earn it back."

"Fine, but I don't have a Super reputation to support me. I'm supposed to be an unknown. I'm supposed to turn up, do my job anonymously and vanish into the night. Lacking a history of good works – I mean, who really paid any attention to me when I was at event sites? - This publicity means that Ali Brent will always be synonymous with the Ice Queen. And no matter what public announcements are made, there'll always be people who'll believe that I'm a

Super-Powered Villainess. I'm not going to be able to get my life back. I thought you realized that."

"I won't let that happen."

"No?" said Ali. "Be realistic. I am. The most important thing we have to do is get Ultra Man back on duty. I'll even admit that it's more important than getting rid of the Ice Queen. If being her and disappearing is the price I have to pay to get you back on patrol, I'm willing to pay it." She sighed and forced herself to relax in her seat. "I've even started planning. How do you think I'd do as a waitress? Just to get me on my feet. I could work my way up to working in a bookstore or mall."

"Damn it, Ali!"

With a crack, the plastic steering wheel shattered under his hands. Splinters flew across the car as Craig grabbed at what remained of the wheel while the car swerved back and forth across the road.

"Craig," screamed Ali, bracing both hands against the dashboard.

He seized the remains of the wheel and hauled on it, pulling the car back into the lane. Fortunately, there was barely any traffic and those cars nearest had been able to dodge away in time.

"What the hell was that about?" shouted Ali, releasing her grip one finger at a time.

Ignoring her, Craig guided the car towards the next exit. "We can't talk about this here," he said. "We'll cause a bloody accident." Ignoring Ali's whispered 'We, who, Kemosabi?' He turned the car into a fleabag motel entrance and stopped the car in front of the office. "Wait here."

He leaped from the car and stalked away. Ali sat and concentrated on her breathing. After a moment, she shook herself and scanned the surroundings. If anyone noticed Craig's crazy driving and notified the police, or worse, the media they could be in trouble. Fortunately, there weren't many cars in the motel parking lot, and drive-by and walk-by traffic was light to non-existent. Even so, Ali remained twitchy and tried to think of a reasonable explanation for a steering wheel with two big chunks torn out of it just in case someone wandered by. She pulled his light denim jacket out of the back seat and arranged it over the wheel. It looked silly, but, with luck, passersby would pay no attention.

By the time she'd arranged the jacket to her satisfaction, Craig was back, motel key in hand. He gave the jacket a puzzled glance but made no comment, starting the car and gunning the engine. Seconds later, he was drawing to a halt outside the ground floor room farthest from the road, having broken several land speed records for driving in a parking lot. Ali unclenched her death grip on the door and wished she had enough spit to swallow. Before she could gather her wits, Craig was out of the car and hauling their bags out of the trunk. She climbed out, locked the car and – lacking the courage to run – followed him through the door he held open. As soon as she was across the threshold, Craig locked the door and grabbed her arm, dragging her across the room. Bags and coats went flying to the floor.

"Craig! What the hell is your pathology?"

"Shut up," growled Craig, hauling her hard against his chest and kissing her.

Ali stiffened, forced her hands between their bodies and pushed with all her strength, to no effect. Craig held her solidly against him. One hand gripped her hips, crushing her intimately against his growing erection. Ali tried for a short arm punch to the gut but couldn't get a good angle.

Craig released her lips and growled. "You're not paying attention. What do I have to do to get you to pay attention to me?"

Ali tried to catch her breath. His arm, tight around her chest, had to be why she could barely draw in enough to whisper.

"You can start by letting go," she said.

"Never again," said Craig. "Not until we get something clear. Do you have any understanding of why I do what I do?"

Ali dismissed the first answer that crossed her mind, deciding that now was not a good time for jokes and shook her head.

"It's really basic, Ali," said Craig, his voice surprisingly calm. "It's not for the money. Hell, I could make an easier, safer living hand-feeding sharks in some show. It's not for the fame. Secret identities and all that make fame irrelevant. Besides, I don't need fame, never did. It's for the same goddamn reason prehistoric man hit woolly mammoths over the head and dragged them back to the cave. I do it for you. For my mate. To keep her safe. I might also save someone else's loved one, but that is secondary. Believe me, waaaaay secondary. First and foremost, I do it for you."

Ali's "Me?" was little more than a squeak before Craig claimed her mouth again. This time his touch was heated, not punishing. He drew the tip of his tongue over her lower lip before sucking it between his own. The light touch of his teeth on the sensitive inner surface drew a whimper from her and she leaned into his embrace.

Craig's grip loosened. One hand drifted up her spine to cup her neck, fingertips brushing the nape of her neck. Ali could feel his grin as she shivered under his touch. He drew back, examining her dazzled expression with some satisfaction.

"I'm not a philosophical kind of guy, Ali. I can't operate on a high moral ground. Some Supers may be able to function that way, but not me. Never could. It was hard when I first started, trying to find a reason to face yet another ravening monster or out of control disaster. But then I'd remember that someone like you could be hurt. Some guy's girlfriend. Someone's sister. I know that when I get a call about a disaster, so do you. Sooner or later you'd be coming to the event site to help the bystanders and I had to make sure there was no residual danger. It all had to be safe before you arrived."

"You can't have thought that. Not for all this time," whispered Ali, resting her hands on his shoulders.

"Sure, I can. Vague concepts like Truth and Justice don't work for me. I need something real. Something solid. Something I can touch," his hands wandered down her spine to cup her buttocks. To squeeze and massage the warm muscle. He watched her shiver and leaned close to nuzzle at her neck. "I know that if you're okay, that you can go to work, come home without being mugged, robbed or getting spam email, then I've done my job. It may not make sense to you or anyone else, Ali, but it's what keeps me getting up every morning. It's what I needed to keep putting on that silly mask."

Color flooded Ali's face. "If that's the case, I haven't helped you much. We never see each other. No dates equals no inspiration."

Craig ran his knuckles down the side of her face and trailed down to the valley between her breasts, fingertips brushing the flesh his gesture exposed. "You may not have seen me, but I've well kept an eye on you," A flash of fire burned in his eyes and Ali trembled, "not that I'm happy to have protected you from afar. I'm telling you right now, that time is most definitely over." He twisted, lifting and dumping her onto the bed and following her down, crushing her between his heavy length and the hard mattress. "You're my girl, Ali. I've known it since the first day I saw you. Wanted you since the first time I saw you- you were arguing with the Dean. I remember, I felt so sorry for the guy, knowing he was completely outclassed and outgunned. I wanted you then, even before I knew your name. I want you now. Unless you move fast, run now, then I'm never going to let you escape me again."

Ali wiggled, rubbing her breasts against his imprisoning arms and her blush deepened.

"I can't get up," she protested. "No fair. You're using Super Strength."

Craig grinned. "I never said I'd make it easy for you. I don't want you to go. Get used to the idea. We either get back into S.S.C., or we go build a different life, but we do it *together*. If I have you, then I could happily flip pancakes for the rest of my life. Don't make the mistake of thinking you're going to escape me, my patience is exhausted."

"Craig, be realistic. The world needs Supers. It's become dependent on _"

"Let me make this clear, Ali, my girl. If the only chance I have to be a hero for the rest of my life is when I climb a tree to rescue a kid and her kitten, then as long as it's our tree, our kid and our kitten, that's the sort of Super I want to be."

Ali finished chewing on her lip, spread her fingers over his chest and gazed up at him. "Never thought you were a cat guy."

Craig ignored the comment, merely tightening his grip on her. "What's your answer, Ali?"

"I don't remember any question."

The corners of his mouth turned up and he nodded. "You're right. I didn't ask. I just ranted." he took her hand in his and raised it to his lips. "Dear Ali, I'm sorry, the ring I picked out is back in my apartment. I'll get it for you later. For now, my love, will you marry me?"

Ali gaped at him for a heartbeat. Two. "You have a ring?"

He nodded, grinning.

"For how long?"

"I'm not going to let you get a swelled head about it, so never mind how long. Just answer. Will you have me for your personal hero?" he laid one hand over his heart. "I promise not to tear down the house, break water mains and dig up the flower beds – unless so ordered."

"No."

Craig tightened his grip until she whimpered, then he transferred his grip to the pillow beneath her. Ali didn't move, didn't so much as breathe, until the tension leaked out of his body and he rolled away.

"It's not going to work," she said, in a voice almost too low to be heard. "Staying together. Too many people have seen our photos side by side. They'll see me, recognize me and know that the guy I'm with is you."

"Don't argue with a certified Super. We tend to get huffy when someone says there's something we can't do. We go all out to prove we can."

Ali sighed and fell silent. He hadn't mentioned love. He'd been territorial, demanding, and passionate. There'd been admiration, lust in his words and his touch, but no words of love. She shifted a little further away from the Superheat leaking from his body. Maybe it was better that he hadn't said the words. It would be so much harder to endure the inevitable separation if he'd declared undying devotion. He was so focused on 'fixing' the problem that he wouldn't even think about the alternatives. Optimism was a necessary part of the Super psyche, just as realism was necessary for an insurance assessor. No matter how she crunched the numbers the odds were still against them.

After a few minutes silence Craig settled beside her on the bed staring at the ceiling. She couldn't tell what he was thinking, and now was not the time to ask. No doubt he'd already paid for the night's stay. She pulled a corner of the quilt over her shoulders. A nap. A brief nap. He'd calm down and she'd be able to think clearly, then they'd talk again.

Ali awoke some measureless time later with Craig's arm flung over her chest, his leg over her hips and his weight pinning her to the bed. As her bladder was yelling at her she tried to slip out from under him. At the first wiggle his grip tightened and both eyes snapped open.

"Where do you think you're going?"

"Bathroom," said Ali, pushing at his arm. "Then out."

His eyes narrowed. "Out for what?"

"For food. Real food."

"Pizza," said Craig, as he rolled off her and reached for the phone book on the bedside table.

While he was distracted Ali rolled the other way, off the bed.

"What do you think you're doing?" asked Craig. "We can call for pizza. They'll deliver."

"I've had enough junk," said Ali, "I want to sit at a table and eat something green that was at one time a vegetable. Food, Craig. In a restaurant."

Craig waved a hand at the thin cardboard furnishings and industrial quality carpet. "I don't think this motel runs to in-house dining, Ali."

"There's a diner across the parking lot. I saw it while I was waiting for you to check in. We can walk across, no problem." At Craig's sulky look, she grinned. "Think of it as a date. Don't I still owe you one or two?"

"I thought we'd gotten past that," said Craig.

Ali blushed. There was a light in his eyes that warned her she was not forgiven for rejecting his proposal. He'd revealed too much of himself, made himself vulnerable and she'd turned him down flat. Revenge was a very real possibility.

"Up you get, I turn nasty if I'm not fed regularly."

"If only you'd told me that sooner," muttered Craig, but obligingly climbed from the bed.

For a diner, Craig had to admit the food wasn't bad, although the service was slow. It could have been a seven-star restaurant and he'd still have damned every minute, every mouthful that kept them there when they could have been back at the motel. It had taken him the best part of seven years to get her into bed, and he was far from finished there. He didn't let Ali linger over her coffee and ordered a couple of slices of pie to-go before she could dither over dessert. Ali had a wicked light to her eyes during the meal, and she'd chatted lightly with the waitress, delaying her and tormenting him. But now that he'd finally cleared the air and marked his territory, so to speak, he wasn't going to endure any prolongation of his self-imposed celibacy. She'd had time to think and reconsider. By now, she'd realized that her refusal was not going to be tolerated. Once back in the hotel room, he wasn't going to accept silence, or self-sacrifice as a reason to avoid the relationship he'd known was inevitable for years. If he could have been confident there were no witnesses, he would have flown them back to their room just to get there a few seconds faster.

He didn't bother trying to conceal his eagerness. Ali was nervous. No doubt mustering her useless arguments. She laughed as she balanced the pie boxes on her arm and watched him fumble with the old key lock. As soon as the door was open Craig hooked an arm around her waist, picked her up and carried her into the room.

"Hey," cried Ali wiggling free to deposit boxes on a side table. "Take it easy."

Craig stepped out of his shoes, tugged his jeans off in one smooth motion. Ali's eyes widened and she backed up until she was pressed up against the wall.

"Listen Craig, this isn't the time, or place."

"Just saving time," said Craig, facing her wearing just his boxers and T-shirt. "You and I have some years of catching up to do. Just to be clear, I want you to look me in the eye and tell me that you don't lust for me. We'll deal with love later. Just for once, say it straight out. If you don't want me, then I'll pack up and get another room."

Ali's curled into fists and she folded her arms across her chest. It was a shock to realize that she did want him. She wanted him because he was Craig. From the top of his curly head to his Super toes, she wanted him. Wanted to feel his hands on her skin. To kiss him hard enough that he wouldn't hear his Super pager. To knock him off his feet. Although, being Ultra Man he'd probably hang in mid-air.

She'd kept him at a distance, using the damned x-rated fan mail, the destruction at event sites, and her father as excuses. While working at the S.S.C., she'd seen the friends and lovers of Supers suffering. Stood by during late night watches while doctors struggled to mend injuries mere mortals would never receive, let alone survive. She'd attended services for Supers like Mr. Crunch's wife and son, The Thump and The Power, when there hadn't been anything at all found of them to bury.

It was hard enough being friends with Supers. At any time, they could overextend themselves in a rescue. Go up against a too-powerful Villain and be hurt. Die. Super Powers could save you from so much, but not everything. Sooner or later, a true hero would step up and take on too much in the protection of an innocent. Just look at what had happened to The Power when he took on a volcano!

But now, it didn't matter. She was leaving the Super life. Leaving Craig. She'd decided. Nothing he, or anyone else, did would change her mind. Once Ultra Man was back on the active roster, she was hitting the road. Which meant now was the perfect time to have her wicked way with him. Perfect goodbye sex. He might not accept her reasons for leaving, now, or ever, but that was just too bad.

"I'm not looking for anything long-term," she said. "I don't want to get married."

"To me, or ever?"

"Both."

"You're wrong, but we'll deal with that later." Craig stalked across the room and started fiddling with the buttons of Ali's shirt. "Right now, do you want me to leave? Get another room?"

"No."

"I warn you, Ali, I'm not *that* kind of boy. You can't just use me. I expect to be respected in the morning."

"Respect, I can manage," said Ali despite the lump that filled her throat. She drew in a deep breath and ran her hands down his solid, warm arms, feeling her own body start to heat. It was hard to get the words out past the ache in her chest. "I lust for you."

A brilliant smile spread across Craig's face. Before she could say another word, Craig scooped her off her feet and tossed her onto the bed. A cloud of purple smoke billowed up from the tangled sheets, filling her vision and clouding her senses. Ali bounced once and lay still, breathing shallowly. Across the room, Craig hit the floor before he even realized he was falling.

Ali groaned and tried to open her eyes. Something sticky on her lashes resisted. She rested for a moment then tried again. When her eyes opened, she instantly regretted it. A blinding headache that had been waiting for the first muscle movement leaped upon her. She held her breath until the sneaky headache retreated a little. Next, she concentrated on trying to unseal her mouth. Her tongue felt swollen to twice its usual size and adhered to the inside of her lips. Her scalp felt tight, and she was convinced that each individual hair had its own headache. Having never experienced a hangover before she thought it very unfair to hurt this much, since she hadn't been drinking.

She raised her head slowly and stared around the room. Shifted a little to test the limits of her bonds. Her neck cramped and spasmed, sending knife-spike agony across her shoulders and down her back. She rested for a moment waiting for the pain to pass, then raised her head again, scanning from side to side as the room came into focus. She was tied, reclining, in an overstuffed brown lounge chair. Bright, early morning sunlight streamed in through wall-to-ceiling windows along one side of the room. Dark, sunburned wood walls held classic artwork in elaborate frames side-by-side with childish drawings stuck to the walls with sticky tape and tacks. Heavy antique furniture was covered with red medical hazard boxes, blue tubing, and intravenous fluid administration equipment. A nearby couch was covered by a thick plastic sheet. Near the door was a rack of oxygen cylinders. Outside the window, she could see thick, tall bushes and trees blocking anything else nearby from view.

She jumped – or tried to – when she heard a rumble approaching. She closed her eyes and sank back against the chair as the door opened. Something substantial was half-dragged, half-wheeled across the room and positioned beside her. Then footsteps retreated and the door closed.

Ali opened one eye, then the other and peered around the room. Empty. She shifted around to face the new arrival and gasped. Craig was unconscious and bound with thin brown string to a chair similar to her own. She twisted her hands and forearms, trying to drag them free. The same thin string bound her. Despite its fragile appearance, the bindings were incredibly strong, without any give at all.

Instead of yielding, it dug deeper and deeper into her skin. Sighing, she sank back, her breath coming in sharp gasps. They were trapped. What had happened?

"Ali?" Craig's eyes snapped open, taking in the room and their situation in an instant. He strained against the ropes, twisting around until he spotted her, then relaxed. He gave her a lopsided smile, "Well, hi there. Glad to see you. We knew someone had stolen the nanotech ropes, now we know who."

"Nanotech ropes?" echoed Ali, twisting her hands again.

"Take it easy," said Craig. "You won't break these. These're long chains of carbon molecules, held together as a small tube. The computer industry's been working on it as the next upgrade from silicon chips. Some guy in some techie lab in California was doing some lateral thinking, trying to come up with new uses and made it into a rope. Next thing we hear, it's been stolen. Guess where it is now?"

"Around us," said Ali, sadly. "This is all my fault. West warned me and I told her to do it anyway."

Craig twisted in his chair to face her. "The 'events conspire' spell? What's the problem? If it is Nuclear Man in the other room, the spell worked, didn't it?"

Ali scowled at him. "Don't be flippant. I didn't realize that it could mean that the Villains would capture *you*."

"Well, it was a risk. Who knows what sort of shape the Universe has to twist itself into to make the spell work? What I don't understand is, how did they know where *we* were? It wasn't as if we'd made a reservation in advance at that hotel. Hell, I just drove into the first parking lot I saw."

"I don't know. Anyway, I'm sorry. This is all my fault."

Craig tested the bindings again, then sank back with a sigh. "Ali, we wanted to catch up with Nuclear Man. If the spell worked, that's great. We certainly weren't getting anywhere following the Jackalopes."

"But we wanted to be the ones doing the tying up," protested Ali. "Not the other way around."

"Jackalopes?" wheezed a voice at the door, "Well, isn't that a kick in the pants? Here I thought it was some sophisticated detective work on your part that brought you to my neighborhood. That you'd done a detailed chemical analysis of a lump of clay I'd left at a crime scene, or you'd used a spy satellite search and a computer-enhanced photograph. Something Super! Ah, well."

A tall man leaned against the doorway. Bald, pale and propped up by a pair of steel crutches, the new arrival did not appear to be much of a threat except, maybe, to his health care plan's profits. His frame was thin and his breath came in shallow gasps. After a pause to gather his strength, he crossed the room, swinging his legs between the crutches rather than walking, until he stood between Ali and Craig's chairs. Resting most of his weight on one of the crutches, he bent down and clasped Ali's fingers where they stuck out beneath the ropes and shook them, then repeated the gesture with Craig. Ali's skin crawled at the chill touch but she thought it better to conceal her reaction.

"Good morning, pleased to meet you. I'm Doug MacLean. Of course, you probably know me as *Nuclear Man*."

He swung around and made his way to a nearby wheelchair, lowering himself carefully to the cushions. He freed his hands and propped the crutches against the wall. Ali couldn't decide whether to be terrified at her current situation or ask Nuclear Man how he was feeling. There was an air of fragility about him that caught at her throat. To her surprise, the Villain met her eye and gave her a broad, reassuring grin. A movement at the door dragged Ali's attention away from Nuclear Man. Before she could react, Craig started swearing.

"Dammit to hell and back," he shouted. "Steve Holtzman!"

The black man at the door bowed and smiled at both of them. "The Shriek, at your service," said Steve, with enviable calm. He carried a tray of drinks into the room and put them on a side table.

The shorter, dark-skinned woman who followed him into the room was also familiar. For a moment, Ali thought Mysterious West had found them, then she groaned.

"Mystress of the Night," whispered Ali.

"Call me Joan, since you're being a friend of the family, so to speak," said the Mystress, tossing her multiple braids back over her shoulder. The bags and charms at her belt jingled as she crossed the room. "Did I hear right? This meeting is a consequence of one of my big sister's spells? Well, looks like she's getting some skill in her old age. But she really has to work on her aim if she's casting spells that get her friends into situations like this."

"Events conspire," said Craig and Joan nodded.

"That'll do it."

"Sister?" gasped Ali. "Oh, my God, you're an evil twin!"

The Mystress laughed, "More wicked than evil."

Ali turned to Craig. "How did you not know they were related?"

"I'm not sure." Craig scowled at the witch. "It seems that I did. It was just never important enough to talk about. Now that I think about it, that doesn't make sense."

"Sis probably cast a 'somebody else's problem' spell so that you'd forget to think about it," said Joan, making herself comfortable on a nearby chair.

"Oh man, I suppose she did." Craig shut his eyes for a moment. "She'd have to."

"I'm glad you're in such an understanding mood," said Nuclear Man. "We have some important issues to discuss, and some decisions to make. It helps when people are willing to approach difficult situations calmly."

"I can do calm," said Craig, wiggling his hands. "Of course, I'd do it a lot better if you loosened the ropes a little."

"We aren't after being stupid, boy," said The Mystress.

"We certainly weren't dumb enough to be caught with our pants down." The Shriek smirked at Craig's boxer shorts. "Literally."

Craig growled, but said nothing. Nuclear Man raised his hands quickly.

"No heckling. I want this to be a friendly meeting, so no low blows." He gave Craig an assessing look. "I can't loosen your ropes, but I can give you a blanket, if you'd like."

"I'm quite warm, thank you," said Craig, putting on stern expression number five. Being tied up was no reason to let a criminal think he'd be easily intimidated. Especially since his only chance to get Ali – and himself – out of here alive depended on getting control of the situation out of the hands of the criminal. Though how he'd do that was a mystery. He made a mental note to speak to Mysterious West about refining her spells, if he ever got the chance, then dismissed that vague anger. He had more important things to worry about right now.

"Good. Well, as I said, I'm Nuclear Man, in case you haven't guessed by now." He directed another broad smile at them, showing pale gums and yellowed teeth. "I'd like you to arrest me."

Craig and Ali sat in silence for a moment. Craig recovered first. "Sure. Fine. No problem. I'd be delighted. Just untie me and we'll call the police."

Nuclear Man's laugh quickly changed to a hacking cough. He wheezed as he reached over his shoulder for an oxygen mask. Joan hurried to his side and regulated the flow of gas before settling the plastic mask comfortably over his face.

"Sure," gasped Nuclear Man, when he could speak again. "We'll do that just as soon as we get a few things settled."

"Sounds like it's pretty settled to me," said Craig. "You are criminals and you're surrendering. Great. Let's get on with it."

"Cr ... Ultra Man," said Ali, leaning as far forward as her ropes would permit. "Take it easy. Wait and hear them out. People haven't been listening to us much lately, and you know how that feels. We can spare the time to listen." She tried to shrug, but the tight bonds limited her movement. "It isn't as if we're going anywhere until we do."

Chapter Eighteen.

Psychic Monthly – but, then, you already knew that.
Esther Reese – famed medium and author – announced on her website today that she had been contacted by the spirits of George and John, who said that they are willing to get together with Ringo and Paul for their long-awaited reunion tour – as soon as someone figures out how to bring them back from the dead.
A message has been sent to the S.S.C. asking that she be notified when someone manifests this ability.

"Great," wheezed Nuclear Man. "I'd hoped you two would be understanding. The issue is that I want to retire. So do Steve and Joan."

"Retire," sneered Craig. "That's one way of saying it."

Everyone in the room ignored him.

"What about Mr. Ooze?" asked Ali. "I don't see him here."

"Well, when we told him about the surrender, he didn't want to go along with it. He said he isn't sick and he isn't interested in trying for a straight life. We talked it over for a long time and finally agreed we'd let … him…," Doug grimace]0ed and leaned back against his chair, breathing deeply for a moment before continuing, "well, he left a couple of days ago, planning to apply for membership in one of the groups on the West Coast. He doesn't like what the heat and salt humidity over there does to him, but says he isn't ready to give up the life he has. Not yet."

"But you guys are?" asked Ali. "You're willing to go to jail?"

Steven and Joan exchanged glances then shook their heads.

"No," said Joan. "Actually, we're not. Not jail. The only one who's willing to do time is Doug. Not that he's got much left. Stevie and me, we're after going straight."

"Somewhat," added Steve, one hand on his hip, the other moving gracefully through the air. "As much as I can."

"Straight?" demanded Craig, pulling at his bonds again, "Do I understand you correctly? You want us to let you go? Just go? After all you've done? All the robberies? The destruction? You want a get-out-of-jail-free card?"

"Yes" said Joan, with a toss of her braids. "Exactly."

"Sorry, but I must have left them in my other pants. There is no way I'm going to go to the police and suggest you be let off," said Craig, straining against his bonds. "You've earned yourselves years inside. Life sentences, if I'm not mistaken. I'm not letting you off, it would go against everything I stand for. Everything..."

"Craig," shouted Ali, then lowered her voice when he jumped and glared at her. "Calm down, you're pontificating and it doesn't suit you."

"They robbed banks and hospitals," continued Craig. "Millions of dollars stolen. Property damage."

"And revealed unethical and dangerous researchers. Exposed medical and scientific practices that we wouldn't have known about without the investigations that happened as a result of their attacks." Ali straightened under the weight of her ropes, "You've got to admit that there's been some balance. Some good out of what they've done. If they'd killed anyone, then yeah, I'd be with you on this. But they didn't, and I'm not. Not completely."

Craig's jaw dropped. How could Ali take their side like this? Before, her opinions on the lack of differences between Supers and Villains had hurt, dammit, but now he felt nothing less than betrayed. She was sitting there, captive to a dangerous group of criminals, and was supporting them.

"Ali, you can't be serious," he said, twisting around as much as he could in that damned chair.

Maybe there was a reason. They'd been separated while unconscious. He leaned forward, trying to get a better view of Ali's arms. No needle marks as far as he could tell, but a sensible crook would inject somewhere less obvious. They'd been unconscious for a few hours. His bladder was uncomfortable, but not urgently over-full. Had that been long enough for them to brainwash Ali? And if they had, would he be able to reverse the damage? He forced himself to stay calm as a more horrible thought occurred. What if she hadn't been brainwashed? What if she really believed what she was saying? He could not see any signs she'd been influenced, but how would he know? He'd never seen anyone brainwashed.

"I am completely serious," said Ali, as if reading his thoughts. "Remember what we found out. Nuclear Man should never have been exposed to those toxins in med school. That doctor is responsible, and he'll never do an hour in court or a minute of jail time because what he did isn't a crime. It was *research*. Nuclear Man's dying because of what that doctor did. On the other hand, he has acted to spare other people similar suffering by exposing dangerous research practices. I think that should count in his favor. Mitigating circumstances."

Craig studied her face, her posture, and couldn't see a single thing wrong. Sincerity shone from every pore. "We aren't the ones who decide that, Ali. If that's the defense they want to use, then they should do it in court. That's how the justice system works."

"Why not? Isn't Justice shown with a blindfold?"

Craig ignored that comment.

"And what about you-know-who?" Ali continued, wiggling her eyebrows. "You know, the one who helped us."

It only took Craig a moment to nod. "Oh, yeah. Her. What about her?"

"You didn't just grab her off the street and drag her off to the lawyers. You listened to her and used your head. Use your own ethical code to decide what to do. I'm just saying perhaps this is one of those times when the legal system is not the place to go if you are looking for *justice*!"

Craig glanced around the room, meeting the eye of every Villain staring at him. They hadn't covered this in Super training. The closest they'd come was how to deal with sexual come-ons. That was not the situation here. The Shriek – Steve, was definitely not his type. The Mystress of the Night was way too old and reminded him too much of the motherly Mysterious West, and Nuclear Man, sitting there with the oxygen mask covering most of his face, looked seven years dead. They didn't look sexy. They didn't even look remotely threatening. In fact, they looked like scared kids hauled up in front of a stern and forbidding headmaster. One thing they had drummed into him in Super class was keeping the Villains talking. Many a Hero's life had been saved by a monologue, or at least, a delaying dialogue.

"If I buy into this," he said, "and I'm not saying I will, then..."

Doug raised a pale hand. "Don't get ahead of yourself, Ultra Man. I know this is going to be a tough sell, so don't pretend to go along with it too soon." His lips lifted in a slight smile. "I'm rather looking forward to convincing you."

Craig straightened, trying to pretend he barely noticed the bonds around his arms, the fact that he was reclining on a chair clad only in his boxers, and put on his dignified face, the one that worked so well at the boring White House banquets. "What methods are you planning on using to convince me, Nuclear Man. Threats? Abuse? Drugs?"

"Good heavens, no," cried Doug, horrified. "If I can't convince you with words, then, well, we have a problem."

"And how would you plan on solving that problem?" asked Ali, and Craig's heart missed a beat.

If they took her hostage, threatened her or hurt her he'd ... he'd follow them forever. Whatever happened, he had to get her safely out of this mess. He couldn't, wouldn't, let her be harmed.

"Running away really fast," joked Steve. "We have contingency plans, don't worry about us."

"I wasn't," said Craig, in chilling tones and had the satisfaction of seeing The Shriek turn pale.

"Quiet, Steve," said Doug, then turned back to Craig. "The fact of the matter is, we don't have a contingency plan. We don't have anything. If we can't convince you, then we are completely in your power." He nodded to Joan and pointed at Ali. "Let her up," he ordered. "Ultra Man, I know you're worried about The Ice Queen's safety, so, as a sign of our commitment to a negotiated outcome, we'll let her loose. Not to leave the house, you understand, but she can get up. Move around." A sad smile crossed his face. "I know how uncomfortable it is to be trapped in a chair."

The Mystress fiddled behind Ali's chair for a few moments. A dull buzz that Ali hadn't been paying attention to stopped, and the tension went out of her ropes. Joan grabbed a handful of carbon tube rope and lifted it over Ali's head. Within a few seconds, Ali was freed.

Ali bit her lip to hold back a scream as blood and sensation rushed back to her limbs. She rubbed at her arms and legs until they stopped complaining, then climbed out of the chair and staggered over to lean against the nearest wall. She kept her back turned toward Craig, unwilling to see the hurt and anger in his eyes. Doug scooted his wheelchair over to her and rested a thin hand on her arm.

Ali suppressed a shudder at the chill touch. In her job, she'd occasionally had to supervise the removal of the bodies of unfortunate victims, but this was the first time a living person had touched her with a hand so deathly cold.

There was a different kind of hurt in Doug's eyes. Obviously, she hadn't been able to control her reaction to his touch. Before he could pull away, Ali covered his pale hand with her own pink, warm, healthy one.

"Ultra Man and I came here intending to capture you," she said, "it helps that you're willing to be captured."

"Ha!" shouted Craig.

"What, exactly, was your plan?" asked Ali.

"Simple enough," said Doug. "After we come to an agreement, I'll go with you to the authorities anytime you like. I just have to have your promise that you'll both swear that Joan and Steve are dead."

"You think people will believe us?" snorted Craig, "Without evidence! You've lost your mind. If I come back with just Nuclear Man, The Shriek and The Mystress will still be listed as 'at large.' They'll never stop searching for you. Besides, Mr. Ooze knows what you were planning. Do you think he'll stay quiet about it?"

"He will if he knows what's good for him. Besides, what's in it for him to talk?" The Mystress's smile was brilliant. "All you have to do it tell the authorities that after years of living with Nuclear Man, Steve and I finally upped and died."

"That's not going to work," sneered Craig. "You were seen, fighting against me, Purple Lightning and West only a few days ago. No one's going to believe you *suddenly* died."

"Of course they will," said Joan. "They'll believe it, because they'll want to."

Craig and Ali exchanged a stunned glance, then Ali nodded slowly. "We've had some experience with people believing impossible things recently. I think we could sell it." She turned to the somewhat-less-than-evil trio. "But what will you do if we let you go? *Why* should we let you go?"

"I'm tired," said Joan, "and my daughter's getting ready to graduate college. She's over in Italy studying magic with the *Arcadia*. She's... I'd like to say that she's inherited my abilities, but the truth is, she's stronger than me. Last time she visited, she told me she wants to join the S.S.C. She's the Mysterious West's biggest fan." Joan covered her face with her hands. "She told me that she knew that *I* was the Mysterious West. Can you believe it? My daughter is so proud of me because she thinks I'm my sister. I can't have her find out that I'm The Mystress of the Night. I don't want her being ashamed of me. And, more importantly, I never want to go into a battle against her. Before she joins up, I *have* to get out of the Villain biz."

"That's all very well," said Ali, "But you have to take responsibility for your previous crimes. Did you see the news report after your last fight? A concentrated level 3 tornado!"

Craig's lips twitched as he tried to hold back a smile. It was nice to have the right person toasted for a change.

"I don't want my daughter visiting me in jail." Joan near tears. "I'm willing to give up magic. That's punishment enough. I deserve it. My sister and Grandma can take it away. They were going to do it years ago, after I called down a storm on my hometown but I was too proud. Too stubborn. I wanted to keep my magic more than I wanted my family. I've changed my mind. Family is more important."

Realizing that he was getting too relaxed, Craig summoned a scowl for Nuclear Man and The Shriek.

"It isn't as if you all made one mistake and are sorry for it now. You've been Villains for years. This isn't some little issue to be negotiated down to a parking fine. You've been tearing up and down the East Coast like natural disasters. You were stealing just a few days ago, and now you want to go straight." He glanced across at Steve. "Straightish, without paying the price."

The Shriek and Mystress looked away, blushing. Nuclear Man didn't appear to be able to summon additional color and met his eyes boldly.

"I do, Ultra Man. And I will. For all of us."

"But why now?" asked Ali. "A few days ago, you were tearing down buildings and robbing banks. What changed? Why did you take the risk of contacting Ultra Man and me? We should just insist that you do jail time. It's not like we have any incentive to ignore your crimes."

"The last lot of money was for Mr. Ooze," said Joan. "He wanted a little something just in case it took him some time to get established with a new group."

"That doesn't explain," said Craig. "what changed? Why do you want to give up now?"

Joan and Steve looked at each other, the floor, the ceiling, everywhere except at Ali, Craig and Doug. Finally, Doug let his oxygen mask drop.

"They're doing it for me, Ms. Brent," he said, "My cancer's spread despite treatment, and I'm getting fragile. The other day, I went to climb out of the shower. I grabbed hold of the safety bar and a bone in my hand broke. Just like that." He raised his bandaged arm and turned to Craig, "I've got family. My mother, my wife, and a daughter I haven't seen for years. I don't dare come near them, as toxic as I am. I'm afraid I'll be ill, throw up and they'll become contaminated. I call them when I can, but I really want to see them, be with them again before ..." He sighed and brought the mask up to his face. "I figured they'd put me in a secure hospital prison. With enough shielding in place, I'm hoping my family'd be able to come up and visit me. I'm turning myself in, on the condition that you arrest me here in Arizona. If I'm arrested and tried here, then, hopefully, they'll put me in jail here, near my folks."

"Your friends still haven't said what they're going to do to go straight," said Craig, "and, believe me, I'm not going to accept any plan that involves living off the interest from stolen money. Any that you still have is going to have to go back."

"Ooze took all the cash when he left," said Doug, slipping his hands back into his crutches and pulling himself to his feet. "Why don't we show you what we've got?"

Joan came forward and put her hands on the handles of the wheelchair, but Doug waved her away.

"No. Thanks, Joan, but for as long as I can keep on my feet, I'm going to walk."

He waved Steve and Joan toward the captives. Swinging along between the crutches, Doug led the way out of the room. Joan took Ali by the elbow and gestured toward the spell pouches on her waist.

"No silliness," said Joan as she guided Ali toward the sliding doors leading out onto the patio. Steve braced himself and started pushing Craig's easy-chair in their wake.

The broad patio outside looked over a crowded clearing. Between the house and the woods, the backyard was filled with row after row of little hutches. Craig could hear many small voices chattering. There was a vaguely familiar scent in the air. One that he hadn't sniffed for years. He inhaled again, searching through his memory for the elusive odor. Doug sank onto a nearby bench and waited as Joan went to the nearest hutch and returned, clutching a small, wiggling creature to her chest. She approached Ali, holding it out in both hands.

"No," cried Craig, straining against his unyielding bonds, "Leave her alone."

"It's okay," crooned Joan, running a finger over the back of the creature in her hands. "This little one doesn't scratch. She's the sweetest little thing."

So saying, she placed the tiny, furry object in Ali's hands. The black and white ball unfurled, and Craig found himself staring at the smallest panda bear he'd ever seen.

"What the heck is that?" asked Craig.

"A Panda Pig," said Doug, proudly. "I was playing with some of the research equipment we collected in between my own personal cancer researches. A little gene splice here, and little genome tweak there, and what do you know, Panda Pig! I heard where this pet SS.C. was looking for a Guinea Pig with Panda Bear markings. I did some research, all ethical I assure you, and figured out how to do it. No pain for anyone involved. Do you have any idea the demand for ordinary Guinea Pigs? The Panda Pig is going to change the whole Guinea Pig market. Each one of our little friends here is going to be worth thousands."

Steve crossed the clearing with another cuddly creature and showed it to Craig.

"We're going to keep tight control on the breeding for a while, at first," said Steve, "Only going to be selling little girl pigs. We don't want breeders going crazy and flooding the market. The female pigs will have offspring without the markings. You'll need both male and female to have the Panda Pig babies."

"So you're going out of the villain business," Ali gasped, "and you're going to raise Panda Pigs?"

Three heads nodded vigorously, and three sets of bright eyes watched Craig for his reaction. Craig groaned and wished he could cover his face with his hands. Beside him, Ali lost the fight for composure and started laughing. Craig growled at her, which only made her laugh harder.

"I don't know what you're so upset about," she said. "You always said you want Villains to become contributing members of society."

"It lacks dignity," muttered Craig finally.

"What do you mean?" asked Nuclear Man (retired).

"A hero is judged by the quality of his villains. His nemeses," cried Craig, spreading his fingers in the closest thing he could get to a helpless shrug. "How do you expect people to take me seriously when they find out mine have just retired to go into the pet breeding business? Oh, God, what will the other Supers say?"

But he couldn't maintain the sulk. Within minutes, he too was laughing.

It took a few minutes – closer to half an hour – to convince Ali to put the little Panda Pigs back into their hutches. When they were safely packed away Ali and Craig – still tied to his chair – were escorted back inside. The atmosphere was relaxed, even social. Joan offered Ali a drink, while Steve settled Doug back into his chair, but the party feeling vanished immediately when Craig cleared his throat.

"All right, listen up. We still have some things to get straight." Craig lay straight in his chair, since he couldn't get into any of his power poses. He realized at once that they weren't necessary. One quick glance around the room showed him that everyone, including Ali, was wearing mother-has-found-out-about-the-broken-vase expressions. He swallowed a sigh. He knew he couldn't relent. "Steve. Joan. You are going to have to turn yourselves in. Whatever you've planned, forget it. You've committed decades' worth of crimes and you have to answer for them in a court of law. If that court decides to let you go, great. I promise to turn up and testify that you turned yourselves in. But there is no get out of jail free card here and I'm not going to let you hand over Nuclear Man ... Doug ... and let him take the heat for you two. I expect you can find someone to run the Panda Pig business for you while you're in jail, but you are going to have to serve some time."

    Joan glanced across at Steve and, to Craig's complete surprise, all they did was shrug. "Well, we can't say we didn't expect it."

    Doug wheeled his chair over until he was beside Craig. "Ultra Man, thank you for even considering our request. We knew that if we couldn't convince you to go along with this idea, then we were sunk. We never prepared a backup plan. If a straight appeal to you didn't work then, that's that. We haven't got any evil card to play. No bomb. No school bus careening toward a bridge that's conveniently out. Nothing like that. Just an appeal to your humanity. Steve and Joan want to return to normal life."

    "After a life of crime, usually the period of punishment comes first," said Craig, in a quieter voice. "Your plan just skips over that part. Tied up like this, I can't force you, but I believe you should all turn yourselves in and do your time. Afterward, hell, even during the time you're in jail, you can sell the silly pigs, but first of all, you should take your punishment."

    "Punishment?" Nuclear man touched pale fingers to his chest. "My cancert, as it grows, it interferes with the beating of my heart. It can't be operated on because of how closely it's wrapped around the heart's wiring center, and, no surprise, chemotherapy doesn't work on me anymore. I'm toast. All I want now is to sit and talk to my family, my friends. I don't know how much time I've got. The doctor who diagnosed me years ago gave me three months to live, and I just read where he was buried this year. He got hit by an ambulance when he was leaving the hospital. A cosmic joke, I suppose, on both of us. Or, maybe, proof that God is a sadist. Either way, I can't guarantee that I'll live long enough to pay for *my* crimes, but I'm going to do my damnedest. I'm not finished with life yet. It is just too interesting. What do you say, Ultra Man? Isn't the ideal of the justice system to convince criminals to give up crime and go straight? Please think again. Joan and Steve want to have a decent life. Let them go. In exchange, I will try to live a hundred years in jail and do my time and theirs. I assure you, the pain I live in is punishment enough for all our crimes and a few more besides. If Steven and Joan had actually died after years of living with me, then I'd still be held responsible for every crime they'd performed at my direction. Let me do this."

    Craig didn't answer. Ali watched impatiently as he drummed his fingers on the chair arm.

    "What punishment do you think will be enough?" she demanded. "Do you really think it will fix things if they all spent a hundred years in jail?"

    "No," said Craig, finally, "and anyway, it's not for me, or you, to decide. They're supposed to go before a jury of their peers."

    "Fine with me," said a smooth, deep voice from the window. "As *their* peer I say they should stay in business."

Joan and Ali spun to face the sliding doors. Craig tensed in his chair.

Framed by the glass squatted Mr. Ooze, his skin glistening with a thin layer crystal green. Beside him were two figures Ali recognized immediately - Major Calamity and The Blast.

"Aw, hell," groaned Steve, then recovered enough to straighten his spine and give the interlopers a superior sneer, "What are you guys doing here?"

Major Calamity swaggered into the room. Ali noticed that he kept one eye on her as he strolled past. She didn't think she counted as much of a threat to a Villain who could tear steel with his bare hands. Then she noticed the way he walked, the cut of his very expensive suit, and the way he brushed his hair back out of his eyes with his little finger. Major Calamity was vain. He wanted to watch her checking him out, hoping to catch her looking at his butt or some such nonsense. Once she realized that, Ali made a point of appearing bored and paid more attention to Ooze and The Blast – who remained in the doorway, blocking that exit.

"Are you really Nuclear Man?" asked Calamity, putting a hand on each arm of Doug's wheelchair and leaning down to peer into his face. "And to think I stayed out of your district because I was worried about offending you." He looked Doug up and down, then laughed. "You look like a strong fart would kill you dead."

"Thank you," said Doug in a flat voice, "I'll be sure not to eat beans."

Major Calamity laughed again, threw his arms wide and transferred his attention to Craig.

"Now, I just dropped in to ask Nuclear Man, as one professional to another, to join forces with me instead of retiring, and what do I find? He's got a going-into-business-together present for me. Wow, Nuclear Man, I'm so flattered."

"Moron," muttered Ali.

"Poseur," said Joan, out of the corner of her mouth. "I've run into him before. He's a Shakespearean-trained actor, so he says, and loves to chew the scenery."

Major Calamity sniffed and pretended to ignore the comment. He strode to the center of the room and assumed Power Posture #1.

"I am so happy that I made this little trip down here. When Mr. Ooze came by to beg me to accept him into my little group, I have to say, I wasn't impressed. What do I need a post nasal drip like him for? But now, I find the witch, the noisemaker, and The Ice Queen, I presume," he bowed and leered at Ali, "all gathered together to meet me. And this, Ultra Man, all tied up with a bow. Well, I'm just so touched. I didn't realize you guys knew it was my birthday."

Ooze glared at Calamity's back but made no protest.

Ali and Joan both groaned.

"Kill me now," said Joan.

"Nah," said Ali, "kill him. The world will thank us."

"That's a plan I can get behind," said Joan, letting her hand drift toward a spell pouch.

This time, Major Calamity turned fully to face them. Behind him, Ali could see Doug was leaning toward Craig's chair, fiddling behind the back. Remembering what Joan had done to free her from the carbon rope, Ali forced a smile on her face and flicked a glance at Joan.

Joan's eyes narrowed and she, too, deliberately ignored Doug's activity.

"Ladies, please," said Major Calamity, assuming a hip tilted, male model pose in front of them, "don't fight over me. I don't do grandmothers, so the path is quite clear for you, my dear Ice Queen."

"Who are you calling a grandmother?" protested Ali.

Beside her Joan sniggered. "Even my daughter could see through your bullshit, Calamity. What the hell are you here for, anyway?"

"Territory, Witch, Territory. We've stayed out of the Northeast and Arizona because we didn't want to get into a jurisdiction battle with Nuclear Man. All this time I thought the press description of him was S.S.C. propaganda. If I'd known he was such a weakling, I would've made a take-over bid years ago. Well, better late than never."

"Better never than never," shot back Ali.

Major Calamity sidled closer. Ali wondered if the man ever walked anywhere. Every move he made was a production number. She remembered that this particular Villain posed for the security cameras when he did his jobs, and it helped her to stay calm.

"My dear Ice Queen. I realize you've probably gone to a lot of work, and maybe even expense, negotiating to take over this area, but we simply cannot have a newcomer moving in on such a rich arena. Heavens, no. I'd be happy to accept you as a recruit," he ran a finger along the curve of Ali's jaw, "even a partner. I think you'll enjoy the fringe benefits."

Ali forced a grin, "You mean you'll let me have sex with Mr. Ooze? How nice."

An optimistic light flashed into Ooze's eye.

"Forget it, sticky," sneered The Blast. "Ain't gonna happen."

Ooze muttered something but made no moves. He surely knew the limits of his power. In this room the only person weaker than him was Ali herself. Ali kept her smile in place and her focus on Calamity. Until Craig was free, they were in a hell of a fix. Major Calamity, on his own, could beat Joan. Steve had used his ability less than a week ago, so he was out. Ali herself had all the Powers of a squashed tomato, and that would be exactly what she'd look like if she got into a fight with Major Calamity.

That always supposed that Joan and Steve weren't going to accept Calamity's offer. Maybe they were leaving the crime biz because Doug talked them into it. What if they weren't willing to go up against Calamity, one of the physically strongest of the Villains? What if they were secretly planning on continuing as criminals with the pet business as a cover?

More importantly to Ali, what would happen when Major Calamity discovered The Ice Queen had no Powers?

Chapter Nineteen.

The London Evening Standard

The UpStairs Maid and The Butler caused considerable damage to the Museum of Modern Art in London today while battling The Rebel in a Blue Dress. The Housekeeper was called in to provide assistance but was distracted by the report of an oil spill in the Black Sea. After examining the oil spill, The Housekeeper handed in her notice and announced her intention of retiring to run a B&B in Bath. The frustrated British Prime Minister has issued an international call to all Super Powered individuals, offering a flat in Chelsea (with a parking space) and a modest annual stipend to any 'halfway decent' Power who'd be willing to relocate to the United Kingdom and take over duties from the British Super Domestic Squad.

"We're retiring," said Joan, to Ali's infinite relief. The witch glared up at Major Calamity. "Not that our plans are any of your business."

"That's where you're wrong, witch. A good commanding officer doesn't make the mistake of letting important assets leave the field of battle before he's gotten good use out of them. Nuclear Man here probably hasn't got more than two or three good jobs left in him, but that doesn't mean I'm not going to keep him around for those *special* jobs."

"You're a slug, Corporal Calamity," said Ali, who'd read the profile on this particular Villain years ago. "I bet you push little old ladies with walkers down the stairs and think it's funny. I did hear you'd graduated from The Three Stooges School of Humor through Humiliation after being tossed out of the Army for failing K.P."

Major Calamity reared back, his smug expression vanishing.

"Don't make the mistake of judging me by these clowns," he growled, waving at Mr. Ooze and Steve. "You will take me seriously."

"I do," called Craig. "Catch."

Calamity spun as Craig leaped to his feet, grabbed the chair that had been his prison and threw it across the room. Joan dove at Ali, pushing them both to the floor as the easy chair, followed by Craig, flew toward them.

Ali struggled up from under Joan, fully expecting to find Craig holding Calamity by the scruff of the neck. Instead, he was sprawled full length on the floor, one hand extended above his head, a length of Carbon Rope stretched between his still-bound arm and the chair. Ali sputtered for a second, then spun to face Doug.

"What's that?" she shouted, pointing at the remaining rope.

"It's on a different circuit," he shouted back, "I wanted to be sure Ultra Man wouldn't get free easily."

"Great," muttered Ali, huddling back against the wall.

Craig was already climbing to his feet.

"Thanks for the warning," he muttered, tearing the armrest free and refocusing on Major Calamity. The chair arm thudded to the floor, still linked to Craig by the Carbon Rope.

Ali stared past them to the window. Mr. Ooze was struggling with The Shriek, who had snatched the plastic sheet off the couch and was trying to wrap it around his ex-partner-in-crime. Crystal ooze was leaking down between them, staining the wooden floor. It was taking most of The Shriek's concentration to avoid stepping in the sticky liquid. The Blast had his hands upraised, and Ali could see the shimmer of power forming around them. Beside her, Joan was muttering as she pushed powders from her pouches into a small velvet bag.

"Go help Doug," ordered Joan, raising the spell bag for a throw, "Don't let him fight. He hasn't the strength for this. Get him out of here."

Ali ducked down as Craig swung at Calamity and sent him staggering back. The chair arm dangling from the rope on his wrist smashed against the floor near her feet. Ali dodged the two fighters, jumped over the overturned chair and ran across the room just as The Blast let loose a bolt of energy, hitting both Calamity and Craig, sending them slamming against the wall Ali had just been huddling against.

Breathing hard, Ali ran - hunched over, as if that helped – to Doug's side.

"Can you do anything?" she demanded, crouching down beside his wheelchair to free the brakes.

"Not today," said Doug, sadly. "I took some meds to settle my stomach a few hours ago."

"Great," said Ali, returning her attention to the fight.

Mr. Ooze was down, unmoving, covered by the plastic sheet. Dribbles of green leaked out to stain the floor around him. Ali wasn't sure if Steve had smothered him or what but was delighted that one attacker was down. Craig and Calamity were on the floor, using wrestling moves and punches that would get them banned from any legal competition. Joan and Steve were concentrating their powers on The Blast, who was edging slowly back toward where Ali and Doug watched. Ali grabbed Doug's wheelchair and pulled him toward the door.

"We can't leave," cried Doug, pushing on the chair brakes. "Help them!"

The Blast shook his hands furiously, summoning power, and raised them to point at Joan. Ali could see the energy rippling around his fingers. Snatching a lamp off the nearest table, Ali brought it down hard on The Blast's head. His knees buckled and he sank to the ground. Joan and Steve froze, mouths hanging open.

"That's a bit cliché, isn't it," observed Doug.

Ali threw a glare over her shoulder. "Things become cliché because they work," she said. Drawing back her foot, she kicked The Blast between the legs.

The Blast, who had been dragging himself up, collapsed to the floor with a faint 'eep' and lay there, shivering.

"That's cliché, too. Are you going to complain?" demanded Ali.

Doug folded his hands neatly in his lap and shook his head. "I'm not saying a word," he replied, as a faint smile pulled at his lips. "Who am I to argue with success?"

A laugh from across the room interrupted Ali's comeback. They all turned to find a red-faced Craig lowering an unconscious Major Calamity to the floor. Joan ran over to kneel near The Blast's head, sprinkling purple powder over his face, but she was laughing at Craig. He turned his back on them all, un-tucked his T-shirt and pulled it down over his boxer shorts. Ali took a few steps toward him, touching him lightly on the shoulder, but he kept his face turned away.

"What's wrong?" demanded Ali, "is anyone hurt?"

"Just the bad guys," said Joan. "Ultra Man took out Calamity while he was distracted."

"I'm sorry I missed it," said Ali. "What distracted him? The Blast going down?"

"Nah," said Joan, still grinning.

"What then?" asked Ali.

"Shut up," said Craig, padding barefoot across the room to check on Mr. Ooze.

"But I want to tell her about the final battle," said Joan, "You have some truly astonishing moves."

"Shut up," growled Craig again.

Steve, Doug, and Ali exchanged puzzled glances.

"What the heck is going on?" asked Steve. "Did I miss something good?"

"Depends on your point of view," Joan started to answer, caught Craig's eye and sealed her lips.

"What do you expect?" demanded Craig, pulling his T-shirt down again and glaring at them all. "I'm fighting in my goddamn underwear."

"Oh, for heaven's sake, what's wrong with that?" said Ali, "Your Super armor is so skin tight I'm surprised that it doesn't cut off the circulation to your brain."

"No, it's not. I had them loosen the trousers," said Craig. "But the most important thing about my armor is that it doesn't have conveniently located," he paused and his blush deepened, "escape hatches."

Steve's eyebrows rose to disappear into his hairline and he moaned his disappointment. Joan collapsed giggling on the floor, and Ali bit the inside of her cheek. It took all of her strength, all her self-control, but she did not laugh. Instead, she looked Craig straight in the eye, batted her eyelashes and said innocently, "I don't understand."

"Honey, he ... um ... his *best* friend...," began Steve, and stopped when Craig raised his hand.

"If you don't know, then I'm not going to explain it." Craig pulled a throw blanket off a chair and wrapped it toga-like around his body. The remains of the chair arm clattered across the floor. "Does anyone mind if we delay any further discussions until after I get dressed?"

Fortunately for Craig's blushes, Steve had brought their luggage from the hotel. While Craig was dressing, Joan cast deep-sleep spells over the defeated Villains, then Steve and Ali helped her stack them in a spare bedroom. When Craig finally rejoined them, Ali was examining the damage Ooze had done to the floor – from a safe distance.

"What a shame. It was a beautiful floor. You're going to have to have the whole lot taken up," said Ali, brushing off the knees of her jeans as she rose to her feet, "and it's going to be tough to keep quiet, because contractors are required to report anything like this ooze to the authorities. Any suspicious ooze has to be disposed of according to some pretty strict regs."

"No. Not really," said Doug, "Mr. Ooze has been living with us for a few years, so we've dealt with these little accidents before. We developed a simple solvent that just dissolves it away. Makes it a non-toxic liquid, easily mopped up."

Ali blinked and felt her jaw start to sag. "Do you suppose you could give the S.S.C. the recipe?"

"Give? No. Sell it? Sure," said Doug with a smile, as Craig cleared his throat.

"Well, isn't this cozy." Craig sauntered across the room to stand beside Doug and held out his hand. The remaining carbon nano cord was still wrapped around his wrist. He looked better, more in command, wearing loose jeans and a shirt. The scowl, of course, was classic Ultra Man.

Doug meekly pulled a gadget out of his shirt pocket and attached it to the rope. A familiar buzz ended as the cord loosened and fell away. In the silence that followed, Ali glanced around. Steve and Joan had stopped smiling and were standing stiff and solemn, side by side and watching Ultra Man. Ali wrapped her arms around her chest and waited. They were all waiting. Craig - Ultra Man - was standing up, dressed and free. If he decided to finish this criminal hunt on his own terms, there was nothing, or little, that they could do to stop him. And with Major Calamity, The Blast and Mr. Ooze neatly wrapped up and snoring in the other room Craig would have no trouble being accepted back into the S.S.C.'s fold. No Super had ever pulled off a capture like this!

Joan, Steve, and Doug, however, would go to jail. An un-negotiated capture, not the surrender they wanted.

Ali shivered and hugged herself tighter. Ali would hit the road and try to rebuild her life. Alone.

Craig caught the carbon rope before it could drop to the floor. He glanced at a nearby empty chair and shook his head.

"I hope you don't mind if I stay standing?"

"Can't stop you either way," said Doug, tilting his head back to stare up at the Super. "What have you decided?"

Silence echoed through the room while they waited for Craig's answer. Ali tried to swallow, but her mouth was too dry. Craig hadn't looked at her, really looked at her, since before the fight and she couldn't help feel that as far as he was concerned, she could do time in the slammer with the others.

Craig folded his arms across his chest in the second Power posture and stared down at them.

"I can't be unfaithful to my - I guess you'd call them my ethics. My commitment to the law. I can't let Joan and Stephen have a pass. It would undermine all that I've done so far as a Power. It would blur the line, for me," he glanced across at Ali, "of the differences between Villains and Supers. You guys might have had good reasons for what you did. You might be able to rationalize it to yourself. You might even, with the help of a good lawyer and sympathetic judge, convince a jury, *but* you have to go through the process. I have to take you in, the legal system has to grind you through. That's the bottom line. I'll put in a good word for you. I'll even turn up, in uniform, at your trial and say that you helped me capture Major Calamity, Ooze and The Blast. Maybe that will help you minimize your time. That is, if my reputation counts for anything after all this." he sighed. "It may not mean much to you, but I can't let you off. It isn't my decision to make. If I rationalize letting you go, who's to say what excuse I'll accept next? What price will buy me next time? I want to get back to work as Ultra Man, but if the price is my honor *as* Ultra Man then the price is way, way too high."

"What do you mean, get back to work as Ultra Man?" asked Doug.

Craig glanced across at Ali, huddled against the wall. She'd already decided to trust them and support them; she wouldn't mind if he gave their story away.

"You must have heard the fuss about the new Villainess, The Ice Queen?" he began.

"Yeah," said Steve, "that's amazing. I've been following Ms. Brent around for weeks and I hadn't seen any sign of a Super Power."

"That's because she hasn't got any. It's all a damn stupid invention of this trash newspaper and it's gotten all out of control! We thought we'd be able to bury The Ice Queen in the fuss that would surround capturing Nuclear Man and his gang. Now you're surrendering, we'll contact the S.S.C. and get things started. Hopefully, arresting you this way will create enough of a fuss."

Doug sighed and glanced around the room. His friends shrugged and nodded.

"You won't make any attempt to run?" asked Craig. "If you give me your word, then I'll make the call. Contact the S.S.C.."

"I have no problem with that," said Doug, "I'm sure that you'll explain in advance to the S.S.C. the terms of our surrender. I have to stay in Arizona. Near my family."

"Craig," said Ali, and was ignored.

"Just remember, in all press conferences and when you talk to your lawyers and everyone, if they ask, you have to say that The Ice Queen never existed."

"Craig?" Ali raised her voice to shout level, "Craig, we have a problem."

Everyone turned to stare.

"Ali, please, this is important," said Craig. "We have to get all aspects of our stories straight before we call the S.S.C. in for the arrest."

"That is part of the problem," said Ali, "or have you forgotten who you're telling them you've caught."

They all faced her with matching blank expressions.

"You, that is, you alone, with no help from anyone, particularly little old Powerless me, have captured Nuclear Man, and The Shriek, and The Mystress of the Night, and Major Calamity, and The Blast, and Mr. Ooze." Ali counted them off on her fingers.

"Okay. Yes," said Craig. "So?"

"Okay?" Ali threw her hands in the air. "In the last four years you and your number one Super Team have never even come close to stopping any *individual* one of these guys and now you are expecting people to accept that you, alone, caught them *all*?"

Craig settled back on his heels and considered this. "Well, we could tell them that you helped a little. That is, not that you haven't been a great help the last few days, Ali, you've been great."

"Good save," muttered The Shriek and grinned when The Mystress elbowed him in the ribs.

"We could say you are really good at Karate or something," finished Craig, glaring at the tall black man.

Ali snorted. "That is so not going to fly it might as well be covered in concrete. People may accept it the first time they hear it reported on TV, but give it enough time, and the talking heads are going to start yammering about how if it was that easy you should have caught them ages ago. Then the members of the church of the perpetually cynical will start preaching about how you're suspected of being seduced from the path of righteousness by this Ice Queen Villainess everyone's been talking about and begin to think that it is some sort of plan to undermine – I don't know – the price of cheese. I don't pretend to understand conspiracy theorists, but you know that eventually the muttering is going to be noticed. In the long run, no one is going to believe you captured six fully powered Villains without help. And then there is going to be trouble."

"She has a point," said Doug. "Maybe we could say that you caught us one by one."

"*All* of you?" asked Ali. "In less than a week? And held you where? And why didn't he notify the S.S.C. or the police?"

"Maybe one of us could betray the others?" suggested Steve.

"Let's not get too complicated," said Craig. "Any story we have to create has to be believable."

"And the best lies stay close to the truth," added Ali. "Easier to remember."

There was a long pause while everyone considered the options.

"We could let Major Calamity et al. go," suggested Doug, "They weren't supposed to be here, anyway.'

"No!" shouted Craig. "Absolutely not. Those guys," he stopped and clenched his fists, drawing air in slowly before relaxing inch by inch. "I will not permit them to escape. I will not choose to take in one Villain team over another. I will not take you lot in simply because you want to be arrested and let them go free because it's inconvenient. Who do you think I am?"

The Shriek appeared to be about to answer that question with a joke but thought better of it and remained silent.

"In that case," said Doug, "the most believable story would be that you had the rest of your usual Super Team help you and in a moment of brilliance and speed managed to capture us, unaware."

"I can't involve Purple Lightning and West. It would destroy their careers to be involved with me right now."

"How?" asked Ali. "You can't tell me that there is no precedent for this. Besides, if you get in front of the news cameras first and talk fast, tell them our version of the story, why won't they believe you?"

"I guess," muttered Craig. "I could call the guys and let them know the story before it breaks. I'm sure they'll back us up. But I want to save that as a last resort."

"I have two problems with this. One personal. One practical," said Joan raised one finger, the mystic symbols painted in silver on her long nails catching the light. "First, this means speaking to my sister about me and you know that is going to cause some severe distortions in the *national* weather system, and the other is, this surrender is not going to be believed for one simple reason – it is insufficiently dramatic."

"I don't agree," said Craig, "I know it will be embarrassing for you, but we will still have to do the perp walk. Everyone will see you being taken into the local police station in cuffs. For Doug's sake, we'll try to arrange it to be at a station with a wheelchair access ramp. If we get enough TV crews there ..."

Joan shook her head. "That isn't enough, Ultra Man. The general public, Goddess bless their adventure-starved souls, are not going to tolerate the end of our Villainous saga being some dull drive up to the front door of a cop shop! Not for *six* Super Villains. They're all descended from the people who cheered the lions. They want sweat! Blood! They want heart-pounding battles on the lip of a cliff top. Last minute rescues from a fate worse than death. They want dramatic rescues over pits of burning lava and bombs being turned off at the very last second, and if they don't get it, they'll be supremely pissed. You think Villains are bad? Just wait until you have to deal with *The Viewing Public*."

There was a longer, more thoughtful pause.

"We need a fight scene, then," said Craig. "A classic battle of good versus evil."

"That should be fun," observed Doug. "And it has to be done in front of reliable witnesses. Or, failing that, a TV news crew."

"And it has to be believable," said Joan. "Which means I get to beat up on my sister one last time."

Everyone turned to scowl at her, and she shrugged. "Well, okay. No weather magic. I promise."

"If we do it right, then no one is going to know it's a setup," said Steve.

"Are you kidding?" cried Ali, "What about Mr. Ooze? He knew your plan to retire. What is to stop him from telling all he knows next time he gets arrested?"

"Oh, I think he'll stay quiet," said Joan, settling back in her chair and buffing her nails on her tunic.

Craig and Ali exchanged a glance, then shrugged.

"Okay," said Craig, "I'll bite. What's to stop him?"

"I told him that I put a spell on him that will turn his Ooze to stone if he ever betrayed us."

"Did you?" asked Ali.

"He thinks so," said Joan with a laugh. "Thing is, if I could have, I would have years ago. Saved a lot of wear and tear on the furniture if I did."

"Well, we're going to have to hope that'll hold him," said Craig, "and that the other spells keep Major Calamity and The Blast under control. But I still want us to try and figure out a plan that doesn't involve the other members of my Superteam. Anyone got ideas?"

"I, for one, think you are doing Oliver a disservice," said Steve, "He'd kick your butt if he knew you were trying to keep him out of this. Don't you think he'd want to take this risk with you?"

"Yes," said Ali.

"Oliver," began Craig, then he paled and sank into the nearest chair.

"Craig? What's wrong?"

"It's just sunk in how fried we are," said Craig. "Control and the S.S.C. are never going to forgive me for this."

"What?"

Craig cradled his head in his hands and did not respond. Ali slid closer to him, wrapping her arm around his shoulder. "Please, Craig, what is it?"

"I've just realized that *all* of the secret identities of my Super team are blown. Every last one of us."

Ali's heart did a left twist, in pike position and took a rapid dive down to her shoes.

"Oh, hell," she whispered as she sagged against Craig's solid shoulder.

It was Nuclear Man's team turn to exchange glances.

"We won't say anything," said Doug. "Promise. We're trying to get the best possible terms for our surrender, and we sure as hell don't want to piss off the S.S.C. in the process."

"You don't understand," said Ali, "We aren't worried about you saying anything."

Craig hunched further down in the chair.

"We're afraid of the S.S.C.," continued Ali. "The only real crime within the SS.C. greater than losing your own secret identity is to expose someone else's. And now I am responsible for outing an *entire team.*"

"We," said Craig, reaching out to take her hand. "We. I'm not letting you take the hit for this alone."

The ensuing silence was broken by a snort from Joan. "Huh, like I haven't known for years that my sister is my sister. We shared a womb."

"You what?" Craig was on his feet staring, then blinked and shook his head. "You know, that's really strange. I've always known that the two of you were sisters, but I never thought much about it. I should have reported it."

Joan rolled her eyes. "This is the downside to the 'somebody else's problem' spell, I have to keep explaining it. We've already discussed this, Ultra Man. Anyone thinking about Lacey and I being related would forget it a few seconds later. The only way to break the spell is to say 'Lacey and Joan are twins' three times."

"Lacey and Joan are twins. Lacey and Joan are twins. Lacey and Joan are twins," chanted Craig and Ali.

"But this isn't going to help," continued Craig. "In fact, it's going to make things so much worse. Bad enough people suspect me of being seduced away from truth and light by a non-existent Villainess, but when they hear that Mysterious West is sister to one, there'll be trouble."

"You guys know the truth, but have you ever heard anyone refer to Lacy and me as sisters?" protested Joan. "Is it in the papers? No. On TV? No! The spell is strong. And if we, and the S.S.C., play it right, that little secret will stay that way."

"Besides, Mr. Crunch told me that Lacey is retiring soon," said Ali, resting her hand on Craig's knee. "If she resigns, and Joan is off the street, perhaps the somebody else's problem spell will hold."

"That only takes care of Joan and Lacey," said Craig, "But it still leaves me, Oliver and you exposed. In addition to you guys, Major Calamity and The Blast have seen me without my mask. Once there are cracks in a secret identity, it starts to crumble fast. On top of that, we have to go home and tell Control that someone was able to track Ali home from an event site, find out where she lived, and observed Supers in their secret identities coming and going from her house. For crud's sake, what would have happened if you and P.L. had one of your parties while Steve was watching you? Do you have any idea how many identities might have been fried?"

"The S.S.C. ignore fraternization outside of business hours. It's human nature to socialize, they can't stop it, so they don't try. But when they find out how many identities have been lost, they are going to be so mad at me." Ali shrank back, struggling to catch her breath. "They may even send me into Protective Custody. Oh, Craig!"

Ali burrowed closer to Craig, only the presence of those watching kept her from screaming. Only a few days ago, her life had been ordered – exhausting, but under control. Now she was discussing S.S.C. policy with criminals. Ultra Man, Purple Lightning, and maybe even Mysterious West's identities were on their way to becoming public knowledge, and there was no way she could think of to fix it.

"I think you're overreacting," said Doug. "We're the only ones who know and we promise, we won't tell. I'll take your secret to my grave. A short trip, but, hey, it's the thought that counts."

Craig ran a hand over Ali's disordered hair and smiled across the room at the dying man.

"S.S.C. research has shown that once *one* person discovers a secret identity there is only a three-month delay before the information has spread to the point of becoming dangerous to everyone associated with that individual Super. No matter how well-intentioned you are, Nuclear Man I have to accept that our identities are going to become public in the worst possible way. Ali's is already out there. Our greatest concern must be preventing the dominoes from falling further. Right now, it's just the Northeast Super Team and us. We don't want it to spread to the whole Super Support SS.C.."

"Okay," said Steve. "Now you're scaring me!"

"Reality does that," said Craig.

"Now we've got an even bigger problem. We have to get arrested in such a way that no one ever suspects that we ever knew the secret identities of any Super. We've got to protect the Super teams," said Doug, then laughed at Craig's stunned expression. "What? You don't think I know what would happen if the Supers had to deal with a mass relocation of their loved ones? I'm a fan of the Super teams. You guys do a lot of good work. Fire rescue, ships lost at sea, puppies up trees and all that sort of thing. You do all the saving the day things that mere mortals wish they could do. It's been proven over and over that the human race needs heroes. With no role model of greatness to emulate, people lose hope. Psychiatrists have proven over the years that the greatest protection against a child falling into a life of crime is a Hero."

"You're a fan?" said Craig, disbelief clear in his voice. "You?"

"Sure. I've been a fan for years." To everyone's surprise Doug reached into his emergency supply bag and pulled out his wallet. He dug through until he found an embossed card and pointed to the Ultra Man Fan club membership number. "See, I'm fan number two thousand and seven. All paid up and everything. I even have the decoder ring."

Ali took the card and turned it over in her hands to look at the issue date. "This is so weird. To get a number this low you had to have joined in the first month after Ultra Man was announced."

"Right after the Mountain Troll incident," said Doug, then laughed at their stunned expressions. "What? Can't Villains admire Supers? Why do you think I committed most of my crimes in his area? It wasn't that I thought you couldn't catch me, you got close a couple of times. It was that I knew that you wouldn't pound me into the ground, just for pounding's sake. I can recognize and value an honorable Super as well as anybody."

"Well, hell," muttered Craig, as Ali shook her head, too tired and confused to even laugh. "My nemesis is in my fan club. Why does that seem to make sense today?"

Now Ali snickered.

Doug thumped the arm of his chair. "Let's get organized. We have planning to do."

"I haven't the faintest idea where to begin," said Craig.

"First of all, we have to call in your crew," said Steve, "We are going to need all the help we can get."

Chapter Twenty.

The Scientific Belgian.

The European scientific medical community is meeting in Brussels this week to discuss the reclassification of Cyborgs.

"It isn't enough to have one artificial arm, or eye, or leg, Super Powered or not, to be a true Cyborg," said Dr. D. Cronenburg in his keynote speech. "If that were all, then a significant number of traffic accident survivors would be so classified. We have to come to some consensus of what minimum percentage of the body is replaced by mechanical parts, and the degree of increased Power over the original flesh is necessary to be considered a Cyborg. I, personally, am holding out for at least 65% replacement, or at least three limbs and one major sensory organ, excluding the tongue, to be classified as a Cyborg. I have not yet decided whether I will give my support to Cyborget, Cyborgoid, or Cyborgish to describe those with lesser replacements."

As it turned out, Craig found it impossible to create a plan from the Villains' point of view. After several hours of futile thought' he handed it over to the 'crime' section to the Villains in the hope that he'd be able to create a 'capture' plan.

"What do you think?" Steve waved a hand at a flowchart. The huge page was decorated with more arrows and circles than the average football play.

"Too complicated," said Craig, trying to decide if it were possible to eat another slice of plastic microwaved pizza and still retain his dignity. With a sigh, he decided four pieces would be too much. "The best plans operate on the 'Keep It Simple, Stupid' principle."

"Don't be so defeatist. We have to have drama," said Steve. "It's not enough to have Ultra Man come up and do a 'grab,' there has to be some crisis for you to prevent at the same time as capturing us."

"Stephen," chided Doug gently, adjusting his oxygen mask. "They are arresting me, not Professor Moriarty. I can't manage drama anymore. I can barely manage a *dra*!"

Craig was surprised to discover he joined in the laughter at that remark. It was getting harder and harder to regard this group as Villains. But when he thought about it, he'd spent more time with these three than he had with any other person – Oliver and Lacey excluded – for the last year. He made a mental note to do something about his social life and found his attention returning to Ali, who was now working her way through a bowl of popcorn. His smile became predatory and, after a moment, it was necessary for him to force his attention back to the discussion. He had to work on two plans. He wasn't going to wait much longer to put the one involving seducing Ali into a wedding ring into action.

"We have to do something special. Something eye-catching," insisted Steve. "I consider it my civic duty to help redeem the reputation of Ultra Man. It's only fair, since we had a little bit to do in wreaking it. I'm sure the S.S.C. will count it in our favor, even if the rest of the world never knows."

"Well, I suppose I could try, one more time," said Doug, with a sigh. "As long as it doesn't involve too much moving about."

"And we'll need help to pull it off," continued Steve. "This plan will work fine if we include Purple Lightning and Mysterious West. They deserve to be in at the kill, so to speak."

"I hope you're ready to face Oliver," said Ali, shamelessly taking the last piece of pizza. Craig scowled at her but was ignored. "He's going to be just the littlest bit pissed when he finds out who you are."

"Certainly, developing a relationship with Oliver was never part of the plan," said Steve, "it just happened. I was coming back here to suggest to Doug that we let Oliver capture us when I ran into you two." Steve let his chin rest in his hands. "I have no idea how Oliver's going to react when he hears who I am. He'll never believe I wasn't taking advantage of him from the start."

"If we're going to ask Mysterious West and Purple Lightning to help arrest Nuclear Man," said Ali, "we need to get them down here for planning sessions. I can't take the risk of calling him. The S.S.C. or the Feds might be monitoring my cell phone. The easiest way would be for Steve to call Oliver and invite him down for a talk. No one will think it unusual if Oliver takes some personal time to visit a boyfriend's family."

"Oh, no, I'm doomed." Steve slid off his chair to slump, dramatically, on the floor. The others ignored him.

"Once we've updated Oliver and persuaded him, he can take the plan back to Mysterious West and make sure that the press is on-site and S.S.C. are under control and far away when we do the arrest," said Craig.

"I disagree with one part of that plan. Unfortunately," said Joan, "I think I need to talk to my sister before we get started. Messages carried back and forth simply won't be enough. It wouldn't do for misunderstandings to screw this up."

"Okay, we'll ask Oliver to bring a friend with him. He's sure to bring Lacey. The two of them have to hang together just in case they get *the call* from Ali." Craig glanced around the table. "Anything else, before we get started?"

"What are we going to do about Calamity and the others?" asked Ali, "They've seen you without your mask, and we don't want them spreading tales about you and Nuclear Man sitting down chatting the day before his arrest."

"Don't worry about it," said Joan, holding up a spell sachet she'd been assembling. "I've been thinking about it. There are some spells that require more Power than I have on my own. If my sister and I combine our strengths then, when we get through with them, those two will feel like the fifth day of a four-day bender and will have the same type of memory loss. We could say they'd been up north raping Grizzly bears and they'd never be able to say they weren't."

Ali had never before been in a room filled with so many low-flying stress pheromones. Even the college pre-exam freak out parties was nothing in comparison with being in a room containing Villains and Supers all waiting for the bovine biological byproducts to hit the metaphorical fan. It would be easier if they were preparing for a fight. They weren't.

It wasn't even a situation where an uneasy truce was coming to an end. It was worse. Far worse.

There were no ropes involved. No threats. No ticking bombs and hostages. Instead, there were several Super Powered beings, chewing their fingernails down to the quick, knowing that in a few minutes equally Powered beings were going to enter the room, identify the occupants and start throwing Power around and no one in the room would be willing to fight back.

Not because of lack of Power.

But because they wanted peace.

Ali pressed both hands to her razor-winged butterfly-filled stomach.

Craig's naked face was flushed, his shoulders hunched as he paced back and forth across the room. He probably didn't even realize that his hands were clenched in white-knuckled fists and that he was periodically punching the air at his sides.

Ali wanted to take his hands in hers and smooth the tension out of them. In a few minutes, poor Craig was probably going to be in the worst position of his Super life. He might have to throw himself between his friends and these Villains - - - and strike the *Supers* to protect the *Villains*.

And there was nothing anyone could think of that would prevent the fight they all expected.

Ali perched on the very edge of the couch cushions. Joan had dithered a while, then decided to put any sort of spell on Ali would be sensed and misunderstood, so Ali remained unprotected.

The door chime had Steve leaping out of his chair as if stung by a cattle prod.

He cast a glance around the room, shuddering. "I guess this is it."

"Smile, boy," said Joan. "You answer the door looking like that, they'll be suspicious right off. You look like you're expecting the Ghost of Christmas Future."

Steve tried to smile. The resulting grimace had everyone groaning.

"Forget it," said Craig. "Now, you look like you have a porcupine up your ass. Just answer the damn door."

"Why do I feel like I'm waiting for the guest of honor at a not-good-surprise party?" asked Ali.

Craig paused in his pacing to shake his head at her.

"I still think this is a big mistake. Not the least because Oliver and Lacey will misunderstand when they see us here, and attack before we can explain. Ali, get ready to get behind the couch."

"Your friends are intelligent people," Doug glanced up from his chair positioned with its back to the door, so that anyone entering the room would have to walk halfway across the room before spotting him. It was generally agreed that seeing Nuclear Man first thing would not get the evening off to a great start. "I'm sure they'll understand."

"There isn't any way to give them a heads up that won't have them coming in 'all spells firing,'" said Joan, "I'm sure I can calm down any weather systems my sister can conjure up."

Craig scowled, but said nothing. Ali watched his fingers clench, relax, and clench again. He couldn't give orders to Joan and, looking as he did right now, as everyone did, there was no way they could convince someone walking into this room that something wasn't going on. Within seconds of crossing the threshold, Lacey and Oliver would come to the obvious conclusion that Craig and Ali were prisoners. If they tried to explain, the next obvious conclusion would be they had been brainwashed by the resident Villains and, after beating Doug and his friends to a pulp, Craig and Ali would be dragged back to S.S.C. headquarters to be 'treated."

And there was nothing Ali could do to prevent it. Nothing she could do to change the immediate future. She pressed harder on her stomach. The butterflies were doing somersaults.

"Do you think it would be better for you and me to meet Oliver and Lacey at the door," said Ali, urgently. "We could tell them that we ran into Steve and ..."

"Face it, Ali," said Craig, "Any way we play this scene, there is going to tension, misunderstandings, and violence. We just have to hope that we can get things calmed down before the twins call down a blizzard."

They both froze when they heard the sound of Steve's voice raised in meeting-strangers tones. A few minutes passed, then the door opened. Before anyone crossed the threshold, Ali was off the couch and had her arms wrapped around Craig, pinning her to his side. She stretched up to clamp her lips hard on his. To her complete surprise, Craig didn't resist. Didn't try to shake her off. Instead, he gripped her hips and pulled her closer.

The first few seconds into the kiss, Ali was hoping that Craig would figure out her strategy and cooperate. He made no move to escape her grip, instead leaned into the kiss, bending her back until her lips parted. Ali's face burned as his tongue invaded her mouth, taking the kiss to a level of intimacy that she hadn't planned to pursue in the presence of friends and Villains.

Craig didn't seem to care that they weren't alone. He took control of the kiss, his tongue delving into her mouth, tangling with hers in an erotic dance that weakened her knees and had her trembling in his arms.

Then she stopped thinking about plans, Villains, or anything at all. Her hands drifted up until they were buried in his thick hair. Her eyes closed and time hung, suspended. Craig's mouth, hands, and warm body, pressed against hers, the only reality. A few years later, she became dimly aware of noise. She opened one eye to investigate. The Shriek, Mystress of the Night, and Nuclear Man were pounding their hands together and laughing. A few feet away stood Oliver, cheering and applauding. When he saw her looking at him, he put two fingers in his mouth and let out a piercing whistle. That was enough to shake Craig's lips loose from Ali's, and he grunted like an annoyed bear as he turned his head to investigate the interruption. Ali felt oddly proud that it took him an instant or two to refocus on the room.

"About bloody time," cried Oliver.

"Time?" muttered Craig.

Beside Oliver stood Lacey, her multicolored turban dangerously close to toppling off her head as she raised one arm to 'whoop, whoop, whoop.'

"You go, girl," shouted Joan.

There was a split second of silence, then Lacey spun to face her sister.

"Hi sis," said Joan, "I missed you."

Lacey ducked, glancing around for a ricocheting spell. She plunged her hands into her oversized handbag at the same time.

"Oliver," shouted Lacey, "Battle stations."

"Way ahead of you," said Oliver, who now had both arms wrapped around Steve's neck and was forcing him to the floor.

"Calm down," shouted Craig, pushing Ali behind him. "Everyone freeze!"

All movement stopped. Oliver and Lacey stared at Craig, then scanned the room. Ali could see the exact second when they recognized each Villain in the room. Then all attention returned to Craig.

"Say, Oliver," whispered Steve, "don't you think you should wait until we've known each other a little longer before starting with the kinky stuff."

Oliver glanced down at his captive. No one had attacked. No spell had burst over them. It was still a mild and cool evening outside, with no sign of abnormal weather. Ali could almost see his thoughts.

They'd walked into a trap.

Villains had Craig and Ali captive.

Then why were Craig and Ali kissing when he came in?

"Oliver," said Craig, "things are not as they appear."

"And *that's* not cliché," said Ali to Doug, who snickered.

Craig glared at them both. "Do you mind? I'm trying to defuse a dangerous situation here."

"Oh, sorry to interrupt. Please, do go on," said Doug, then turned his chair so that he faced the new arrivals, calmly ignoring the fact that Oliver had Steve in a half-Nelson, and there was a spell package in Lacey's upraised hand. "While you're doing that, may I offer anyone tea? Coffee? Dinner is ready. For dessert, we have pie. Coconut cream. Joan said it was your favorite, Ms. Henley, or may I call you Lacey? Joan has told us so much about you."

"What's going on here?" asked Oliver, still maintaining his grip on The Shriek's neck.

"We invited Ultra Man and his charming companion here, to arrest us. It was suggested that you might like to be involved," said Doug, folding his thin hands over his chest. "But if you don't mind waiting, we can have pie first."

"Your spell worked, Lacey," leaning out from behind Craig, Ali waved her hands to demonstrate that she wasn't tied up. "Events Conspired to bring us here."

Craig gave a helpless shrug and moved across the room to stand beside Doug, who gave a little wave.

"See. I'm standing in the presence of Nuclear Man."

"Well, Hell," said Lacey, gesturing to Oliver to release Steve. "This is going to be one for the books."

Then she walked across the room to stand facing her twin. After a pause, The Mysterious West hauled The Mystress of the Night into a massive hug.

"Hi, sis, I've missed you too."

Craig studied the room's occupants with considerable interest and not a little suspicion. Emotions were flying everywhere. If he was not mistaken, now that the adrenaline was fading, Oliver had a fully-fledged atomic-powered sulk coming on and, if they were not careful, the tenuous truce between the twins wouldn't last five seconds. Craig felt himself settling into Power Pose #1, opened his mouth and found that he had nothing to say. He had no idea how to deal with the complicated relationships before him. Hell, he didn't even know how to deal with his own relationship with Ali. In fact, he suspected that Ali was planning on doing a midnight flit sometime soon. It was the noble, self-sacrificing thing to do. Almost... he grinned, cliché. But he wasn't going to accept it. He had to take his stubborn woman in hand and explain one or two things to her. The memory of that kiss set various parts of his body to sitting up and begging. Okay, he had three or four things to say to her, but it would have to wait.

He glanced around the room. From the look of things, he wasn't the only one with something to say.

"Okay. Everyone!" They all turned expectant faces to him. "I'm declaring a one-hour time-out. Go to your corners and talk it over. I want no character aspersions. No raking over old grievances. No illegal holds. No low blows. And, especially, no weather disturbances." The twins giggled and he frowned at them. "Seriously, any anomalous weather will have the S.S.C. down on us faster than our friend Lightning. Now, I'm trusting you to deal in an adult manner with whatever angst you think needs to be vented. I'll be back in an hour and I'll want to see all wounds staunched, all bruised egos treated, and everyone on their best behavior and prepared to play well with others."

So saying, he spun on his heels and exited into the gardens. Ali, Powerless neutral party, was the best person to arbitrate what was going to go on in there. He might not like the fact that Ali could see things from the Villains' point of view, but at this moment, with these Supers and Villains, her attitude was essential to peace. He hadn't thought about that before. Ali, with her sarcastic wit and refusal to bow to anyone, wasn't being utilized to her fullest potential. There had to be some job she could do that would make better use of her particular talents. Her vision. Her sympathy. He'd mention it to Mr. Crunch, just as soon as he was certain that Crunch wasn't going to fire him – outright or out of a cannon.

And while she was sorting out that emotional chaos in there, he was going to give some serious thought to how the hell they were going to fix the rest of this damned mess.

He wasn't gone three seconds before Oliver and Lacey had grabbed Ali and squeezed the air out of her. Ali struggled free of the group hug and tried to get her thoughts in order. First a mauling, well, a mutual mauling, with Craig, and now this.

"Congratulations, Ali," cried Oliver, kissing her cheek. "If I'd known all it would take was leaving you two alone for a few days, I would have locked you two in the basement closet years ago."

"What the hell is your problem, Oliver?" asked Ali. "Don't you recognize a classic film Noir distraction technique? The kiss-me-you-fool maneuver?"

"Looked real to me," said Lacey, and there was a general murmur of agreement from the watching Villains.

"It's supposed to look real," said Ali, "That's why it worked."

Oliver took a step back and regarded Ali with a scowl. "Are you telling me that you and Craig still haven't gotten it together?"

"What 'it'? I have no idea what you mean."

"When I captured...," Steve shot a glance at Joan. "We captured Ultra Man and Ice Queen, Ultra Man was down to his boxers and she was on the bed."

Ali blushed. "That isn't I mean... We weren't...I was fully dressed."

"You mean, you stopped them?" Lacey glared so hard at Steve that he took several steps back.

"Hey! Look, I'm sorry. I didn't realize!"

"That's none of your business," cried Ali, and was ignored.

"Hell, we've been trying to get these two together for years," shouted Oliver at Steve. "We don't need any ham-handed interference from ..."

"Oliver! Enough!" shouted Ali. "We have more important things to talk about."

"No, we don't," said Joan, with commendable calm. "My sister and Oliver are going to help arrest us. Done deal. You and Craig are much more interesting. Why didn't you go with him, just now?"

"I have no idea what you're talking about."

Lacey ignored Ali and shook her head at her sister. "You would not believe the dance this child has sent that poor boy on. Years, he's been chasing her. Shocking tease that she is. Unless I'm mistaken, that just now was their first kiss."

Joan tut-tutted as Steve snickered. "Now, that I do not believe. Ultra Man, sexually frustrated? Good thing the Villains didn't know."

"Don't you tell anyone," said Ali. "Anyway, it's none of your business what's going on, or not going on, between Craig and me. You have other, more important issues to work out."

"Ain't nothing going on half as interesting as this," said Steve, with a smirk.

"Oh, that angst stuff can all wait." Joan waved her well-decorated fingers. "Lacey and I have been yelling at each other since long before you were born. We're in no hurry for the next fight."

"Listen, you guys have got things to work out before we can get started planning your spectacular arrest scene. We haven't got time to worry about the non-existent relationship between Craig and me."

"Non-existent? Girlfriend, you will be the death of me yet. You and Craig are so overdue. If you don't sort it out now, you'll find all sorts of other reasons to keep delaying it, and, frankly, my nerves are wrecked."

Oliver glanced around the room, spotted a loose, soft rug thrown artistically across a couch and grabbed it. In an instant it was wrapped around Ali and they were out of the door. No one attempted to prevent the kidnap. In fact, the Villains and Super witches crowded the window to wave bye-bye as Olive and Ali zoomed out into the night.

"You'll never find him," gasped Ali as guinea pig hutches, trees and bushes blurred past.

"Dooon'tttt uneddddresttttttimate meeeee," said Oliver.

A few twists and dodges later and Oliver slid to a halt at Craig's feet.

Craig pushed away from the tree he'd been leaning against. "What? What?"

"You two sort it out," said Oliver, dumping Ali, blanket and all, into Craig's arms. "Don't come back until you do."

"Well, this is interesting," said Craig, but made no move to set Ali on her feet.

Ali took a few seconds to get her breath back before she started struggling. Fully intending, Craig could tell, to get out of his arms and put as much distance as possible between the two of them.

He didn't wait. Tensing his shoulders, he bent his knees and pushed his feet against the ground. Gravity thought about it for a moment, then surrendered. In seconds, they were airborne and well above tree level.

A few minutes later, he had achieved what he considered a safe cruising altitude. Despite the dry Arizona air, he was able to find a low-lying cloud and flew into it. Once enveloped in the soft, faintly dusty smelling mass of moisture, he flipped over so that he was flying with his back to the ground with Ali reclining on him. He wrapped his Super-heated arms around her and held her close.

"What the hell are you doing?!" Ali gasped – a combination of decreased oxygen and surprise. "Didn't you learn your lesson last time?"

His grin broadened as she wrestled within his grip, trying to find a way to stay up in the air that didn't require full body physical contact.

"Yeah," said Craig. "You'd think I'd learn my lesson. Silly me, I guess you're gonna have to hit me again." He waited until she balled her fist and raised it. "But first, let's go back to that interesting conversation we were having last night. You know, the one where you told me you lusted for my bod." He wiggled his eyebrows at her until she couldn't hold in the laugh. "You do remember, don't you?"

"I have no idea what you're talking about," said Ali with an attempt at dignity - failed.

Craig shifted his grip until one hand cupped the back of her head and he drew her closer. "In that case, my dear Ice Queen, let me improve your memory."

Flight Powers gave a guy a small advantage when it comes to kissing. When you're on the ground, there is that small differences-in-height issue that had to be addressed when maneuvering in for a kiss. It was hard to find a girl who was just the right height for a straight-in lip lock. But, Craig discovered as he hauled Ali up his chest, if you could fly, you could just adjust your positions a little until everything lined up perfectly.

And, there was the added advantage of knowing that no one knew where they were, nor could they interrupt them for some considerable time, leaving him free to take his time and really enjoy himself.

Knowing his captive, he started with a full force, overwhelm-her kiss, covering her lips with his and holding it until she was breathless. Then he switched to little teasing kisses, wandering over her face and returning to her mouth to explore its soft smoothness and sweet depths.

As minutes passed without any threatening moves from Ali, Craig settled into the kiss with heat and passion, until her arms rose to wrap around his chest and all the tension leaked from her body. She lay on him and yielded her mouth, face and neck to his exploration.

Eventually he drew back and studied her face. He took a little pride in her stunned expression and half-closed eyes. A glance around told him they'd drifted out from the protection of the cloud and they were now in danger of frightening some migrating birds. He shifted his shoulders and directed them back toward shelter. Ali blinked and shook off her kiss-induced distraction.

"What are you up to now?"

"Getting us a little privacy "

Ali scowled at him.

"Whose fantasy are we playing out now?"

Craig studied her for a moment, then remembered, "God, no, Ali no. Nothing like that. Give me a break. This isn't anyone's fantasy script. This is just me, winging it. But if you tell me your fantasy, I'd be happy to fulfill it." He wiggled his eyebrows hopefully, but Ali turned her face away. "Oh, come on, don't make a guy beg. You can't complain that I don't do what you want, or consider your feelings, if you never tell me what they are. I've been waiting for years for you to just tell me what you want in a guy, so I could work on convincing you I'm exactly that."

Ali shifted a little until her elbows were on his chest and she rested her chin on her palms, staring down at him.

Craig steadied her, placing both hands on her hips, which had her eyebrow winging up, but she smiled instead of pushing him away.

"Okay," she said, "let me tell you first off, reading all your groupies' lust fantasies made me nauseated – and, I'll admit it, jealous. They didn't have any inhibitions about letting you know what was on their minds. Every second line was 'I love you, Ultra Man.' Every time I read those words, it made it harder for me to get near you. I didn't want to be one of the crowd."

"Ali, love," Craig sighed and tightened his grip. "What do I have to do to convince you, there never was a crowd for you to get lost in? There has only ever been you."

She blushed and pressed her heated face against his chest. Without looking up, she whispered. "My fantasy's never been about a specific guy. It's that I've wanted someone I could snuggle with in front of a fire. You know, simple, quiet, but meaningful affection. I want to feel cherished. Special. I want to feel that I'm the most important person in his world."

They changed direction in an instant, rocketing toward to ground.

"I can do cuddly," said Craig, as they fell out of the sky. "I can do open fire. Just you wait."

Ali held on for dear life and closed her eyes as the ground charged toward them. Craig judged the flight precisely. They swooped down, then there was a nausea-inducing lift and drop and Ali was back on the ground, barely able to keep her balance.

While Craig scraped an area of ground free of decaying wood and stones with his foot and collected a few armfuls of fallen branches and leaves, Ali wrapped the thin blanket around her shoulders and struggled between the need to laugh or weep. He was so damned *cute*! The way he kept glancing over his shoulder at her as if watching for her approval of his arrangement of twigs. Checking to see if the little ring of rocks he'd created around his makeshift fire pit was – she didn't know – *elegant* enough for her? Was she really that demanding that a full grown adult Super would tremble if she frowned at the lopsided pyramid of wood he was about to ignite for her benefit?

Apparently so. When Craig finally waved at the flickering fire pit with a ta-da gesture, and she smiled in response, his face lit up so much that she began to fear she'd been a sincerely obnoxious individual in the past. Had it really been so hard for her to say anything nice to him?

For Heaven's sake, Ultra Man, the most Power-laden Super living was almost doing the happy-me dance because she smiled at him.

"I like it." Just watching him work left her feeling warm and soft. She stared at the curls framing his face as if she'd never seen them before. Loving him had crept up on her. Sometime, when she wasn't paying attention, Craig Duane had climbed into her heart, made himself comfortable, and stayed. Now, that was a Super ability no one had warned her about. She took two steps forward, shook the blanket free of her shoulders and reached up to wrap it around them both. Together they stood, side by side, contemplating the shriveling leaves and blackening wood. Craig slipped one arm around her shoulder and turned her to face him.

He slid his other hand up to cup her chin.

"You think this fire is good," he whispered, "You should see what else I can do to keep you warm."

He slid the blanket from around her and spread it on the ground.

Ali stepped back, or at least she tried to. Before she could move her feet, Craig had lifted her into his arms and was lowering her to the blanket. He knelt beside her, watching her face warily.

"I don't bite," said Ali.

"You've done everything but," said Craig, lying down beside her and running his fingers around the curve of her jaw. "However, I don't think I'd mind much if you did."

He stretched out on the blanket behind her, easing her head down to rest on his arm, both of them facing the flickering firelight.

"I've thought about holding you like this, a lot," said Craig, pressing his lips to her hair. "Of course, in my daydreams we're at some exclusive hotel resort, maybe a snow lodge, and the fireplace is this huge stone thing and we're lying on a thick rug with – well, you don't drink wine, so maybe hot chocolate. Soft music playing in the background. All the traditional stuff."

"Nice thought," said Ali, with a small wince. With all the gifts nature had seen fit to bestow on Craig, she really should have found some Charm to add to the Strength and Flight and *stuff*. Perhaps, on reflection, maybe not.

"I wanted our first time to be special. Roses and soaking in a Jacuzzi by candlelight."

"This is special,' said Ali grabbing him by the ears and pulling him down to kiss.

Craig cupped her face in both hands and delved into the kiss with a gentleness that was distinctly unsatisfying. He brushed his lips across her, barely making contact. His hands wandered down her ribs, missing her breast by inches. Ali tightened her grip on his head and tried to deepen the kiss. Immediately, she discovered one disadvantage of using force on this Super – if he wanted to be an immovable object, he could.

Ali relaxed her grip and shifted away from Craig. He started kissing a path down her neck – at least she thought he did, the touch was so light she wasn't sure.

She ground her teeth and glared at the top of his head. What the hell was wrong with the man? Did he want to make love to her or not?

It finally occurred to her that the man who could crush bricks to dust with his hands was stroking her skin as if afraid she'd shatter.

He was afraid of hurting her.

Ali shifted under him, struggling to free her arms.

"Babe, please don't change your mind," whispered Craig as he kissed a path across her jaw. "I'd die."

Ali seized his wrist and pressed his palm, firmly, over her breast.

Startled, Craig's hand flexed around her soft flesh, his thumb flicked her nipple. "Ali?"

"If you want me to know that you're making love to me, Mr. Duane," growled Ali, "You're gonna have to touch me as if you mean it. I'm tougher than I look, or haven't you figured that out by now?"

Craig gaped at her as she threw her other arm around his neck and lifted herself up to rub against his already heated body. "I'm strong, Ali, I've got to be careful. I don't want to hurt you."

"You wanna make it with me, you're gonna have to put some effort into it," Ali's hand drifted down his chest, tugged at the button of his jeans and down further to cup and mold the fabric against his erection. "Make me feel it."

"Well, if you're sure?" The corners of his mouth quirked up in an evil grin. "We Supers are here to give satisfaction, ma'am."

"That's my boy."

Ali sighed, lowered her head to rest on Craig's chest and relaxed into his embrace. Immediately, her head came up again as she felt herself begin to sink down his body. She glanced around, went 'eep' and clenched arms and legs tight around Craig's body.

To her complete shock she – and Craig – were floating above the trees. Ali studied the distant ground, with the dying fire, crumpled blanket and their clothing scattered to the four corners of the clearing.

"What the hell happened?"

Craig laughed as they began a slow descent. "I dunno. I don't remember deciding to fly. It just happened."

When he caught Ali's glare, he continued. "Well, it didn't seem right to you know, do it, with you lying on the ground. Not on stones and twigs and stuff. I didn't want to hurt you, so I sort of lifted you into my arms. And then, well, I got distracted."

Ali shifted her grip until she was holding on more securely around his neck. "I see."

Craig gripped her buttocks and supported her as they sank toward the ground. "Okay, I got a lot distracted."

Ali could tell the exact moment Craig touched down. One moment she was resting easily in his arms, then her body weight returned. Before she could slide free, Craig caught her and waited until she unwrapped her legs from around his hips and got them back on the ground.

She stepped back as soon as she was certain her legs would support her. She turned and grabbed the blanket, wrapping it around herself and she searched for her clothes.

"Where the hell is my bra?"

"I dunno." Craig hadn't moved. He was still standing where he'd landed, staring at her with a smug, but brilliant smile on his face.

Ali blushed. "You had it last."

Craig scanned the clearing, then laughed and pointed up. Her bra dangled shamelessly from an overhead branch.

"How the hell did it get up there?"

"I dunno. I was distracted at the time."

Craig crouched slightly, then lifted off the ground. He floated up to where the lost bra had landed, pulled it loose, then descended. He folded it carefully and held it out to her in both hands.

Ali stared for a moment, then started laughing. She couldn't help it. There was Craig – Ultra Man – standing naked except for a very mangled shirt half hanging off his shoulders, holding out her bra as if it were a precious trophy. There she was, completely naked except for a thin blanket, accepting it. She stepped up, pressed her lips against his heated cheek. "I want you to know that you're my hero," she whispered.

"Good to know." Not satisfied with the chaste kiss, Craig pulled her close. "Tell me, why did it take so long for us to get together? Were you waiting for some sign? Was it the chocolates? Absence of chocolates? Perfume?"

Ali laughed and pushed the hair back from his forehead and snuggled closer to his Super-heated body. "None of the above. I guess the worst thing I've ever done is read those blasted fan fantasies. It seemed like every second line they were saying 'I love you, Ultra Man", and it cheapened the emotion for me. I couldn't....wouldn't let myself feel anything for you. Not when there were so many crazy women saying the same thing. I couldn't bring myself to be like them, crazy about you, and keep my self-respect."

"Aw, Ali. That is so sweet and so dumb."

Ali slapped him across the chest. "You read them! You know how they sounded."

Craig laughed. "Silly Rabbit. Of course, I did. I was looking for dating tips. Man, I was so desperate, I was taking advice from a fifty-year-old witch and a gay guy. There were no depths I would not descend to if I could only get a date with you."

"And all along all you had to do is be accused of ..." Ali frowned, "I forget. Why are we on the run again?'

"Don't ask, the whole set up never made any sense to me. All I know is I want to get back. No. Wait." He smiled down at her. "My priorities have changed. What I want is you! Ultra Man, the S.S.C., all that is secondary."

He waited a moment, but Ali remained silent.

"Your turn, Ali cat. What do you want? And remember, be honest."

Ali ran her fingertips down the side of his face and across his lips. Craig nipped at them and caught them, briefly, in his teeth.

"I guess," she sighed. "Okay, I know I want you. I love you, Craig Duane."

"I'm so glad you said that. I love you and want you, too." Craig's grin became feral. "Let me show you what I want you for."

Some unmeasured time later, Craig pulled the blanket across their naked bodies and stared up at the stars.

"Ali, I've figured it out, why you were so mad at me. Why you hate your Dad."

She blinked in surprise. She hadn't realized he'd remembered that conversation, and she certainly hadn't expected him to bring that up. "And this would be?"

"It offends you when someone strong, someone who should protect and guard the weak and defenseless, uses their power against them. Your Dad's job was to make sure no one ever hurt you. Didn't hurt your spirit or your pride. Instead, he abused his position. Every time he played a trick and humiliated you, he failed in his dad duty. He tried to wear you down and make you weak. Make you his victim so that he could feel powerful. I'm glad that he failed. Practical jokes aren't funny when they're vicious attacks in disguise. They undermine a person's confidence in the universe. Water fountains shouldn't spray up your nose and make you choke. You should be able to go to bed without looking for short sheets and drink your lemonade without looking for spiders and flies in the ice cubes. You shouldn't have to worry when you walk down school corridors that someone hasn't put a 'kick me' sign on your back."

"Spiders? Flies. I didn't hear about that one." Ali gave a weak smile and brushed her fingertips over his chest. "And what does that mean about you?"

"I finally know what I'm supposed to apologize about." He took a deep breath and looked her in the eye. "Ali, I'm sorry for any time I made someone feel helpless. I'm sorry for any memory I, as Ultra Man or my civilian self, gave someone that makes them cringe years later. Most of all, I'm sorry for every time I laughed when someone else was hurting."

"That's what you feel, is it?"

Craig responded to her smirk with one of his own.

"That's some of it." His hands tightened around her shoulders. "The rest of it is, I love you. I want you, and I'm going to spend the rest of my life making sure no one gets to hurt you." He pressed his lips against her forehead and started nibbling his way down the side of her face. "After all," he whispered when he got level with her ear, "there has to be some benefit to being married to a Super Power."

Warmth spread through Ali's body, pooling in her belly. Craig cast a look at her again, and she found herself wanting to reach for him. Keeping him naked, biting his muscular butt, dragging him off somewhere safe and quiet for a few years seemed like such a good plan.

"Comedian," Ali snorted, when she had her hormones back under control, "We may be able to beat the Villains – with their cooperation. I'm more worried about the S.S.C. I'm sure I know that I'm going to have to be relocated. There is no way the gang-of-four are going to allow us to be anywhere near each other. The security risk is too great."

"That doesn't matter, Ali, because I'm going to tell them they can relocate both of us, and it has to be together. Being with you is more important than anything else. Get used to having me around, oh Ice Queen, 'cause I'm gonna be right beside you for a long time."

"You think it," said Ali. "You may even believe it. We're going to do it your way and I have no say in the matter?"

"Exactly."

She smiled and patted him lightly on the shoulder, "You go on thinking that," she said, "if it makes you feel better."

"Is that a yes?" asked Craig.

"I'll think about it and let you know."

"Not good enough, Ali cat. I want to hear you say it. I've got a vacancy for a partner. Membership of this team is limited to two. I think you've got all the qualities I need in the person I want guarding my back. You're sweet, funny, loyal and determined," he touched a fingertip to her nose, "and I love you. So, tell me, do you want the job? Will you marry me?"

The world took another spin and dip. For a moment, Ali wasn't certain that Craig hadn't swept her up into the air again. But no, she was still safely on the ground, naked except for Craig's shirt and half a blanket. Not the circumstances she'd imagined as a child when she'd daydreamed about receiving a marriage proposal, although she would admit, a naked Craig, even if he wasn't on one knee and holding a massive ring, had nothing to be ashamed of.

"No matter how it turns out?" asked Ali.

"When it's you and me against the world, oh my Ice Queen. I'm betting on us."

"In that case, yes. Just ..." she paused just long enough for Craig to look worried.

"What?"

"If that ring you've got waiting for me is a diamond, could you take it back and switch it for another stone. Somehow I don't think I like the idea of wearing *ice*."

Craig and Ali managed to find their way back to Doug's isolated home and were walking back from the tiny, but remarkably well equipped, guinea pig maternity unit when a bundle of fur jumped out from under a hutch and bounced rapidly past them into the undergrowth. Ali jumped behind Craig, being careful not to clutch at him. One didn't touch a Super in a high-risk situation. You might slow him down that crucial split second and lead to his defeat.

"What the heck?" cried Craig, stumbling a few steps after the creature.

Ali peered over his shoulder into the darkness. The animal stopped just out of reach and glanced back at them while wiggling its whiskers.

"Well, I'll be damned," cried Ali, "a Jackalope!"

"He really has them, then."

Craig laughed and reached to wrap an arm around Ali's shoulders as they watched the silly little creature with its tiny curved horns sitting neatly between long floppy ears. After a moment, their vision adjusted to the dim light and they saw dozens of the creatures hopping through the clearing.

"Good grief, they're all over the place. I wonder where they came from?"

"Who knows," said Craig, pulling her in front of him and sliding his arms around her and resting his chin on her shoulder. "I wonder if they're going to sell these, too. I think they'd be a hit."

Ali glanced toward the open porch doors. Doug was reclining in one of the easy chairs, apparently asleep. In the corner, Lacey and Joan were talking quietly as they passed a photo album back and forth. Oliver and Steve were seated silently at opposite ends of a couch.

"I gotta say, I don't much feel like going back in there,' said Craig. "For one thing, we've been gone for more than an hour and I don't need to be faced with Oliver's 'I know what you've been up to' smirks. And for another, I have no idea what to do. How are we going to arrange for a sufficiently dramatic capture?"

"Steve seemed to think he had a plan."

"It's too elaborate. The more complicated the machinery, the less it takes to screw it up."

"Well, why don't you look at it like directing someone who likes to overact," suggested Ali. "Let him run through it how he thinks it should go, say 'thank you that was nice but next time, don't do this, this and this.'"

Craig cast her a suspicious look. He'd briefly been involved with the college amateur dramatics club. Right now, he couldn't be sure of the dates. Had that been before or after Ali had arrived on campus? Her smile was entirely innocent, which meant she'd probably seen one of the productions he'd been in. Damn. Damn. Damn.

"Okay," he said, after a pause. "Let's go find out what Mr. De Mille wants us to do."

It took hours to hammer out the planned capture. Shortly before dawn, Joan showed Craig and Ali to one of the many spare rooms in the house – while smiling benignly. Ali's attempt to get separate rooms was overridden by both Villains and Supers. Despite his lecherous intentions, it hadn't taken long for Craig to pass out. Ali waited until Craig was sleeping the sleep of the just and sexually exhausted, then she crept out of their room and down to the main floor. She was not surprised to find Stephen with Oliver, Lacey with Joan, and Doug all sitting quietly in the wood-paneled living room. Ali peered over her shoulder – the staircase behind her was empty.

"Okay. You have something you want and I have something I need to do." Closing the door without a betraying click she walked into the center of the room. "Let's make a deal."

Chapter Twenty-One.

Police band radio.
"All Units. S.S.C. alert! Fugitives Ultra Man and Ice Queen spotted in downtown Phoenix".

It had taken a whole day to get the plan sorted out, equipment purchased and the site selected. Joan had searched six costume stores before she'd found one with an Ultra Man suit in stock. It was made of thin plastic, a size too small and not tailored well – or, indeed, at all. It was very much of the one-size-fits-nobody family of clothing. With a little luck, the heat-pressed seams would hold up for just one fight scene, otherwise, well, the world would see more of Ultra Man than they'd ever seen before.

Craig appeared surprised when they'd found, for some reason, that Ultra Man paraphernalia had been flying off the shelves in the last few days. Ali couldn't decide if people were showing support for the missing Super or taking their last chance to pick up collector's items before S.S.C. announced Ultra Man was now a Villain, and pulled them.

Now that the moment for action had arrived, Ali could barely breathe even though her role was fairly simple. The parking lot they had chosen for the 'capture' scene was overlooked by some mostly empty warehouses. Her building, chosen since it had the best view of the parking lot, stank of years of captive mold and antique dust. She sprayed a filthy window with cleaner and rubbed away several years of accumulated muck. Once the glass was clean enough to satisfy her, she opened the leather case at her feet and started assembling the camera tripod. It took her about fifteen minutes to get all the equipment out of the bag and properly positioned.

Craig slipped through the half-open door and wrapped his arms around her from behind. He pressed a soft kiss to her hair and peered over her head down onto the pavement.

"How're things going?" asked Ali.

"Good. We're at five minutes and counting. Before we start, I just wanted to give you a present. Something for you to hang onto until I get home and can give you your ring." He grinned down at her, nervously. "I picked this up yesterday when I got the uniform from the costume store."

Ali stared at the bright silver box resting on the palm of his hand for a full minute before accepting it. She pulled the top off to reveal a small green and bronze plastic magnet.

Half laughing, she lifted it out of the box, turning it over in her fingers.

"Craig? Why in the world did you get me this? I have a box of them in my office."

"Maybe," Craig flushed, "but I noticed that you don't have my logo magnet on your fridge. Under the circumstances, I'm going to insist that you have one from now on. I'm not asking for you to take the others away, I just want to join the gang."

Ali turned the small piece of magnetized plastic over and over in her fingers. "How do you know I don't have you on there already?"

"I looked the day you asked me to order take-out," he paused and ran a fingertip down the side of her face. "I gotta tell you, Ali, that hurt. Hurt more than I thought it would. All I want you to do is add me to the list."

Ali stared for a few seconds then started laughing. "Oh you poor, dear neglected Super. I didn't leave you off intentionally, and it certainly wasn't because I wanted to hurt your feelings. Did you think I *chose* to leave you off? You silly boy. It's because I keep running out of them. I can't keep anything with your logo on in stock. Pens, magnets, note paper- whatever we're giving out at event sites, people all want your logo! I never have one left over to take home with me. That's the only reason you're not there."

"Well, damn," Craig laughed and shook his head. "That is one explanation that just didn't occur to me. What a waste of all that sulking and hurt feelings. Ah, well, at least you have one now." He folded Ali's fingers around the tiny magnet. "Understand me? This one doesn't get given away."

"Deal," said Ali, and kissed him.

Ali peered out of the window at the empty parking lot across the street. "Almost show time."

"Did Steve say how Oliver reacted to his confession?" asked Craig.

Ali gave a shrug. "They're still speaking to each other. Steve says he's hopeful. After all, who else can understand the demands of a Super Hero's life better than a Super Villain?"

Craig shook his head as one side of his mouth twitched, but he couldn't keep the laugh in. He leaned against the dusty wall until the spasms ended.

"So, they're still dating?" he asked.

"Apparently," said Ali, "Oliver said that the only reason he got so bent out of shape is that he was upset at himself for not recognizing a Villain when he was sitting across the table from him in a restaurant."

Craig chuckled. "I suppose. But he should remember, he introduced The Shriek to you, and then I met him as well without realizing who he was. We were all fooled. Amazing what a difference a little tiny mask makes."

A movement outside caught his attention.

Ali joined Craig gazing out of the window and together they watched a battered van drive into the lot and take the only available disabled parking place. A figure emerged from the driver's side, glanced about and went toward the back of the van. The figure transformed into a purple blur that raced down the Sunday empty street, paused in the parking lot long enough to resolve into Purple Lightning. The purple light surrounded the van for a moment, then was gone again. When Ali and Craig looked at the front of the van again there were familiar figures slumped in the van's front seat.

"That's Ooze, The Blast and Calamity in place," said Ali, "How much longer 'til show time?"

"Things should be heating up soon."

Ali nodded, activating the video camera and aiming it at the parking lot. She made sure one last time that she had the van centered in the shot. Then she checked the battery and memory disc. It wouldn't do to fail just because they ran out of memory at the wrong moment.

Down in the parking lot, Nuclear Man climbed slowly out of the back passenger door and waited. A few seconds later, P.L. returned. Instead of running at his top speed, he jogged into the lot, circling the van a few times. With each rotation stray newspaper pages, dust and grit rose from the pavement to dance in the air behind him. Nuclear Man turned his face toward the van, one hand raised to shield himself from the flying debris. On P.L.'s fourth circuit, Nuclear Man leaned forward and vomited directly in P.L.'s path. Ali winced. Even though she'd been the one to think of the fake emesis trick – and helped Doug hide bladders of half set-jello mixed with diced carrots under his shirt – the sight was nauseating. P.L. tried to dodge, but one foot appeared to catch on the corner of the mess and he flew across the parking lot, crashing into a pile of cardboard boxes.

P.L. made one feeble attempt to regain his feet, then collapsed.

Craig winced. "I am so going to owe him one for faking that fall."

"If anything permanently stained his new clothes you may never get into his good books again," muttered Ali, tightening the focus and zoomed in on the struggling Super, "Damn it to hell, here come the noble members of the press ahead of schedule! I thought we had a good ten minutes yet."

Although they wanted – nay, *needed* the press involved they'd wanted to get the scene well and truly set before they arrived. Several TV news vans screamed around the corner, bumping against each other as they jostled for the lead. When they skidded to a halt, Nuclear Man grinned at them and hobbled a little further away from the van. A strong wind stirred the rubbish around him.

"Hells Bells," groaned Craig, pointing at the lead TV van. "Who invited them?"

Ali stared, then started cursing.

The door of the TV van opened and Tye Dye leaped out. Right on his heels came Urban Renewal, closely followed by a camera-laden man and a woman struggling under the weight of her TV-ready makeup. In the parking lot Nuclear Man paused, then crutched his way behind his van as fast as he could

"No. No," cried Ali. "We don't need any more Supers. They'll spoil everything. This is supposed to be *your* capture!"

Craig shook his head at the panicked note in her voice but turned his attention skyward. There, on schedule, was The Mysterious West. Ignoring the additional Supers on the ground, West flew directly at Nuclear Man. West, Ali suspected, was trying to get to the fragile Villain first, to protect him from Urban Renewal. Tye Dye must have been worried about losing the arrest as he activated his Power, drenching the gathered Supers, Villains and TV crews in color.

Ali froze as the light built. Craig leaped, pulling her down below the window ledge. Even with their eyes shut tight they sensed the color and light filling the room. The blue wept. The red smelt of fire. Ali clutched at the only surety in her world, crawling into Craig's embrace to hide.

"What the hell?" cried Craig, curling himself around Ali, "He's been amplified!"

"The Colonel gave him a new suit."

The light above their heads died suddenly. Craig and Ali emerged inch by inch, reluctant to expose themselves to another color attack.

"That moron. I'm going to kill him dead," said Craig peering over the window ledge. Down in the parking lot Mysterious West lay sprawled across Tye

Dye, both of them unconscious at Nuclear Man's feet. Urban Renewal was noisily retching, too caught up with his own misery to take any action. "If this had been a real Villain situation, he would have just screwed us all."

"Do you think the camera survived?"

"After that blast? I doubt it. No time to check right now, just let it run. The press is here anyway. If they can't record, or transmit, at the very least they'll be witnesses."

"Do you think West is badly hurt?" asked Ali

"I can't tell. Even if the S.S.C. drops Tye Dye back to second-string, they're going to have to hide him. West is going to fry his ass for this stunt. Well, Ms. Ice Queen, do you think it's time for us to save the day?"

Ali grinned up at him and nodded. Craig lifted Ali until she could put both arms securely around his shoulders then he squeezed them both through the window. They drifted up and across the road, beginning their descent from behind Nuclear Man. Even with the air rushing past her ears Ali could hear the excited cries of "Ultra Man" from the microphone-wielding reporters on the other side of the street.

It was a good thing they weren't actually counting on the element of surprise, thought Ali, *with all these pointing loudmouths around.*

Nevertheless, Doug did not react to the noise. Instead, he continued to focus his attention on the fallen Supers at his feet.

"Soften your knees" warned Craig as they came in for a landing, "Fall over rather than hurt your legs."

"I've been dropped by you before," said Ali, with a grin, "I haven't fallen yet."

Craig had only a few seconds to chuckle then they hit the ground a few feet behind Nuclear Man, who spun to face them. Ali danced to the left, jumping out of range as Nuclear Man squeezed another bladder of liquid, and vomited in her general direction. Before he could straighten, Craig closed with him and threw a succession of punches.

Ali ducked behind Nuclear Man and kicked at his crutches, missing by inches. Nuclear Man, Ali and Ultra Man shifted back and forth across the buckled asphalt. A stray blow with a crutch had Ali diving to the ground, pretending injury, while Nuclear Man turned to face the more powerful threat. Ali stayed on the ground, crawling until she was positioned between Nuclear Man and another of the ubiquitous piles of cardboard boxes.

"Okay," she called, backing away as Doug shuffled toward her voice. "Come on back. A little more, little more."

When Doug was in position, Ali came to her knees, leaned forward and grabbed him around the waist. As he collapsed, she boosted them both up and back. Together, they fell into the middle of a pile of cardboard boxes. A cloud of feathers and pillow stuffing exploded over them. Ali took the worst of the blow, cushioning Doug with her body. He was surprisingly light and she held him carefully, fearful of breaking the thin bones.

Before the feathers could settle, Craig rushed over to them, grabbed Ali and dragged her to her feet. Together they stared down at the fallen Villain.

"Are you okay?" whispered Ali, obeying Craig's elbow nudge and putting her hands on her hips, her feet slightly apart. The Power Stance she'd seen in pictures so often made her feel ridiculous.

Doug opened one eye and grinned, raising his thumb. Then he slumped back, concentrating on his breathing.

"I'm just great," he said, softly, then raised his voice, "Oh, Ultra Man, you've beaten me fair and square."

"Stick to your lines," muttered Craig, then stepped back, dragging Ali with him. "Better yet, shut up and lie still." Raising his voice, he called to the approaching news crews. "Stay back! Call the Hazmat team! Call the S.S.C.! We need medivac for the Super Team and Nuclear Man."

Ali shifted until she was standing profile toward their audience, glared down her nose at the TV crews who ignored Craig's warning and were now running across the parking lot, cameras and microphones at the ready.

"Stand back," she screamed, annoyed at the squeak in her voice. "This is a Nuclear Man site. Are you all made of lead? Do you ever want to have children? Or do you want them to have three noses and nine eyes?"

The charge faltered, then halted. A few at the back headed in the other direction.

"Get back now," commanded Ali, dropping out of the power pose and waving her arms. "Get back and stay there. Don't any of you dare to go anywhere until the Hazmat team arrives. You and all your equipment will all need to go through Decontam."

The crews exchanged nervous glances, and Ali decided to get a little revenge. She sauntered over to the nearest on-air talent and whispered.

"Just for our records, you might want to write down your name and the names of your next of kin and pin it to your clothing," she said, her face solemn "just in case. Makes identification easier later."

The slender woman clutched at her throat and staggered away, her face ghost pale under her TV-ready makeup.

"Traitor! Stand and face me."

Ali spun. Across the buckled asphalt stood Tye Dye, his new Super suit splattered with simulated Nuclear Man's emesis. Tye Dye brushed at the stains, then raised his head to glare at Ultra Man. "You've betrayed everything the Supers and the S.S.C. stands for, Ultra Man. Surrender now!"

"Oh, good grief." Craig rolled his eyes and sighed.

The last thing he needed at this moment was to waste time with this particular idiot. He turned, his damned plastic mask slipped crookedly across his face. He pushed it back up in time to see Tye Dye assume Power Pose #7 – arms raised, legs spread – beside a TV van. A camera crew scrambled across the crowded asphalt, swinging their equipment back and forth between the two Supers. After the first color blast, Craig doubted that the TV camera still worked, but the crew couldn't be certain, so they were sticking with what they knew. If it looks like it will bleed, try and get it on film.

"Stand down, Tye Dye," said Craig. "The stuff in the news about me was a load of sh... a big misunderstanding."

"Stop right there, traitor," shouted Tye Dye as colored waves formed around his outstretched hands.

"No, Tye Dye, No!" shouted West from her place on the ground.

Tye Dye ignored her and concentrated. Color leached out of the buildings, equipment – even the people surrounding him.

"Tye Dye," shouted Craig, but the other Super continued to power up.

"Tye Dye," came a shout. The Mystress and The Shriek jumped from the van, landing on either side of Ali. The Mystress pushed Ali into The Shriek's waiting arms and raised her hand, spell pouch at the ready.

"Everyone, get back," shouted Craig, "Get down."

Tye Dye spun to face the newly arrived Villains.

"Traitorous bitch," cried Tye Dye to Ali, releasing his power. "Taste the consequences of your betrayal!"

Before the color pulse could reach Ali, The Mystress and Mysterious West both threw spell pouches. The powers and powders collided over Ali's head. For a moment there was silence as the colors froze mid-air, the spell powders released, mixed, blended – then exploded. Colored clouds billowed out and down, first enveloping Ali, The Shriek, and The Mystress, and flooding across the asphalt toward Craig.

Before Craig could command his feet to move, a hard, purple blur hit him at waist height, throwing him to the ground beside Nuclear Man. Craig pushed his mask back into place and tried to get up. P.L.'s over-regulation weight pressed him to the asphalt.

"Stay down, man," hissed P.L. "Keep your eyes shut. You're not wearing your real mask, remember?"

"Did you get Ali?" whispered Craig. It was true. His cheap plastic Halloween mask was no protection. Even with his arm covering his face, the amplified color leaked through. He swallowed hard against rising nausea. "P.L., did you get Ali?"

When he did not reply, Craig started struggling against P.L.'s confining weight. "Who got Ali?"

"Stay down, man," said P.L. as he lifted his weight from his friend. "You haven't got your armor on. Stay down. Act stunned. West and I will deal with this."

"No," Craig pushed him off, struggled to his feet and was halfway to the van before what he saw penetrated his mind.

Leaning against the multicolor streaked van were three skeletons draped with scattered fragments of fabric. Craig took two more steps toward it before P.L. caught his arm.

"It's too late, Ultra Man," cried Purple Lightning. "Tye Dye's Power mixed with the witches' spells have killed Ali, The Shriek and The Mystress."

Craig stared at the pile of tumbled bones. Time stretched as he struggled to make sense of what his eyes were telling his brain. There was the multicolored van. There were bones. Ali had been standing there. She wasn't there anymore. Craig's chest was one frozen, aching mass. He tried to draw in air but his body resisted. If he breathed, he might think. If he breathed then time would start moving again and he'd have to face the possibility - the distant, horrible possibility that Ali was ... was ... Time clicked into motion again, oxygen reached his brain and Craig turned to face his friend.

"*Are you serious?*"

Of all the possible responses Craig expected to his question, being sucker punched in the stomach was not one of them. But that was just what P.L. did. Gasping for air, Craig bent double. P.L. grabbed him by the shoulders and pulled him into a close embrace.

"Let it go, Ultra Man," shouted P.L. "Ali was a worthy agent. We will all miss her."

Craig gripped P.L.'s arm and squeezed - hard. "You are both deafening and smothering me. Let go."

"Not just yet," whispered P.L., running his hand over Craig's curly hair and giving the cheap plastic mask a tug to pull it back into place. "The news crews are watching us, so act broken up for a few minutes. Cry or something. West is talking to Urban Renewal."

"What about?" mumbled Craig to P.L.'s armpit – making a mental note to speak to The Colonel about upgrading P.L.'s deodorant.

"Hush," said P.L.

Craig hushed just in time to hear Mysterious West's orders to Urban Renewal.

Get Tye Dye the hell out of here. Look at the damage. Innocent bystanders injured. Villains… *S.S.C.* personnel *dead!* You *do not* want to be here. Take Tye Dye into custody and get him the hell out of here before Ultra Man gets loose." P.L. chuckled, softly. "And there they go, Tye Dye in the lead by a nose. Urban Renewal tight on his heels. I don't expect they'll stop running until they see polar bears."

"Can I straighten up now?"

Overhead, they both heard the familiar heavy thump of the Chinook. P.L. relaxed his grip and he and Craig straightened to watch as the S.S.C. helicopter circled, looking for a place to land.

"Now, *this* is going to be interesting," muttered Craig.

P.L. and Craig watched as protective-suited Norman was lowered down from the Chinook. Once on the ground, Norman ignored them. He trotted by, his Hazmat boots thudding on the pavement, an oxygen cylinder and mask tucked under his arms. The winch retracted, and then lowered again. Craig and P.L. froze, gaped and came to attention, both paling as far as their complexions would allow. Mr. Crunch, dressed in his familiar steel grey Captain Smash Super suit freed himself from the winch, then strolled over and halted a few feet away, his solid face impassive. Craig's heart sank.

Silence settled over the TV crews as they realized who had emerged from the Chinook.

Captain Smash? Out of retirement? Cell phones appeared out of pockets and bags, and crews – still hoping their equipment was functioning – focused on the solid Super. A few talking heads rushed toward Captain Smash, only to halt and retreat when he turned and stared at them.

After effectively defeating the TV reporters, Captain Smash stalked over to where West lay, her leg at an odd angle.

"We'll have medical transport for you in a moment," said Captain Smash assured her.

West gave him an odd smile and settled back. "No hurry."

Finally, Captain Smash crossed to where P.L. and Craig waited.

"Sir?" said Craig.

"Gentlemen," said Captain Smash looked around the damaged parking lot, taking in the camera crews, the skeletons, Norman administering oxygen to the fallen Nuclear Man, then resumed staring at the Supers. "Seems you've been having a busy morning.".

"Just doing our sworn duty, sir," said P.L.

Craig glanced past his boss and groaned.

A last figure had descended.

Mr. White glared around the damaged parking lot.

"Where is the Villainess, *The Ice Queen*?" demanded Mr. White.

"There never was a Villainess, The Ice Queen," began P.L.

"Stop denying!" shouted Mr. White.

"If you will let me finish," said P.L. "There never was a *Villainess*. There was, however, Ali Brent, employed by the S.S.C. as a Site Supervisor. She was brave enough to volunteer to go *undercover* to assist Ultra Man with his plan to capture Nuclear Man. Unfortunately, during the final battle Ali was killed, along with the Villains - The Shriek and The Mystress of the Night, when two spells interacted badly with Tye Dye's Power and reduced them all to that."

P.L. pointed at the pile of multi-colored bones.

Craig gaped at his friend. Where the hell had that story come from? It could only have been planned. No way P.L. could have thought up that lie on his feet. Who had helped him? Where had the bones come from? And, most important – where the hell was Ali?

White stalked over to scowl down at the mess. "I would have preferred if she'd been brought in to be questioned. We still need to complete an investigation into her vandalism."

"I believe you will find that Ali Brent's location can be verified for every one of those fraudulent event sites," said Craig. "Any vandalism was the responsibility of those people planning on perpetrating insurance fraud. Ali was in no way associated with those crimes."

The head of Oversight sniffed. "You still need to explain yourself, Ultra Man."

"But this is not the time or place," said Captain Smash gripping both men's arms and pushing them further away from each other.

It was then that Craig realized he'd stepped forward until he was nose to nose with Mr. White.

"Purple Lightning," said Captain Smash, "this site needs to be held secure. Stay here. The local Super team is on its way. Mr. White, you should leave. Return to the Chinook where I asked you to wait. This location is not yet secured, and we cannot guarantee your safety. P.L., you keep an eye on those Villains still in the van. Tye Dye's blast must have knocked them out, and I don't want them escaping just because no one is paying attention to them. The Mysterious West will aSS.C. Nuclear Man to the hospital and receive medical care herself. We can arrange for her to stay with him until we can arrange for his safe incarceration. A Hazmat unit is being transported down here as we speak. Ultra Man, I need you to come with me."

"Sir?" Craig fell into step behind the retired Super, "Where is Ali?"

"Ultra Man, please remember what I told you about security. We are being recorded." Captain Smash tilted his chin toward the watching news crews.

"After Tye Dye released his amplified Power, I doubt there is a working camera anywhere in the next three states," hissed Craig, and leaned closer to his lawyer. "Where did P.L. take Ali?"

There was the thump of displaced air and three Supers fell – literally – out of the sky. The local Super team had arrived and they were not pleased.

The Sky Man – whose only Power was flight, and was therefore used by his team as a Super-Powered Taxi – stayed in the air, seated cross-legged on his Super-levitated Skateboard and watched as his teammates gathered round to glare at Ultra Man.

"Out of your area," grumbled The Gorilla, rising up on his toes to tower over Craig and Captain Smash.

"Professional demeanor, gentlemen," whispered Captain Smash and glared at both of them until The Gorilla squeezed Ultra Man's hand in simulated congratulations.

"Your team is to assist P.L. in securing this site until transportation arrives. Please ensure that nothing is contaminated over there," Captain Smash indicated the pile of bones near the van with a glance, "until the forensic team arrives."

He turned and led Craig over to the watching news reporters. A tidal wave of questions rose. Craig didn't even raise his head in response. There was nothing he wanted to say to the eager public. Tye Dye's blast was sure to have destroyed all the film. They needn't have bothered trying to stage a public capture. That idiot had ruined everything.

Captain Smash raised his hand and waited until the press fell silent.

"Very well, ladies and gentlemen, I understand you have to go back to the antique method of recording known as paper and pencil, so I will speak slowly. First question."

"Captain Smash, did you come out of retirement because you are the only Super capable of arresting Ultra Man?" A few of the press held mini voice recorders and cell phone cameras, but the rest scribbled frantically on borrowed notebooks.

Despite his heavy mask, Captain Smash managed to wipe the smug smile of that reporter's face just by turning in his direction. Craig didn't wonder what expression could be seen. He'd been on the receiving end of Mr. Crunch's frowns more than once. In Craig's opinion, they should be listed as one of his Powers.

"Ultra Man has been engaged in the pursuit of Nuclear Man for the last week. At no time has he committed any crime. Exactly why should he be arrested?"

"The kidnapping," cried one reporter.

"Federal fugitive warrant!" shouted another.

Captain Smash raised his hand again. "You will have to speak with Mr. White about that. It has been he who has been releasing information to the press, alleging improprieties. The S.S.C. is confident that at all times Ultra Man has been in compliance with the highest possible standards of behavior required of our employees."

"Why hasn't Ultra Man spoken to repudiate the accusations?"

Craig raised an eyebrow, more at the college level words than the question. Before he could respond, Captain Smash jumped in.

"Pursuit of a dangerous Villain is a tense, dangerous, and time-consuming business. It isn't as if Ultra Man could call a timeout, come to your studio, be fussed over and annoyed by your makeup department and answer facetious questions, when to do so might compromise his pursuit. Really, I don't know what you expect of us. If you want entertainers, get entertainers. If you want Supers to deal with Villains, you are going to have to grant us the time to actually do the job!"

Craig held his breath. The number of times Mr. Bendit had lectured them on dealing with the press, and here was Captain Smash reading them the riot act. Craig said a brief prayer of thanks that he was present to witness it. As he raised his eyes skyward he saw the familiar shape of the Chinook rising, and heading away, north.

He watched as the Chinook vanished into the distance and started to form his own suspicions as to where Ali had gone.

"What about the murders?" demanded one reporter. That brought Craig's attention back to the press in a hurry.

"What?" Craig blinked and P.L. stiffened.

"The Shriek and The Mystress of the Night are dead," said another reporter.

Before Craig could speak Captain Smash was there, in full lawyer mode. "That term is not used to describe the deaths of Villains who die while resisting arrest. I suggest you be more careful when you write your news report. As it is, we of the S.S.C. cannot yet confirm the deaths of The Shriek or The Mystress of the Night. They were observed at this Event site and are no longer visible. It may take some time and significant forensic study of the remains before we can confirm their deaths."

"What about the Ice Queen?" demanded another, pointing to what was now a puddle of water.

Captain Smash managed a surprised expression. "Who?"

"The Ice Queen," chorused the news crews.

"The S.S.C. has never issued a statement in support of the existence of any such Villain or Super - *The Ice Queen*."

Craig snorted and was ignored.

"We were in the process of gathering data," continued Captain Smash.

"But she was here," cried an unnaturally skinny blonde. "We saw her die."

"You did?" asked Captain Smash. "Please describe your experience. When did a Super-Powered entity announce her title was Ice Queen?"

The woman reddened – which highlighted the edges of her pancake makeup. "We saw a woman on the site with Ultra Man. The same woman he kidnapped from the front of the S.S.C. building."

Captain Smash produced a small notepad and pen from somewhere and made a few notes. "You saw her closely enough to make a positive identification?"

"Yes!"

"Where were you standing?"

"Over there," she pointed to her TV van.

"And she was?"

"Over there - with known Villains," she sounded very smug about that last.

Craig's face reddened. One of these days he was going to...

"Hmmmm. About two hundred yards," Captain Smash made another note. "Interesting. And you know this woman – by that, I mean she is a friend, a colleague, someone you could reliably identify at a distance of two hundred yards, in the middle of a Super/Villain battle. You are one hundred percent confident that you know, without a doubt, that the woman you saw was... what did you say her name was?"

The reporter paused and glanced around at her colleagues for support. "The Ice Queen? Ali Brent?"

"And you know this because?"

Craig lowered his head so no one could see his smile. No one knew that the secret identity of Captain Smash had been a successful prosecution lawyer – after he'd risen through the ranks to serve as Captain in the NY police force. Poor girl. She had no idea what she'd gotten herself into. It was likely that she'd end up reading the cat-up-a-tree stories in Nowhere, USA for the rest of her career.

"Um….. the Vice President's sister's news reports."

"Ah, indeed. That young woman was quite upset to have lost a bidding war with another young lady, who was never identified by the S.S.C. at her own request. The Vice President's press secretary will be issuing a retraction later today." Captain Smash smiled at the gathered reporters. "I hope you are not suggesting that the S.S.C. pays its employees enough that our insurance adjusters can afford to bid millions of dollars for a date?"

There was a nervous laugh from the reporters and Craig felt the knots in his shoulders releasing. It might not be the plan that he'd created with his team and the Villains, but it seemed to be working.

Thank God. Craig froze and stared up at the sky again. He knew the S.S.C. policy. When there was any question of loss of security, when there was a person with newly manifested Powers, the S.S.C. went into 'snatch and run' mode. They would swoop down and collect the new Super and all their family members. Then, when everyone was safely confused, helpless and in S.S.C. control, negotiations began about what sort of life the Super and Family would be permitted to have. If the S.S.C. decided they couldn't trust the family to keep secrets, the family stayed where the S.S.C. put them.

And now Ali had vanished.

She didn't have a Power, but she did have a lot of secrets. Craig reached out and grabbed the convenient carrying handles built into Captain Smash's suit.

"Excuse me, ladies and gentlemen," said Craig, "There will be another news conference later, when you've collected new equipment and we have more information. You will be notified of time and place. Right now, Captain Smash and I have another appointment."

With that he pushed off the ground and launched himself and his struggling lawyer into the air.

"Ultra Man," cried Captain Smash. "We have to go back. There is a scene to secure. Villains to arrest."

"The local team is there. So are P.L. and West. They can hold the site. I don't care who gets the credit for the arrest as long as Nuclear Man's looked after." Craig had to pull Captain Smash close so he could be heard. The Halloween costume did not come equipped with communications gear. "We have something more important to do. Where the hell is Ali?"

"Ultra Man, you have responsibilities back there."

"And I am not letting you take Ali away from me." Craig tightened his grip on Captain Smash's shoulder. His boss might be Super Indestructible, but Craig was Super Strong and they'd never put what would happen if those two forces met to the test. "Why don't you take a guess which is more important to me right now?"

The lawyer was silent.

"Call ahead." Craig clenched his hands on the handles again and tried not to let his teeth chatter. "Call them. Tell them to circle back and pick us up."

"Ultra Man."

"Call," shouted Craig and slowed his speed. The rush of air into his eyes was blinding him. They had to come back, and they had to come before Crunch realized that there was no way for Craig to pursue. He had no idea where they were going, and no way he could keep up. "Call, or we find out if you can really survive a fall from this height, because I'm not stopping. I'm going to follow as long as I'm able. I'm not going to land. This costume is thin plastic. The mask isn't protecting my eyes and my hands are already freezing. It won't be long before I let go or I crash into something. Well, Boss, what are you going to do?"

Ali woke strapped into one of the passenger seats in the back of the Chinook. She blinked rapidly and rubbed at her still watering eyes. When she recovered, she would track Tye Dye down, she decided, and explain to him why he should never activate his Powers ever, ever again. Then, when his bones had healed and his bruises faded, she would explain it to him again just to be certain the message was received. When her eyes cleared enough to focus, she saw she was not alone in the back of the Chinook. Mr. White, without his entourage for a change, was seated directly across from her glaring as if he suspected she'd vanish if he took his eyes off of her. A few seats away sat Mr. Hackham scribbling as usual in his notebook.

"When you talk to the press, you can make it clear that I never had any Superpowers," said Ali, loosening her seat belt and sitting up, "That I was never involved in any of the event sites attributed to the Ice Queen, and that anyone going through with insurance claims is going to be explaining themselves in court."

"And good morning to you," Mr. Hackham raised an eyebrow. "Still the professional, Ali, how gratifying."

"Glad you think so, *Nigel*," shot back Ali, "As far as I can see the only professional people in this situation have been me, Norman and Craig. The S.S.C. really screwed up big time."

"It certainly seems so, doesn't it?" The lawyer nodded absently then beckoned to the waiting co-pilot. "Time to go."

The co-pilot paused. "Sir? We haven't heard back from Site Examiner. He hasn't declared the site secure yet. We're waiting to hear where the Hazmat tank is and are standing by to fetch it."

"I believe I gave you an order. The ground Hazmat tank is on its way. Two Super teams are on site and can control the situation until then, don't you agree? So it is safe for you to obey the orders of the person who signs your paycheck." Mr. Hackham's voice was mild, but the co-pilot was moving toward the cockpit before he'd finished.

Ali swallowed a grin. The liquid Nuclear Man had been tossing around was half-set jello mixed with carrots, which meant that no one in the neighborhood was in any danger. She settled in her seat and waited for Mr. Hackham to speak. He, however, started making notes in his book and ignored her until the Chinook started trembling, and finally took off.

"The silent treatment won't work with me, Nigel," said Ali. "I've worked directly for you, for far, far, *far* too long, and I know all your tricks. Most of the time I don't care enough one way or another to object, but today, I only have one nerve left and you're tap-dancing on it. What happens now?"

Mr. Hackham glanced up, folded his hands over the notebook and smiled.

A particularly strong jolt shuddered through the Chinook. Ali clutched her chair arms as Nigel's pen and notebook flew across the floor.

"What the hell?" Ali turned and shouted toward the cockpit. "Guys? Hey. Take it easy."

In the cockpit the pilot continued to concentrate on his flying as the co-pilot levered himself out of his seat and joined them in the cabin.

"Lock it down or lose it," he said, picking up the straying notebook and tossing it in Nigel's general direction. "I'm going to open the bay doors for a few minutes."

That statement shook Mr. Hackham's legendary calm and he gasped and clutched his notebook and briefcase to his chest.

"Are you crazy? While we're still up in the air? Why?"

"We are sort of designed to do that, sir," said the co-pilot. "We're dropping down a few hundred feet to where the turbulence is less. It will be windy for a few seconds, but don't worry, we've opened doors in flight before and survived." The co-pilot attached the hail-Mary cable to a hook on his belt and smirked at the lawyer. "Ultra Man and Captain Smash are outside, flying alongside us."

Nigel swallowed, nodded and tightened his straps. Ali slipped hers open. She felt a little lurch under her heart and some deep tension loosened. Whatever his plan, she had to be ready. She zipped the front of her jacket closed and wiped sweaty palms on her jeans. If necessary, she'd leap into his arms as soon as he dropped off Mr. Crunch and they'd fly away.

With the downdraft from the propellers and strong winds, Craig – carrying Captain Smash – did not so much 'come aboard' the Chinook as get blown in. Ali, Nigel and the co-pilot clung to the walls and seats and concentrated on staying inside while the winds battered their eardrums and blew everything that wasn't nailed down out the door.

The bay door rattled and groaned closed against the pressure of the wind, and Ali breathed a sigh of relief when the outside world was firmly shut out. Pushing handfuls of hair back off her face she glanced back and forth between Craig, Mr. Crunch and Mr. Hackham. Crunch looked severely put out, which was for him the equivalent of an erupting volcano. Hackham appeared baffled. Craig, however, was stern, intent, and worried until his eyes stopped watering and he caught sight of Ali. Within heartbeats he was at her side, both arms tight around her. Ali struggled against the pressure of his arms, and the seat belts, but managed to get her arms around his shoulders. For the first time in her experience, instead of pumping out Superheat, Craig was chilled.

"Stupid trick," chattered Craig, his lips pressed to her wind-tangled hair. "They should have known it wouldn't work."

"What trick?"

"They're trying the divide and conquer thing, Ali cat."

"I thought you were staying to secure the scene," said Mr. Hackham, most of his attention on the senior lawyer.

"Purple Lightning shook off the effects of Tye Dye's attack and took over," said Craig. "The local Super team are on site. With all the Villains in medical and magical restraint, there was no need for us there, and I wanted to make sure you didn't 'disappear' Ali while my back was turned."

"The very idea," protested Mr. Hackham.

Ali snorted.

"Really, Ms. Brent, that is most inelegant."

"Like I care."

"Ms. Brent."

"Come off it, *Nigel*, I'm not your employee anymore. I don't have to take your attitude and your fake accent. I quit, remember? And no matter what happens next, I still won't be in a position to answer to you. So just shut up."

"It's a real accent," said Nigel, shrinking back into his chair. To Ali's surprise, he seemed almost hurt. "I was born just outside of Oxford."

"Well," Ali began.

"And Mr. Crunch will confirm that we were already preparing to rehire you, with no interruption in benefits, no loss of seniority, after we'd had a chance to calm the situation down." Mr. Hackham flipped open his leather notebook. "See, I even have a notation, reminding myself to call on you tomorrow."

"That will not be happening," stated Mr. White, surprising those who had forgotten he was present. "Ultra Man and the Ice Queen still have to answer for their crimes."

"Give me a break," groaned Craig. "Will someone please explain to this moron that there is not, and never was, an Ice Queen?"

"There is sufficient evidence ..."

"There is no evidence," Craig finally released Ali and crossed the shuddering interior of the Chinook to stare down at the head of Oversight. "Nothing. Nil. Nada. None. No evidence outside of your twisted, conspiracy-minded mind. Do you hear me? NONE!"

Mr. White pulled himself upright in his chair and assumed a smug attitude. "I have the authority to enforce your incarceration until I am satisfied with your answers to my questions, Ultra Man, so I suggest you modify your attitude in short order or I might forget to begin the interrogation for a year or so."

"You do not have the authority to disappear me, you idiot," began Craig.

"This guy is a complete pain in the butt," muttered Ali to Mr. Crunch. "Everything gets out of control when he's around. Can't we just knock him out or lock him up somewhere 'til this is sorted out?"

"Dream on," whispered Mr. Crunch, adjusting his grey mask. Then raised his voice. "Don't be ridiculous."

Ali jumped, but realized he wasn't speaking to her. Mr. Crunch was frowning at Mr. White.

"Ultra Man has never been accused of, or even implicated in a crime," continued Mr. Crunch, "He is, still, a respected member of the Super Teams, and exonerating Ms. Brent will be the simplest of tasks. The times of the Ice Queen's alleged attacks are well documented, and Ms. Brent's location at each of these times is easily verified. Additionally, with her assistance, Nuclear Man has been captured."

"You can't know that," shrieked Mr. White. "The Ice Queen has been a criminal since she first came on the scene. How do you know that this wasn't a setup since the beginning? Nuclear Man's plan! He's up to something, and he's used the Ice Queen to seduce Ultra Man."

"Lucky Ultra Man," muttered Mr. Hackham.

The only one who heard him was Ali, who blushed. Mr. Crunch and Craig both started shouting at once. Mr. White screamed back, red in the face.

"They need to be arrested. Held in a secure facility until this whole mess is straightened out," cried Mr. White.

"Every time he says something, it just gets worse," moaned Ali, as Mr. Crunch started citing the need for proof. The rule of law, innocence before guilt, all long-standing legal niceties which Mr. White seemed determined to ignore. Ali clenched her fists, climbed free of her seat and stepped between the shouting men.

"There hasn't been a crime, you moron," shrieked Ali, and everyone stopped.

Ali tried to calm her breathing and kept her attention on the aggravating Mr. White.

"There never was a provable Ice Queen sighting. It was all a..." she sought desperately for a word. "The Ice Queen is entirely fictional. She never appeared in public and, certainly, never committed a crime. Every news report, event site was entirely the creation of the minds of other people. Not, I repeat, *not* the result of any action of a member of Super Support Corp."

"Exactly," said Mr. Crunch, smiling at them both.

Ali almost sagged against Craig in relief. Mr. Crunch was supporting them. Had said so in front of the moron from Oversight.

"The Virginia attack!" said Mr. White, his color still high, pointed at Ali. "All that criminal vandalism. She has to be held accountable for that."

"Aren't you listening?" said Mr. Hackham, with a slight smile, "The Ice Queen did not perform any vandalism. It was the work of the farmer. All the reported Ice Queen events are examples of criminal attempt to defraud insurance companies. The S.S.C. did, indeed, issue statements to that effect."

Ali glared at the back of Nigel's head, her fingers itched to slap him. They'd issued those statements all right, then said they'd retracted them and issued a 'we don't know' statement. Damn them, anyway. Their S.S.C. asses were well and truly covered. Hers had been hung out in the wind.

"That's beside the point," shrieked Mr. White and Ali flinched away from the rage in his voice.

Until they got this moron out of the way, there was no chance of them getting this settled quickly or easily – or at all. Ali could almost feel the light bulb appearing above her head.

"Oh, my God," gasped Ali. "It's his Superpower. Mr. White! I just realized, he's just like the Computer Destructo Woman. He doesn't even have to think about it. His power just leaks out that way."

"Ms. Brent," said Mr. Crunch in quelling tones, "you are not helping."

But nothing could suppress Ali's excitement. She pointed and her boss turned, staring at the suddenly grinning Mr. White.

"I have a Power?" he whispered, awe filling his voice. "I really have a *Power*?"

"Well," she stammered, 'It's obvious when you think about it."

"What is it?" asked Mr. White.

"Um... It's ah ..."

"She doesn't like to say," broke in Craig, casting Mr. White an embarrassed grin, "It's not like it's a first-string level ability. She doesn't want to raise your hopes and then disappoint you."

Mr. White's joy faded and the scowl started to return.

"It's a hidden power," said Mr. Crunch, quickly. "One that works better if it's kept a secret. A monkey's paw Power."

"Not from me. I want to know. What is it?"

"It's that you induce *Chaos*," said Ali.

Instead of being offended Mr. White's smile returned. "You know, I think I've noticed that in the past. Is that really a Power?"

The members of the S.S.C. exchanged stunned glances. Was the moron truly believing this?

"Well, yes, for you. In you," said Ali, crossing her fingers behind her back and praying that Mr. White was as Super crazy as the most pathological seven-year-old who'd ever jumped off the top of his parents' house dressed in pajamas with a towel tied around his neck. "I've noticed that whenever you're around, people's blood pressure goes up, they get irritable. No one can think calmly or logically. My goodness, yours is a really dangerous Power! You make people crazy!"

She pressed her hands against her throat and did her best to cringe away and look terrified.

"But, unfortunately," said Mr. Crunch catching the ball smoothly and laying a sympathetic hand on the paper-pusher's shoulder, "it's not directional, and it wouldn't be much use on one of our more active, physical, Super teams. I'm afraid we'll have to hold you in reserve, for special occasions."

Mr. White's eyes were round. "But I can have a logo?" he gasped, "A Super title? A doll?"

"Certainly," crooned Mr. Crunch, turning Mr. White and leading him away toward the back of the Chinook where an emergency containment unit was hidden, "we'll have to discuss what would be the most suitable use of your special abilities. Or maybe we should think about putting you in the protected program. It's not as if we can leave you wandering around. My God, think of the destruction you might wreak! How the world would suffer if a Villain were to capture you and turn your ability to Evil! Yes, protection is the way to go. Mr. White, I'm sorry, but we have to take you into custody. There are some papers for you to sign giving us authority to keep the world safe from you. I believe you designed these forms."

"Yes. Yes," cried Mr. White, nodding vigorously.

A heavy door slammed behind them.

Mr. Hackham watched them leave. "We'll have to move fast," he said, thoughtfully grabbing a bundle of papers out of his case and hurrying after the other lawyer. "Get him to sign over authority. Get him into the relocation program before he has a chance to think. Once the fog clears, he'll see right through us. Still, even if he does wake up, jumping through the legal hoops to get out of the relocation program will keep him out of our hair for a few years."

Craig sank into the nearest chair, wrapped his arms tight across his chest and started shaking. Ali searched through the storage bins until she found a couple of folded blankets. She wrapped both around Craig's body and legs and then pulled him into her arms and hugged him tight. Craig grinned as he rested his head against her chest. He didn't move even when the two lawyers returned, Mr. Crunch having taken the time to change out of his old Super suit.

"I'd forgotten how those old fabrics chafed," he said, settling into the chair that faced Ali and Craig's.

"Ali's reinstated again, isn't she?" said Craig from his comfortable position. "Everything goes back to normal today."

"Hardly," said Mr. Hackham. "There has been far too much publicity. No matter what explanation we offer, there will be long-term repercussions from these events. Surely you must realize that."

"But this is the perfect time," protested Craig. "Back at the site. Captain Smash, here, just publicly confirmed our story. There is no Ice Queen. Now you have to go back to S.S.C. Headquarters and back it up. Finish it. Say it. Tell them I picked Ali up to take her to a secret event site or something. Tell them that she'll be returning to her previous duties, with the S.S.C.'s thanks and a promotion would be a nice touch."

Mr. Hackham sighed and rolled his eyes. "Ultra Man, you have a delightfully simplistic view of life. Just because she didn't have a Superpower doesn't make her secret identity any less important. SS.C. policy is quite clear. Ms. Brent's loss of anonymity is as significant as with any Super. Any employee of the S.S.C. She cannot return to her previous life. Ah, now, if only Mr. White hadn't made such a fuss. We know he's responsible for the photo leak, the FBI involvement, and another egregious announcements. The more I think about it, the more I am inclined to believe you may be right about our absent friend, Mr. White. Chaos followed him, everywhere. Perhaps we should have him tested." Nigel raised an eyebrow toward the other lawyer.

"Waste of time," Mr. Crunch slumped back in his seat, "Do you really want to replicate his Power? Can you imagine any scenario where you would want him on a battlefield?"

"Not unless he was the target," said Craig.

"What, may I ask," said Mr. Hackham, "was your plan now? Purple Lightning and Mysterious West updated us on the way down here, without alerting Mr. White, of course. I must admit, I could not comprehend how you thought capturing Nuclear Man would aid your case."

"Distraction," said Craig. "I thought that if we gave them a really dramatic story, they'd forget about the Ice Queen. Drown her in waves of press releases about something juicier. Something with proof."

Hackham cast a sad smile in their direction.

"Ah, children. It warms my old heart to see such idealistic optimism. Such naiveté."

"Your snotty attitude is not helping," said Ali, "If you had backed us up at the beginning, this hell would not have happened. So don't go superior at us. Your time to help was ages ago, when we all swore up and down that there was no Ice Queen. You failed us. Now is the time for you to redeem yourself and fix this!"

Nigel Hackham had the grace to look embarrassed. "I realize that the confusion..."

"Confusion, hell," shouted Craig, "You all chose not to believe us. We swore by everything we hold sacred, and yet you just let it all spin out of control. Now we want to get our lives back. You have a great piece of crime-fighting theater to use, several tons of press waiting to hear whatever story we decide to give them, so, come on, what's the problem? Why aren't you taking advantage of it?"

"There is no way we can take Ms. Brent back in these circumstances," said Mr. Hackham, "I do apologize. You are indeed correct that we didn't fully understand what you were trying to tell us."

Craig snorted and Ali waved her fist under Hackham's long nose.

"Unfortunately," continued Mr. Hackham, leaning back in his chair, "we have to deal with reality. Your secret identity is blown, Ms. Brent. There has simply been too much publicity. You cannot return to work at S.S.C. without attracting public scrutiny. At the moment, if I were to guess, you are the second most famous face on the planet. Second only to Ultra Man. The press will not give up such a juicy story, particularly when they ever hear a hint that a powerless person was involved in the capture of the most dangerous criminals of all time."

Craig gathered himself to argue but stopped when Mr. Crunch raised his hand.

"I think what we forget here is that the world currently believes that both Ali Brent *and* The Ice Queen are dead!"

"Dead?" Mr. Hackham raised one eyebrow and stared across at Ali. "Did I miss something? She appears remarkably alive to me."

"Me, too," said Craig. "I don't know whose idea it was, but P.L. was spouting some nonsense back at the event site about Ali, The Shriek and The Mystress of the Night being reduced to skeletons by Tye Dye."

"Exactly," said Mr. Crunch. "Now, think before you answer, Ultra Man, and keep in mind the number of the members of the press who were standing by, observing the events. Is there any possibility that The Shriek and The Mystress of the Night are still alive?"

"Ah." Craig folded his arms across his chest and glared at the lawyer. Dammit all to hell and back again. Ali, his team and the Villains must have gone behind his back and created this story. His teeth ground together as his suspicions grew. When P.L. and West had left yesterday to update the S.S.C. about the planned surrender/capture of Nuclear Man and his friends, they must have dropped hints to Tye Dye so that he'd come to the event site just in time to be framed for the 'deaths' of The Shriek and The Mystress. The only question left in his mind was whether Ali's 'death' had been planned, or an unintended consequence.

He cast one sidelong look at Ali and had his answer.

Ali put her hand on his arm.

"I'm sorry, Craig. They're right. The Shriek and The Mystress are dead and if we want them to stay dead, so is Ali Brent. No matter what tale we spin or how thoroughly we b s. the press, if we let them have any hint that The Shriek and The Mystress survived, then as soon as they have a moment to think, they'll be after me. Forever! It's just too good a story. And with all that going on, we'll never be able to have a relationship. Even if I appear in public with *a female*, albino dwarf with eczema, the press is going to speculate about whether *she's* Ultra Man in disguise."

"Ms. Brent is quite correct, "said Mr. Hackham. "It would never be safe for you, or her, to be seen in public again, unless it is as Ultra Man and Ice Queen."

"Ali can't be Ice Queen," shouted Craig. "The Ice Queen's dead!"

"I understand, but my first concern is SS.C. security. We cannot risk it just so that you two can remain friends. Not with this level of scrutiny."

"This isn't a *friend* situation," cried Craig, rattling the walls of Chinook. "We're getting married."

"Obviously not," whispered Ali.

Craig spun, seizing her by the arm and pulling her out of her seat and into his lap. Before she could even squeak he had both hands cupping her face and was staring up at her.

"Ali. I may not be certain of many things, but I know I'm not listening to any plan that separates us. That's my bottom line. Hear me?"

She tried to nod but couldn't get a muscle to move. Instead, she gave him a warm smile. "Yes."

"That is your final word?" Mr. Crunch's deep voice rumbled through the tiny space.

"Yes sir," chorused Ali and Craig.

"No matter what the cost?"

They didn't hesitate. "Yes, sir."

"Very well." Mr. Crunch nodded to Mr. Hackham, who sat back. "Under the circumstances, we won't be able to kill off Ultra Man any time in the near future. Too many people will start speculating about his allegiance, and whether this was a sanctioned hit, and we don't need that sort of reputation. We should use the alternative."

"Kill off?" cried Ali, tightening her grip on Craig. "What alternative?"

Mr. Crunch smiled at her. "My dear Ms. Brent. This is hardly the first time a Super has created such a public furor. No matter what we say, there will always be civilians who will use the last week's publicity as an excuse to distrust Ultra Man. When a Super loses the public's confidence and Heaven knows, we do need their good-will to function, especially considering the mess we make, or has completely blown their secret identity, we recycle them."

"Recycle?" echoed Craig.

"Exactly," said Mr. Hackham. "It's not as if truly useful Super Powers grow on trees. Good Heavens, when you think of it, the majority are as insane and useless as Tye Dye. It amazes me that we manage to field useful Super teams at all. Consequently, when the situation gets this bad, we usually arrange for a dramatic, heart-rending fatal accident for the affected individual. Then, after a suitable period of time, we announce the discovery of a new Super."

"But people must notice the new one has the old one's Powers," protested Ali.

"Hardly," said Mr. Hackham, "Have you? We've had some experience with this situation, Ms. Brent, and we've gained some skill in the matter. We emphasize different aspects of the Supers Powers. For example, our friend Ultra Man here. The announcement will be that he is going to officially retire, because he cannot work with people suspecting his motives and he is deeply grieving the loss of you, Ms. Brent, his one true love. There will be the occasional, carefully scripted public appearances, at baseball games and the like, where he will gently throw out the opening ball and refuse to sign autographs. That role will be played by one of the weaker third strings, wearing Ultra Man's uniform – we have a couple whose only Power is limited range flight. Meanwhile, Craig will go to a relocation facility and concentrate on learning new skills - martial arts, or something similar. In a few months, in a new Super suit, with a new color scheme and logo, we will present him to the world. A flying martial artist, or something like that." Mr. Hackham gave Mr. Crunch a speculative look. "That actually sounds like a good idea. We haven't had a Super Ninja. Do you think our Craig could learn enough to pull that off?"

Mr. Crunch gave it a moment's thought. "Possibly. He's fast enough. Most people won't be able to see him clearly enough to swear that he isn't actually using sophisticated karate and judo moves."

"You'd do this?" asked Ali. "We were told that if we lost our identities the SS.C. would dump us. Why do you make such a fuss about identities when you've got a plan?"

"We want you all to be careful," said Mr. Crunch. "Have you any idea how much work this is? How expensive? Take Captain Fabulous, for example. It costs millions a year for his security because he hasn't got a working secret identity, and most of that is forfeiting security deposits since he has to change apartments so often. We've given up buying him houses." He regarded them thoughtfully, then continued in a quiet voice. "It took over a million to recycle my son."

"*The Power*'s still alive?" cried Craig. "I thought he died when Mount St Helen's blew."

"That's what we wanted everyone to believe," said Mr. Crunch. "He had a bad year, with accidental civilian fatalities at a few sites and being too late to help with that ship sinking. Shouting at the press while drunk in uniform didn't help, so we recycled him." He gave them both a rare smile. "Can you guess where he is now?"

"Urban Renewal," said Ali instantly, remembering the verbal sparring at the charity bash. The Power and Ultra Man had been in competition since Craig was 'discovered.' And the sparing had carried over into Craig's relationship with Urban Renewal.

"Exactly," Mr. Crunch nodded.

"What about Mrs. Crunch? The Thump! She's listed MIA too."

"She was looking to take things easy. Retire. It gets hard to throw a good punch after a few decades on the job. Now she works intake down in Decontam."

Ali gasped remembering the squat, square woman with the colored fingernails, then started laughing.

"What are you going to do about Oliver?" asked Craig. "Mysterious West is willing to retire, but Oliver wants to stay on the job. He's kind of distinctive. No way people are going to accept another black Super Speeder is a different person."

"Purple Lightning will not be recycled," said Mr. Hackham. "The current publicity has been directed at you, not your team."

"Ah." Ali and Craig looked at each other.

"Didn't he say?" began Ali.

Both lawyers froze, then scowled.

"Exactly what are you implying, Ms. Brent?" asked Mr. Crunch.

"Nuclear Man, The Shriek, The Mystress. They all know my and his secret identities," said Craig. "Even if – and I'm sure they will intend to keep the secret - but even so, you know what the research shows, in a few months P.L.'s identity will be compromised."

"Ah. Yes." Mr. Hackham stared at his pen. "You know, I have an interesting idea. Why can't we have Super Ninja twins? With both of you in head to toe Ninja suits no one will have any hint of who you are and with Oliver's Super Speed, he doesn't even have to learn much of a martial art. Who is going to say what technique he used to knock the Villain out if they didn't even see his hands move? This is one of those occasions where the existing mythos will assist us." He chuckled and began to sketch. "We could even keep the two of you on the same team. You're used to working together."

Craig scowled, then relaxed a little. "I suppose. I had a brown belt in Judo before my Super Powers kicked in. What are you doing?"

"Designing your new suits." Mr. Hackham glanced up.

"Doesn't The Colonel do that?"

Hackham sniffed. "The Colonel has no sense of style. I do the design, he makes it work."

Ali started to laugh. Three years in the SS.C. and there was still twists and secrets within that she was yet to learn. Maybe it would turn out that the scary Control secretly worked with Big Brothers/Big Sisters on her days off. Or not. More likely, not.

"I don't have a Power. what are you going to do with me?" said Ali.

"You actually have a choice, Ms. Brent. We can put you both into the relocation program. Craig can go on to become a Super, and we could create a nice, quiet married civilian personal life for you both."

"Or what?"

"Well, the other alternative is somewhat more complicated." It was Mr. Hackham's turn to exchange a glance with Mr. Crunch. "There are, as you know, a very few people who go public admitting to being involved with the S.S.C. It is a difficult life, but it has its rewards. It just so happens a vacancy just this moment fell available. It will take a bit of work to get you assigned to this job. It's a political appointment, but I think we'll be able to finagle it for you and you'd be able to carry it off with style."

"Take it," said Craig.

"But what are they talking about?" asked Ali.

"A job for which you are uniquely qualified because of your flexible attitude toward Supers and Villains, and your complete understanding of the impact they have on society. You'll replace Mr. White," guessed Craig, hugging her. "The rest of it, my disguise, my secret identity, can be arranged so I can be your husband without revealing that I was ever Ultra Man."

"The more I think about it, the more the idea of Super Ninja appeals to me," Mr. Hackham muttered to himself. "A full body mask would do much to solve the secret identity issue. I wonder if I can get anyone else to change their costume?"

"Yeah," said Craig, "and we need new dolls. A complete set of Super Clean Up squad dolls. We need Site Examiner, Site Supervisor, building and cleaning crew dolls, and don't forget the Transport buses, Norman's van and the Chinook."

Ali cast Craig a brilliant smile and he blew her a kiss in reply.

"You must be joking," Mr. Hackham stared at them open-mouthed. "Who'd buy them?"

"I will," said Craig, putting his arm around Ali's shoulders. "All of them if I have to, to create a demand. And as soon as people realize they're hard to find, they'll become rare, expensive collector's items and you'll never be able to keep up. Besides, it is about time that the SS.C. made everyone realize that the S.S.C. isn't just the Supers. Flying around knocking down buildings isn't *all* that the SS.C. does. The Clean Up squad are not given full credit for the contribution they make."

Ali leaned forward and kissed Craig. "Unless you gentlemen don't believe we contribute. Do either of you want to go on record saying that?"

Both lawyers shook their heads.

"Good," said Craig. "That's settled. Now, I think we've kept the ladies, gentlemen and parasites of the press waiting long enough. Let's go find some and announce my retirement."

Epilogue.

Washington Post.
The SSS announced today that the remains collected from the Phoenix Super event site were indeed those of The Shriek and The Mystress of the Night. The bodies will be transported to the S.S.C.'s secret Cemetery of Super Beings for Hazmat internment. Out of respect for the innocent civilian members of The Shriek's and The Mystress's families, no announcement will be made regarding any information discovered concerning the secret identities of these two Villains. The newly appointed chairperson of the Paranormal Oversight Committee, Ms. Amber Waves, has issued a statement supporting this action.

Phoenix Evening News.
Nuclear Man Declared Too Fragile To Stand Trial!
The terrifying criminal, Nuclear Man, has been held in a secure medical facility in Phoenix, Arizona since his arrest by Ultra Man and the Northeast Super Team. Today, doctors, holistic practitioners and other medical personnel who have examined the criminal, have announced that Nuclear Man is too ill to be subjected to the rigors of a court trial.

Nuclear Man's lawyer, Mr. Bendit, has announced Nuclear Man intends to elocute fully regarding his crimes in the presence of a Superior Court Judge from his hospital bed sometime in the near future - as soon as one can be found who is willing to go within ten feet of the infamously toxic criminal.

The retired Super, Ultra Man, when contacted for comment, has stated that he intends to be present when the elocution takes place to provide support.

A month later.
The messenger stepped through the metal detector and handed a small box to the security guard. Both box and messenger went through the machine without activating a single beep.

"Clear," said the guard in a bored voice and signed the clipboard.
After collecting the signature, the messenger retreated at high speed out of the newly-built maximum security hospital. He knew who the prison contained, and he planned on having children in the future. Consequently, he broke a few land speed records getting away from the place. (To the joy of a local traffic cop, who was waiting to catch those few persons who visited the facility.)

The guard passed the parcel over to a pale, over-muscled colleague also dressed in lead-impregnated clothing. This one tucked the parcel under his arm and proceeded down dull grey corridors, through a succession of locked and barred doors, until he came to a small glass-fronted office. The doctor within glanced up at his arrival and came out to scan the return address label. After verifying the sender's name was on the approved list, he accepted the box and set off down another secure hallway.

The radiation detector pinned to his collar beeped every now and again as he talked but stayed a comforting blue.

He paused, finally, at a wide one-way window and stared in at this prison's only occupant.

Nuclear Man, oxygen mask on his face, lay in a La-Z-Boy recliner in the center of a bright, cheerful room. Medical scanners were placed, discreetly, in a bookcase behind him. A wide screen TV, with all the audio-visual technology any geek could desire, occupied a whole wall. The remaining walls were covered in bright wallpaper and clumsy childish paintings. The middle-aged woman reading in a nearby chair shifted uncomfortably from time to time under the weight of her protective clothing, while the teenaged girl who sat at the other side of a chess board smiled up at Nuclear Man, waiting for his next move.

The doctor tapped in his security code and then knocked before entering the room. Somehow, he could never bring himself to bully the fragile Villain who was as polite to him as he was to his own mother.

"Dr. Carter," said Nuclear Man, his voice a husky whisper barely audible over the hiss of the oxygen mask, "Thank you for letting my wife and my daughter stay over last night. We really appreciated it."

"We don't get many people asking for permission to use our guest rooms," said Doctor Carter, "and according to my orders, they can drop by any time – just as long as they don't bake any files into cakes."

"Not going to happen," said Nuclear Man, smiling. "That would be a waste of good cake."

"I suppose," said Dr. Carter as he took a quick glance at the radiation detector clipped to his collar. "I've had some more interview requests. *The Scientific Belgium* has had an amazing response to your first interview, now they want to arrange a follow-up. They want to know all you've learned about dangerous research practices and how to avoid being an unwitting volunteer. *News Of The Screws* wants to talk to you about your personal life."

The doctor smiled nervously at Mrs. Nuclear Man, who laughed.

"Phone interviews, I assume," said Nuclear Man, grinning.

"Well, yes. Naturally."

"Certainly, I'd be delighted." Nuclear Man nodded toward the box. "Is that for me?"

The doctor placed it on the nearest table, unwilling to put anything into the fragile Villain's shaking hands. Nuclear Man struggled with the tape for a moment, then his wife came to her feet and used her knitting needles to tear the tape. Dr. Carter wondered yet again why she and this young girl – and this prisoner - were allowed so many exceptions to the usual Prison rules. Dr. Carter and his team of guards maintained their vigilance, determined Nuclear Man would never be free to wreak havoc on the world again. Although how he would stage an escape armed only with knitting needles and an oxygen mask was a problem Dr. Carter had not resolved in his own mind.

Still, this facility was more like a high priced medical resort than a prison for a toxic and dangerous criminal. While the S.S.C. continued to fund it, and its many luxuries, they got to set the rules. The thousands of doctors begging to come here and study the multiple-cancer-ridden, highly toxic, still-living

Villain were all turned away – by the still popular but retired-Ultra Man's express orders. But news reporters were granted unlimited access. Well, almost unlimited. The S.S.C. permitted Nuclear Man to be fussy about which reporters he spoke to. The AMA was still screaming about the fall-out (ha), and public outrage that arose after the Nuclear Man spoke at length and passionately about the reality of being subjected to medical research. The S.S.C. had gone as far as assigning Nuclear Man his own secretary and legal team to deal with the AMA's protests.

Dr. Carter watched his controversial charge search through his package, revealing boxes of cookies and other junk foods. At the very bottom was a pile of magazines and photographs.

Nuclear Man lifted out the first magazine, read the front cover, held it out for his wife and they both laughed

Front and center on *Pet Fancy* magazine was a photo of tall, black man, and a tiny Jamaican woman. The title below identified them as the winners of the two-million-dollar Panda Pig award. A brief story teaser on the cover noted that Steven Holtzman and Joan Henley-each holding a tiny, little Panda Pig – were donating their reward, and most of their expected profits, to various medical charities

"Yes, I think I'll enjoy reading this," said Nuclear Man.

He handed the magazine to his wife and lifted out the last, carefully wrapped item. He peeled back the plastic lid to find a large piece of cake – frosted half bronze and green, half silver and blue.

"Ah," he said, tears coming to his eyes, "a little left-over wedding cake."

Nuclear Man and his family passed around photographs of a wedding party, and eventually permitted Dr. Carter to take a peek.

There was nothing to identify who was getting married in these shots, Dr. Carter realized. Everyone was wearing masks! Even the bride. It was clear that, whoever they were, they'd taken a trip down to Vegas to get married at a cheesy Super Team chapel. Sure, standing outside the Super logo-decorated chapel, the bride seemed to glow with happiness and the groom was as proud and pleased by his good luck as anyone could reasonably hope at a wedding. They were surrounded by actors dressed as a variety of Supers. From the look of things, a Captain Smash double had been chosen to give away the bride, the Mysterious West actress took the part of Matron of Honor, and a sadly overweight Purple Lightning clone wearing the old-style uniform had been the best man. Still, there was no way of knowing why they'd sent photographs of a Super wedding party to Nuclear Man.

The doctor watched as the criminal and his family carefully cut their section of cake. Yesterday, he'd been sent a camera with strict instructions. Even if he didn't understand them, given who had issued them, he intended to obey. He waited until everyone was distracted by sugar and cream before snapping away.

It was a photo destined never to be seen outside of the S.S.C., but the original soon found its way to the bottom drawer of Mr. Crunch's desk. Nuclear Man and his family eating cake together and celebrating the health, happiness and marriage of Ultra Man and The Ice Queen.

The end.

Update:
Computer Destructo Woman graduated from college with a Ph.D. in Abnormal Psychology and currently works as a counselor for the S.S.C. Her Super pSychosis Clinic is located on a farm in the mountains of north New York state. On her weekends off Computer Destructo Woman enjoys hang-gliding.

Panda Pig Associates ™ has become one of the world's most successful pet companies, with its Jackalope, DoDon't's and pigmy elephant lines of genetically augmented pets. Their intelligent monkey series was discontinued after one of the animals escaped and became the governor of a Midwest state before anyone realized its genetic heritage.

Despite the S.S.C.'s best efforts, periodically there are still Ice Queen sightings. Conspiracy theorists claim that the actual Ice Queen is so dangerous she is held – with the aliens – in Area 51.

Amber Waves, Head of the Paranormal Oversight Committee, lives with her husband Theodore, a martial arts instructor, in North Dakota. She has been known to become hysterical at backyard parties if anyone offers her ice for her drink.

**By The Same Author
Available on Amazon Kindle**

FANTASY ROMANCE
The Use of Changing Magic, book one.
The Complexity of Changing Magic, book two

REGENCY ROMANCE

Ridiculous!
Obstreperous
Ruined Forever
Gentlewoman Urgently Seeks Husband
Crimes of the Brothers

CONTEMPORARY FANTASY

First Destroy All Giant Monsters
The Adventures of a Super Hero's Insurance Adjuster

What Authors and Reviewers are saying about D.L. Carter's first novel, *The Uses of Changing Magic*

"D. L. Carter has crafted a fantastic tale of magic and romance that will enthrall you and leave you hungry for more. The world she has built is fascinating, filled with rich characters and sizzling sexiness. This page-turner will keep you up all night. I can't wait to read what comes next from her!"
~Ann Charles, National Award-Winning Author of the *Deadwood* Mystery Series."

"D. L. Carter takes you on exciting journey of magical sex, enchanted adventure, and High King intrigue of Elves and mortals. Don't miss this thrilling new fantasy romance!"
~Jacquie Rogers, author of *Much Ado About Marshalls*.

"A compelling fantasy romance that delivers a double shot of heat and magic!"
~Amber Scott, Kindle Bestselling author of *Irish Moon* , of the *Moon Magick* Series.

www.ingramcontent.com/pod-product-compliance
Lightning Source LLC
Chambersburg PA
CBHW022354040426
42450CB00005B/181